CW01674443

Outlooks

Outlooks reveals the rich and diverse contribution that visible and confident lesbian and gay publics have made to the visual world. Asking such questions as whether there is a need for a specifically queer perspective on past art, how have lesbian and gay artists responded to the AIDS crisis and society's attempts to censor homosexual art, *Outlooks* analyses the involvement of lesbians and gay men in visual culture.

Offering a sense of something shared with others, this volume provides a space for lesbian and gay artists to exhibit their work and discuss its relationship to society. In critical essays, it allows for a wide ranging theoretical and historical discussion of the activities of lesbian and gay men as consumers and producers of art and shows how much has been missed by a heterosexist approach to art history and the study of culture.

Richly illustrated with over forty images, many the work of the contributors, the book includes statements by contemporary lesbian and gay artists, photographers and performers as well as critical articles by art historians, cultural theorists and lesbian and gay activists.

Emmanuel Cooper on Francis Bacon
Richard Dellamora on Warhol and postmodernism
Sunil Gupta on race and queer art
Richard Kaye on the gay icon of Saint Sebastian
Wendy Leeks on Ingres and the lesbian viewer
Reina Lewis and Katrina Rolley on lesbians and the fashion spread
Thaïs Morgan on lesbianism and nineteenth-century aestheticism
Carl Stychin on the censorship of lesbian and gay art
Simon Watney on the visual poetics of mourning

With statements from contemporary artists: Robert Farber, Sadie Lee, Veronica Slater, Lawrence Steger and Iris Moore, Matthew Stradling, and Cherry Smyth on Tessa Boffin.

The editors, **Peter Horne** and **Reina Lewis**, both teach in the Department of Cultural Studies at the University of East London.

Outlooks

Lesbian and gay sexualities and visual cultures

Edited by Peter Horne and Reina Lewis

London and New York

First published 1996
by Routledge
11 New Fetter Lane, London EC4P 4EE

Simultaneously published in the USA and Canada
by Routledge
29 West 35th Street, New York, NY 10001

© 1996 Peter Horne and Reina Lewis, collection and editorial material;
individual chapters © authors

Designed and typeset by
Tek-Art Croydon Surrey

Printed and bound in Great Britain

All rights reserved. No part of this book may be reprinted
or reproduced or utilized in any form or by any electronic,
mechanical, or other means, now known or hereafter
invented, including photocopying and recording, or in any
information storage or retrieval system, without permission in
writing from the publishers.

British Library Cataloguing in Publication Data

A catalogue record for this book is available from the British Library

Library of Congress Cataloguing in Publication Data

A catalogue record for this book has been requested

ISBN 0–415–12467–0 (hbk)
ISBN 0–415–12468–9 (pbk)

Contents

Figures

Contributors

Emmanuel Cooper is a writer, critic, potter and broadcaster. He is a regular contributor to *Gay Times*, *Creative Camera* and *Time Out*. His books include *Henry Scott Tuke, a Monograph* (GMP, 1987), *The Sexual Perspective: Homosexuality in Art in the Last 100 Years* (Routledge, 1994), *Fully Exposed: The Male Nude in Photography* (Routledge, 2nd edition 1995) and *People's Art: Working Class Art, 1750 to the Present Day* (Mainstream, 1994). He is based in London.

Richard Dellamora is a Visiting Scholar at the Center for the Study of Theory and Criticism, University of Western Ontario for the winter term of 1996. He is the editor of *Postmodern Apocalypse: Cultural Theory and Practice at the End* (New Cultural Studies Series, University of Pennsylvania Press, 1995) and author of *Apocalyptic Overtures: Sexual Politics and the Sense of an Ending* (Rutgers University Press, 1994) and *Masculine Desire: The Sexual Politics of Victorian Aestheticism* (University of North Carolina Press, 1990). He lives in Toronto.

Robert Farber died while this book was in press. He was an artist/painter working in a variety of mediums. He exhibited in New York at the Paula Cooper Gallery, Artists Space and the Project Room at the Museum of Modern Art. His work has also been shown in many galleries and museums outside Manhattan, including the 1992 'Read my Lips' exhibition at Tramway in Glasgow. In 1993 he was awarded a fellowship from The Edward F. Albee Foundation and he is featured in a book of interviews entitled *Muses from Chaos and Ash: AIDS, Artists and Art* (Grove Press, 1993). He lived and worked in New York City.

Sunil Gupta is an Indian-born, Canadian citizen who lives and works in London. At various times he is a cultural activist, an artist, a photographer, an editor, a teacher and a curator. In 1995 he curated a British exhibition for Africus – the first Johannesburg Biennale. Also in 1995 he held the Essex Fellowship in Photography.

Peter Horne (joint editor) teaches a course on lesbian and gay cultures at the University of East London, where he helped to plan, teach and co-ordinate one of the first undergraduate degrees in cultural studies. He has recently contributed an article on homosexual identity to *Modern Times: Reflections on a Century of English Modernity*, produced by the Cultural Studies Department at the University of East London.

Richard A. Kaye has studied at the University of Chicago and Princeton University. His essay in this volume is adapted from his book in progress, *Voluptuous Immobility: St Sebastian and the*

Decadent Imagination, which explores the figure of Saint Sebastian from the nineteenth century until the present. His articles and reviews have appeared in *The New York Times*, *The Nation*, *The Village Voice*, *Boston Review*, *Arizona Quarterly*, *The Wallace Stevens Journal* and *Studies in English Literature*. He lives in New York City.

Sadie Lee left her art foundation course in 1986 disillusioned with the art institution atmosphere. She did not paint again for five years. In 1992, her painting *Erect* was chosen as the promotional poster for the BP Awards at the National Portrait Gallery, London. She has since exhibited at the Mall Gallery, London, Victoria Art Gallery, Bath, in the Hunting/Observer Prize and the ICA 'Art for Equality' exhibition for Stonewall. She was co-organizer of 'Exposing Ourselves' at The Worx, London. Her first solo exhibition, 'Venus Envy' was at Manchester City Art Galleries. She lives and paints in Soho, London.

Wendy Leeks is senior lecturer and course leader in Visual Culture at Leeds Metropolitan University. Her doctorate, a psychoanalytic interpretation of the pleasures of viewing paintings by J.A.D. Ingres, particularly for a lesbian spectator, was awarded in 1990. Her interests are psychoanalytic, feminist and lesbian/gay perspectives on visual culture and lesbian spectatorship.

Reina Lewis (joint editor) lectures in the department of Cultural Studies at the University of East London. Her writings on contemporary lesbian culture and practice have appeared in a number of journals. She is the author of *Gendering Orientalism: Race, Femininity and Representation* (Routledge, 1996).

Iris Moore is a performance artist and writer whose solo work and collaborations with Beth Tanner and Lawrence Steger have been seen widely in North America. *Rough Trade*, a collaboration with Lawrence Steger, also toured the United Kingdom. She has received funding from several state and city arts councils in the United States and a recent commission for a work, 'Sentimental Discipline', from the Portland Art Museum, Oregon. Her writing has been published in various literary, art and performance magazines.

Thaïs E. Morgan is an associate professor of English at Arizona State University, where she has worked extensively with the interdisciplinary Humanities Program. She has written many articles on contemporary literary theory and Victorian studies. Her most recent books include *Victorian Sages and Cultural Discourse: Renegotiating Gender and Power* (Rutgers University Press, 1990) and *Men Writing the Feminine: Literature, Theory, and the Question of Genders* (State University of New York Press, 1994).

Katrina Rolley is a freelance fashion historian. She has written extensively on dress as an expression and communication of lesbian identity. She is the principal author of *Fashion in Photographs 1900–1920* (Batsford, 1992) and is currently working on a book entitled *The Lesbian Dandy: The Role of Dress and Appearance in the Construction of Lesbian Identities* (Cassell, forthcoming).

Veronica Slater is an artist and lecturer who lives and works in London. Exhibitions have included 'Along the Lines of Resistance', 'Genitals: External', 'Intervening Spaces', 'Visions of Paradise' and 'The Borrowed Image' (touring the United Kingdom in 1995–6). Her work is in public and private collections and has received awards from Northern and North West Arts. She also teaches at the 'City Lit' and is currently involved in a programme of research involving artists from India, Australia and New Zealand.

Cherry Smyth is a journalist and author of *Queer Notions* (Scarlet Press, 1992). She is co-curator of the London Lesbian and Gay Film Festival and author of the first study of contemporary lesbian visual art, *Damn Fine Art by New Lesbian Artists* (Cassell, 1996).

Lawrence Steger is a video and performance artist whose solo performances have been presented widely in the United States and in the former West Germany. He collaborated with Iris Moore on the performance piece *Rough Trade* and with the video artist Suzie Silver on various works. His video collaboration with Patrick Siemer, *It Never Was You* was premiered at the London Lesbian and Gay Film Festival in 1995 and has toured extensively. He has received numerous grants and awards from city arts funding bodies in the United States.

Matthew Stradling studied painting at St Martin's School of Art and gained an MFA from the University of Reading. His work has been included in various national exhibitions and he has had several solo shows in London, notably 'Luxuria' at Battersea Arts Centre and 'Penetralia' at the Edge Gallery. His work has been collected by Derek Jarman, Marc Almond and the Princess Anita of Malaysia. He now works from a studio in north London.

Carl F. Stychin is a lecturer in the school of law at Keele University. His research interests include lesbian and gay legal studies, an area in which he has written extensively. He is the author of *Law's Desire: Sexuality and the Limits of Justice* (Routledge, 1995) and co-editor (with Didi Herman) of *Legal Inversions: Lesbians, Gay Men, and the Politics of Law* (Temple University Press, 1995).

Simon Watney is a writer and critic based in London. His most recent book is *Practices of Freedom: Selected Writings on HIV/AIDS* (Rivers Oram Press and Duke University Press, 1994).

Acknowledgements

We would like to thank Rebecca Barden at Routledge for commissioning this book and for remaining calm and encouraging in the years it took to complete. Finding contributors was not always easy, and a number of people helped with suggestions, telephone numbers and contacts: we are grateful to Susan Collins, Emmanuel Cooper, Sally Dawson, Robert Farber, Paul Holloway at the Ferens Art Gallery, Hull, Veronica Slater, Simon Watney and Lola Young. We are also grateful to Susannah Radstone for her advice. Reina Lewis would like to thank Suzanne Hamilton for saying all the right things on many crucial occasions.

Tessa Boffin had decided to write a piece for this book shortly before she died in 1994. We are extremely grateful to Cherry Smyth for agreeing to write the article in Tessa's stead. We were particularly pleased that Tessa chose to write about her performance practice rather than her photography and that Cherry was able to continue with this focus.

Sadly, we also have to commemorate the death of another contributor to this book: Robert Farber died of AIDS late in 1995. We are particularly pleased that he was able to finish his chapter, and modify it to reflect on his experiences as his illness grew more serious. From our contact with him we know he will be greatly missed for his humour and strength, as well as for his outstanding work.

Introduction

Re-framed – inscribing lesbian, gay and queer presences in visual culture

Peter Horne and Reina Lewis

This book is an exploration on the part of artists, art historians, critics and theorists of how we might inscribe lesbian and gay sexualities, identities and desires into accounts of past and current artistic production and its reception. It takes the reader into accounts of the past (Part I), into statements by practising artists of the present day (Part II), and into discussions of a broad range of contemporary visual cultures that includes photography and the consumption of popular culture, as well as the traditional categories of fine art (Part III). These interconnecting parts share a concern with the relationship between visual theory and our understanding of sexual categories. This is characterized in various ways: art historians insert a queer perspective into the consumption and historiography of past art; contemporary artists refer to, quote and adapt the codes and styles of past artists; lesbians read same-sex pleasures into fashion magazines in a way that is both with and against the grain of ostensibly heterosexual imagery. In these and other ways, contributors to this book remove the presumption of a heterosexual viewer, construct alternative traditions and find means of inscribing a queer presence in the play of spectatorship to be accessed within the product, whatever the sexual identity of the artist/producer who created the work or the heterosexual postulations of the text.

In recent years, the term queer has re-emerged as some people's preferred description of themselves and/or their work. Queer has sometimes been defined by its transgressive difference from what are perceived as heterosexist norms. It has also been taken to encompass a variety of desires and hybrid identities, countenancing elements of play and sexual practice, which also transgress the norms of what some have seen as more ostensibly 'politically correct' forms of gay and lesbian identity. In the construction of what has come to be known as queer theory, the work of Judith Butler has been influential in articulating a sense of lesbianism as a contingent category. She argues that lesbianism does not express an inner essence but is rather a meaning produced in opposition to dominant forms of gender, forms which are given the effect of being natural by virtue of the repetition of their performance (Butler 1991). Butler opposes the idea that the lesbian can be defined in relation to prior regulatory notions; rather, she understands herself as someone who is eligible for the category of lesbian because of an attraction to the dissolution of the boundaries that identify what is masculine, feminine or even heterosexual. Moreover, Butler argues that what is signified by the terms heterosexual, lesbian or queer will change over time. Once all gendered identities are seen as performative and transitory, the heterosexual is not uniquely separated from the lesbian or gay. The adoption of lesbian or gay or queer identities throws up the kinds of contradictions and instabilities that the regulatory definition of gender as natural tries to suppress.

This book, while retaining lesbian and gay in its title, is aligned to queer in that we would also see all sexual identities as contingent and transitory, in the sense of being formed in active (though not necessarily conscious) response to dominant identificatory norms which themselves need to be deconstructed. But we consider that the terms lesbian and gay still denote identities with which more people wish to be affiliated. Also, queer is currently discovering its own history. In this process points of continuity between queer and lesbian and gay visual histories are emerging as well as points of difference. This book is poised at this particular cusp. It is driven by the dynamic of a double movement: it addresses lesbian and gay visual cultures in a way which foregrounds art produced by lesbian and gay, or queer, artists but also goes beyond that to attend to the potentially queer reception of visual material from the past and the present, regardless of its sexual point of origin. This creates a space to consider the production of queer meanings, since in a heterosexist society the queer reader has often to be ever resourceful and imaginative in the production of alternative sexual pleasures. One form that this imagining takes is the envisaging of other gay readers: Eve Kosofsky Sedgwick illustrates this in the *Epistemology of the Closet* when she invites the reader to consider a solitary gay listener to a Judy Garland song, marooned in middle America away from the urban gay cultures, imagining other consumers enjoying similar pleasures of self-identification in the music (Sedgwick 1991: 144). This vision of camp appreciation as the assumption of shared pleasures points to the importance of cultural production in the formation of lesbian and gay identities. It also points to the ways in which both identity and community may have to be thought of differently in the case of lesbian and gay experiences. Camp is but one form of twentieth-century gay culture. This book hopefully also offers further senses of something shared with others, be it a visual code, a way of reading, or a question about the dominance of heterosexuality. Both readers and their envisaged others may be variously identified as lesbian, gay or queer: categories which may themselves be interpreted in a number of different ways. What is common in all these discussions is the sense that in modern cultures the presence and meaning of same-sex desires are inseparable from modes of power, which both censure and produce sexualized identities, whatever their provisionality. This volume wishes to put these issues at the centre of visual enquiry in an intervention that encompasses artistic production, cultural activism and the academy.

The past twenty years have seen the growth of interdisciplinary and radical academic work which has addressed the issues of power and culture in modern societies. Questions of class, gender and ethnicity have been at the cutting edge of much of this exciting cultural theory, linked to both the development of university departments of cultural studies, and the various revisions of the previously autonomous disciplines. Attention to these concerns has entered the realm of the art historian and the critic, though often with a greater delay than in other areas. Revisions, such as the social history of art and feminist art history, have found that their need to re-inscribe class and gender has not been met simply by identifying the role of working-class or women artists. Rather, this type of re-inclusion has itself raised methodological questions about writing, power and historiography. One might expect the strategies for the inclusion of lesbian, gay or queer sexualities within the narratives of modern culture to raise similar questions about the paradigms of explanation and analysis. Instead, there is often a resistance to re-addressing theory in the light of these sexualities. This tendency is even present in some postmodern theory. Postmodernism is often characterized in terms of a dislocation or decentring of the major forms of modernist representation and the loss of those grand narratives of modernity which implied an unproblematic sense of progress (even, or especially, if this is achieved through struggles between opposing forces propelling the action). In one dominant version, that of Fredric Jameson (1991), discussed here by Richard Dellamora, emphasis is placed on the loss of agency produced by the dissolution of individual and spatial boundaries in the disengaged experience of the (post) modern world of electronic media. Some postmodern theory is haunted by such senses of loss.

The view from the position of those marginalized or made peripheral within the previously dominant narratives of modernism and modernity is often quite different (see Mercer 1994). Gay art theorists, such as Douglas Crimp, have seen the resource which postmodernism offers (Crimp and Rolston 1990). The dissolution of the sense of difference between high and popular cultures and the defence of appropriation as an aesthetic strategy have provided lesbian and gay activists with the theories and practices to be used in a new assertive politics of the street in the vital visual art of AIDS demonstrations. Similarly artists have used the mixing of codes and media within postmodern practice to explore new ethnic identities unconnected to imperialist and colonialist narratives of origin. In the experience of the diaspora there is a felt need to recognize difference but also to challenge the primitivism and Orientalism that has had such an enduring presence in modern and modernist western visual cultures. One of the potentials of postmodern theory is to challenge the idea of modernity's clean break with past discourses of subordination and exclusion. Yet, it is all too common for the postmodern theorist who is not lesbian or gay to ignore the implications of new sexualities and new negotiations of issues concerning power and the image. This is redressed by Dellamora's intervention in this debate within this volume. The tendency in some postmodern theory to write out (homo)sexuality is even more disturbing when we recognize that one of the main contributions of academic revisions and activist polemics has been to constitute visual theory as a field that cannot but be concerned with the engendering and racialization of the gaze.

In this light, lesbian/gay/queer theorists are in an advantageous position. Rather than regretting the loss of a putative centre in a sovereign subject who is implicitly white, male and heterosexual, they frequently weigh the supposed losses of postmodernism against the benefits of postmodern permission to pleasure and habits of appropriation that account for much of the vivacity of contemporary gay culture. Indeed, one could say that lesbians and gays have always had to be post-modern in the sense of having to form identities out of appropriations and adaptations of existing codes, not least in order to resist definition and co-option by medical and legal discourse.

Strategies for the inclusion of sexuality within the narratives of modern culture are unsettling to the existing paradigms and raise difficult questions of the categories to be used. How are we imagining the gay, lesbian or queer identities and modes of spectatorship that animate this book? When we first told someone that we were editing a book on lesbian and gay sexuality and visual culture, he (a heterosexual man) asked us if were going to be 'outing' past artists? There was a sense of threat involved in such an expectation, and an assumption that it would be natural for a book on lesbian and gay art history to simply reclaim past and present visual artists as lesbian or gay, and that the meaning of such terms would be obvious. Anyone remotely concerned with lesbian and gay or queer theory would know that the application of these categories to past and present artists is contentious and the politics of outing, in any case, debatable. However the idea of outing artists, or the provision of spaces within which artists can come out on their own terms, is important. Unlike the case of feminist art history, where the putatively gendered subject of the woman artist is always out,[1] the lesbian and gay artist, critic, historian and reader is often rendered invisible unless they make a point of coming out. However, 'coming out' and 'outing' can imply a rather uniform notion of a closet which is present in the same way for all, and a simplified idea of self-affirmation in escaping from it. This model has been accused of setting a white male middle-class agenda which is inappropriate to the experience of those negotiating complex identities or occupying several different identities in different contexts (Smyth 1992). There is also a problem about what one would be outing artists as. If the term homosexual is a modern medicalized construction, only invented by the sexologists of the latter part of the nineteenth century, so the liberationist idea of the gay identity can only be applied to those involved in the cultures of the moment of gay liberation and after. Moreover, recent theory has questioned assumptions in the use of these terms, in so far as they imply a political identity resting on self-recognition and the liberation of a unified inner self (Butler 1991).

Still, the desire to discover past gay and lesbian artists, to produce a tradition, to invent a history, is understandable: a need that this book recognizes, but also problematizes. Obviously, all the practitioners in this book are happy to be identified with a project of this title (and some that we approached were not); being in this volume, is one way of coming out. But this does not imply that the contributors to this volume all make the same identification with any of the terms lesbian, gay or queer, or interpret the meaning of these terms in the same way. Several artists in this book would wish to be known as artists who are lesbian, gay or queer, and whose sexuality is relevant to their work, but they would not necessarily wish to be known under the composite terms lesbian artist or gay artist. These latter terms seem to foreclose meanings and restrict their audience. However, whether or not they wish to be so labelled, they also find that the identification of their work as the product of a 'gay' artist may still determine meanings even where the artist is not using codes which are exclusively gay: Sadie Lee's paintings of female nudes aroused censure in Manchester City Art Gallery, because the work was identified as lesbian-produced, unlike the other (presumed male-produced) canonical nudes in the gallery. Thus artists not intending to restrict their work to a gay audience may find their work bound to their sexual identity, whether they like it or not.

As well as attempting to reach a wide audience without having the work's meanings confined by the artist's sexuality, artists also deploy visual strategies that will be particularly accessible to specific viewing communities. The production of images which are multicoded, gives gay readers a privileged access, without prohibiting more general meanings. Veronica Slater's use of a Gluck self-portrait references a gay iconography that allows a privileged access to the visually literate gay reader who recognizes both the lesbian identity of the quoted artist and the lesbian codes of the Gluck image. This, of course, demonstrates that the desire to tie meanings to a point of origin in a sexualized personality can operate for the lesbian and gay reader as well. But these meanings may be found in alternative traditions, or sets of codes recognizable to those accustomed to the exclusions of dominant homophobic cultures. The constructions of such interpretive communities can be seen as a collective expression of negotiated identities rather than as the immediate outlet of true sexuality assumed in common sense.

Rather than just outing individual artists, it is possible in the analysis of certain historical contexts to discern the emergence of codes, used by more than one artist, to construct alternative meanings. This approach, which tends here and elsewhere (Dellamora 1990) to centre on the nineteenth century, demonstrates how dominant models are reused by homosexuals to formulate alternative identities and spectatorial positions, often by appropriating existing mainstream myths and images. Thaïs Morgan discusses how the homoerotic 'monoculture' of the Pre-Raphaelite Brotherhood with which Swinburne and Solomon were associated found expression in the appropriation of lesbian themes from Sappho (already popular as a Greek 'classic') and homosocial narratives from the Bible. This type of approach may not out individuals as gay (Swinburne's sexual orientation can only be guessed at, for example) but looks at the codes that artists of diverse sexualities have used in forming oppositional strategies to the restriction of gender categories. This is not intelligible outside of a social context – particular formations of homophobia provide the occasion for the emergence of different gay codes envisaging different values and identities. As Morgan demonstrates, the exchange of and response to images, poems and letters was a fundamental device in the 1860s and 1870s through which were constructed perverse and homosexual identities and through which individuals could articulate their shifting allegiance to or denial of (as was the case with Swinburne's denunciation of Solomon) counterhegemonic socio-sexual identities in circulation. Also in this volume, Richard Kaye traces the process by which Saint Sebastian was appropriated and constructed as a gay icon, emphasizing how the Saint's significance altered as gay identities and agendas were differently constructed in different periods.

The ways in which artists and readers relate to dominant cultural forms can vary. Kaye's reading of the shifting cultural codes used to represent Saint Sebastian demonstrates how the gay significance of iconography is read through negotiation with dominant/high cultural meanings. Other work, in contrast, can be understood as a more straightforward rejection of dominant forms, drawing on other codes generated within gay cultures, as in the output of Andy Warhol's Factory. Here, the gay artist's opposition to what was experienced as the masculinist forms of the dominant aesthetic of Abstract Expressionism found an alternative visual resource in the camp appreciation of popular culture. Later gay artists, including some in this volume, continue to find that the protocols of Abstract Expressionism taught in their art education excluded a sense of themselves as gay or as having alternative aesthetic sensibilities, and have often turned back to the codes of the nineteenth century. Some, like Matthew Stradling, have re-used both the gay icon of Saint Sebastian and the gay-coded stylistics of Aestheticism to articulate a late-twentieth-century gay sensibility. However, others like Robert Farber have found an enormous resource in a practice and discourse like Abstract Expressionism which values authenticity. Indeed, the very emphasis on gesture and origin which some find obliterating, in the context of AIDS can be transformed into an ethos of testimony and presence in the face of potential annihilation. What makes Farber's work so telling is the way that he deployed different forms of record: transforming the self-referentiality of Abstract Expressionism into a painterly form that can accommodate and interact with the record of contemporary AIDS activism and a recall of how past forms of mourning found a collective expression. The AIDS pandemic has produced a need to build new forms and cultures of mourning that speak to the particularity of the AIDS experience and how this has repositioned or questioned accepted personal and professional wisdom about the expression of grief and its representability. Simon Watney here analyses the specific effects of AIDS on male gay communities. In particular, he considers the impact of shared multiple losses and the need this creates to find appropriate forms, both personal and collective, for expressing grief and making public witness, as well as educating a population composed of individuals with very different histories of the virus and the syndrome.

This volume is concerned in some ways with how artists conceive their work (not least in our artists' statements), but also with how meanings are produced by readers. If we no longer see the author in the role of owner of the text's meaning, we can locate the generation of meaning in the interaction between reader/viewer and text. This allows for both the specificity of different reading positions and for the interaction of subversive readings with dominant or preferred meanings. It thus becomes possible to analyse how the queer reader can find queer pleasures in texts which may appear to be ostensibly heterosexual. This process of reading against the grain is one that recognizes the preferred, or in this case heterosexual, meaning of the text at the same time as it realizes the possibilities of alternative pleasures. The interaction of subordinate and dominant/heterosexual meanings in the case of diverse images is examined in this volume by Wendy Leeks, Reina Lewis and Katrina Rolley. They discuss how the lesbian viewer, who has assumptions different from those of a paradigmatically heterosexual female viewer, may make distinctively lesbian readings at the same time as she shares pleasures that might previously have been assumed to be heterosexual alone. It may not be that the lesbian viewer simply makes subversive readings, but that the possibility of a shared lesbian/same-sex pleasure was already there in the text. Is this a deviant reading of the dominant against the dominant, or did the dominant always have the deviant within it? In other words, queer reading does not aim to discover a gay origin but to trace the spaces for multiple readings within the text. In this way, Leeks re-reads Ingres's *Stratonice* series to analyse how the images produce the possibility of a lesbian visual pleasure. The recognition of the suppressed female knowledges and gazes in Freud's case study of 'Dora' in his 'Fragment of an analysis' is used to open up the paintings to new possible readings: Leeks identifies the marginalized female gazes within the picture plane to argue that there is already encoded within the Ingres series the availability of a position for an active female/lesbian viewer. Similarly, Lewis and Rolley re-examine psychoanalytic theories of narcissism to see how the ostensibly same-sex space of the fashion magazine produces homoerotic codes and permits a lesbian pleasure that can simultaneously desire to be and to have the beautiful female model that is the object of the woman reader's desiring gaze.

Another approach concerned with the viewer's response takes homophobia itself as the object of study. Carl Stychin, Richard Dellamora and Emmanuel Cooper all assess how the operation of homophobia within both dominant and even supposedly radical cultures can paradoxically destabilize the terms of the heterosexual dominance they seek to uphold. For radical discourses this throws texts into contradiction and causes problems of analysis. Dellamora, for instance, argues that Fredric Jameson actually stymies his own project by his need to disavow the body and homosexuality. His suppression of the homoerotic character of camp leads him to ignore a model of agency that would resolve his (political) problem of the non-agency of the postmodern split un-subject. As Stychin and a number of artists emphasize, we must also attend to the explicit forms of censorship that homophobia produces. Attempts at suppression and other overt uses of power can, in fact, give publicity to the queer work that they want to stifle. As Stychin demonstrates in his discussion of the controversy over the American National Endowments for the Arts funding policy, the internal instabilities of homophobic anxiety call into question the security of the very heterosexual identities that Senator Helms and others seek to defend. It is no coincidence that so much of the moral panic in America has centred on the visual arts; it is not just sex acts but their representation that endangers the mythically pure 'America'. Both homophobic and gay discourse presuppose that representation is central to the formation and maintenance of identity. Stychin is specifically concerned with how the law, which appears as an arbitrator rather than a producer, is itself another form of representation. It is in this context of shifting terms – which change not just from our own efforts, activisms and theories, but also in response to attack and the need to counter-define – that writers and artists are choosing how to identify themselves and their work.

The analysis of the effects of the power to censor must be matched by attention to other processes which have stifled the plurality of voices, even within cultures of opposition. One reason for the popularity and political purchase of queer is that it promises the inclusion of those previously excluded. Although the earlier lesbian and gay movements wanted to question all forms of sexuality, they have come to be seen by some as formations that marginalized difference in the production of a gay 'ethnic' identity that in practice was white, middle-class and male. Such a response ignores the attempts of black and white lesbian and gay activists to acknowledge and deal with exclusions, and to recognize the difficulties of negotiating the demands and appeals of often conflicting sexual and ethnic identities. In the 1990s, queer has been associated with a willingness both within and beyond the gay movement to recognize diverse and contradictory sexualities and lifestyles. With this recognition and the gaining of more cultural spaces for the exhibition of black art, there is new work being produced which explores and challenges sexual and ethnic identities. In some cases, this uses aesthetic codes actively to construct new hybrid entities, and in others it pushes at the limits of identity itself in work which is not easily contained within existing formulae for sexuality and ethnicity. This cultural activity is not happening in a political and material vacuum; Sunil Gupta's essay explores the ways in which black and Asian artists in Britain have found or fought for spaces within which to explore these issues of sexuality and identity. He traces a development from the context of funding by the Labour-controlled Greater London Council, which in the early 1980s embraced a rainbow coalition of previously marginalized constituencies, to new international contexts offered by exchange and communication within and beyond Europe. With these changing points of reference, new communities of reading visual images are emerging.

The present moment is one in which developments identified as queer are encouraging new perspectives on past work. For Emmanuel Cooper, it is possible to look back and assess how current queer work was anticipated by artists who have either been at odds with the modernist tradition or can be reclaimed in a queer perspective now that their sexuality can be more freely discussed. Cooper's analysis of the posthumous outing of Francis Bacon reveals not only the effort that critics previously made to 'in' an artist who was always out for anyone who wished to see it, but also reconsiders twentieth-century art in relation to an emergent aesthetic of transgression, desire and the body which was present in past practice and is now receiving more overt attention.

As seen in this volume, gays and lesbians have often looked back with a sense of transformative possibility: camp and gay plundering of the past is not just nostalgia, but marks an active reincorporation that is self-knowing. While, as Kaye argues, the appropriation of Saint Sebastian pre-dates the postmodern, his reactivation as a plague saint at the time of AIDS illustrates the strategic provisionality of (gay) identities: the categories we use now are necessary to make sense in the world, but not only do they not relate to any essential 'us', they may signify different things at different times. Similarly, Stradling and Lee re-examine gay visual codes to find new contemporary meanings with a self-knowing narcissism whose irony disputes the possibility of an essential truth or a singular gaze. In other words, recognition of one's own processes denotes a self-conscious subjectivity that, like camp, does not yearn for authenticity. For Stradling, the representation of an idealized, eroticized body foregounds the pleasures of the nude and links the rarefied realm of fine art to the denigrated sphere of the pornographic. The beautiful, if anguished, bodies of aestheticism may speak to a gay sensibility, but as Stradling comments at the close of his piece, this idealization is being reconsidered in the context of AIDS. For Slater, the context of AIDS along with that of the family, produces a representation of the body that is not idealized, but is mutable and temporal. The disintegration of the ideal male body, like her complex positioning of the female body, speaks to a physicality that is fragile and compromised. Here, again, the physicality of paint re-enters as a trace and an object in its own right. For Stradling, and Lee also, the decision to paint rather than use more 'modern' technologies, offers a route into a visual past that other means would obscure. They share a tendency to paint portraits whose monumentality is postmodern in its self-conscious construction of a facade, creating personae that are dressed up and self-knowing, ironically offering the temptation of the (fantasized) truth of an individual.

Contestation over the authenticity of gendered bodies and the fixity of individual natures is elaborated further in the performance work of Iris Moore and Lawrence Steger, and Tessa Boffin. In the case of Moore and Steger, the interchangeability of the gendered roles in their collaboration calls into question the stability of all forms of identity and of the popular cultural images they appropriate. The famous Sharon Stone knicker(less)scene from *Basic Instinct* takes on a whole new meaning when alternatively reproduced by a woman and a gay man, resituating revisionist strategies that aimed mainly to reverse a (gender or class) bias. The performative identifications staged in this new type of work question all the terms of social identification. Tessa Boffin's self-presentation as lesbian boy and queer dyke, described here by Cherry Smyth, signalled the sort of gender-fuck identifications that queer might offer lesbians (like the gender-fuck that gay liberation offered gay men). Tessa's masquerade performance of lesbian drag both offered the materiality of her body and denied any attempt to make a single truth of it. Whereas male gender-fucking at the time of gay liberation was frequently criticized as a misogynist parody of femininity, now, parody is not only fashionable but critically respectable. Once femininity and masculinity are both seen as forms of masquerade naturalized by repetition, women can parody femininity as well. Though we wonder, in the light of the mainly male popular cultural take-up of transvestism (Kurt Cobain *et al.*), whether the radical potential of new queer gender-fuck will turn out to have its transgressiveness assimilated by the dominant. New forms of masquerade have further radical purposes: for artists such as Lawrence Steger and Iris Moore, it is clear that masquerade offers not only a radical critique of gendered and sexualized positionalities, but also challenges the way that audiences read.The desire to produce an author as owner of the text and origin of its meaning is frustrated when the two performers can take either role or speak any part, not wanting to produce a formal play, but creating a series of unique events. This challenge to the ownership of fixed meanings allows them to experience a temporary relief from the burden of authorship and gender while they watch the other perform 'their' part. In the circulation of positions within such performances, disruptive and disorderly desires are envisaged in a queer intervention into hegemonic, often masculinist, representations of gender.

A postmodernist emphasis on pleasure, combined with this new queer interest in performance and spectatorship suggests possibilities for a cultural analysis that moves beyond the critique of objectification to a belief in the pleasure and potentials of looking and voyeurism. In terms of the female gaze, this context marks a shift that allows us to discuss how lesbians and women look for or with pleasure at other women, without being simply re-appropriated as masculinist. Queer has great potential for visual theory, particularly when it is conceived as a new mode of spectatorship. However, while some would see queer spectatorship as untrammelled by previous notions of identity, we think that it is important to consider how queer as a mode of viewing may itself be differently inflected by the agent's experience of being positioned by pre-existent regulatory discourses or, equally, of assuming identities developed in resistance.

It is significant that the emergence of an interest in the performative is linked to the issue of AIDS. The AIDS context electrifies the depiction of the body and adds an urgency to the need to recognize the diversity of activities and identifications: when being realistic about who does what with whom can save lives, the need to accept the shifts of sexualized object choice are crucial. For Boffin, this was a political imperative that meant focusing on fantasy as well as reality. With the development of safe sex material the erotic re-emerges as both a product of and vehicle for safe gay sex, illustrating the changing but crucial role of representation in the formation of sexualized identities. This is typical of the processes by which lesbian and gay readers find and create meanings from diverse visual sources.The exercise of and reflection upon this gaze in themselves produce new spaces for the articulation of homoerotic pleasures.

This volume is in part one such space; it is a space in which artists can come out in terms that they choose and make statements about their work, some entering into a form of communication different from their usual, primarily visual, discourse. It also provides a space to consider theoretically and historically the activities of lesbians and gay men as viewers responding to artists' adoption of the existing canon of high culture. And it gives space to consider the creation of communities of viewing in the development of new canons and codes for representing and questioning sexual identities, formed and reformed in resistance to heterosexual norms and to the homophobia that is analysed in several pieces. It is also a space for the historians, critics and artists to consider their own positions as spectators (see also Davis 1994: 5), sharing with other lesbian, gay or queer viewers an intent to find visual pleasures and give scope to fantasy and desire.

Note

1 Though we recognise that some of the early work of feminist art history did require the effective 'outing' of women artists in the struggle to re-attribute to women their mis-attributed work. See Greer 1979 and Parker and Pollock 1981.

References

Butler, J. (1991) 'Imitation and gender insubordination' in D. Fuss (ed.), *Inside/Out*, London: Routledge.
Crimp,P. and Rolston, A. (1990) *AIDS Demo/Graphics*, Seattle: Bay Press.

Davis, W. (1994) 'Introduction', in Davis (ed.) *Gay and Lesbian Studies in Art History*, New York and London: Harrington Park Press, Haworth Press.
Dellamora, R. (1990) *Masculine Desire: The Sexual Politics of Victorian Aestheticism*, Chapel Hill and London: University of North Carolina Press.
Greer, G. (1979) *The Obstacle Race: The Fortunes of Women Painters and Their Work*, London: Secker & Warburg.
Jameson, F. (1991) *Postmodernism, or the Cultural Logic of Late Capitalism*, London: Verso.
Mercer, K. (1994) *Welcome to the Jungle: New Positions in Black Cultural Studies*, London: Routledge.
Parker, R.and Pollock, G. (1981) *Old Mistresses: Women, Art and Ideology*, London: Routledge Kegan Paul.
Sedgwick, E.K. (1991) *Epistemology of the Closet*, Hemel Hempstead: Harvester Wheatsheaf.
Smyth, C .(1992) *Lesbians Talk Queer Notions*, London: Scarlet Press.

PART I

Queering art history

Chapter One

Queer spectacles

Emmanuel Cooper

Queer art remains a paradox. What it is and what forms it takes virtually defy definition, though its spirit informs work by many young artists, and its existence seems to be as much concerned with lifestyle – evident in street demonstrations, parades and nightclubs – as shown on the walls of art galleries. Queer art is part of a widespread, if often diffuse, reaction to a perceived complacency about art which claims to address issues around gay and lesbian identity, and the way this fails to acknowledge the political shift from art directed at lesbians/gays, to that seeking a wider and more general audience.

The importance of queer, 'this violent rejection and despoliation of the norm by the exiled' (Derbyshire 1994: 45), and its ability to open up the question of how lesbian and gay identity has been theorized and represented in art, is a vital part of current debates. For not only does queer address the perceived need to bridge the huge gulf that separates 'the reportedly homosexual from the presumably heterosexual, and the questionably white from the allegedly Black' (Reid-Pharr 1993: 31), but it is part of a widespread continuing debate concerned with individual and collective identity, and the conflict between what concerns us as individuals and what can – and should – be made public. While the assertive, rebarbative and confrontational concept of queer is not intended to offer solutions, it has stimulated productive debate around rapidly changing identities, and raised the question of the degree to which queer takes up and develops existing ideas.

Within this discussion, the death of Francis Bacon in 1992 can be seen as an opportunity to discuss his work as a painter in the light of queer culture. His death marked an end to the old traditional school of politeness, and perhaps the start of something new. Bacon, a latter-day Edwardian gentleman, invariably smartly dressed, wealthy, debonair, bachelor and vaguely aristocratic, fond of booze, food, gambling and sex, led a privileged and, despite massive publicity in recent years, a remarkably private life in which the media, public and friends conspired with the artist to ensure a veil of secrecy was cast over the turbulent events of his life, and on any specific queer reading of his work.

I want to use Bacon's death as an opportunity for re-appraisal, a moment to examine the concept of queer and the emergence of queer culture in the light of the work of artists who have produced transgressive art in the 1970s and 1980s. The roots of queer culture in the field of visual art, however complex, can be identified in work as diverse as the turbulent paintings of Bacon, the large-scale photographically based screen-prints of Andy Warhol and the sexually explicit photographs of Robert Mapplethorpe, as well as in the graphics of Keith Haring and the agit-prop based work of David Wojnarowicz, who were involved in art and direct action around the AIDS epidemic. Such discussion inevitably questions the extent to which queer art is as new, challenging and transgressive as its image may imply, a theme taken up here. The argument put forward is that queer art, though taking particular forms today, is part of a continuing search for a visual language which expresses the hopes, anxieties, desires of queers/gays/lesbians/dykes/bisexuals.

While the notion of queer presents a series of contradictions around issues such as integration/confrontation, and problems around assimilation/opposition, it is also a crucial focus for arguments around the adoption of changing concepts of queer/gay/lesbian/dyke/bisexual identity at a time when who and what we are is under close scrutiny. As AIDS continues to take its toll, the necessary adjustments can never be fully resolved but must be constantly reviewed, throwing into question the aims and intentions of cultural production. AIDS, above all, has heightened awareness of the fragility of life, and the need to assert confidence and affirm identity. The extent of the AIDS epidemic continues to be a significant element in critical definitions of contemporary sexual behaviour, attitudes and sensibilities.

Debates around the concept of queer have been brought sharply into focus as part of a response to a profound questioning of identity, as issues around civil rights and illness are forcing us to look at who and what we are. This chapter attempts both to identify elements of a queer tradition which, though never labelled as such, have been emerging for over 20 years, and to discuss the ways in which artists who are gay have often found challenging, even confrontational, ways of subverting mainstream culture and inserting their own odd, even perverse perspectives on a largely unsuspecting and often unsuspicious public.

WHAT IS QUEER?

Much, if not all queer culture is concerned with aspects of social transgression, whether involving a variety of same-sex relationship, and/or cultural confrontations. Fundamental to queer culture is the questioning and exploration of desire, investigating how it is shaped and perceived, and in what forms it can be expressed. One of the most disruptive and potentially liberating aspects of queer culture, with its possibilities of participation and activism, has been the rejection of fixed notions of sexuality. This has not only challenged conventional notions around gay/lesbian identity, often perceived as white, materialistic and thirty-something, but has also questioned clear defining lines between the sexually transgressive and the normative concept of straight. In an area which has tended to be seen as essentially objective, that is disembodied and universal rather than personal and specific, queer culture insists that discussion is about the freedom of individuals to choose whatever sexuality they wish.

Despite all the writing on queer culture, no simple definition has emerged which encompasses its breadth or suggests its implications[1]. But this absence of a handy definition does not invalidate the significance of queer, nor do the challenges posed by queer culture with its associations of malfeasance, unlimited boundaries and desire for pleasure and play, limit its effect. While many aspects of queer culture are concerned with specific acts of social transgression, such as outing public figures, or highlighting the anti-gay attitude of the church through the disruption of religious services, for many individuals it is in the public expression of same-sex desire that the assertion of queer is most strongly expressed. Much of this centres around fetishism, and the ultimate excesses of bodily sensation and sado-masochism (s/m) with its connotations of deviancy and 'kinky' sexuality. In an effort to claim images of their own sexuality 'lesbians have looked to gay male culture and produced images of a so-called sexual fringe – images of fisting, sex toys, and sado-masochistic scenes that refuse, or at least attempt to refuse, assimilation by mainstream culture' (Fernandes 1991: 38) – a feeling expressed more directly in the effort to select 'the most frightening, disgusting or unacceptable activities and transmute them into pleasure. We make use of all the forbidden symbols and all the disowned emotions...' (Califia 1979: 19).

The radical status of queer culture as a powerful force for change, with its continuing agenda of challenging and confronting existing modes of representation, has not been unproblematic. Jeffrey Weeks recognized this when he posed the question 'Does sado-masochism involve a submission in dangerous fantasies of violence, or is it no more than a harmless playing out of eroticised power relations?' (Weeks 1986: 81). While on the one hand queer can be seen as an expression of growing confidence and security, critics within both the lesbian and the gay communities, provoked by the hedonism of the 'pleasure at any price' principle, see s/m as replicating and exaggerating traditional heterosexual power relationships, and that rather than opening up new ways of relating, s/m is a denial of feeling.

Lesbian-feminist proponents of s/m argue that while they regard it as a liberating practice, it is so only within a lesbian-feminist context. It can, they argue, 'equalise a power imbalance in a love relationship, but only between members of the same sexual caste ... but it would be extremely self-destructive for any women to play *either* role in an s/m relationship with any man' (Samois 1979: 8). They also acknowledge that discussion and consent must always precede 'the eroticised exchange of power negotiated between two or more sexual partners' (Samois 1979: 2). The law takes a different perspective. The prosecution of consensual gay s/m sex in the Operation Spanner trial in the United Kingdom dramatically brought home the limitations of legal acceptance and the legal limitations placed on the individual to give consent.

Aspects of lesbian/dyke/gay/queer culture around s/m were brought sharply into focus in the United Kingdom with the publication of Della Grace's book of theatrically staged photographs *Love Bites* (Schulman 1991), which centres on the idea of lesbians' 'pleasuring of their own bodies' (Fernandes 1991: 38). An American artist working in London, Della Grace took debates about lesbians and s/m which had been raging on America's West Coast since the late 1970s, and presented them in photographic form to a largely unsuspecting audience in Britain. In the United States Gayle Rubin was writing on lesbians and s/m in the late 1970s, while Pat Califia's *Macho Sluts* and the regular publication *On Our Backs: Entertainment for the Adventurous Lesbian* continued the argument.[2] Sado-masochists 'have all argued at various times that they do not lead stunted lives, do not do harm to others, are perfectly capable of healthy relationships, and should not be considered by definition to manifest some defect of personality' (see Rubin in Samois 1979: 29). Later, artist and critic Joyce Fernandes argued that s/m is a means of providing 'feminists with the most powerful strategy with which to confront a culture still enmeshed in prescriptive images of women as mothers, nurturers, and sexual satisfiers of male desire' (Fernandes 1991: 35).

Grace's erotic photographs featured 'portraits of lesbians from the punk, leather, and s/m and bar communities' (Schulman 1991: 4) involving carefully staged scenarios of women acting out s/m fantasies, many of which parody the dress and stance of gay men and the fantasy leather-gear depicted in the art of Tom of Finland. Items of leather and rubber clothing, caps, vests and such-like, and emblems of sexual domination such as dog collars, studded belts and chains, together with long black rubber gloves and a range of different-sized dildos, usually associated with men, were here being used – and abused – by women. The book launched a wide-ranging debate in Britain. This not only questioned the success of the images, but raised the wider issue of the appropriation of s/m by dykes.

The book received a mixed reception. Two feminist bookshops in London refused to sell it, either fearing prosecution under the Obscene Publications Act, or because they thought Grace had betrayed the politically correct lesbian consciousness. Supporting sisters and brothers, wearing s/m gear, picketed the shops offering copies of the book for sale. The controversy was fuelled by Paul Burston's review article 'Falling from Grace' in the free weekly London newspaper *Capital Gay* (21 June 1991). His enthusiasm was met with a storm of protest from outraged lesbians and gay men.

Interviewed by Burston in the article, Della Grace acknowledged that some of her images may be seen by some lesbians as unacceptable, saying:

> My purpose is to provide images of my sexuality and the sexuality of the women I identify with, who are part of a

> community which is considered 'politically incorrect'. SM dykes have been ostracised, labelled 'fascists' or 'pseudo-men'. The women I photograph are women who want to express who they are. In Britain especially, lesbian sexuality is so invisible. I want women who see my book to recognise that they're okay, that there's nothing wrong with them.[3]

A lively series of letters followed Burston's article, with readers of *Capital Gay* expressing a wide range of opinions. Eugenia Oakes (Oakes 1991) found them 'insulting'. She not only thought Burston's article a 'patronising wank', but she had little time for the photographs saying 'they are not good, important or ground breaking', and that they offered 'no examination of female desire'. Anne Marie Smith, for PUSSY (Perverts Undermining State Scrutiny) and OutRage disagreed in the paper the following week (Smith 1991). The photographs, she wrote, 'capture the ways that pro-sex lesbians, especially s/m dykes, are playing with gender roles'.

The basis of much of the criticisms of Grace's photographs was that the images aped the power relationships of men, that the book had been reviewed favourably by a man who was in effect telling lesbians what to do, and, compounding this view, that the book had been published by Gay Men's Press, a male-dominated publisher.

Many women found the images disturbing. Some sympathetic observers such as Reina Lewis were finally 'half convinced', saying, perhaps with an unintentional element of wit, that '*Love Bites* offers a multiplicity of positionings which has, in the end, convinced me of its liberating potential' (Lewis 1994: 87). 'But', she added, the images 'are overwhelmingly coded with sadomasochistic referents and this still troubles me.' Reina Lewis went on to detail her doubts about the images, saying that not only do they make strong references to s/m but that they 'display precisely a lack of a clear morality that so troubles some feminists about postmodernism's celebration of diversity and contradiction'.

Challenging the concept of static sexualities, one of the themes underlying Della Grace's concern with a dramatically changing lesbian/dyke identity, was taken up in his *Capital Gay* review by Paul Burston, a gay man, who confessed to finding the images erotic, and thereby transgressed the gender code of sexual desire. In focusing on confrontation, and rejecting conventional feminism in favour of 'queer feminism', Grace's work was part of a wider movement of artists, identifying as queer, responding to a growing sense of urgency around the AIDS epidemic, to the perceived indifference of government and the need for a full and direct educational programme.

ART AND DIRECT ACTION

The emergence of grassroots direct-action organizations in the 1980s and early 1990s was part of a protest against the indifference and inactivity of government agencies, drug industries and religious institutions in the face of the AIDS epidemic. ACT-UP (AIDS Coalition to Unleash Power) was set up in the 1980s in the United States, followed by Queer Nation in New York, and OutRage in the United Kingdom. All carefully targeted their demonstrations and other activities around discrimination, AIDS education and censorship. The proliferating cultural forms addressing the prejudice and fear around the 'AIDS crisis' have not only sought to counterbalance the distortions and misrepresentations of mainstream discourse, but have raised fundamental questions about the relevance of art and its role in the epidemic. Such movements have also been spurred on by homophobic legislation. In the United Kingdom, Clause 28, enacted in the 1980s, ensures that same-sex relationships are denied equivalent heterosexual status. In the United States, the action of the far right has succeeded in censuring cultural expressions of sexual difference.[4]

Keith Haring and David Wojnarowicz[5] , two artists in the United States whose work embraced both their own involvement in direct-action groups and their concern with the AIDS epidemic, each devised a highly distinctive visual language, much of which was intended to convey their anger, frustration and sorrow. Both artists were part of queer culture, using visual art as a means of raising political issues around gay identity and the AIDS epidemic.

Trained as a graphic artist, Keith Haring (1958–1990) called on his skills as painter, graffiti artist and designer to work directly on the walls of nightclubs and the sides of buildings, to decorate cars as well as design posters, T-shirts and badges to produce sensitive and effective images addressing aspects of the epidemic. Many examples of his art have become modern icons in their successful combination of text and image. Ever alert to the graphic possibilities of presenting information, Haring occasionally made use of dramatic black-and-white drawing, some employing the graphic style of comic books, to suggest the horrors of the epidemic, while other work makes inventive use of strong areas of colour to catch the eye. In all his art the seriousness of the message is softened with a thread of wit and humour.

Aimed at an audience outside the art gallery, Haring took his work to people, making it attractive and accessible, but also hard-hitting and graphic. One of his most effective images was that of a red triangle on a black background with a pattern of interlinking silhouette figures covering their eyes, ears and mouths in a modern version of 'see no evil, hear no evil, speak no evil', illustrating the slogan 'Silence = Death', the emotive protest at the refusal by authorities and individuals to acknowledge the size and significance of the epidemic. A black-and-white version of the theme, which also included the slogan 'Ignorance = Fear', has been blazoned across T-shirts, posters and badges.

Haring, described by his biographer as 'an unparalleled phenomenon in contemporary American art, and the most populist artist of his time' (Gruen 1991: x) was diagnosed as HIV-positive in his teens, and devoted much of his artistic output to addressing the epidemic, seeking, above all, to make people aware of, and respond to, human needs. Haring not only brought art and direct action together in a unique way, but he successfully blurred for ever the boundaries between graphic and fine art.

David Wojnarowicz (1954–1992) was one of the first artists to recognize the importance of art as part of a strategy against public indifference, government inactivity, and the reluctance of the art establishment to deal with the issue of AIDS. From the start of his work as an artist, Wojnarowicz operated outside the confines of art galleries, choosing to reject the idea of consumer art, in favour of that which had contemporary relevance, was ephemeral and uncollectable, with no resale value. On one occasion he stencilled designs with spray paint on streets and abandoned warehouses along the Hudson River, combining powerful motifs with apt words or phrases to direct more clearly the viewers' response.

Adopting an agit-prop approach forced Wojnarowicz to simplify his images, often combining minimal motifs with text to explore directly his own life and experience, so disrupting any formal separation between form and content. Wojnarowicz's combinations of image and text in a hard-hitting updated agit-prop style successfully called on the turbulent events in his life, both as a youth coming to terms with his sexuality, and as an adult who rejected many of the commercial and exploitative values of the contemporary society.

Many of Wojnarowicz's ideas were expressed in the 'Sex Series', a group of large-scale collages. These included images of a fetus, a picture of Jesus, police dressed in riot gear, and a microscopic image of the AIDS virus to evoke the fear and prejudice around the epidemic. The Rev. Donald Wildman, executive director of the American Family Association, denounced the work, pointing out that, tucked away among the images, there were depictions of gay sex-acts. In the process of circulating the blow-up section of the work, and drawing it to the attention of the media, Wildman succeeded in giving it enormous publicity, thereby ensuring that the work was seen by a much wider audience.

Queer culture, mainstream art

A major characteristic of much art by gay men, and to some extent that by lesbians, has been its alienation from late modernism because the forms and conventions of mainstream art did not offer the range and meanings required. Within mainstream culture, the art of the post-pop era was seen as an ineffectual vehicle for conveying the complexities of particular 'minorities' – a point taken up by the curators of the widely publicized and highly prestigious 1993 Whitney Biennial Exhibition. In their selection, they centred on a determination to break with modernist orthodoxy around the primacy of form rather than content, actively encouraging artists from 'minorities' to contribute, and in their choices considered what the work was saying as well as what it looked like.

Six openly gay and lesbian artists were selected to be in the exhibition, and showed work which was directly concerned with their own lives and experiences.[6] This, in fact, fitted in well with the avowed intention of the curators to feature the work of 'minority' artists, with a perceived emphasis on '(exotic) identity'. African-Americans, native Americans, Latinos and Asians as well as self-identifying gays and lesbians were represented.

Despite their widely differing concerns, what all such 'minorities' have in common is the way their work has become the focus for far-reaching debates about what forms art should take, what audience it should address, how such art is evaluated, and what is its motivation. All of the 'cultural producers' within such 'minorities' are likely to be as suspicious of the new, whether concerned with theory or practice, as they are of the established modes of discussion and communication because they have often been formed outside the direct needs of the groups involved.

The curators also tended to favour new rather than established artists, and sought to limit their previous obsession with the avant garde by putting a strong emphasis on 'message'. Such a public disregard for modernist concepts in so high-profile an exhibition highlights the perceived limitations of the movement which has dominated art for so much of the twentieth century. Modernism, it appeared, had simply failed to convey the nuances and subtleties required by artists today.

One response to the 'objectivity' of modernism was for artists who were gay or lesbian to develop a highly coded language, much of which concerned identity and desire. Robert Mapplethorpe (1946–1986) was one of the few openly gay artists who not only operated in the mainstream, but also produced photographic images of gay culture which, despite their highly aestheticized presentation, were transgressive and sensational. Having established a reputation as a portraitist and photographer of flowers before he became a chronicler of the subcultural activities and rituals of gay New York, Mapplethorpe was able to present his more queer work by relying to a large extent on his professional status. His images were accepted and purchased by a range of widely different audiences, some lured by the idea of being fashionable and chic, others because the work had an authenticity in reflecting the complexity of gay desire.

Like many queer artists, Mapplethorpe called directly on his own experience, presenting it in a form which was able not only to reflect that experience, but to communicate his desire effectively to others. The autobiographical aspects of his s/m images, his love of and desire for black men, and his own participation in s/m rituals, were crucial to a contemporary concern with attempting to speak for yourself while also seeking to indicate that involvement to others. In reflecting his personal involvement and translating it into something wider and more general, Mapplethorpe broke for ever the unspoken vows of silence which had restricted images of gay life to boys by the pool, or endless images of youthful, muscular men.

The status of Mapplethorpe as an icon of gay culture is reinforced partly by the continuing controversy which surrounds his work, and partly by the way it serves as a reference for other artists. This is not only because of the often hard-hitting documentary aspects of Mapplethorpe's images, but also because they touch on the sensitive issue of relationships between white and black men, and the political questions this involves. His images of youthful black models, produced in the late 1970s and 1980s, are either idealized by placing them (often literally) on a pedestal, or totally objectified by showing only a section of their anatomy – dismembered and disembodied fetishizations or photographic celebrations of desire – aspects of Mapplethorpe's work defined by Kobena Mercer (Mercer 1994) as 'troublesome'.

The extent to which Mapplethorpe's work can usefully be identified as queer calls into question the whole concept of queer as something completely new, and particular to the 1990s. Mapplethorpe's presentation of the acceptability of his own involvement in deviant aspects of gay subcultural life can be readily identified as queer in the way it transgressed accepted boundaries. An established artist-photographer, Mapplethorpe aestheticized his subject and formalized his approach, yet his images have a confrontational element, describing the Other with vivid accuracy. Like much queer art, his images sought to subvert mainstream prejudice, making use of available opportunities to present alternative and challenging views.

However, Mapplethorpe's work remains 'troublesome', and presents difficulties which cannot be ignored just because the work reflects lived experience. While his work has been celebrated by many gays and lesbians as an unselfconscious demonstration of 'gay aesthetics' which rightly have to be defended against homophobic, anti-intellectual, anti-art attack from the American right, many people of colour, including gays and lesbians, are critical of what they perceive to be its elements of bald racism.

PHANTOMS OF DESIRE

Significantly, while Eugenia Oakes was virulent in her attack on Della Grace's photographs in *Love Bites*, she had nothing but praise for the photographs of gay icon Robert Mapplethorpe. 'Robert Mapplethorpe was closely, passionately and precisely in touch with his sexuality' she wrote, adding 'The visual language he developed had a purity of vision that distilled the power of sex' (Oakes 1991). She saw little that was problematic in the power relationships implicit in Mapplethorpe's images, or in the use of black models by a white photographer.

Such criticisms lay at the centre of the installation *Notes on the Margins of the Black Book* by the black American artist Glenn Ligon, included in the 1993 Whitney Biennial Exhibition. For his installation, Ligon appropriated Mapplethorpe's images of black men, remounted them and placed them alongside dozens of separately framed excerpts from the many public and quasi-private statements made about Mapplethorpe and his work by luminaries such as Stuart Hall, James Baldwin and Audre Lord as well as by friends and acquaintances.

> It is the way that black people are marked as black (are not just 'people') in representation that has made it relatively easy to analyse their representation, whereas white people – not there as a category and everywhere, everything as a fact – are difficult, if not impossible, to analyse, *qua* white. The subject seems to fall apart in your hands as soon as you begin. (Richard Dyer)

> Mapplethorpe appropriates the conventions of porn's radicalised codes of representation, and by abstracting its stereotypes into 'art' he makes racism's phantoms of desire respectable. (Isaac Julien and Kobena Mercer)

One of the most incisive statements about Mapplethorpe and his contemporary Andy Warhol came from the artist himself, who observed:

> Mapplethorpe's relation to Warhol includes an ability to mirror the doubts and prejudices of his spectators, to make them see what they do not want to see. (Glenn Ligon)

Far from being critical of Mapplethorpe's art, Ligon suggests that, like the art produced by

Warhol, Mapplethorpe's photographs reflect the repressed desires of the viewer 'to make them see what they do not want to see', an aim to which most artists would aspire. In concentrating on his own desires and fantasies, Mapplethorpe revealed what many desire, though they may be unable to recognize, in the way his highly focused images unite aspects of pleasure, the forbidden, and danger. They are likely to continue to be controversial both within and outside of the queer/gay/lesbian/dyke/bisexual culture and are far from being dismissed as history.

QUEER AVANTGARDISM

Queer and the avant garde, while appearing to be following similar paths, are in fact in total conflict. While queer represents radical social/cultural/artistic change, the avant garde is essentially a manifestation of modernism and a move towards more remote and elitist forms of art. Embracing both the transgressive aspects of queer, and the exploratory qualities of the avant garde were qualities evident in the graphic art and films of Andy Warhol (1928–1987).

When looked at from the present perspective, Andy Warhol's life and art can also be seen as part of queer tradition, reflecting as they did, his personal history, often explored in camp, as well as the presentation of shifting, unfocused sexualities. Holly Woodlawn, a transvestite and one of the stars of Warhol's films, when asked to define her sexuality on a television chat show ('What are you? Are you a women trapped in a man's body? Are you a heterosexual? Are you homosexual? A transvestite? A transsexual?'), replied 'But darling, what difference does it make so long as you look fabulous' (Grover 1989: 42).

Warhol's own dark obsessions took a more coded form in his art which defy any simple readings. 'Everything was just how you decided to think about it' (Warhol, quoted in Bockris 1989: 121). In the 1960s and 1970s, Warhol created brilliant icons of famous and familiar people – stars, political figures, royalty and even the Pope – adding to a basic black-and-white screen-printed image areas of bright colour to highlight the eyes, lips, hair and so on, on a close-up portrait which filled the frame. The use of mass-produced, mechanically printed images was both a denial of the uniqueness of art, and a recognition of fame and familiarity.

Warhol's obvious parodying of glamour was in contrast to his abiding concern with photographs of violent disasters which appeared in the popular press and which featured in his 'Death and Disaster' series. These depicted automobiles, planes or train crashes, and the electric chair, with Warhol refusing to comment, aligning himself 'with the spectator who looks on the horrors of modern life as he would look at a TV film, without involvement' (Lippard 1970: 97). These seemed to be more intimately bound up with his own melancholic and introspective nature. 'Violence is what people want, so we're giving it to them. That's the secret of my success – just give people what they want' (Warhol, quoted in Bockris 1989: 366).

Looking back on Warhol's work with a knowledge of his life revealed in the spate of biographies following his death, his depiction of car smashes and street accidents in huge grainy black-and-white blow-up screen-prints, seem like a metaphor for the secrets of his own life, for his own desires and self-destructive actions, and a reflection of his bleak and deeply cynical view of humankind. His use of contemporary icons such as portraits of Marilyn Monroe or his life-size black-and-white prints of Elvis Presley appeared to speak directly to the gay community while ostensibly being aimed at – and welcomed by – a general audience.

Common to all queer artists is a concern with self identity, with who and what we are, of artists articulating their own experiences. None made any attempt to universalize their art but allowed viewers to draw on it in their own way. Little wonder, perhaps, that the keepers of the ivory towers of modernism have reacted strongly to such work, adopting a defensive attitude towards what they clearly perceive as a threat to its academic concerns. They argue that such work is an interference in the so-called steady progression and accumulative project of knowledge which attacks the basis of a universal, classical art.

Writing in *Culture of Complaint*, Robert Hughes articulates conventional anxieties around this work, deploring what he sees as the limitations posed by such an approach, and the use of technical process rather than artistic skill.

> The self is now the sacred cow of American culture, self-esteem is sacrosanct, and so we labor to turn arts education into a system in which no-one can fail. In the same spirit, tennis could be shorn of its elitist overtones, you just get rid of the net. (Hughes 1993: 6)

Hughes's bitter and overstated rejection of what he sees as the ultimate retreat into the highly selective shores of postmodernism, with the turning of the inquisitorial eye inwards rather than outwards, ignores the needs within a society which appears to be growing more anonymous and remote, to validate, at least in part, the individual rather than the collective experience. In the work of Andy Warhol, apparently superficial and decorative, there appears to be a denial of content. '*Time* magazine would ridicule him, but you know Andy didn't care. It was advertising. It gave him publicity' (Paul Warhola, quoted in Bockris 1989: 144). The absence of 'content', and the use of mechanical techniques rather than artistically skilled processes such as drawing, were all part of the removing of the net as far as critics such as Hughes was concerned.

If the conflict between the public face and the individual experience is a well established aspect of art, what is new is that this is now openly and freely acknowledged. From this work has come the paradox, identified by Hughes, that while the art may be more personal and revealing in consciously avoiding an objective perspective, decoding and reading the work places increased demands on the viewer in acknowledging metaphors and recognizing the extent of allegorical references. From this complexity have come accusations of elitism, an aspect of postmodernism many artists were setting out to confront.

Subtle state of amorous desire

Autobiography, expressed in the work of artists as diverse as Mapplethorpe, Haring, Wojnarowicz, Warhol and Grace, all of whom were as much concerned with pushing at the boundaries of art forms as well as content, was fully explored also in the work of the highly acclaimed, but artistically conventional painter Francis Bacon. The driving force for much of their work was the artists' experience and the significance of personal revelation. Within gay culture, much of the conflict between what is experienced and what can be expressed can be identified as the 'subtle state of amorous desire' that Roland Barthes called 'languor' (Barthes 1990: 155).

In this context, David Hockney's paintings of the 1960s and 1970s immediately spring to mind. In his early 'coming out' paintings of the late 1950s and early 1960s, he expressed an endearing preoccupation with his own exploration and acceptance of his sexuality. In a *faux naïf* style, he amalgamated aspects of contemporary gay life, such as messages on lavatory walls, with gay heroes like Walt Whitman, and minimal but pertinent text from popular songs ('Lover Boy') to suggest the delights and importance of self-discovery, asserting the need for a 'confessional' art which transgressed the confines of modernism. Significantly, commentators and critics of Hockney's paintings rarely discussed the subject of this work at the time, and indeed neither did they have to hand a ready language with which to do so, nor were such concepts openly admitted in discussion of art.

In contrast to Hockney's insightful and relatively unproblematic paintings, there has been much art where the amorous subject 'according to one contingency or another, feels swept away by fear of danger, an abandonment, a revulsion' (Barthes 1990: 29), sentiments Barthes identifies as anxiety.

It is often in this work that the most challenging and ultimately most subversive aspects lie. It is particularly evident in the work of Francis Bacon which, though operating outside of any sort of acknowledged queer – or even gay – subculture, may yet be identified as some of the queerest art of the twentieth century.

The split, the divide, the conflict, between Bacon the homosexual and Bacon the highly successful twentieth century artist posed great problems for both him and the art establishment. He was fond of quoting his own version of T. S. Eliot's notorious nihilist lines in *Sweeney Agonistes*:

> That's all, that's all, that's all, that's all
> Birth, and copulation, and death.

While defining the material reality of life, these words brush aside the importance of emotional feeling, of experiences which may disrupt the transition from birth to death. For Bacon, it was a highly effective deflecting action, encouraging the identification of broad general themes in his work rather than any further probings into the more problematic aspects of his paintings and what events informed them.

Yet it is hard to think of an artist whose life and work were so intimately bound up together. Violence, destruction, despair, anguish, fear, are the sort of highly emotive words applied to his painting – all reflecting Barthes's analysis of anxiety – themes developed below.

Analysis of anxiety

Bacon's death at the age of eighty-two in 1992 can be seen as a significant moment, a turning-point, the end of a tradition in which major issues around the work and life of a highly acclaimed artist were discreetly passed over in favour of more formal discussion of form, use of colour, historical precedents and such-like. Certainly on his death the floodwaters, pent up for years, burst, and a spate of obituaries and biographies gave, only too readily, graphic, often explicit details of his life and loves of which there had previously been only hints and nods.[7]

Discussion of Bacon's life – and death – is significant not only because of his queerness, but because of the often fabulous claims made for his status. In his tribute to Bacon after the artist's death, (*Guardian*, 29 October 1992) Grey Gowrie, now chairman of the Arts Council, described Bacon as 'the greatest living painter and the greatest British painter since Turner', a view endorsed by many critics, artists and writers. Similarly, in an eightieth-birthday tribute (*Guardian*, 26 October 1989) the artist Howard Hodgkin described Bacon glowingly as 'the world's greatest living painter since Turner', a view echoed by George Melly. Nicholas Serota, director of the Tate Gallery, though more circumspect, was still fulsome in his praise, saying 'Bacon was not only the greatest British painter of his generation, but also recognised as one of the outstanding post-war artists' (*Guardian*, ibid.).

Such glowing praise is rarely offered lightly, and seems even more surprising given that in many ways Bacon was an old-fashioned and very traditional easel painter. Though he preferred to paint on the back of the canvas because he liked its raw, untreated surface, Bacon used the traditional materials and form of the artist and he worked in oils; he insisted on expensive gilt frames for his work and on having his pictures glazed – devices which accorded them status when shown in a gallery. Glazing, whether intentional or not, often resulted in the viewer's own reflection being mirrored in the image. This element of theatrical presentation also ensured that, at one level, Bacon's work never seemed anything other than established and conventional.

More significant than the presentation of his work was Bacon's use of academic composition. A limited range of colours with black and red predominating, a strong sense of drawing, and figurative compositions meant that Bacon resisted abstraction, and turned instead to artists as diverse as Velázquez, van Gogh and Picasso for their bold, often confrontational choice of subject matter.

Respect for Bacon's work accumulated as the artist aged. Prices for his paintings rose dramatically, and journalists started to devote many column-inches to his work and his often enigmatic utterances. Attention increased as he approached his eightieth birthday. Bacon showed little reluctance to be photographed, invariably appearing fitted out in smart leather bomber jacket and posed, like the phoenix, amongst the piles of detritus in his studio, or in his favourite Soho drinking hole. Melvyn Bragg's now infamous *South Bank Show* (9 June 1985) made Bacon's sexual interests clear when the artist pointed out that his taste lay in the direction of his own sex, thus disrupting Bragg's comments about artist's models.

The press have had problems dealing with his private/public life; some journalists often managing to come up with conflicting views in the same article. The greatest difficulty has often been over Bacon's 'private life', and the extent to which he had, or had not gone public about his homosexuality. Caroline Lees, reporting on the beneficiary of Bacon's will (*Sunday Times*, 30 August 1992), claimed that Bacon 'made no secret of his homosexuality', while adding in the same article that 'the artist's reluctance to have his personal affairs discussed in public was legendary'. She presumably did not see the two statements as contradiction. In a report on his death, the *Daily Telegraph*, (4 May 1992) described Bacon dismissively as 'the homosexual artist', an identification in terms of sexuality they would never dream of applying to heterosexual artists.

Homosexuality lay at the heart of the enigma about Bacon. While his sexual preferences were a fact well known within a privileged section of the art world and a small coterie of friends and acquaintances with whom he drank and gambled, they were not placed within the public domain until Bacon was well into his seventies. There seem to be two aspects to this decision. One was Bacon's own contradictory attitude towards talking about his work. 'If you talk about it, why paint it' (*The Times*, 2 September 1989) was a favourite diversionary device; if that did not seem sufficient, he often presented a fatalistic view, saying, 'We live, we die, and that is all' (ibid.). The other aspect was Bacon's own attitude towards, and understanding of, his homosexuality.

Two of his often told anecdotes were about his youth and homosexual adventures. He was banished from his home in Ireland by his brutish father (who also had him beaten) after being caught dressed in his mother's clothes, and also discovered having sex with the grooms who managed his father's stable. Apart from these melodramatic incidents, Bacon said little in public about his sexuality, and the obituary notices had few direct quotations from the artist on the subject.

Lord Gowrie, in his obituary in the *Guardian* (29 April 1992) wrote:

> He told me that he (Bacon) had come to the view that homosexuality was an affliction, that it had turned him , at one point in his life, into a crook. The crookishness, not the sex, was a source of shame and if he talked at all , it was his nature to tell everything. We both liked Proust and agreed that the beginning of *Cities of the Plain*[8] said all that needed to be said about being homosexual.

In an interview with art critic Richard Cork (*The Times* Saturday Review, 16 March 1991) shortly before his death, Bacon was more blunt and direct about his sexuality, when, commenting on the public reception of his work in this country, said:

> Oh, they don't like my work here at all. Maybe it's the savagery they find in it, or maybe it's the homosexuality which I suppose is in my work. I don't go about shouting that I'm gay but AIDS has made it all much worse. People are very, very odd about it.

Perhaps equally as important as Bacon's own ambiguity towards discussing his work, was the difficulty the art establishment had in acknowledging Bacon's subject-matter. This was partly because critics did not want to see what was implied by the work, and partly because, just as in the work of David Hockney, they did not have an established language to use. Modernist orthodoxy had put forward the view that to be meaningful, art had to be abstract, that it should avoid depicting particular events or people, but had to seek out some essence which could be conveyed as much spiritually as literally. Clearly Bacon's work presented a dilemma. Much of it was self-evidently about particular events depicted with violence and passion, and while the emotional impact of the work could be acknowledged, the specific subject-matter was more problematical.

Peter Lennon (*The Times*, 15 September 1983) could only hint at Bacon's subject-matter, saying 'what painters and poets do for you is unlock the valves of sensation and bring you nearer to a kind of reality.' It was not a reality Lennon chose to identify. Nor was it acknowledged by Michel Leris, the distinguished chronicler of Bacon's work, who comments that Bacon's 'searing' paintings 'express the human condition as it truly and peculiarly is today: man dispossessed of any durable paradise.'[9]

For the painter R. J. Kitaj, such generalizations would not do. Quoting Picasso, he wrote that 'It is not sufficient to know an artist's work. It is also necessary to know when he did them, why, how, under what circumstances', adding 'Bacon might not agree with that, but I do' (*Guardian*, 26 October 1989). Ironically perhaps, Picasso was one of the few artists whose work Bacon openly admired, and like Picasso he invariably worked from memories of people (or photographs) rather than actual life.

'Why, how, and under what circumstances' are aspects of Bacon's work which have been thoroughly raked over in the flood of biographies and articles published since the artist's death, though none has been incisive about the artist's close involvement with his subject-matter. For Bacon's retrospective at the Tate Gallery in London in 1989, he collaborated in the preparation of a commentary on each painting, giving background information and any relevant autobiographical details. In the event, the artist withdrew this material at the last moment and the commentary has never been issued.

Deprived of, or choosing not to acknowledge, the 'facts' which inform particular pieces of Bacon's art, critics have been only too ready to fall back on generalities which reinforce the mystery and mysticism of the work, rather than offering any real analysis of it. For example, Brian Morton, writing in the *Times Educational Supplement* (7 June 1985) said that his painting 'communicates a tremendous physicality, both of paint and its image', and that 'much of his work has had to do with the uneasy relationship between the physical body and the spiritual nature', while the plastic qualities of paint are 'thoroughly humane and wholly sympathetic'. A convenient ploy to suggest that this is all there is in Bacon's work, which, under a veneer of art historical generalizations, subverts a closer discussion of the sort of 'tremendous physicality' with which the artist grappled.

The late Peter Fuller had little sympathy with Bacon's subject-matter, which he slightingly parodies (*Daily Telegraph*, 28 October 1989) as 'lonely figures still throwing up in lavatory bowls beneath naked light bulbs, [who] occasionally ... hunch together on couches for some barbarous act of congress, or be sprawled disgorging their abdomens'. Nor did Fuller admire Bacon's use of paint, saying that he 'applied pigment as if he hated the stuff, dragging it across the raw, unsized canvas which drains it of beauty and of all semblance of life.' Lest we feel the homophobic boot is not well and truly slammed home he added, for good measure, 'Bacon's technical inadequacies seem to me to be inseparable from his spiritual dereliction.'

Fuller's critical rejection of Bacon's art and, I suspect, all that Bacon represented, was a view not shared by other critics who often made grandiose claims for his talent (see earlier references). More problematic is how Bacon, and the critics, regarded Bacon's homosexuality. At least the art critic Tim Hilton acknowledged the sexual dimension of Bacon's art, writing in purple prose that 'Bacon's art is about risk, catastrophe, murder and an abandoned but private sexuality' (*Guardian*, 29 April 1992). Cautiously, he made no attempt to identify what the 'private sexuality' referred to. Richard Cork was less ambiguous, writing grandly 'With characteristic honesty, Bacon has never made any attempt to hide his homosexuality. Some of his finest and most erotic paintings depict male figures embracing and making love' (*The Times* Saturday Review, 16 March 1991), something of an understatement for the energetic and often violent actions pictured.

Francis Bacon was a queer artist in the old-fashioned sense when queer was a term of abuse, a recognition and disapproval of divergent sexual tastes. In his own words, he was not gay – he disliked the word – and preferred to be labelled queer. There is little indication to suggest that he was touched by the ideas and concepts of gay liberation, but rather that the movement brought an unwelcome intrusion in what he regarded as his private life. At the time of the Stonewall riots in 1969 he was nearly sixty and his lifestyle was resolutely pre-liberationist in style and attitude, and his international reputation well established.

As much as any artist, and more so than most, he poured his emotions and feelings into his art, often basing his compositions on specific incidents in his life. His love affairs were often stormy, and frequently ended in violence. One of his former lovers, Peter Lacey, an ex-RAF pilot who played the piano in Dean's Bar, Tangier, died on the opening day of Bacon's 1962 Tate Gallery show. Undeterred, Bacon attended the opening and publicly at least acted as though nothing untoward had happened. There was a similar catastrophe some ten years later when Lacey's successor, George Dyer, also died a violent death at his own hand on the day of Bacon's larger and even more important retrospective which opened at the Grand Palais in Paris in 1971.

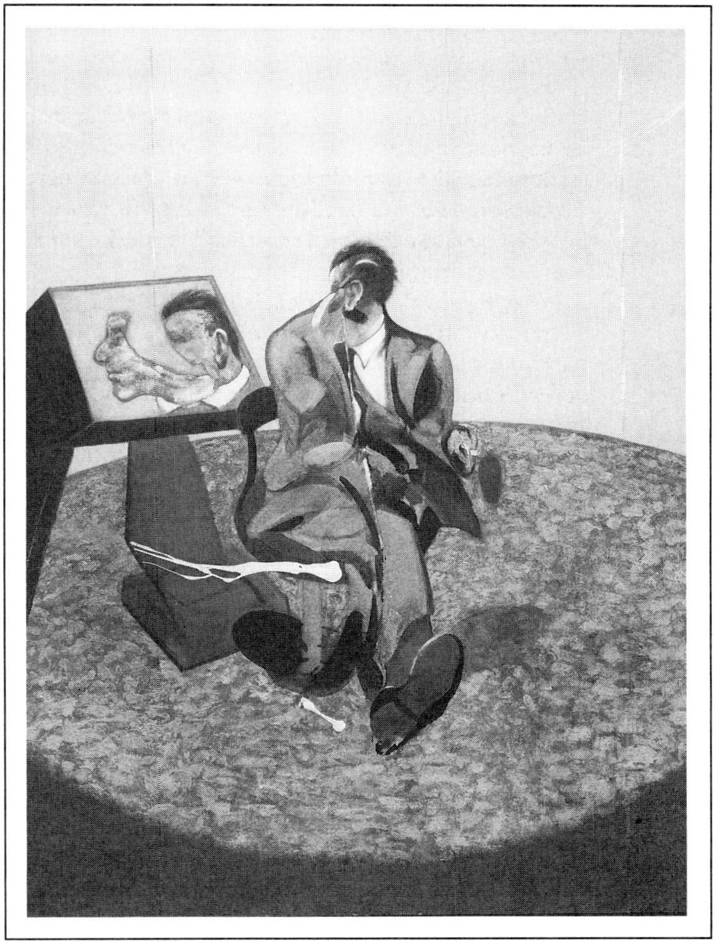

Figure 1.1 Francis Bacon, *Portrait of George Dyer in a Mirror* (1967–8), 78″ × 58″, oil on canvas
Fundacion Coleccion Thyssen-Bornemisza, Madrid.

While Bacon, the urbane and ultra-cool artist, acted out his part, his paintings give some idea of his inner turmoil and anger. His paintings of Dyer present his lover as twisted, distorted and virtually disembodied. One portrait, *Portrait of George Dyer in a Mirror* (1967–8), shows Dyer sitting in what looks like an office swivel chair, his disembodied face, split down the centre, reflected in a lectern-like stand. On the painting are two splurges of white paint splashed across the surface reminiscent of semen defacing the image. Whether indicative of the sexual dimension of their relationship, or of the need to assert a particular personal expression of possession, even in an image, it was Bacon going public on a profound and deeply important aspect of his emotional life.

Bacon could almost have said, as his acknowledged mentor Picasso had claimed some time before, 'My work is like a diary. To understand it, you have to see how it mirrors my life.' Certainly this is the starting-point for any real assessment of Bacon's queer art – art which for all its establishment form, continued to explore deviant, highly personal and transgressive emotions. But such work is only effective if it succeeds in conveying its meaning, and if we recognize the sort of language being used. However reticent Bacon was in disclosing the specific subject of his work, he was totally uncompromising when he came to putting it on canvas. It is there to be recognized, and from it we get not only an indication of the turbulent emotional life of the artist, but more importantly an insight into our troubled decade.

Queer outlooks

'The personal is the political', the slogan which stirred the heart of every radical involved in personal politics in the 1970s, has taken on new significance in the 1990s. In an atmosphere in which 'political correctness' has become as oppressive as the prejudices it seeks to attack, a search for a private and a public ethic, about who and what we are, has become even more vital. What often ravishes us, as Barthes has said 'reaches us through a ring, a rip, a rent' (Barthes 1990: 192), and it is the opportunity for such encounters which are opened up by queer culture.

Some understanding of what is happening today can be obtained by looking back at our recent past and identifying those spaces where queerness has seeped – or even burst – in, to the horror of some and the delight of many. In one sense, queer cultural politics, as the New York critic Robert F. Reid-Pharr has argued, 'must necessarily be the politics of the moment, the politics of action, the politics of bombast, the politics of innovation, and most especially the politics of joy' (Reid-Pharr 1993: 38).

In reassessing the importance and development of queer art, its cultural roots, often lying deep within the individual experience, must inevitably be open to a wide range of readings. Francis Bacon lived most of his life ducking and diving to avoid any gay or queer label, despite the directness of much of his subject-matter, and in this respect we need to desanitize his powerful and emotive images. This art is important because not only does it push at the boundaries of what images of the figure can suggest, but because in reflecting the vividness and depth of emotional life, it reveals a great deal about our current times. Discussion of the subject of homosexual relationships in Bacon's paintings will strengthen rather than diminish them, because while at one level they specifically address issues of gay life, they also reflect the turmoil of feelings and desires many experience in a rapidly changing world.

Bacon, like Mapplethorpe and Warhol, was adept at remaining silent when appropriate, while continuing to produce the sort of pictures he wanted. These artists represent significant turning-points in the rebellion/integration of gay/queer art, moments we can now start to recognize. The publication of Della Grace's book, and the Whitney Biennial Exhibition are equally significant events in responding to and helping to define queer culture, presenting very clearly the dilemma of consolidation/separation.

Almost intrinsic to queer culture is that it is fleeting and unpredictable, it cannot be encouraged or promoted in any regular or routine way, but must exist in the cracks and rips. If this is something which artists in the past have made use of, then this is something to be celebrated rather than denied.

Notes

1 It is significant to note that in his edited book of writing on homosexuality, *A Queer Reader* (London: Fourth Estate, 1993), Patrick Higgins offers no definition of the term queer. For a useful discussion of the concept see Simon Watney,

'Queer epistemology: activism, "outing", and the politics of sexual identities', *Critical Quarterly*, edited by Isaac Julien and Jon Savage, (Oxford: Blackwell, 1994)

2 See Gayle Rubin, ' The leather menace: comments on politics and S/M' in *Coming to Power: Writings and Graphics on Lesbian S/M*, rev. edn, Boston: Alyson Publications , 1982; Pat Califia, *Macho Sluts*, Boston: Alyson Publications, 1988; *On Our Backs: Entertainment for the Adventurous Lesbian*, published six times a year by Blush Entertainment Corp., San Francisco.

3 Della Grace in 'Falling from Grace' by Paul Burston, *Capital Gay*, 21 June 1991.

4 In the United Kingdom Clause 28 restricted the power of local authorities to 'promote homosexuality', while in the United States Senator Jesse Helms, a North Carolina Republican, proposed legislation in summer 1989 to restrict federal funding for the arts by the National Endowment for the Arts in response to, among other things, a retrospective exhibition of Robert Mapplethorpe photographs partly supported by the NEA. A version of his restrictive language was adopted for NEA guidelines.

5 Sadly, both artists died of AIDS-related illnesses.

6 These included Barbara Hammer, Zoe Leonard, Cheryl Dunye, Glenn Ligon, Mark Rappaport and Sadie Benning, all of whom dealt explicitly with 'homo(sex)uality'.

7 The first biography was by Daniel Farson, a long-standing friend of Bacon's, *The Gilded Gutter Life of Francis Bacon* (London: Century, 1993), which drew on his friendship with the artist and his intimate knowledge of Soho. Andrew Sinclair's *Francis Bacon: His Life and Violent Times* (London: Sinclair-Stevenson, 1993) is a more serious and detached study.

8 Marcel Proust, *Remembrance of Things Past: Cities of the Plain,* trans. C. K. Scott Moncrieff and Terence Kilmartin, vol. 2 (London: Penguin, 1983), 623—56. This incident describes a casual sexual meeting between M. de Charlus 'whose ideal is manly precisely because (his) temperament is feminine' and Jupien, a tailor. The 'objective' account identifies the sorts of sexual signals involved and the (often) crossing of social boundaries. Proust goes on to identify different sorts of homosexual liaisons, though the overall picture is distanced and objectified.

9 Michel Leris, *Bacon* (Phaidon Press), quoted in Peter Lennon *Times*, 15 September 1983.

References

Barthes, R. (1990), trans. R. Howard, *A Lover's Discourse: Fragments*, London: Penguin Books.
Bockris, V. (1989) *Warhol: The Biography*, London: Muller. For a different perspective on Warhol see Crone, R. (1970), trans J.W.Gabriel, *Warhol*, London: Thames & Hudson.
Burston, P. (1991) 'Falling from Grace', *Capital Gay*, 21 June.
Califia, P. (1979) 'Unravelling the sexual fringe: a secret side of lesbian sexuality', *The Advocate*, 27 December.
Derbyshire, P. (1994) 'A measure of queer', in *Critically Queer*, ed. Isaac Julien and Jon Savage, Oxford: Blackwell.
Fernandes, J. (1991) 'Sex into sexuality: a feminist agenda for the '90s', *Art Journal*, Summer.
Grover, J.Z. (ed.) (1989) *AIDS: The Artist's Response*, Columbus: Ohio State University.
Gruen, J. (1991) *Keith Haring: The Authorised Biography*, London: Thames & Hudson.
Hughes, R. (1993) *Culture of Complaint*, London: Oxford University Press.
Lewis, R. (1994) 'Dis-Graceful images: Della Grace and lesbian sado-masochism', *Feminist Review*, 46, Spring.
Lippard, L.R. (1970) *Pop Art*, London: Thames & Hudson.
Mercer, K. (1994) *Welcome to the Jungle*, London: Routledge.
Oakes, E. (1991) *Capital Gay*, 28 June.
Reid-Pharr , R.F. (1993) 'Queer art at the Whitney', *Fuse Magazine*, XVI (4), May/June, Toronto, Canada.
Samois, (1979) *What Color is Your Handkerchief?: A Lesbian S/M Sexuality Reader*, Samois, Berkeley.
Schulman, S. (1991) Introduction to *Love Bites: Photographs by Della Grace*, London: Gay Men's Press.
Smith, A.M. (1991) *Capital Gay*, 5 July.
Weeks, J. (1986) *Sexuality*, London: Tavistock.

Chapter Two

Absent bodies/absent subjects

The political unconscious of postmodernism

Richard Dellamora

Commemorating the twenty-fifth anniversary of the Stonewall riots, *Art in America* published a set of interviews with a dozen gay and lesbian artists in June 1994. One of the points that emerges is the overriding significance of Andy Warhol to a new generation of queer artists. Deborah Kass, for instance, says:

> I find Andy so fascinating because he was the first queer artist – I mean queer in the political sense we mean queer. While some of his homosexual contemporaries were into coding and veiling and obscuring, Andy really made pictures about what it was like being a queer guy in the '50s. He was the first big queer-boy artist and he really made these pictures of the inside of his queer brain, from the women's shoes on. (Cotter 1984: 57)

It is characteristic of queer politics as Kass understands it both to mythologize Warhol as the 'first queer artist' and, in the same breath, to demand a historical analysis of the situation in which he became the characteristic artist of his moment. As Kass implies, Warhol arrived in New York at a time when Abstract Expressionist painters were beginning to affirm the existence of 'the artist as a masculine solitary, his artwork as a pure statement of individual genius and autonomous will' (Jones 1993: 630). In the 1950s, Warhol responded with the whimsical defiance of his ink and gold leaf drawings of women's shoes and nude young men. In the Pop Art paintings of the early 1960s, he challenged the terms of artistic presence and expression that underwrote the aesthetic of Action Painting. Rejecting gesture and direct touch, he devised a method of painting with silk screens that placed the artist and his assistants at a deliberate, ironic distance from artistic making. We are now becoming aware that Warhol and other gay Pop Artists such as Jasper Johns and Robert Rauschenberg were neither alone nor the first to challenge the dominance of the male heterosexual model of artistic genius. If there is a particular moment at which this debate begins to be engaged, it may well be the occasion of the 'Lecture on Nothing' that John Cage delivered in 1949 to the Artists Club, a bohemian group that 'became the primary arbiter of what would be called abstract expressionism' (638). Warhol's fey, nonconfrontational drawings of the 1950s, then, are tactical responses in a contest between queer artists and critics, on the one hand, and assertively straight ones, on the other.

This context in sexual politics needs to be remembered when one considers the exemplary role that Warhol has acquired in the very different context of contemporary critical theory. Particularly in the work of Fredric Jameson, who describes Warhol as 'the central figure in contemporary visual art' (1991: 8), Warhol has come to be regarded as *the* representative artist of postmodernity. For Jameson, however, postmodernism is a negative term that implies a loss of historical awareness, in particular 'the unity of a single great collective story ... – for Marxism, the collective struggle to wrest a realm of Freedom from a realm of Necessity.'[1] Postmodernity, in Jameson's characterization, instead celebrates 'the *societé de consommation*, with its consumption of images and simulacra, its free-floating signifiers and its effacement of the older structures of social class and traditional ideological hegemony' (1981: 92). Taking Warhol as the representative figure of this epoch, Jameson poses against him the loss of the pursuit of collective good that Marx and Engels worked to gain for both the proletarian subject and the vanguard intellectual.

Curiously, in presenting Warhol, Jameson forgets the sexual politics within which Warhol's work and attendant critical debates developed. In this respect, Jameson replicates the amnesia for which he indicts the postmodern subject. As we shall see, this blindness permits Jameson to repeat allegations against Warhol that resemble the assaults launched against him in the 1960s by critics such as Hilton Kramer. At the same time, Jameson's affect-laden prose exploits the sensationalism he condemns. Jameson refers to the characteristic affect of postmodern culture as 'a camp or "hysterical" sublime' (1991: 34).[2] The reference recalls Susan Sontag's argument in 'Notes on "Camp" ' that 'homosexuals, by and large, constitute the vanguard – and the most articulate audience – of Camp'. Further, she contends: 'Jews and homosexuals are the outstanding creative minorities in contemporary urban culture .... The two pioneering forces of modern sensibility are Jewish moral seriousness and homosexual aestheticism and irony' (290). By aggressiveness towards Andy Warhol, Jameson attempts to defend his position against homosexual contamination. At the same time, by giving 'a camp or "hysterical" sublime' a central place among his analytic terms, Jameson attempts to adapt the subversive energies of camp to his own purposes. The 'absent subjects' of my title are the gay cultural practitioners of the 1950s and 1960s, whose sexual politics Jameson ignores. The 'absent bodies' belong to men with sexual and emotional ties to other men. The 'political unconscious' is the gendered, sexualized metanarrative of the opening chapter of Jameson's *Postmodernism, or The Cultural Logic of Late Capitalism* (1991). This underlying fiction is motivated by an attraction/repulsion towards sex between men that requires both the exclusion of gay subjects and the lapse of the straight-identified male body into the maelstrom of sensation. The unanticipated consequence of repression is that the straight-identified male subject comes to experience itself only negatively, that is, in terms of absence. This absence, which Jameson represents in terms of the vanguard intellectual's inability to comprehend the meaning of contemporary experience, much less to intervene in it, is doubled by a sense of bodily loss that is as demoralizing as it is intensely pleasurable.

Jameson's recoil from Warhol, his envious delight of the subject dissolving in sensation, and his anxieties about the loss of agency in the public sphere pertain to a general class of straight-identified, male left intellectuals, in particular, vanguard marxists. In eliding Warhol's specifically gay subject position, Jameson masks the gender and sexuality of his own. Doing so, he necessarily re-inscribes yet again the homosexual/heterosexual dichotomy (Sedgwick 1990: 11). The price of the tactic is even more costly since if Jameson were willing to acknowledge his homoerotic investment and that of male intellectual culture generally, he would open a way for moving beyond this particular point of impasse in sexual and cultural politics. He could then recognize the agency that Warhol and other queer artists actually exert. And he would probably also find that rather than dismissing 'the willed euphoria' of the entire range of minority politics,[3] he would be able to acknowledge the existence of far more 'points of resistance', to use Michel Foucault's phrase, than he now does. Moreover, as Foucault remarks:

> Just as the network of power relations ends by forming a dense web that passes through apparatuses and institutions, without being exactly localized in them, so too the swarm of points of resistance traverses social stratifications and individual unities. And it is doubtless the strategic codification of these points of resistance that makes a revolution possible. (96)

In this essay, I argue that the 1984 journal article which provides the opening chapter of *Postmodernism* is engaged in a tacit critique of aspects of Ernest Mandel's *Late Capitalism*. Jameson draws his highly schematic view of the structure of capitalism from Mandel. Nonetheless, and despite insisting that radical politics must be based on class-consciousness (1991: 331),[4] Jameson's view is consonant with the current consensus among avant-garde intellectuals in the United States that Marx's view of '(the proletarian) class as subject of history' fails to provide an adequate basis for radical politics (Foster: 140). The psychological 'thickness' of Jameson's postmodern subject works to subvert the attempt to represent the class subject as a signifier of historical truth. In Jameson's essay, gendered representations refer to a masculine sensation of bodily absence that is both cause and effect of a perceived loss of agency by the postmodern subject. This absence may be construed as the loss of *self-presence*, by which I mean a conscious sense of self generated by ability to act that includes awareness of bodily contour and movement. Absence is obviously related to a loss of confidence that history has a class subject, but it is just as strongly related to a crisis within the construction of normal masculinity.

Although it is evident that Jameson deplores this loss, it is pertinent that Warhol's postmodern aesthetic develops in conscious criticism of the insistence by the Abstract Expressionists on presence in their painting. Warhol's work either signifies such presence parodically, as in the oxidation paintings of the late 1970s, or achieves an equivalent by erasing signs of artistic presence through banal subject-matter and mechanical technique. It is this process that I refer to when I say that Warhol exploits the position of an *unsubject* in devising what has paradoxically proven to be a remarkably indelible signature. But by unsubject, I mean something else as well. Warhol was marginalized not only by being effeminate and gay but also in virtue of factors of class, ethnicity, regional, and religious background. In this essay, I have chosen to emphasize works in which Warhol uses the occasion of a 'portrait' of admired fellow artist, Robert Rauschenberg, as a way of constituting Pop Art as a mode of gay agency that includes historical recuperation. In other words, I have chosen an example in which Warhol engages precisely in the work of memory that Jameson generally denies postmodern culture and Warhol in particular. True, Warhol invokes American national myths in reconstructing the past, but he does so in ways that participate in them while holding them up to the scrutiny of a permanent outsider.

Double bind

In the essay, Jameson represents bodily absence in displaced fashion by means of a number of shoe-images, and especially pictorial images by van Gogh and Andy Warhol. He analyses the sensation of absence in theoretical terms in section IV of the essay, without title in the book but named 'The hysterical sublime' in the earlier version.[5] Jameson argues that the 'camp or "hysterical" sublime' is a 'euphoria' experienced within postmodern spaces which are 'felt as incompatible with the representation of the body .... The world ... momentarily loses its depth and threatens to become a glossy skin, a stereoscopic illusion, a rush of filmic images without density. But is this now a terrifying or an exhilarating experience?' (1991: 32, 34). Later, in an unfolding metanarrative of the loss of bodily presence, he situates the experience within his feeling of being lost in the 'hypercrowd' (1991: 40) of registrants at the annual meeting of the Modern Language Association held at the Bonaventure Hotel in Los Angeles in 1982. Jameson observes: 'So I come finally to my principal point here, that this latest mutation in space – postmodern hyperspace – has finally succeeded in transcending the capacities of the individual human body to locate itself' (1991: 44). In a bodily code, this 'principal point' is the telos towards which the essay moves. In what follows, which, in another code *should be* the goal of the essay, namely the restoration of self-presence in a newly reformulated politics, Jameson finds himself stymied. He is unable to affirm the capacities of representation, agency or subject-formation that he believes to be necessary for the recovery of a radical politics.

The work of reconstituting the subject, which I take to be the most significant work of Jameson's text, is performed by a narrative of the loss and recovery of agency. The turns of this narrative are so evident that Jameson can scarcely be unaware of them – however much he may fail to recognize the sexual politics involved. Indeed, the failure of such recognition helps account for the double bind with which the essay ends. Jameson shows no ability to analyse the transcoding between theoretical concerns and anxieties of gender and sexuality that occurs in the text even though, in ending, he seconds Louis Althusser's assertion that the postmodern subject must be gendered.

Jameson's metanarrative has a context in the struggles over the meaning of masculine existence that have engaged various groups, including feminists and gay men, in the United States for the past quarter century. One of the key figures in that context is Warhol. The appropriation of camp taste in Pop Art of the early 1960s was part of a conflict that took place between newly assertive gay men in avant-garde culture and other members of the American, East Coast male elite: whether Jewish, liberal, or, as in Jameson's case, on the political left. Critical attacks marked by homophobia were part of the campaign. Although Jameson sometimes adopts a 'Gee whiz' stance in celebrating 'utopian' aspects within 'even the most degraded type of mass culture' (1979: 144), he affords no such indulgence to Warhol. Jameson writes as though he were oblivious of the criticisms that Rudolf Arnheim, Hilton Kramer and other critics levelled against gay artists such as Warhol, Johns and Rauschenberg.[6] Nevertheless, a less defensive consideration of Warhol could show how, within his own terms, he addresses the questions of representation, agency and the subject that have been so troubling for theory. Entering high culture from an acknowledged position of cultural deficit – as an awkward, effeminate young man, as a boy from a coal-mining town, and as a Roman Catholic of Slovak lineage – Warhol carried on his own subversions of gender and other institutional formations. Paradoxically, he turned his position as an unsubject into one that expresses agency and sociality while renovating art and simultaneously engaging in a thorough critique of the fashioning of subjects and communities through representation.

Jameson ends the opening chapter of *Postmodernism* by presaging the return of the subject. This return, however, appears to be as distant as it is yearned for. He writes:

> The new political art (if it is possible at all) will have to hold to the truth of postmodernism, that is to say, to its fundamental object – the world space of multinational capital – at the same time at which it achieves a breakthrough to some as yet unimaginable new mode of representing this last, in which we may again begin to grasp our positioning as individual and collective subjects and regain a capacity to act and struggle which is at present neutralized by our spatial as well as our social confusion. The political form of postmodernism, if there ever is any, will have as its vocation the invention and projection of a global cognitive mapping, on a social as well as a spatial scale. (1991: 54)

The utopian promise of a regained agency is troubled by its very desperation. Not once but twice Jameson puts in doubt the possibilities of representation and self-presence that he invokes. In addition, he confesses to a 'confusion', both 'spatial' and 'social', regarding issues of representation.

Jameson insists that political action requires at least the conceivability of making a set of representations of the real world. In the course of the essay, however, he argues that in the most recent moment of capitalism, that of multinational capital with its attendant nuclear and electronic technologies, 'the truth' becomes, in effect, unrepresentable. Accordingly, the function of ideology, in the Althusserian sense of 'articulating' scientific knowledge in relation to 'the experience of daily life', is at present not possible at all (1991: 53). Still, Jameson remains wedded to an iconic model of representation even when he phrases the issue as the need 'to think the impossible totality of the contemporary world system' (1991: 38).[7]

The paradox he expresses could be used to articulate approaches to individual and collective agency that do not depend on positing a need for totalizing representations. In postmodern culture, moreover, global theories like that of Mandel on the three stages of capitalism since 1800, which

Jameson adopts, can become counter-effective. Instead of enabling the transformation of reality, they can exacerbate an already pervasive sense of paranoia by raising it to the level of abstract thought. Jameson observes:

> Insofar as the theorist wins ... by constructing an increasingly closed and terrifying machine, to that very degree he loses, since the critical capacity of his work is thereby paralyzed, and the impulses of negation and revolt, not to speak of those of social transformation, are increasingly perceived as vain and trivial in the face of the model itself. (1991: 5-6)

Jameson himself exaggerates this tendency by translating Mandel's argument out of its historic specificities and into a reductive typology.

Both the image of the machine and that of the 'global cognitive mapping' (1991: 54) of a postmodern political practice are at odds with another view of contemporary culture that Jameson includes in an earlier essay. In 'Reification and Utopia in Mass Culture' (1979), he observes:

> The only authentic cultural production today has seemed to be that which can draw on the collective experience of marginal pockets of the social life of the world system: black literature and blues, British working-class rock, women's literature, gay literature, the *roman québécois*, the literature of the Third World. (141)

This observation, if pursued, could offer a way out of desperation, paranoia, and impasse by means of a politics practised most frequently at micropolitical levels between shifting coalitions of individuals and groups. Although this approach too depends on theory, it does not depend on claustrophobic theoretical machines.[8] Moreover, the suggestion is very much in accord with those offered by a number of other North American analysts of postmodernism.[9] But Jameson remains sceptical of a politics of difference which he fears might reflect mere 'stylistic and discursive heterogeneity without a norm' (1991: 17).

If the advantages of a decentred politics are obvious and if examples of agency are already evident, why not take advantage of these openings? Here the centrality of the hysterical sublime to Jameson's experience of postmodernism is highly relevant. The simultaneous celebration and denigration of the hysterical sublime figures both attraction to and repulsion from the dissolution of the bounds of the male subject. This condition needs to be refused because it undoes precisely those conventions of a stable masculinity that Jameson depends on in order to be able to represent himself as an agent. But the attractiveness of the hysterical sublime prevents Jameson (and, in his view, the postmodern subject) from relinquishing the sensation. Hence a double bind.

It is important to keep in mind that the existence to which I refer is social. Although lived by individuals, it is also represented in the subject-position of much theoretical discourse. Jameson figures this gendered investment in theory in the Introduction to the book, where he employs René Magritte's painting, *Le Modèle rouge* (1935), as an analogue of the relation between postmodern culture and postmodern economy. Apparently, Jameson considers this relation to be fetishistic since Magritte's image illustrates the Freudian concept of the fetish by representing male feet as part-objects metamorphosing into boots in a continuing, reciprocal process. Magritte suggests the psychological mechanism of displacement by the absent referent of the foot/shoe, namely the maternal phallus. Also absent but implicitly referred to is the cathected subject, who is both male and homosexual.[10]

COLOUR IT SEPIA

Jameson offers a nostalgic portrait of effective masculine interpretation in Martin Heidegger's well-known commentary on Vincent van Gogh's painting, *Old Shoes with Laces* (1886) (Figure 2.1). Jameson understands Heidegger's reading as a collaborative effort with the painter in raising a feminine/feminized subject to the level of general significance. In the process, however, Jameson begins to evacuate signs of artistic, in particular, bodily presence from the work of art. In analytic terms, this loss also implies the loss of the possibility of a work of art's signifying a coherent set of social relations.

Jameson represents the male body in displaced fashion as a fetish-object, namely shoes of a peasant woman. In the essay, 'The origin of the work of art', Heidegger interprets the painting as expressing a totality of which the shoes are the incarnating sign:

> There is nothing surrounding this pair of peasant shoes in or to which they might belong, only an undefined space. There are not even clods from the soil of the field or the path through it sticking to them, which might at least hint at their employment. A pair of peasant shoes and nothing more. And yet.
>
> From the dark opening of the worn insides of the shoes the toilsome tread of the worker stands forth. In the stiffly solid heaviness of the shoes there is the accumulated tenacity of her slow trudge through the far-spreading and ever-uniform furrows of the field, swept by a raw wind. On the leather there lies the dampness and saturation of the soil. Under the soles there slides the loneliness of the field-path as the evening declines. In the shoes there vibrates the silent call of the earth, its quiet gift of the ripening corn and its enigmatic self-refusal in the fallow desolation of the wintry field. This equipment is pervaded by uncomplaining anxiety about the certainty of bread, the wordless joy of having once more withstood want, the trembling before the advent of birth and shivering at the surrounding menace of death. This equipment belongs to the *earth* and it is protected in the *world* of the peasant woman. From out of this protected belonging the equipment itself rises to its resting-in-self.
>
> (Heidegger 662–3)

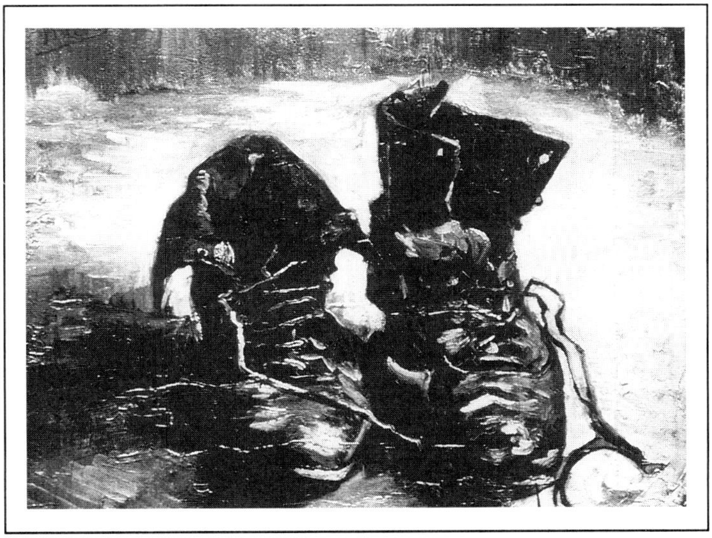

Figure 2.1 Vincent van Gogh, *Old Shoes with Laces* (1886)
Rijksmuseum Vincent van Gogh, Amsterdam.

Heidegger's analysis provides a representation in which the depiction of an object refers to a totality that becomes comprehensible through a double act of interpretation, first by the artist, then by the critic. In this way, representation of an object becomes the rhetorical figure of an accessible truth. He continues:

> What happens here? What is at work in the work? Van Gogh's painting is the disclosure of what the equipment, the pair of peasant shoes, *is* in truth. This entity emerges into the unconcealment of its being. The Greeks called the unconcealment of entities αληθεια. We say 'truth' and think little enough in using this word. If there occurs in the work a disclosure of that which *is* in that, what, and how it is, then there is here an occurring, a happening of truth at work.
>
> In the work of art the truth of what *is* has set itself to work. 'To set' means here: to bring to a stand. Something that *is*, a pair of peasant shoes, comes to stand in the work in the light of its being. (664–5)

Jameson supplements this reading with his own, which I will return to in a moment. He remarks that Heidegger's interpretation has 'a satisfying plausibility' (1991: 8), an equivocal phrase that masks both scepticism and envy of the ease with which Heidegger moves from a painting to a world-picture.

The production of this picture depends on how gender functions in the passage. To Heidegger it is important that the shoes are a woman's and that the land that she treads is female: 'In the shoes there vibrates the silent call of the earth, its quiet gift of the ripening corn and its enigmatic self-refusal in the fallow desolation of the wintry field.' Jameson obliquely indicates awareness of the gender-coding by noting that, in commenting on the passage, Jacques Derrida has referred to the shoes, as 'a heterosexual pair, which allows neither for perversion nor for fetishization' (1991: 8). Yet Jameson errs since Derrida's text, 'Restitutions of the truth in pointing [pointure]' is a ' "polylogue" (for n + I – female – voices)', in which no single statement can be said to express Derrida's own view. Secondly, in Derrida's text the shoes are referred to as bisexual not heterosexual.[11] They are both vulval, with 'the dark opening of the worn insides', and phallic, 'the equipment itself rises to its resting-in-self'. Jameson's slip is another symptom of the bisexuality repressed thoughout the chapter. It is in this sense that, as in the case of the implicit fantasist of the Magritte painting, the male subject of theory is characterized by disavowed homosexual desire.

Jameson describes Heidegger's analysis in implicitly gendered and sexualized terms. It translates 'the meaningless materiality of the body and nature' into 'the meaning-endowment of history and of the social' (1991: 7). He makes the 'earth' yield cultural meaning. By drawing attention to the male work of cultural production, Jameson indicates signs of a competitive gender-anxiety in the quotation. Heidegger cites female reproductivity twice, both as the earth that bears a 'gift' and as the woman who gives birth, while simultaneously demonstrating through his writing the higher because intellectual productivity of the male couple of artist and mediating theorist who together generate the *'world'*.[12] Artist and critic give birth to the work of art as an interpretive act and thereby transcend the female bodies of the land and woman.

In addition to Heidegger's reading, Jameson offers his own, which sublates Heidegger's heterosexual obsessiveness by rising to a yet more abstract level of theory. Where Heidegger emphasizes the totality of peasant existence, Jameson concentrates on the painting as a sign of artistic self-awareness in Mandel's first stage of capitalist development. According to Mandel, between 1848 and the 1890s, technology was dominated by 'machine production of steam-driven motors'.[13] The division of labour characteristic of this stage is mirrored in the optical specialization of van Gogh's activity. Emphasizing this sensate aspect of artistic production, Jameson isolates it from metaphors of copulation and birthing while preparing the ground for his argument that art becomes increasingly sensational in the late twentieth century. With regard to van Gogh, sensation, restricted and reduced to the visual, becomes more abstract both *ipso facto* and as an allegorical sign of the artist at work under an intensified division of labour. Jameson's interpretation exaggerates the work's abstraction by neglecting its tactile qualities, which mesh with its optical ones, and by stressing its function as a sign of Mandel's totalizing view. These displacements yield utopian results; the painting becomes

> a Utopian gesture, an act of compensation which ends up producing a whole new Utopian realm of the senses, or at least of that supreme sense – sight, the visual, the eye – which it now reconstitutes for us as a semi-autonomous space in its own right – part of some new division of labour in the body of capital, some new fragmentation of the emergent sensorium which replicates the specializations and divisions of capitalist life at the same time that it seeks in precisely such fragmentation a desperate Utopian compensation for them. (1991: 7)

The work of theory in this passage, which moves in the direction of postmodern 'space', occurs at the expense of body. Jameson dissociates the painting from the bodily work of making that is evident in the painting. This sublimating process occurs also in Jameson's use of the word 'body', which is displaced from an individual human being to 'the body of capital'.

It is characteristic of the level of abstraction in the chapter that the painting of shoes by van Gogh that Jameson reproduces is not the same as the one that Heidegger discusses. Moreover, as Meyer Schapiro has pointed out, Heidegger's reading is adrift. Having tracked down which painting, of a possible number of eight, Heidegger had in mind, Schapiro argues that the shoes are not a peasant's nor are they a woman's. Rather, the painting appears to be of a pair of shoes that van Gogh wore while in Paris in 1886–7. To Schapiro, this connection suggests that the painting is an exercise in meditative attention to what Schapiro regards as 'the personal and physiognomic in the shoes' (1968: 206).

Canvassing the debate between these two writers, Derrida observes that while Schapiro criticizes Heidegger for projecting reference onto the image, Schapiro ignores his own projection of van Gogh's presence into the painting. Moreover, Derrida makes a convincing case that in characterizing the owner of the shoes as 'an artist..., a man of the town and city', and – later – 'a brooding, self-observant drifter' (205), Schapiro identifies image and maker with his own self-image as an aesthetic, urbane European, in exile in New York City. In translating van Gogh from his own self-conception as a peasant-artist into a prototype of the alienated modern artist, Jameson repeats the gestures of appropriation – of artifact and artist – that Derrida questions in Heidegger and Schapiro's accounts of the painting.[14] Jameson's reading effaces the painting both as a set of bodily gestures and as a mode of self-meditation. To that extent, the attenuation of the subject is a projection on Jameson's part.

PHOTOGRAPHIC NEGATIVES

Jameson next proceeds to contrast van Gogh's shoes to the 'Diamond Dust Shoes' series by Andy Warhol. As in the discussion of Heidegger/van Gogh, the particular image in question is of little interest to Jameson; nor is he interested in the transformation of the image that Warhol achieves by using a photographic negative, a transformation that underscores the fact that the image is no 'real' or 'true' representation. Jameson does not specify which painting in the series he refers to; rather, his concern is with the works as a category. Jameson argues that the image, which is based on a photographic negative of rows of women's dress shoes, converts shoes into fetish-objects that lack both affect and meaning as signifiers of a totalizable truth.[15] Or rather, their resistance to interpretation is precisely what characterizes them as signifiers of postmodern culture. Jameson, moreover, argues that they construct no subject-position for the viewer: 'Nothing in this painting organizes even a minimal place for the viewer' (1991: 8), an observation that, in context, continues the process of evacuating the subject already underway in Jameson's re-interpretation of van Gogh's painting.

Jameson responds to the painting with an excess of affect that is oddly disjunctive with the preceding analysis.

> Here...we have a random collection of dead objects, hanging together on the canvas like so many turnips, as shorn of their earlier life-world as the pile of shoes left over from Auschwitz or the remainders and tokens of some incomprehensible and tragic fire in a packed dancehall. (1991: 8)

The 'we' of these lines clearly feels itself to be the object of emotional violence. Moreover, it occupies a subject-position as subject of what Jameson later terms the hysterical sublime. The inscription of Warhol's image into Jameson's critical discourse, complete with its own cathected subject, is an act of translation, remarkable for the aggressiveness with which it effaces Warhol's efforts to resist the projection of emotional affect onto representations.

In a recent exhibition at the Achenbach Gallery in Frankfurt, Germany, a black-and-white painting in this series was hung next to a multiple-image portrait of Marilyn Monroe. At a 90-degree angle hangs a single-image, silkscreened portrait of Elizabeth Taylor similar to ones made by Warhol in 1963. In front of the painting of shoes is a stack of Warhol's simulated Campbell's Tomato Juice boxes. In this setting the fetishized character of Warhol's imagery and its metonymic relation both to 'commodity' and to 'woman' is altogether evident. Two sets of displacements, however, tend to demonstrate the fact that these objects are commodity-fetishes. First are displacements in the technical processes whereby the images are made: for instance, the use of pre-existing photographic images and the intervention of the silkscreen process between them and the images of Liz and Marilyn that appear on the canvas. The silkscreen process leaves signs of choices made by the fabricators of the images, who are probably persons other than Warhol himself.[16] In the shoe painting, use of a negative image demonstrates the mechanical, phased process whereby photographic simulacra of reality are fashioned.

The second set of displacements has to do with the type and repetition of the objects represented in the shoe picture. Although this aspect is characteristic of the world of advertising and of Warhol's commercial images of shoes drawn in the 1950s,[17] the number of shoes draws attention away from particular objects to the general category of 'shoes', to their status as commodity-objects and as representations of American class-values, aspirations and investments.[18] Juxtaposed with images of Liz and Marilyn, both the objects that are human and those that are inanimate tend to be flattened on a single horizon of commodity-use, replication, advertisement, circulation, availability, redundancy and, finally, disposability.[19] This mode of presentation emphasizes the prescribed character of the fetish-object as well as of the gaze of the subject. The sense of displacement of the subject that troubles Jameson and apparently triggers his response operates for Warhol as part of an analytic process that resists the viewer's tendency to invest himself (or herself) in the images as fetishes. In other words, Warhol constructs not a neurotic effect but an alienation-effect.[20]

Warhol's attention to this range of issues places the series of shoe-images within the terrain of conceptual art. This observation is consistent with Jameson's contention that the relation between artist and work of art has become increasingly abstract and disembodied in the late twentieth century.[21] Nonetheless, Warhol is present to these works in a number of ways. For one, he has chosen to produce in a high-art tradition that provides an alternative to the tradition that overemphasizes art as a uniquely personal mode of expression. In the late 1940s, Warhol was enrolled in the program in Pictorial Design at Carnegie Tech in Pittsburgh. There he came under the influence of ideas promulgated by Laszlo Moholy-Nagy at the New Bauhaus or Institute of Design in Chicago, 'a fashionable, in the sense of hip, if financially shaky institution in the 1940s'. Moholy's book, *Vision in Motion* (1947), which includes images of photographic negatives, was 'the most influential text in American art education of the period'. In the book, Moholy writes:

> People believe that they should demand hand execution as an inseparable part of the genesis of a work of art. In fact, in comparison with the inventive *mental* process of the genesis of a work, the question of its execution is important only in so far as it must be mastered to the limits. The manner, however, whether personal or by assignment of labor, whether manual or mechanical, is irrelevant.[22]

In adapting this approach to image-making, Warhol later invented the idea of artistic signature as trademark, not the trademark of an authorial style, handling, or mythic iconography but the literal trademark of consumer products or star-images, images that convert an individual into a trademark of himself or herself. Displacing himself as subject in this way, Warhol has *become* a subject – so that when we see an image of a coke bottle or of Liz, we read not 'Coca-Cola' or 'Elizabeth Taylor' but 'Warhol'.

Jameson appropriates this process when he chooses one of the 'Diamond Dust Shoes' series as the cover image on the dust jacket of *Postmodernism* (Figure 2.2). The image of the Warhol painting refers as much to the author's name as to the title of the book. In this way and together with Jameson's by now well-known critique of these images, the Diamond Dust Shoes become the trademark of 'Jameson', theorist of postmodernism. Such mimicry might be considered the sincerest form of flattery despite Jameson's expressed scepticism about the effectiveness of such moves as a mode of analysis of artistic and commercial production (1991: 9). Yet, as I have argued, Jameson's translation of Warhol elides precisely the approach that the painter developed from his position of cultural deficit.

Jameson also underestimates the status of Warhol's paintings as individual works of art. The silk-screen process, without hand and at times with the intervention of assistants, results in unique registers of images that 'stop time', demanding that the viewer stop and look closely even if the trademark character of the image invites a look-at-a-gulp. Although Jameson mentions the prominence of shoes in Warhol's commercial work, he ignores the series of shoe-portraits of celebrities that Warhol exhibited in 1956 and which were included in the Frankfurt installation. It is probable that Warhol was familiar with comments in Sigmund Freud's study of Leonardo that connect male homosexuals with shoe fetishism.[23] Freud argues: 'Fetishistic reverence for a woman's foot and shoe appears to take the foot merely as a substitutive symbol for the woman's penis which was once revered and later missed'.[24] Warhol responded to this suggestion by using shoe-images in ways that both acknowledge and ironize their fetishistic significance within psychoanalytic theory. Among the mid-1950s collages, for instance, he includes a tribute to Christine Jorgensen that comments on the fetishistic aspect of transexuality.[25] Jorgensen is a Danish transsexual famous for being the first to undergo a change of sex. Jorgensen made use of medical technology to turn his body into the 'substitutive symbol' of a woman. No more appropriate 'symbol' of Jorgensen could be found than a shoe-fetish, which also symbolizes the loss of something that never existed in the first place.

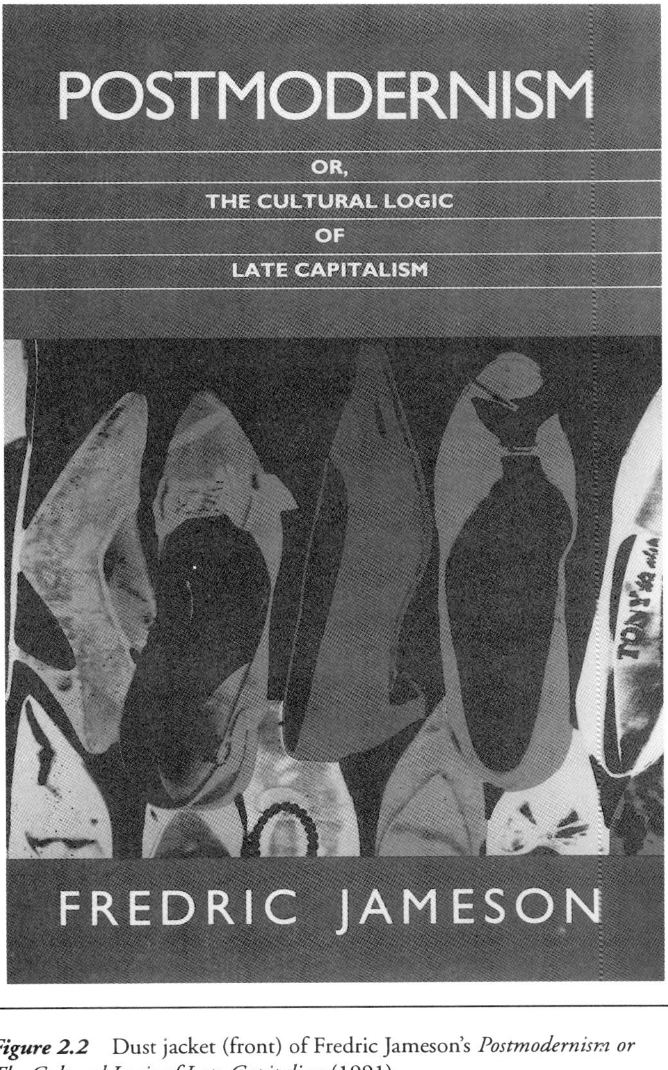

Figure 2.2 Dust jacket (front) of Fredric Jameson's *Postmodernism or The Cultural Logic of Late Capitalism* (1991)
Durham: Duke University Press, 1991. © ARS, NY and DACS, London 1995.

Both the Diamond Dust Shoes and the earlier shoe-portraits use camp style and subject-matter to register Warhol's resistance to masculinist approaches to artmaking. The shoe-portraits flaunt their refusal of the aesthetic of Abstract Expressionism.[26] At the time, Warhol also attempted unsuccessfully to arrange an exhibition at the Tanger Gallery of the images that are still misleadingly referred to as his 'private "boy drawings" '.[27] As Bradford R. Collins has commented: 'The submission was refused, of course: in the context of the conservative social attitudes of the decade and the masculine atmosphere of Abstract Expressionism, such subject matter was unacceptable.'[28]

The hysterical sublime

Jameson frequently makes use of Freudian analytical technique – as, for instance, when he refers to 'a kind of return of the repressed in *Diamond Dust Shoes*, a strange compensatory decorative exhilaration' (1991: 10). However, the phrase, 'return of the repressed', better refers to Jameson's text than to Warhol or to the 'Diamond Dust Shoes'. Far from attempting to conceal his 'swish', Warhol very much performed it. Gay reference is evident in particular works of art, in his collaborations with other individuals, in group projects, and in the 'alternately glacially ironic and self-distancing but also aggressively "deviant" and exhibitionistic milieu of New York pop culture of the 1960s, a culture that first centered around [Jack] Smith but soon shifted to Warhol' (Moon 37). In these activities, Warhol and others adapted gay camp taste in art that was at once hip, commercial and a mode of high culture.

In Jameson's text 'intentional repression' triggers 'the mechanism of conversion' that produces the affect of the hysterical sublime. Continuing from the passage cited above, Jameson contrasts to the glint of diamond dust on the surface of Warhol's paintings 'the august premonitory eye flashes of Rilke's archaic Greek torso which warns the bourgeois subject to change *his* life: nothing of that sort here, in the gratuitous frivolity of this final decorative overlay.'[29] Jameson invokes Rilke's Apollo in order to draw a nostalgic contrast between what Hal Foster has referred to as 'transgressive strategy and utopian desire' (Foster: 151) in modernist art and what Jameson sees as apocalyptic euphoria in Warhol. Yet the surprising introduction of Apollo at this point suggests that Jameson is engaged in his own process of fetishizing the paintings. He compares their glinting surfaces with the 'light' shining from Apollo's skin – I say 'skin' because the torso of Apollo referred to in the poem is headless: 'If there weren't light,/ ... its skin wouldn't gleam like the fur of a wild animal,/ and the body wouldn't send out light from every edge as a star does' (147). The conversion is double. Jameson converts the painting's image into a (male) fetish-object. But it also becomes the target of phobic anxieties about the gleaming surface of the male body.[30]

Just as Heidegger in responding to the van Gogh shoes indulges in a sort of fetishism that 'reduces history to nature',[31] Jameson indulges in another kind of fetishism, one that reduces history to aesthetics. Not only is sexual and emotional attraction between men suppressed so also is the particular 'transgressive strategy and utopian desire' involved in the politics of gay liberation at the end of the 1960s and early in the 1970s. This moment of political affirmation is one referent of the Apollo-figure. Apollo is traditionally an androgynous figure, whose gender-crossing connotes the attempt that first-wave gay theorists such as Dennis Altman made to imagine a desire that would undo the construction of gender.[32] The commodification of gay existence during the 1970s followed by the onset of AIDS abruptly checked such hopes. Other references in Jameson's comments on 'Diamond Dust Shoes' – the 'tragic fire in a packed dancehall' and 'Auschwitz' – refer in displaced fashion to other moments in recent social history: the gay discotheques of the 1970s, the sexual euphoria that some gays found in that decade, and the catastrophic losses to AIDS in the years following.[33] Jameson's reference to the 'deathly quality' (1991: 9) of the Warhol shoes particularly resonates in the context of the new crisis.

About 'euphoria', not just Andy's or that of other gays but even more so that associated with the 'intensities' of postmodern urban space (1991: 29), Jameson is ambivalent. Describing the experience of being inside the Bonaventure Hotel, he speaks of the loss of a sense of bodily self in the 'hypercrowd' (1991: 40) that throngs the spatially confusing public spaces.

> You are in this hyperspace up to your eyes and your body; and if it seemed [to you] before that that suppression of depth I spoke of in postmodern painting or literature would necessarily be difficult to achieve in architecture itself, perhaps [you may now be willing to see] this bewildering immersion as the formal equivalent in the new medium.(1984: 83)[34]

The sensation of 'bewildering immersion' is the ultimate condition of the postmodern subject. Jameson uses his experience of the Bonaventure as a metaphor for the central condition of postmodernism, the state of the hysterical sublime, 'incompatible with the representation of the body' (1991: 34):

> The sublime was for Burke an experience bordering on terror, the fitful glimpse, in astonishment, stupor and awe, of what was so enormous as to crush human life altogether: a description then refined by Kant to include the question of representation itself – so that the object of the sublime becomes now not only a matter of sheer power and of the physical incommensurability of the human organism with Nature but also of the limits of figuration and the incapacity of the human mind to give representation to such enormous forces. (1991: 34)

At this moment, when the power to represent either the body or the world is lost, Jameson explicitly introduces the topic of homosexuality by describing this state as 'a camp or "hysterical" sublime' (1991: 34). The condition of the hysterical sublime is dystopian in the extreme yet Jameson has argued that theorists need to seize on those aspects of postmodern culture that, in however debased, occluded or confused a form, permit some expression to 'intolerable, unrealizable, properly imperishable desires'.[35] Thus, he also characterizes the Bonaventure as a 'complacent and entertaining (although bewildering) leisure-time space' (1991: 44). The question arises, then, what about camp's associations with specifically gay culture? What 'imperishable desires' belong to men who have sex with other men? Is Jameson in some way signalling that sexual and emotional ties between men also have a part in utopian experience and aspiration?

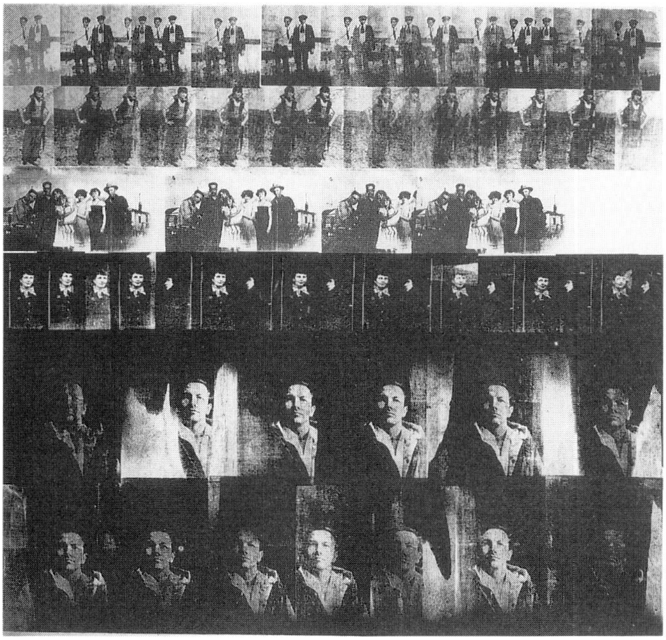

Figure 2.3 Andy Warhol, *Let Us Now Praise Famous Men* (1963), 6′10″ × 6′10″, silkscreen ink on canvas.
Private collection. © ARS, NY and DACS, London 1996.

LET US NOW PRAISE FAMOUS MEN

Jameson's ambivalence about the hysterical sublime underlines the need in critical theory specifically to address questions about male relations and the male body, its felt needs and fantasies. Jameson contends that postmodern culture is characterized by 'the waning of affect', the disappearance of the depth model, and the loss of a historical sense.[36] Yet at times Warhol instates a gay subject of postmodern culture in ways that invite the viewer not to sacrifice either affect or history but rather

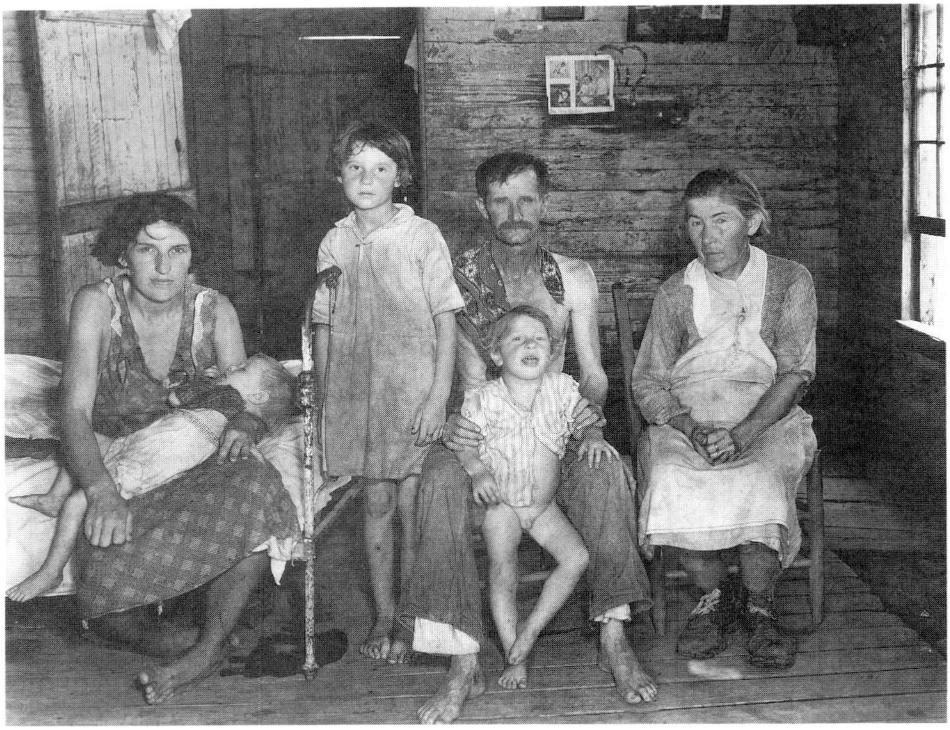

Figure 2.4 Walter Evans, *Sharecropper's Family, Hale County, Alabama* (Ivy, Ellen, Pearl, Thomas and Bud Woods and Miss Milly Gallanin) (1936)
Courtesy Library of Congress, Washington DC.

to experience them differently. Consider another leading theorist of postmodernism, Jean-François Lyotard, who also associates postmodernism with contemporary aesthetics. Like Jameson and other commentators, he credits 'the general idea' that 'we can observe and establish a kind of decline in the confidence that, for two centuries, the West invested in the principle of a general progress in humanity' (77). Unlike Jameson, however, Lyotard poses the possibility of a responsible response. The 'post-' of postmodern need not 'signify a movement of *comeback, flashback,* or *feedback,* that is, not a movement of repetition but a procedure in "ana-": a procedure of analysis, anamnesis, anagogy, and anamorphosis that elaborates an "initial forgetting" ' (80). In this section, I trace the operation of this process, at once individual and collective, in a number of works by Warhol. It is characteristic of his method that he accomplished it not by transcending the conditions of contemporary existence but by working through them.

Let Us Now Praise Famous Men (1963) (Figure 2.3) is one of at least five works done by Warhol early in the 1960s that combine images by fellow Pop artist, Robert Rauschenberg, together with what look like snapshots from the Rauschenberg family album. The best known of these images, in the third row from the top of the painting, is a family portrait taken in 1926 at Port Arthur, Texas, where Rauschenberg's father dug postholes for the local light and power company (*Rauschenberg*: 13). The image anticipates the photographs that Walker Evans took for James Agee's *Let Us Now Praise Famous Men*, a 'documentary report of the late 1930s about three tenant farmer families in the southern United States'. Nan Rosenthal reports that when the project was complete, the report was rejected for publication by the journal that had commissioned it because it 'was insufficiently patronizing toward its subject'. After publication, it fell out of view until it was reprinted in 1960. In 1962, a photograph (Figure 2.4) of the Bud Woods family group included in the volume was shown at an exhibition of rural photography from the depression years mounted at the Museum of Modern Art.

Although the Rauschenberg group is not destitute, they are sufficiently ordinary to make comprehensible Rauschenberg's quip about 'being "poor white trash" '.[37] In the version in the Michael D. Abrams collection, the repeated silkscreen images of the photograph have been printed in a sepia-coloured ink that signifies temporal distance, evoking nostalgia. Yet, as I have indicated, the immediate art-context of the use of this image is one of the recovery of work that had originally been ignored because it made readers uncomfortably aware of the indignities suffered by other Americans.

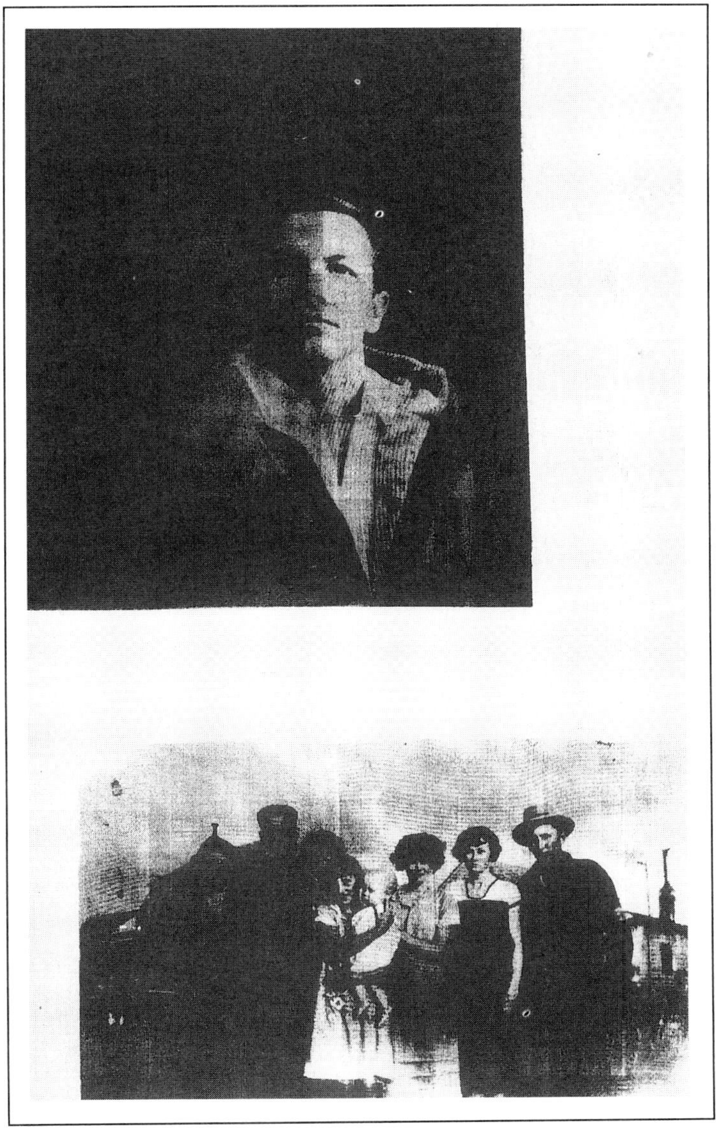

Figure 2.5 Andy Warhol, *Young Rauschenberg #1* (1962), 35″ x 22″, silkscreen on canvas.
Private collection. © ARS, NY and DACS, London 1996.

The use of sepia as well as the repeating image demonstrates the codification of the image within a sign system in which what actually once was becomes a symbol of 'then'. In other words, Warhol manipulates the image to visualize the sort of loss of a historical sense that Jameson deplores. This loss can in turn serve to anaesthetize those who, like John Kennedy during his 1960 primary campaign in West Virginia, were shocked to discover the extent of rural white poverty. Warhol manipulates the images, however, so as to undercut the sentimental dislocation signified by the use of sepia. He (or his studio assistant) indicates the disruptive effects of deprivation by cropping the third image from the left so as to delete Rauschenberg's parents. To the far right, as in a number of the disaster pictures of the early 1960s, he introduces a white blank, the only open space in the painting. The white space comments on the mechanical character of the production of the original photographic images. At the same time, the blank functions as a metaphor of temporal gap or rupture, of mortality.[38]

Beneath this row of images is a repeating image of a photograph of Rauschenberg as a young, successful artist. In other handlings, for example in *Young Rauschenberg #1* (1962) (Figure 2.5), the portrait is placed above the family group, which invites the 'before' and 'after' reading of a conventional American success story: rural obscurity to begin with, personal achievement and celebrity afterwards. The images even invite reading in terms of 'cause' and 'effect': anonymity and relative deprivation prompt a dramatic upward mobility. Warhol's staging of the images draws attention to their status as a myth. This analytic presentation, however, resonates with history, in part because the 'hero' is a bohemian artist, in part because both the subject of the painting and its painter were old enough to have experienced the Great Depression. The space between the two different kinds of image functions as a metaphor of the distance that both men covered in a generation. For Warhol, whose father emigrated from Slovakia and worked in a coal mine, the myth is also biography and autobiography.

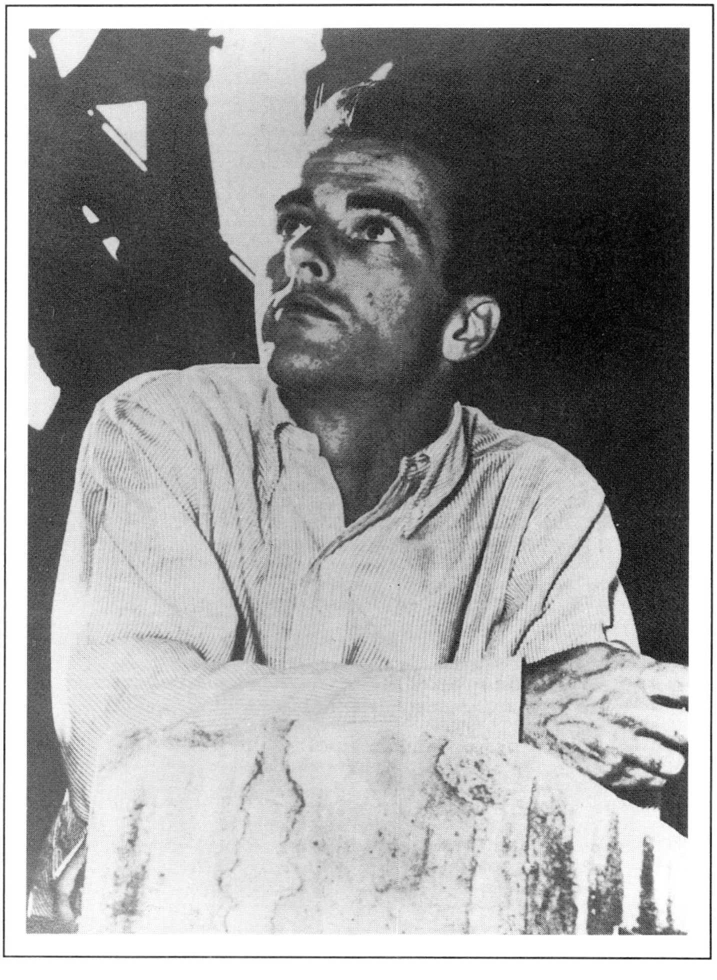

Figure 2.6 Publicity still of Montgomery Clift
Date and provenance unknown.

In *Let Us Now Praise Famous Men*, Warhol repeats the portrait-image, overlaps it, erases it with irregular white spaces or heavy inking. The repetitions highlight the conventionality and reproducability of celebrity; the manipulations suggest its temporality. The pose and lighting of the original photograph specify the masculine character of this version of the myth. With head lifted and eyes raised above the viewer, the image recalls Hollywood publicity stills, in particular a shot of Montgomery Clift (Figure 2.6).[39] Richard Dyer, who classes these images as 'male pin-ups', argues that the look up and away spiritualizes the male body while valorizing the ideal of straining, which he regards as the central suggestion of male pin-up imagery: 'it is precisely *straining* that is held to be the great good, what makes a man a man' (72). Straining in this painting, however, is straining with a difference since it is expressly loaded with the urgencies of social mobility – and dislocation – of working-class Americans born either shortly before or during the depression. Moreover, the fame refer-red to in the title is marked as the fame of a male who is homosexual. Rauschenberg, who was better known in 1963 than Warhol was, and Jasper Johns were both prototypical Pop artists as well as gay men; they also were lovers.[40] Warhol's homage to Rauschenberg, then, is homage to a man who was able to overcome the stigma of homosexuality.

Gay reference in *Let Us Now Praise Famous Men* works with other aspects of the painting to undercut univocal interpretation. These displacements destabilize the subjects of the images represented while enacting Warhol's strategy of return – of gay men to each other and to others, to workers, to women, to family, and to the patterns of self-improvement in America that Warhol both acknowledges and calls into question. The element of resistance in this affirmation should not be underestimated since Warhol was negating the assertion, urged in the preceding decade, that fags were Commies, child molesters, in short, some monstrous Other (D'Emilio 1989, 1983). Warhol's counter-assertion was: 'I am another; I am one of you'.

In *Let Us Now Praise Famous Men*, Warhol was able to turn his position as an unsubject to good use. If one were to pursue the question of how his work continued to be marked by gay reflexivity, one would consider an ever-changing range of practices. Warhol did other 'unsubject' works in the early 1960s. These works – referring to newspaper reports about anonymous deaths in major accidents; the 'car crash' pictures, whose iconography is drawn from sensational photographs in the print media; the electric chair series; the images of falling and fallen suicides; the images of racial violence in Birmingham, Alabama; the images of the *Thirteen Most Wanted Men*, a twenty-foot-square mural commissioned by Philip Johnson for the exterior of the New York State Pavilion at the 1964 New York World's Fair and covered over by direction of Governor Rockefeller – all these images play with a public exposure, even a publicity, which leaves subjectivity a blank (*Andy Warhol: Death and Disasters*: 106; Stuckey: 16). This extreme sense of alienation between the subject and its public appropriation register Warhol's awareness of his psychically and socially exposed position. Warhol also was a frequent collaborator with young gay men, most notably in his adaptation of underground film technique in both experimental and commercial filmmaking, often dealing with homosexual material, between 1963 and 1969.[41]

Engendering the subject

In the final lines of the opening chapter of his book, Jameson invokes the name of Althusser in arguing that critical theorists have yet to address the need to theorize the relationship between the Lacanian symbolic and the issues of agency and representation in postmodern culture. In his essay, 'Freud and Lacan', Althusser contends that the formation of the contemporary subject, whose existence is necessary to the functioning of late capitalism, occurs through the processes of education and family life. Althusser especially emphasizes this inculturation as a process of gender formation. Commenting on Lacan's *'Symbolic Order'* (162), Althusser argues that 'Lacan demonstrates the effectiveness of the Order, the Law, that has been lying in wait for each infant born since before his birth, and seizes him before his first cry, assigning to him his place and role, and hence his fixed destination' (163). A feminist might respond that in this instance as usual, critical theory limits its attention to the male subject. In the essay, however, Althusser at least acknowledges the fact that the gender formation of women is also central to the constitution of the economic order (162).

In 'Postmodernism, or the cultural logic of late capitalism' Jameson transcodes 'Lacan's account of schizophrenia' (1991: 26) from psychoanalysis to aesthetics. Jameson remarks: 'I must omit the familial or more orthodox psychoanalytic background to this situation' (1991: 26). In response, Jacqueline Rose has observed that Jameson elides precisely the psychoanalytic etiology that has made schizophrenia especially a female condition (116). The exclusion of this context guarantees other significant absences. Rose points out 'the omission ... of any women artists from his account of postmodern cultural production, and more specifically of those who might be said to make the representation of sexual difference, or sexual difference *as* representation, their chief object of concern'. Rose also observes that 'the concept of representation that is at stake' for Jameson 'seems to bring with it a kind of nostalgia for direct and unmediated vision', for 'a moment or an epoch when vision was direct and possible, when the viewing subject looked out on and greeted the world, and greeted too, without perversion or aggressivity, the other human subjects who peopled it' (117). I would add to these comments that, in the context of the opening chapter of *Postmodernism*, the subject of this innocent gaze is a heterosexual male, that is, that he occupies the position of Heidegger/van Gogh and that instating this position, even if equivocally, requires Jameson to negate not only feminine difference but also differences within masculine existence, in particular, feminized male homosexual difference.

Recent gay critique has associated schizophrenia with the play of visibility and invisibility within the regime of closeting. Commenting on the Russian dancer, Nijinsky, for instance, Michael Moon writes:

> The strain of being a visible and intensely mystified embodiment of the open secret of male homosexuality in Paris and London in the decade or two after the epochal downfall and death of Oscar Wilde no doubt played a significant part in what was diagnosed as Nijinsky's schizophrenic disintegration in his late twenties, at the end of World War I. (29)

In *Postmodernism*, Jameson belatedly begins to attend to sexual contexts of schizophrenia. He adds to the discussion of Lacan a footnote that refers the reader to Lacan's discussion of the Schreber case, which Freud analyses in terms of 'a regression to a passive homosexuality' (Wollheim: 157). In this limited way, Jameson provides a trace of male–male desire in his account of schizophrenia.

In failing to address the psychoanalytic structure of schizophrenia, Jameson ensures that the play of gender in his text will act out rather than act on the implications of Althusser's reflections. The dissolution of the subject in the hysterical sublime, however, also functions as a symptom of Jameson's resistance to contemporary marxist theory. This resistance shows in two ways: first, in Jameson's preoccupation with 'the unavoidable representational problem that there is no "late capitalism in general" ' (1991: xx); and second, in his evacuation of the revolutionary subject. As for the problem of representation, one might argue that Jameson's reduction of Mandel's model of capitalist development to a thumbnail sketch is more problematic than Mandel's portrayal of that development within *Late Capitalism*. Mandel's account of capitalist expansion in the nineteenth and twentieth centuries persuasively illustrates his general thesis that '*the accumulation of capital itself produces development and underdevelopment as mutually determining moments of the uneven and combined movement of capital*' (85). He also provides a credible account of the functioning of this inverse relationship in the relation between postcolonial economies and multinational corporations since the end of the Second World War (556–61). In the light of this analysis, there appears to be no need for a representation of ' "late capitalism in general" '. Mandel provides a good basis for understanding the effects of further capital accumulation in the metropolitan countries.

More problematic is the apocalyptic turn that Mandel takes in the final chapter, in which he argues the imminence of the revolutionary overturn of the capitalist economy by a 'working-class' whose 'cultural and political horizon' is ever 'widening' (585). The subjects of this revolution are unitary, and Mandel uses terms like 'workers' and 'democracy' in altogether reified fashion. In contrast, Jameson presents a postmodern subject who is not transparent but thick – even if only with sensation. In positing this subject, Jameson indicates how different is his assessment of political possibility in the waning years of the century.

The movement of the narrative of 'Postmodernism, or the cultural logic of late capitalism' is not toward the recovery of capacities for representation and agency but towards an occluded subject altogether suitable for the *fin de millennium.* This process is symptomatic of blockage at both the social and psychological levels. Yet the impasse, as I have tried to show in analysing the position of Andy Warhol, is by no means the only or even a necessary outcome of postmodern theory and practice. Avoiding this impasse, however, requires the continued work of engendering theory, including Jameson's; of attending to the specificities of experience of those subject to hegemonic masculinity; and of an inventive use of macro- and micro-politics in both metropolitan countries and elsewhere.

Notes

1 Fredric Jameson, *The Political Unconscious*, 19.

2 References to Jameson unless otherwise noted are to *Postmodernism, or, The Cultural Logic of Late Capitalism.*

3 In a long Conclusion, Jameson addresses 'what (rightly) struck some readers as a crucial missing component of the program essay, namely, the absence of any discussion of "agency" ' (1991: xviii). In context, agency refers to 'the "micropolitics" that corresponds to the emergence of' a 'whole range of small-group, nonclass political practices' (1991: 318). Jameson dubs these practices a ' "bad infinity" characterized 'by the willed euphoria of some metaphysical permanent revolution'. He continues:

> I think myself that that euphoria is a compensating formation, in a situation in which, for a time, genuine (or"totalizing") politics is no longer possible; it is necessary to add that what is lost in its absence, the global dimension, is very precisely the dimension of economics itself, or of the system, of private enterprise and the profit motive, which cannot be challenged on a local level (1991: 330)

4 See section IV, 'Groups and representation', of the Conclusion (1990: 318–31).

5 1991: 32; Jameson, 'Postmodernism, or the cultural logic of late capitalism', 76.

6 Craig Owens has connected issues of representation in critical theory, including Jameson's, with the idea of theory-as-phallus, that is, the idea of theory as a gendered site that requires the exclusion of feminist theory/practice from the discourse of straight-identified male poststructuralist theory ('The discourse of others', 64-7). In 'The signification of the phallus', Jacques Lacan writes: 'the phallus is the privileged signifier of that mark in which the role of the logos is joined with the advent of desire' (287). See Jane Gallop's discussion of the essay, including her discussion of Jameson's comments on feminists, Lacan, and the phallus (ch. 6, especially. 134-6). Attention to feminine/feminist difference would lead inevitably to the gender-analysis of male theory itself, a fact which provides a powerful reason for theorists such as Jameson to ignore feminist work. Hence, too, the customary tendency to marginalize and denigrate gay cultural practices.

7 Charles W. Haxthausen discusses the Peircian meaning of the word 'icon' (67).

8 I think, for instance, of Teresa de Lauretis, 1984 (ch. 6), 1986, 1987 (ch. 1).

9 Hal Foster, 139–55; Ross, 228–32.

10 The relevant passage in Freud is quoted below. See the articles 'Phallic woman, phallic mother' and 'Disavowal (denial)' (Jean Laplanche and J.-B. Pontalis, 311–12; 118–21).

11 A voice refers parodically to 'the obvious bisexuality' of the shoes. Derrida provides a basis in Freudian dream-theory for making such a reference: 'Bisexual symbolization remains an irrepressible, archaic tendency, going back to childhood which is ignorant of the difference of the sexes.' To this observation, another voice responds: 'So it is always necessary to hold in reserve a sort of excess of interpretation, a supplement of reading – which is decisive, to tell the truth – for the idiom of a syntactic variation'. (Derrida, *The Truth in Painting*, 268, 278). In stating that 'Derrida' refers to the shoes as 'a heterosexual pair', Jameson (hetero)sexualizes Derrida's text, excluding exactly that 'excess of interpretation' to which the preceding citation draws attention.

Jameson's misreading of Derrida has also been noted by John Frow in 'Tourism and the semiotics of nostalgia', 141.

12 Contrary to Jameson's reading, the passage from Heidegger could be read in another way. The 'world' of the peasant woman may be her cultural product rather than that of the male artist and male critics and theorists.

13 Cited by Jameson 1991: 35.

14 Derrida, *The Truth in Painting*, 259, 272.

15 For three different images in this series see *Retrospective*, plates 390, 391, 392. I use the term 'image' because the image, which Jameson refers to no single painting by Warhol, appears to be *Jameson's* summary notion of such an image.

16 For a discussion of the serigraphs, see Marco Livingstone, 'Do it yourself: notes on Warhol's techniques', in McShine (ed.), *Andy Warhol*, 74.

17 Illustrated in McShine, (ed.), *Andy Warhol*, 42, 64.

18 Crone, *Andy Warhol*, 63.
19 Crone has pointed out that at the beginning of his career as a Pop artist Warhol was aware of these aspects of the star system, including its relation to middle-class fantasies and aspirations (*Andy Warhol*, 68-9).
20 Crone argues that Warhol was an admirer of Bertolt Brecht ('Form and Ideology', 70–2).
21 Stuckey, 'Warhol in Context', 24.
22 Rosenthal, 'Let us now praise famous men', 37, 40, 41.
23 See Crone, *Andy Warhol*, 63.
24 Freud, *The Standard Edition*, 11: 96. At the end of his life, Warhol was producing images drawn from Leonardo's *The Last Supper*, a key image of love between men in both Roman Catholic and nineteenth-century aesthetic culture. One hopes that Warhol, who did a series of Cow-images in the mid-1960s, knew as well the following passage from Freud's study:

> When ... the child becomes familiar with the cow's udder whose function is that of a nipple, but whose shape and position under the belly make it resemble a penis, the preliminary stage has been reached which will later enable him to form the repellent sexual fantasy' of cocksucking. (*Standard Edition*, 11: 87)

25 Fig. 219 in Crone, *Andy Warhol*.
26 See Rosenthal, 'Let us now praise famous men', 41–2.
27 McShine, 'Introduction', *Andy Warhol*, 19.
28 Collins, 'The metaphysical nosejob', 48; also Crone, 'Form and ideology', 74.
29 1991: 10; italics mine.
30 Between the terms of comparison in the text fall 'Rimbaud's magical flowers "that look back at you" ' (10).
31 The phrase is Paul de Man's; see *Allegories of Reading*, 142.
32 For the tradition, see Dellamora, *Masculine Desire* (1990), 242 n. 18. See also Adam, *The Rise of a Gay and Lesbian Movement*, ch. 5.
33 The strong period-sense of New York gays when faced with the onset of AIDS is registered in Andrew Holleran's short story, 'Friends at Evening' in Holleran 1986.
34 I cite the earlier version in order to retain the second-person references, which I place in brackets. These are removed from the 1991 text.
35 Jameson, 'Reification and Utopia', 141.
36 1991: 11-12, 18-21, as well as the discussion of Warhol's *Diamond Dust Shoes*; see also Dan Latimer's discussion (118–19).
37 Rosenthal, 'Let us now praise famous men', 47, 48, 49.
38 The white space is analogous with the strobe cut used by Warhol in his films (Crone 1989: 89–90).
39 Reproduced in Dyer, 62.
40 Personal information is from Jonathan Katz. See also Collins, 48.
41 See, for example, his collaboration with Gerard Malanga who attached poems to thermofax images from the Death and Disasters works (*Andy Warhol: Death and Disasters*, 24–7); see also Ehrenstein.

References

Adam, B.D. (1987) *The Rise of a Gay and Lesbian Movement*, Boston: Twayne.

Althusser, L. (1984) 'Freud and Lacan', in *Essays on Ideology*, London: Verso, 147–71.

Andy Warhol: Death and Disasters (1988) Houston: The Menil Collection.

Collins, B.R. (1988) 'The metaphysical nosejob: the remaking of Warhola, 1960–1968', *Arts Magazine* 62 (February): 47–55.

Cotter, H. (1994) 'Art after Stonewall: Twelve artists interviewed', *Art in America* 82 (June): 56–65.

Crone, R. (1987) *Andy Warhol: A Picture Show by the Artist*, New York: Rizzoli.

____ (1989) 'Form and ideology: Warhol's technique from blotted line to film', in Gary Garrels (ed.), *The Work of Andy Warhol*, Seattle: Bay Press.

Davis, M. (1989) 'Heavyweight contenders', *Interview* 19 (August): 148, 178.

de Lauretis, T. (1984) *Alice Doesn't: Feminism, Semiotics, Cinema*, Bloomington: Indiana University Press.

—— (1986) 'Feminist studies/critical studies: issues, terms, and contexts', in Teresa de Lauretis (ed.), *Feminist Studies: Critical Studies*, Bloomington: Indiana University Press.

—— (1987) *Technologies of Gender: Essays on Theory, Film, and Fiction*, Bloomington: Indiana University Press.

Dellamora, R. (1990) *Masculine Desire: The Sexual Politics of Victorian Aestheticism*, Chapel Hill: University of North Carolina Press.

de Man, P. (1979) *Allegories of Reading: Figural Language in Rousseau, Nietzsche, Rilke, and Proust*, New Haven: Yale University Press.

D'Emilio, J. (1983) *Sexual Politics, Sexual Communities: The Making of a Homosexual Minority in the United States:*

1940–1970, Chicago: University of Chicago Press.
—— (1989) 'The homosexual menace: the politics of sexuality in Cold War America', in Kathy Peiss, Christina Simmons, and Robert A. Padgug (eds) *Passion and Power: Sexuality in History,* Philadelphia: Temple University Press.
Derrida, J. (1982) *Margins of Philosophy,* trans. Alan Bass, Chicago: University of Chicago Press.
—— (1987) *The Truth in Painting,* trans. Geoff Bennington and Ian McLeod, Chicago: University of Chicago Press.
Dyer, R. (1982) 'Don't look now', *Screen* 23 (September–October): 61–73.
Ehrenstein, D. (1989) 'The filmmaker as homosexual hipster', *Arts Magazine* 63 (Summer): 61–4.
Foster, H. (1989) *Recodings: Art, Spectacle, Cultural Politics,* Seattle, Washington: Bay Press.
Foucault, M. (1980) *The History of Sexuality. Volume I: An Introduction,* trans. Robert Hurley, New York: Vintage.
Freud, S. (1971–4) *The Standard Edition of the Complete Psychological Works,* trans. and ed. James Strachey in collaboration with Anna Freud, 24 vols, London: Hogarth Press.
Frow, J. (1991) 'Tourism and the semiotics of nostalgia', *October* 57 (Summer): 123–51.
Gallop, J. (1988) *Reading Lacan,* Ithaca: Cornell University Press.
Haxthausen, C.W. (1990) 'Translation and transformation in *Target with Four Faces:* the painting, the drawing, and the etching', in *Jasper Johns: Printed Symbols,* introd. Elizabeth Armstrong, Minneapolis: Walker Art Center: 63–75.
Heidegger, M. (1964) 'The origin of the work of art', in Albert Hofstadter and Richard Kuhns (eds), *Philosophies of Art and Beauty,* New York: Modern Library: 649–701.
Holleran, A. (1986) 'Friends at Evening', in George Stambolian (ed.), *Men on Men: Best New Gay Fiction,* New York: New American Library.
Jameson, F. (1979) 'Reification and Utopia in mass culture', *Social Text* 1 (Winter): 130–48.
—— (1981) *The Political Unconscious: Narrative as a Socially Symbolic Act,* Ithaca: Cornell University Press.
—— (1984) 'Postmodernism, or the cultural logic of late capitalism', *New Left Review* 146 (July–August): 53–92.
—— (1991) *Postmodernism, or, The Cultural Logic of Late Capitalism,* Durham: Duke University Press.
Jones, C.A. (1993) 'Finishing school: John Cage and the Abstract Expressionist Ego', *Critical Inquiry* 19: 628–65.
Katz, J. (1990) 'Sexuality in the art of Johns and Rauschenberg', paper, Fourth Annual Lesbian, Bisexual and Gay Studies Conference, Harvard University, Cambridge, Mass., October 28.
Lacan, J. (1977) *Ecrits: A Selection,* trans. Alan Sheridan. New York: W.W. Norton.
Laplanche, J. and J.-B. Pontalis (1973) *The Language of Psycho-Analysis,* trans. Donald Nicholson-Smith and introd. Daniel Lagache, New York: Norton.
Latimer, D.(1984) 'Jameson and post-modernism', *New Left Review* 148 (November–December): 116–28.
Livingstone, M. (1989) 'Do it yourself: notes on Warhol's techniques', in Kynaston McShine (ed.), *Andy Warhol: A Retrospective,* New York: Museum of Modern Art.
Lyotard, J.-F. (1993) *The Postmodern Explained: Correspondence, 1982-1985,* trans. Don Barry, *et al.*; ed. Julian Pefanis and Morgan Thomas, Afterword by Wlad Godzich, Minneapolis: University of Minnesota Press.
McShine, K. (1989) 'Introduction', in Kynaston McShine (ed.), *Andy Warhol: A Retrospective,* New York: Museum of Modern Art.
Mandel, E. (1976) *Late Capitalism,* trans. Joris De Bres, London: New Left Books.
Milan Women's Bookstore Collective (1990) *Sexual Difference: A Theory of Social-Symbolic Practice,* trans. Patricia Cicogna and Teresa de Lauretis, Bloomington: Indiana University Press.
Moon, M. (1989) 'Flaming Closets', *October* 51 (Winter): 19–54.
Owens, C. (1987) 'The discourse of others: feminists and postmodernism', in Hal Foster (ed.), *The Anti-Aesthetic: Essays on Postmodern Culture,* Port Townsend, Washington: Bay Press.
Rauschenberg: An Interview with Robert Rauschenberg by Barbara Rose (1987) New York: Vintage Books.
Rilke, R. M. (1981) *Selected Poems,* trans. and commentary by Robert Bly, New York: Harper & Row.
Rose, J. (1988) 'Sexuality and vision: some questions', in Hal Foster (ed.), *Vision and Visuality,* Seattle: Bay Press, 115–27.
Rosenthal, N. (1989) 'Let us now praise famous men: Warhol as art director', in Gary Garrels (ed.), *The Work of Andy Warhol,* Seattle: Bay Press.
Ross, A. (1989) *No Respect: Intellectuals and Popular Culture,* New York: Routledge.
Schapiro, M. (1968) 'The still life as a personal object: a note on Heidegger and van Gogh', in Marianne L. Simmer (ed.), *The Reach of Mind: Essays in Memory of Kurt Goldstein,* New York: Springer Publishing Co.
Sedgwick, E. K. (1990) *Epistemology of the Closet,* Berkeley: University of California Press.
Sontag, S. (1966) 'Notes on "Camp" ', in *Against Interpretation and Other Essays,* New York: Farrar, Straus & Giroux.
Stuckey, C.E. (1989) 'Warhol in Context', in Gary Garrels (ed.), *The Work of Andy Warhol,* Seattle: Bay Press.
Warhol, A. (1985) *America,* New York: Harper & Row.
Watney, S. (1989) 'The Warhol Effect', in Gary Garrels (ed.), *The Work of Andy Warhol.* Seattle: Bay Press.
Wollheim, R. (1971) *Sigmund Freud,* Cambridge: Cambridge University Press.

Chapter Three

Out of the maid's room

Dora, Stratonice and the lesbian analyst

Wendy Leeks

> ... camp recognition doesn't ask, 'What kind of debased creature could possibly be the right audience for this spectacle?' Instead, it says what if: What if the right audience for this were exactly *me*?
>
> ... And what if, furthermore, others whom I don't know or recognise can see it from the same 'perverse' angle? Unlike Kitsch – attribution, the sensibility of camp-recognition always sees that it is dealing in reader relations and in projective fantasy (projective though not infrequently true). (Sedgwick 1991: 156)

> In 'Dora' what was terrifying was that these archetypical servants were put by Freud himself in 'the maid's room' – that is, in the notes.
>
> ... Freud didn't give the servant-girl enough recognition. Never do you see her in the body of the text – she is always in the kitchen, in her station: she appears in the notes. When Freud speaks of Dora's sexual initiation, entirely acquired from books, it is automatically attributed to the normal sources of this sort of pernicious education – it is probably the maid's doing. (Cixous 1986: 150 and 152)

THE QUESTION IS . . .

Contemporary cultural analysis recognizes that the viewer or reader is the place where meaning happens. This movement towards looking at the spectator, derived in part from psychoanalysis, has been fuelled particularly by those identified, or self-identifying, as on the margins of mainstream culture. For these spectators understanding their relations to cultures and pleasures, as consumers and as contributors, is urgent. The consequences of this shift in focus to relations of consumption have been major for academic practice. Here the position of the analyst – the scholar or critic as reader or spectator – and how it affects interpretation has become a subject for enquiry and critique. Much of the impetus for these enquiries into what psychoanalysis terms the countertransference, or the analyst's fantasies, identifications and investments in the case, has come from areas of academic activity often seen as marginal or eccentric – including feminist analyses, black and post-colonialist studies and lesbian and gay or queer studies. Many critiques developed from these 'margins' have revealed the pleasures enjoyed by the analyst occupying a position at the centre of dominant discourses : they have focused on the discourse of the analyst who is 'one of them' – white, male and heterosexual. What about the fantasies, pleasures and position of the analyst who is 'one of us'?

The analyst in question here and now is 'exactly *me*'. This analyst has to be characterized as a white, feminist, lesbian art historian[1] who, in this instance, happens to get pleasure from certain paintings by Ingres of the story of Antiochus and Stratonice. The questions being posed are:

How does she get this pleasure?

What is the nature of this pleasure?

What does this examination contribute to lesbian and gay/queer theory?

To answer these questions I turn to psychoanalysis as the theoretical basis of my investigation of pleasure and desire and also because my relation to the paintings is tied to my knowledge of feminist critiques of Freud's analysis of Dora. My pleasure in these images is connected to affinities between the paintings and the Dora case, linked, in my mind, by a shadowy figure of a maid.[2]

WHAT DID DORA SEE?

In 'Fragment of an analysis of a case of hysteria' (1905) – the Dora case – Freud describes this unsuccessful treatment of a young woman with hysterical symptoms. The case history has proved important because it was there that Freud's failure to see the operation of countertransference, to recognize that his own fantasies and unconscious desires fundamentally structured his interpretation, became manifest. Freud attributed his failure to Dora's having terminated the analysis before its completion and also, as he wrote in a footnote, to his inability to recognize the importance of Dora's lesbian love for Frau K :

> The longer the interval of time that separates me from the end of the analysis, the more probable it seems to me that the fault in my technique lay in this omission: I failed to discover in time and to inform the patient that her homosexual (gynaecophilic) love for Frau K was the strongest unconscious current in her mental life. I ought to have guessed that the main source of her knowledge of sexual matters could have been no one but Frau K. (Freud 1977: 162)

Cixous suggests the countertransference caused Freud to underestimate the significance of the maids. References to these women are marginalized, consigned to the 'maid's room' of the footnotes. Freud presumes the maids responsible, in their ideologically-constructed role of seductress (the role ascribed to the nursemaid consistently in Freud's fantasies[3]), for Dora's illicit sexual knowledge. He also gives this role, again in the footnotes, to Frau K – sexual informant, seducer, betrayer/sexual object, used, discarded. Frau K is shut up in the maid's room, where all 'improper' sexual knowledge and each 'debased creature' in the case is consigned. Also in the footnotes Freud speaks of Dora's lesbian desire, revealing his discovery of it to the reader but not telling Dora. (Would telling her have been to act like a maid?) Dora's lesbianism itself belongs, of course, in the 'maid's room' too.

A series of characters occupy, or resist, the place of the maid in the case history, there to be that little something that the wife does not supply. The K children's governess was seduced by Herr K and then thrown over. He told her he 'got nothing from his wife' (Freud 1977: 146). Dora is propositioned by Herr K at the lake with the words: 'You know I get nothing out of my wife' (138). Freud is enlisted to treat Dora by her father, who says: 'You know already that I get nothing out of my wife' (57). Freud is given a fortnight's notice of the termination of the analysis by Dora. He says: 'That sounds just like a maidservant or a governess – a fortnight's notice' (146). But who employed whom? Cixous writes:

> Freud in relation to Dora was in the maid's place. It is Freud who was the servant girl, and that is what is intolerable for Freud in the Dora case – that he was treated as one treats maids, having been fired the way you fire a servant-girl. There is no failure worse than that. The knot, the crux of the Dora case, is that Dora was afraid of being the maid, and, on the other hand, she was afraid of being nothing, like her mother. (Cixous 1986: 152)

It becomes clear in rereading the case that Dora was resisting identification with the maids (resisting being used and discarded) and with the wives/mothers (resisting becoming 'nothing'). But also and primarily she was resisting a position as an object of exchange between her father and

Herr K (with Freud acting in some sense as their surrogate and instrument). In order to preserve his amicable relations with Herr K and safeguard his affair with Frau K, Dora's father was willing to give his daughter over to Herr K. Caught within these circles, where could Dora's resistances have taken her except into illness?

Freud, on the other hand, also resists identification with the maids, with the hysteric, with the feminine. His vehement disavowal of these feminine positions both forces and enables him to retreat into an overdetermined masculinity. He aligns himself with what he sees as the successful and powerful characteristics of Herr K and Dora's father (the bourgeois 'man of means'), and with the 'scientific' objectivity of his own profession and the tone and assertions of the body of the text.[4]

For everyone 'in' the Dora case, the position of the maid is negative. For Dora, the positions of wife and mother seem negative too. But for Freud, Dora must be persuaded, or helped to realize, that she desired to be (could have been/should have been) Herr K's wife. For Freud himself being identified with the maids is an offence against both his gender and class positions. To him Dora should be either a girl, uncorrupted by the contaminated knowledge of the maid (or Frau K) and therefore with a passive, unresisting, inchoate sexuality, or a wife and mother. Her class position makes the 'maid's room' an improper place for her to be. She should become legitimate mistress of the house and not illicit mistress *to* Herr K. Her class and her gender together rule out, in Freud's eyes, the possibility that she could or should have any other place. Dora's lesbian desire is said by Freud to be the 'strongest unconscious current in her mental life' (162). According to him she does not know of its existence and he does not tell her (so she cannot know unless she 'got it' from Frau K or the maids). For him, this desire has to be strong and ***unconscious*** in order to cause Dora's rejection of Herr K (and her father); in order to cause Dora's rejection of Freud and to cause his failure; in order to cause Dora's symptoms, creating her unhappiness by forcing her to resist her 'proper place'. Seeing Dora as lesbian – when he finally does so – is a negative image for Freud, but not necessarily for Dora: we only have Freud's words for it.

Yet there is an important element in the case history which may throw some light, or some doubt, on how Freud saw Dora and the question of what Dora saw. In the session interpreting Dora's second dream she recalled a visit to the art gallery in Dresden where she saw Raphael's painting the *Sistine Madonna*:

> She remained *two hours* in front of the Sistine Madonna, rapt in silent admiration. When I asked her what had pleased her so much about the picture she could find no clear answer to make. At last she said: 'The Madonna'.
> (Freud 1977: 135–6, original emphasis)

This is significant in many ways for Freud's interpretation of the dream. But the information about Dora's reaction to the picture, and Freud's interpretation – in a long footnote – of what the picture meant to Dora, are also interesting for what they show of Freud's preconceptions, speculations and investments. Freud did not find out from Dora what it was about the Madonna that pleased her; he presumed to know: 'The *Madonna* was obviously Dora herself' (145).

> *If* the analysis had continued, Dora's maternal longing for a child *would probably* have been revealed as an obscure though powerful motive in her behaviour. (145, emphasis added)

For Freud, then, what Dora saw in the picture was herself as mother. Therefore what pleased her was narcissistic identification with the image as an ideal image of self in a wished-for role as mother.[5] Freud's footnote of 'supplementary interpretations' is interesting also for what it goes on to say:

> The numerous questions which she had been raising latterly seem to have been belated derivatives of questions inspired by the sexual curiosity which she had tried to gratify with the encyclopaedia. The subjects which she read up in it were *presumably* pregnancy, childbirth, virginity, and so on ...

> These improper words seemed to point to a second and *oral* source of information, since the encyclopaedia would not cover them. I should not have been surprised to hear that this source had been Frau K herself, Dora's calumniator. In that case she would have been the person whom Dora generously spared, while she pursued others with an almost malignant vindictiveness. Behind the almost limitless series of displacements which were thus brought to light, it was possible to divine the operation of a single simple factor – Dora's deep-rooted homosexual love for Frau K.
>
> (Freud 1977: 145–6, emphasis added)

Again, dirty maids' talk is linked to Dora's love for Frau K and placed in the 'maid's room' of the footnotes.

Freud tells us what he thinks Dora saw when she looked at the *Sistine Madonna* in Dresden. What did Freud see when he looked at the same picture? Freud seems to have forgotten his own reaction of some eighteen years previously, but it is recorded in a letter he wrote on 20 December 1883 to his then fiancée (later wife) Martha Bernays:

> Now I happened to know that there was also a Madonna by Raphael there and I found her at last in an equally chapel-like room and a crowd of people in silent devotion in front of her. You are sure to know her, the Sistina. My thoughts as I sat there were: Oh, if only you were with me! ... The painting emanates a magic beauty that is inescapable, and yet I have a serious objection to raise against the Madonna herself ... Raphael's Madonna is a girl, say 16 years old; she gazes out on the world with such a fresh and innocent expression, half against my will she suggested to me a charming, sympathetic nursemaid, not from the celestial world but from ours. My Viennese friends reject this opinion of mine as heresy ...[6]

The nursemaid appears again. Dora's relation to the *Sistine Madonna* image is characterized by Freud as narcissistic identification: Dora sees herself. Freud, on the other hand, sees an object of desire different from him, a sexual (and illicit?) object that makes him wish his 'legitimate' sexual object – his fiancée – were there. Did Freud, perhaps, see in Dora what he saw in the *Sistine Madonna*? This same footnote makes reference to the significance of Dora's wordplays with names – where proper names show 'improper' associations. What about the name Dora that Freud gave to Ida Bauer?

> In *The Psychopathology of Everyday Life*, Freud disclosed that when he searched for a name for Ida Bauer, 'Dora was the only name to occur'. Dora was the name of a servant in the Freud family who had been his sister's nursemaid. She had been forced to give up her own name, Rosa, as it was his sister's name. Through his choice, or lack of choice, Freud revealed his recognition that in his mind, as in Ida Bauer's, servitude was a metaphor for femininity. At the very same moment, however, Freud also conferred his wish that like Rosa, the servant woman who gave up even her name, Ida Bauer make her peace with servitude. To escape a feminine fate is the prerogative of the son, not the daughter.
>
> (Ramas 1985: 176)

All this may reveal the complexities of Freud's unconscious fantasies and desires, but what about Dora's? Freud can be a desiring subject seeing an object of desire when he looks at the *Sistine Madonna*, yet he cannot allow this for Dora. But *what if*? What if a lesbian Dora saw in the *Sistine Madonna* not herself, or not *only* herself, but another who was not entirely other (different): self and other, mother, loved and lover? Freud's words do not tell us; Dora the hysteric who loses her voice cannot tell us; the lesbians and the feminists in the maid's room can only fantasize and gossip.

In the Dora case the position of the maid can be seen to stand for many elements. For Freud the maid is sexualized, enticing, seducing, betraying, subordinate, subservient, Other. His disavowal of identification with the place of the maid is a major factor in the failure of the case. We, however, can see that the maid also stands for femininity. She is part of the formula for 'woman' in the middle-class, heterosexual, sexual economy that is the setting for the case history; a formula completed by the 'boss's wife'.[7] Important here is that the maid's place, assigned by the middle-class hegemonic structure, secured by dominant ideologies of class and gender, is marginal yet necessary to that structure. The maid is the Other or 'outsider' *inside* the family space, the despised (working-class) whose barely tolerated presence sustains the status and integrity of the 'insiders' (bourgeois family unit), while at the same time apparently threatening to disrupt it. She is also, in the Dora case and a more general sense, the one in a position to see, to acquire knowledge of the 'goings-on' in the family and to impart it – in a 'below stairs' way. Furthermore, the place of the maid is associated in the discourses of the Dora case with lesbianism. What if, instead of refusing to be placed as the maid, the analyst were actively to adopt that position, or to recognize that, in many respects, that *is* her position?[8]

What's in it for the maid?

The nineteenth-century French painter J.A.D. Ingres is probably best known for his lavish and peculiarly distorted female nudes, most famously *The Turkish Bath* (1863). This might be cited as a prime example of an image produced from and for the fantasies of white, heterosexual males.[9] Apart from nudes and portraits, Ingres is also noted for repeating subjects and motifs, and the *Antiochus and Stratonice* pictures are an example of this.[10] Again, the narrative of Antiochus and Stratonice is tailored to heterosexual male fantasy.

The story is in classical works including Plutarch's *Lives*[11] and is based on the historical characters Seleucus I Nicator, his wife Stratonice and his son by a former marriage, Antiochus. Seleucus was a successful general under Alexander the Great and when the emperor died in 323 BC he became king of a large part of the old empire. The story is that Antiochus is stricken with love for his stepmother Stratonice and is dying because of the impossibility of his desire. No one knows the cause of his illness until the doctor Erasistratus feels Antiochus's heart race, notices this has happened when Stratonice has walked into the room and realizes love for Stratonice is the cause. He tells Seleucus, who gives Stratonice to Antiochus and divides up the kingdom so that both men can rule.

This narrative re-enacts the exchange of women between men that Lévi-Strauss describes as the process which establishes kinship structures and social relations: a social contract that sanctions desire and avoids incest[12]. In terms of fantasy fulfilment, the story presents a happy conclusion to the Oedipal dilemma. In the narrative Antiochus is able to 'have' Stratonice because she is his stepmother, not his mother. However, the extreme response of Antiochus to his desire – that it, or his resistance to it, makes him ill to the point of death – indicates that the desire involved is the (any) son's repressed unconscious desire for the (their own) mother. The story thus in a disguised way (an example of Freudian displacement) embodies the fulfilment of the son's greatest wish : to achieve his outlawed and repressed (unconscious) desire for his mother without suffering the father's threatened punishment of castration.

Pleasure for the heterosexual male is therefore easily available from the narrative. In painting, the subject had been treated by many artists before Ingres. It had been set as the competition piece for the Prix de Rome in 1774 and won by Jacques-Louis David, later to be Ingres's master. Ingres's first version of the subject has been dated at 1801 because on the reverse is a sketch for *The Ambassadors of Agamemnon at the Tent of Achilles*, the competition piece with which Ingres won the Prix de Rome in that year. David and the other artists who had painted the subject combined the two vital moments of the story into one composition – the doctor's discovery and the king's ceding of his wife. In terms of pleasure, the son gaining possession of the mother must be the most important moment. Yet Ingres never represents it. In all his versions only the most dramatic and also most ambiguous moment is shown, the moment of discovery when the father's reaction is not yet known. It could be argued that anyone viewing the pictures and knowing the story already knows what the outcome is, however, the fact that the action is arrested at this moment before the 'happy ending' has major consequences for viewer identification and pleasure.

In examining the pleasure of the lesbian analyst, I will concentrate on three paintings in the series : the Chantilly oil (1840), the Philadelphia oil (1860) and the last painting (1866) now in the Musée Fabre, Montpellier.[13] All contain the figure of the maid at the door, probably representing the servant/confidante of Stratonice mentioned in some of the literary sources and often included as a more prominent figure in paintings of the subject.

The Chantilly and Montpellier versions are similar in most respects, both containing the full cast of characters in their usual (within the series) places and poses. The Montpellier picture is slightly bigger than the earlier painting and reverses the composition left-to-right. The Cleveland oil is an unfinished sketch for the Chantilly picture commissioned by the Duc d'Orléans. The 1860 Philadelphia oil is different in several respects, including a pair of mourning hounds in the foreground and showing, in my opinion, a moment perhaps a split second earlier than the other versions. In this picture Erasistratus looks at Stratonice but his stance indicates thought rather than discovery. Ingres's tracing of this work (Musée Ingres, 867.2194) reworks the doctor's pose so that his left hand, resting on the bed in the painting, is raised. This sets up a sequence across the four works : the Philadelphia oil shows the thought, the tracing 'discovery' and the Chantilly and Montpellier paintings show full realization of cause and consequences. For simplicity I will focus on the Chantilly picture (Figure 3.1) with its completely elaborated architectural setting and positioned characters.[14]

In this the three males are grouped together on one side of the composition, over against Stratonice, their opposite and Other, the object of their desire (Antiochus, Seleucus) and of their gaze (Erasistratus, Antiochus).[15] The heterosexual male spectator[16] needs to identify with these male figures, primarily with Antiochus, in order to achieve a fantasy fulfilment of his wish to (re)possess the mother in the outcome of the story. Such an identification presents problems because of the moment at which

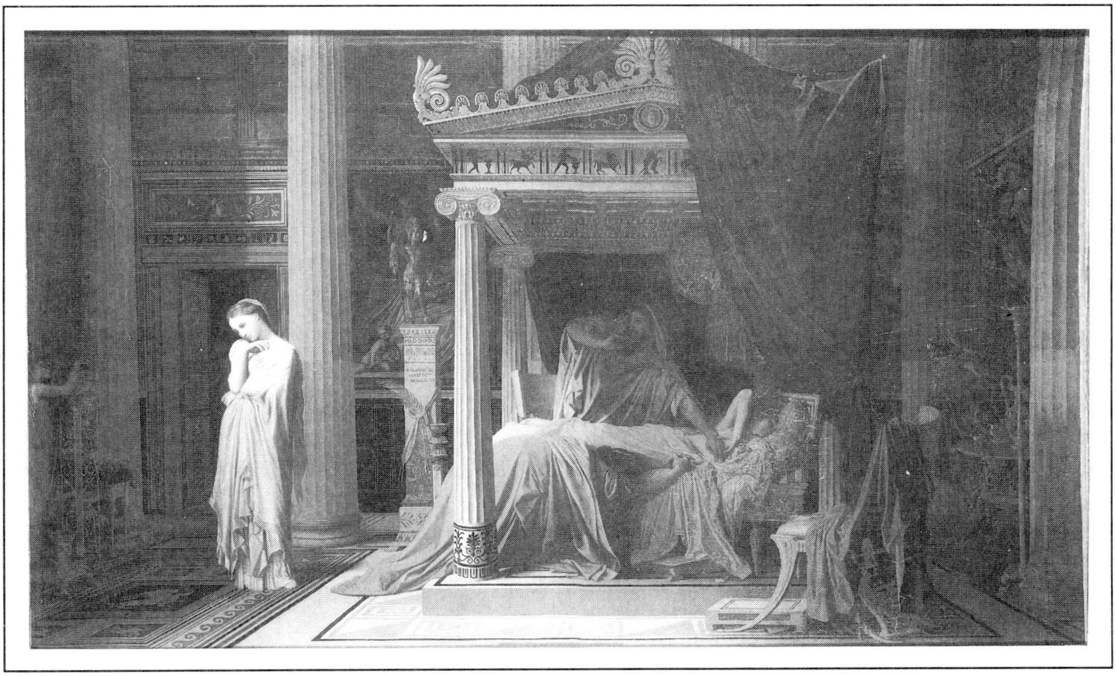

Figure 3.1 J.A.D. Ingres, *Antiochus and Stratonice* (1840), oil on canvas 57cm × 98cm
Musée Condé, Chantilly.

the action is 'frozen'. Not only does Ingres not show the exchange of Stratonice, he also freezes the male characters in positions of weakness.

Antiochus ought to be the main focus for straight male identification. But according to conventional signs of masculinity (and masculinity as a construct depends upon signs and conventions) he is a deficient, unsatisfactory hero. The statue of Alexander presiding over the scene should indicate Antiochus, through Seleucus, as heir to martial might. Here it just adds to the pathos of the warrior prince reduced by love to a helpless invalid. The frescoes of Hercules in the background also refer back to Antiochus, again setting up a contrast between what he should be – the strong man – and what he is – weak. The elements stressing activity bring the passivity of Antiochus into sharper relief, and passivity is an attribute conventionally associated with femininity. Furthermore, Antiochus has been brought low by the intensity of his desire and his attempts to suppress it. He must not and cannot reveal or speak of his desire, yet it is revealed by symptoms involuntarily appearing on his body which are read by the doctor. Antiochus is an hysteric, and as we see from Freud, the hysteric is always a feminized position.[17]

Seleucus, father and king, should also be a strong focus point for the straight male viewer. In the Chantilly painting the figure is nothing more than a mound of clothing with beseeching arms – very unsatisfactory. In the Louvre drawing (*c.* 1807) Seleucus huddles against the wall with his head in hands and clutches his sceptre. Instead of signifying his kingly dignity and power this seems to suggest power and strength reduced to an empty symbol. In the Philadelphia painting even the symbol of power is abdicated, with Seleucus's long sceptre propped against the bed post. The king, blind to the cause of his son's illness and literally laid low with grief, is virtually a dead letter in the pictures.

Erasistratus seems more satisfactory as the site of identification for the heterosexual male spectator. He is the male who sees and understands, who 'reads' and interprets the signs. In this role he puts together the meanings within the scene, the activity of the spectator outside the painting (as seer and site of meaning). The active gaze of the male heterosexual viewer can 'become' Erasistratus's gaze (and 'possess' Stratonice by sight). Even here there are difficulties. Erasistratus is also feminized to an extent in that his reactions are hysterical like those of Antiochus. His fingers-on-lips gesture suggests he is intent on keeping the secret,[18] but his extravagant bodily gestures give it away to anyone able to see and interpret (as the viewer can). The Louvre drawing also indicates that the doctor is not a perfectly powerful seer and bringer of knowledge (attributes that in Lacanian terms belong to the Symbolic Father and the Law), because he is shown as lame and with a crutch.

In the Louvre drawing and subsequent versions the strong, upright, seemingly self-possessed figure is Stratonice. If the males are 'deficient' in masculinity, their deficiency appears linked in some way to her. According to Lacan, the central illusion of gender identity and the fantasy that secures heterosexuality is that the male appears to have the phallus (but does not) and the female appears not to have it but to be it (that is, for the man, and therefore to be what he lacks/wants/desires). In these pictures the males are lacking, their power is at an ebb. It will be restored in the continuation of the narrative : Antiochus will be brought back from the brink of death and made a king, Seleucus will regain kingly status, by the exchange between them of the woman Stratonice. This will be effected by the third term, Erasistratus, bringing knowledge and representing the social order and its rules. At the surface level the narrative represents exogamy as described by Lévi-Strauss. At a deeper level it also represents transgression of the incest taboo. In Lacanian terminology, Ingres's pictures can be said to show Stratonice as phallus. The woman as phallus must be repossessed by the males by being exchanged between them in order to guarantee their masculinity (by being the adjunct of a male the woman/phallus supplies his lack). At the point in the story where the action is frozen, Stratonice has not been communicated between the males, so they still lack the phallus and are feminized (castrated).

The problems of identification for the male heterosexual viewer are also problems around pleasure. Under the guise of exogamous exchange, the narrative of Antiochus and Stratonice expresses the son's unconscious desire for the mother. Although the story seems to fulfil this ultimate fantasy it also transgresses the incest taboo. This conflict is insistently registered in Ingres's treatments of the subject. A complex of associations within the images underlines the danger of this desire. In the images the threat does not come from the father, who should punish the son's outlawed desire by castration, but from the woman as object of desire or the sight that incites desire.

Stratonice, alone, aloof, at a distance from the action yet the cause of it, is the Other of the male characters. Her capacity to incite desire and her danger come from this Otherness. The danger is indicated by key elements in the elaborate settings of the pictures. The frescoes, the statue of Alexander and the armour all point to Antiochus as hero. The wall paintings compare him to Theseus, killer of the Minotaur, and Hercules who killed the serpents and rode in triumph with the woman/goddess at his side. In the serpents fresco (Chantilly oil), the figure of the nurse mirrors Erasistratus's gesture (in reverse). He indicates the connection between Antiochus and Stratonice and she points out a connection between Stratonice and the snakes. Theseus also heroically overcomes a monster (Cleveland oil) and Antiochus similarly battles against his monstrous desire. His useless armour hangs above his head, his bed having become a battlefield where he wrestles with the desire provoked by the sight of Stratonice.

Stratonice connotes 'to-be-looked-at-ness'[19] for all who see or refuse sight within the paintings. Grief blinds Seleucus to her significance, which has to be revealed by Erasistratus. For Antiochus, the sight of Stratonice is the problem. Woman as object within sight and the danger attached to sighting her are heavily stressed. But Antiochus's shield, bearing a representation of the Medusa's head, indicates another dangerous aspect of vision – the baleful power of female sight. In the Perseus legend the Medusa's power is that any man she looks at is turned to stone. Perseus holds up his shield like a mirror in front of her and deflects her paralyzing gaze back onto herself. He cuts off her head and annexes her power by placing it on his shield.

The detail of the Medusa head is a further instance of references to sight in these pictures. Specifically, the Medusa reference draws attention to Stratonice's action as viewer, counteracting her presumed primary function as the object of sight. It is easy to overlook the object of her gaze because she is not looking at the couch. In all the painted versions the angle of her look is at a sphinx decoration in the floor mosaic. This links the apparently aloof Stratonice with the discovery taking place outside of her vision, because the sphinx is a recognized symbol of medical knowledge.[20] It connects Stratonice to the doctor's 'scientific' knowledge, but by a contrast. It implies that Stratonice's knowledge – of the discovery and by extension her knowledge(s) in total – comes to her indirectly, mediated through a register of signs of a different order that is mythic, mystical and prescient.

Stratonice is associated with danger, an occult intelligence and a dread force through the sphinx, the murals and the Medusa shield. These are linked to her Otherness and the threat this presents to the males. By exercising knowledge and problem-solving (like Oedipus) the males in the story of Antiochus and Stratonice 'solve' this dilemma of the woman. Stratonice ceases to be a problem when she is brought back under the control of the men and her threat is neutralized by the exchange. In the Oedipus legend solving the problem leads to disorder and the disruption of the generations. Here that tragedy becomes comedy, in the proper sense of a happy ending. The father is not killed, the right ordering of the generations and the succession is preserved. The exchange cements the relationship between the men. Nevertheless, in its mythic dimension the story cannot have a happy ending. The disguised incestuous wish cannot be licensed, either socially or psychically, and this conflict is repeatedly signalled in Ingres's treatment of the subject by the inclusion of the sphinx motif, referring back to the Oedipal drama and the danger of the woman. Because the exchange of the woman is not shown, this danger is not 'neutralized'.

It is unsatisfactory, perhaps impossible, for the straight male spectator to identify with Stratonice as this would be an offence against and a threat to their masculinity. Stratonice must necessarily be presented as Other (different, the phallus, the prize) for the story and the picture to work for heterosexual male pleasure. Because she is Other, Stratonice as seer constitutes an object of dread or distrust for the heterosexual male onlooker. For the female spectator, an apprehension of Stratonice with a capacity for sight and insight opens up an increased possibility of pleasurable identification. Stratonice as seer and phallus acquires an authority and power that could mitigate the masochism involved with the female spectator's identification of the character as an item or 'victim' of exchange between men. Associations that are negative for the straight male spectator can become positive for the female viewer (lesbian or straight).

Also, the female viewer, or more specifically the female viewer/analyst, might recognize in the figure of Stratonice a correlation with the complex significations of 'woman' under patriarchy. This recognition, in a sense of step back from identification with the place of the character, is likely to give satisfaction to the feminist analyst. She sees that the narrative and the images repeat the putting into place of the woman. Her satisfaction comes from revealing a flaw in the discourse of mastery, revealing the cultural construction of this apparently natural position, the presence of counter-transference and what 'they' do to 'us'.[21]

In the paintings under discussion, there is another character who sees, the peripheral or threshold character of the female watching from the doorway – the maid. More than Erasistratus, this character mirrors the activity of the spectator outside the painting. The characters in the room are a spectacle for her while she is unnoticed by them. This shadowy figure is a voyeur and 'reminds' the spectator of their own voyeurism. She is in a position to view, with her active gaze, the 'goings-on' within the room and within the family, to interpret the signs and know the secrets – just like the spectator outside the picture. Fantastically, but still unsettlingly, just as we are the only ones who can see her, she is the only one who could see us.

There is no indication of a reaction by this figure to the scene viewed, but her presence reiterates the notion of secrecy that attaches to the scene. As voyeur, seeing but unseen, the figure emphasizes the guilty nature of the secret being revealed and introduces a possibly judgemental aspect. In a sense, the act of voyeurism by the spectator outside of the painting is placed under scrutiny by this watcher within the painting. The censorial or judgemental attributes of this figure in the doorway are attributes that should be exercised by the (symbolic) father. In the paintings neither of the father figures, Erasistratus and Seleucus, exercise this function. Both are flawed in that they do not perform the primary function (in Lacanian terms) of the symbolic father – prohibition. The father *should* prevent the son from satisfying his illicit desire. The suggestion that what is happening in the pictures is illicit comes in large part from the watcher at the door, acting as censor not only of the scene in the room but also of the watcher outside the painting (the son outside the painting, the male heterosexual viewer).

Ascribing this censoring role to a female figure means that all 'negative' or dangerous elements that threaten the pleasure of the heterosexual male spectator are vested in female characters. The fathers are benevolent, their judgemental or condemnatory functions excised. The division along the normative, ideological (illusory) axis of masculinity–femininity is confused, compounding the deficiencies of the males, on one hand, and the dangerous power of the females on the other. The presence of the *female* censor indicates the impossibility of the exchange of the female (the son cannot 'have' his mother).

The concentration of negative (for the straight male) aspects on the female concentrates straight male identifications on the males in the scene, even though this involves a degree of masochism. It means the male spectator repeats the manoeuvre of waiting for a promised pleasure – here the exchange promised by knowing the story, in the dissolution of the Oedipus complex the promise of becoming like the father in time. If this male spectator were to identify with the maid his pleasure in the foreground scene would be undermined. For this spectator identification with the foreground 'heroes' seems essential to pleasure. The maid acts as a reminder of the existential 'outsiderness' of viewers outside of the picture, re-instating the distance between viewer and viewed, self and Other. Again, the maid also stands for social subordination, her class position being on the border between the inside and outside – of the room, the palace, the family, and so on. For the straight male spectator – for Ingres, for Freud – identification with the maid is insupportable; they must cling to the masculinity of their gender identification.

The feminist analyst, however, has nothing (except her class position?) to lose in identifying with the maid. In effect her identification with this figure reverses the polarity of the normative gender division, a subversion in line with her political project. Still, this is at the level of intellectual satisfaction, not desire as such.

The spectator who gains the most through identification with the maid is the lesbian spectator. At the moment when the action is frozen the 'little circus' of heterosexual exchange does not work any more. I can identify with the maid most readily because she marks the impossibility of the male heterosexual fantasy; she is the 'proof' that the exchange of Stratonice – in my fantasy, set in train by the painting that I view – cannot take place. At this moment of suspension neither Stratonice nor the maid are under the control of the males. Stratonice, at this moment, is not wife or mother (she has not become 'nothing') and the maid is not the object of the boss's illicit desire. The watcher/censor and Stratonice are invested with phallic power and are paired by the significations we have seen operating across the pictures. My projective identification with the woman in the doorway projects me into fantasy pairing with Stratonice. In this scenario the two females retain their power and together escape the cycle of male control. They can exit together through the open doorway, with their own (lesbian) desire, leaving the males locked in hysterical impotence.

WHAT REMAINS TO BE SAID?

> Having reached a definite conclusion, I find more remains to be said. The 'more' revolves around Dora's love for Frau K. around her lesbianism ... The 'more' I have to say is about the beauty, the eroticism, the affirmative quality of that love ... And somehow beauty and affirmation, sexuality as pleasure and joy rather than as murderous assimilation, seem to find their place only as a supplement to the political, theoretical argument. (Gallop 1985: 217–8)

The 'something more' of lesbian desire has frequently been assigned to the postscripts, footnotes or other textual asides in feminist theoretical writings.[22] An important aspect of lesbian and gay/queer studies of culture has been to instate the fact of lesbian and gay desire into the main body of the text. This analysis of the analyst's pleasure aims to contribute to that process.[23] I believe it does go some way in analysing how my pleasure in these images can come about, and to some extent the nature of that pleasure. But there is something more to be said. A great deal of pleasure in producing this analysis comes from the affirmation of lesbian desire and fantasy; from wresting an Other pleasure from the very bedrock of heterosexual male fantasy. The problem is that this tells us next to nothing about lesbian desire: it tells us that lesbian desire *is*, but not *what* it is.

If the lesbian spectator lays claim to her fantasy it is only in the face of the picture as object, that is within the terms of the composition as it is, structured by masculine, heterosexual fantasy. The lesbian spectator's network of identifications may revise the meanings of the representation, but cannot totally escape the terms of the representation. Similarly, analysis of the Dora case can reveal the countertransference and its effects but cannot make Dora speak. Neither can the lesbian analyst escape the (masculinist) terms of Lacanian psychoanalytic theory. According to those terms, Stratonice *is* the phallus and the maid, exercising the father's function as censor/judge, *has* the phallus. Logically, when the spectator identifies with the maid she is cast in a system which characterizes her desire in terms of masculine, heterosexual libido.

Psychoanalytic theory has not yet developed satisfactory explanations of any female desires. It cannot explain lesbian desire(s) but explains them away as a slightly distorted mirror of stereotypical heterosexual relations – the maid is transvestite, not lesbian.[24]

Dora could not say what it was about the *Madonna* that pleased her. The fact of her lesbian desire would not be spoken. Now it is possible to speak of lesbian desire, up to a point, in academic arenas. That affirmation is necessary. The celebratory aspects of queer may be necessary too, but lesbian theory and queer theory have not yet gone far in developing the means to discover what lesbian desire is, and how it is.

Notes

1 This 'me' is an intersection of positions, significantly different from the me I think is writing. This 'me' is made up by you, of course, in your here and now of reading.

2 See Bernheimer, C. and Kahane, C. (eds) (1985).

3 See Griggs, K. (1973).

4 See Forrester, J. (1984): 4–8.

'The nurse/mother is a well-known feature of the Freud lexicon: in his childhood, they appear as Nannie/Mater; in the Leonardo essay, we are shown them in the Virgin and St Anne. But we only find them in the Dora story in retrospect, after the analysis has been broken off. Freud could neither recognise himself as Madonna, nor as nursemaid. In the final session, he knew immediately to place Dora in the part of maidservant or governess, giving a fortnight's notice, but could not draw the appropriate conclusion that, whoever was playing the part of servant – and Cixous and Gallop point out Freud's reluctance to recognise himself, rather than Dora, as the wage-earning employee, being put out the door – the other party must be the employer, and most probably the mistress of the house. Once more Freud misses his chance to place himself in the transference – once again, because he could not adopt the position of woman.' (Forrester 1984: 7)

5 Lacan's concept of the Mirror Stage is a necessary background to this discussion, but there is not space to go through it here. See Grosz, E. (1990); Mitchell, J. and Rose, J. (1982); Lacan, J. (1979).

6 Quoted in Forrester, op.cit., p.4.

7 '... seduced by the boss and then eliminated for having been seduced by the boss. Women's situation carried to the paroxysm of horror. So, the servant-girl is the repressed of the boss's wife.' (Cixous 1986:150)

8 The issues of class position and identification that are so much a part of the Dora narrative are also crucial to the analysis being conducted here. My self-identification as a migrant from the working class must be of significance.

9 I have argued elsewhere the possibility of interpreting *The Turkish Bath* differently (Leeks 1986). In my doctoral thesis I consider more fully issues of lesbian spectatorship in relation to Ingres's work (Leeks 1990).

10 The versions are:

a) Drawing, Musée des Beaux-Arts, Boulogne-sur-Mer, *c.* 1801.
b) Drawing, Musée du Louvre, Paris (RF 1440), *c.* 1807.
c) Drawing on tracing paper, Musée Ingres, Montauban (867.2193), *c.* 1807.
d) Oil, location unknown (Wildenstein catalogue W164), 1825.
e) Oil, Cleveland Museum of Art, Cleveland (CMA66.13), *c.* 1834 (W224)
f) Oil, Musée Condé, Chantilly, 1840 (W232).
g) Oil on paper fixed to canvas, private collection, Philadelphia, 1860 (W295).
h) Drawing on tracing paper, Musée Ingres, Montauban (867.2194), *c.* 1860.
i) Watercolour, oil, graphite on paper fixed to canvas, Musée Fabre, Montpellier (844.1.1), 1866 (W322).

11 For written sources and pictorial treatments before Ingres's see Stechow, W. (1945).

12 See Lévi-Strauss, C. (1969); Rubin, G. (1975); and Cowie, E. (1978).

13 For reproductions and discussion of the series see Condon, P., Cohn, M. B. and Mongan, A. (1983); and Wildenstein, G. (1956).

14 Stratonice is set apart on the left looking downwards and to the left, away from the bed. Her chin is resting on her hand. Behind her is an open door with a female figure about to enter looking in. To the left is another female servant tending an incense holder. Between Stratonice and the bed is a pillar and a raised, inscribed plinth bearing a statue of Alexander the Great which seems to preside over and look down upon the bed. Behind the statue is a wall painting

depicting Hercules strangling the serpents (in the Cleveland oil the fresco in this position is of Theseus killing the Minotaur). The bed is on a dais surmounted by a baldacchino. Seleucus is hunched at the foot of the bed with his face in the bedclothes. Antiochus has his head turned away into the pillows. His left arm tries to prevent Erasistratus from feeling his heartbeat. Erasistratus is standing behind the bed with his left arm outstretched to feel Antiochus's heart. He looks at Stratonice, with his right arm bent and his fingers on his mouth in consternation. Antiochus's armour is inside the canopy above his head. To the right of the bed a figure supports itself against a pillar with its head on its arms (sometimes described as Antiochus's friend) and another crouches under a table with her head cradled in her arms (sometimes called Antiochus's old nurse). On the right-hand wall is a fresco of Hercules in a triumphal chariot with Pallas Athene.

15 My argument depends upon feminist readings of Lacanian psychoanalytic propositions which there is no space to elaborate here. See Mulvey, L. (1989).

16 This formulation, or 'straight male', are used throughout in order to indicate that I have made no assumptions about the pleasures of gay male spectators. References to masculinity are all in connection with the ideological construction of heterosexual masculinity. No presumptions have been made about the masculine identity of gay males. Analysis of gay male viewer positions is outside the scope of this study, beyond my competence and, I feel, not my role to undertake.

17 See Cixous and Clément (1986).

18 Like all maids – even those who are doctors – Erasistratus turns out to be unable to keep it to himself and betrays the secret to the father.

19 Mulvey (1989): 19.

20 Stechow (1945): 231.

21 On the face of it, the satisfaction gained by feminists reviewing the Dora case. For instance:
C[atherine Clément]: Listen, you love Dora, but to me she never seemed a revolutionary character.
H[élène Cixous]: I don't give a damn about Dora; I don't fetishize her. She is the name of a certain force, which makes the little circus not work any more. (Cixous 1986: 157)

22 See Cixous and Clément (1986): 153ff; and Gallop (1985).

23 The move 'out of the "maid's room" ' has been quite literal in this case. The present analysis is a reworking of part of my doctoral thesis where, in an ironic mirroring of the Dora case, I placed the extensive references to lesbian desire and the lesbian spectator in the footnotes.

24 See Mulvey (1989): 33.

References

Bernheimer, C. and Kahane, C. (eds) (1985) *In Dora's Case: Freud, Hysteria, Feminism*, London: Verso.

Cixous, H. and Clément, C. (1986) *The Newly Born Woman*, Manchester: Manchester University Press.

Condon, P., Cohn, M.B. and Mongan, A. (1983) *Ingres – In Pursuit of Perfection: The Art of J.A.D. Ingres*, Louisville, Ky and Bloomington, Ind.: J.B. Speed Art Museum and Indiana University Press.

Cowie, E. (1978) 'Woman as Sign', M/F 1, 49–63.

Forrester, J. (1984) 'Freud, Dora and the untold pleasures of psychoanalysis', *Desire: ICA Documents*, 1, London: Institute of Contemporary Arts.

Freud, S. (1977) 'Fragment of an analysis of a case of hysteria', *Pelican Freud Library*, 8, Harmondsworth: Penguin.

Gallop, J. (1985) 'Keys to Dora', in Bernheimer, C. and Kahane, C. (eds) *In Dora's Case: Freud, hysteria, feminism*, London: Verso.

Griggs, K. (1973) 'All roads lead to Rome: the role of the nursemaid in Freud's dreams', *Journal of the American Psychoanalytic Association* 21, 108–26.

Grosz, E. (1990) *Jacques Lacan: a feminist introduction*, London: Routledge.

Lacan, J. (1979) *The Four Fundamental Concepts of Psychoanalysis*, London: Penguin.

Leeks, W. (1986) 'Ingres Other-wise', *Oxford Art Journal* 9 (1): 29–37.

—— (1990) 'The "family romance" and repeated themes in the work of J.A.D. Ingres', unpublished PhD thesis, Department of Fine Art, University of Leeds.

Lévi-Strauss, C. (1969) *Elementary Structures of Kinship*, Boston: Beacon Press.

Mitchell, J. and Rose, J. (1982) *Feminine Sexuality: Jacques Lacan and the Ecole Freudienne*, London: Macmillan.

Mulvey, L. (1989) *Visual and Other Pleasures*, London: Macmillan.

Ramas, M. (1985) 'Freud's Dora, Dora's hysteria', in Bernheimer, C. and Kahane, C. (eds) *In Dora's Case: Freud, hysteria, feminism*, London: Verso.

Rubin, G. (1975) 'The traffic in women: notes on the political economy of sex', in Reiter, R.R. (ed.) *Toward an Anthropology of Women*, New York: Monthly Review Press: 157–210.

Sedgwick, E. K. (1991) *Epistemology of the Closet*, New York and London : Wheatsheaf.
Strechow, W. (1945) ' "The love of Antiochus with faire Stratonica" in Art', *Art Bulletin*: 221–37.
Wildenstein, G. (1956) *The Paintings of J.A.D. Ingres*, London: Phaidon.

Chapter Four

Perverse male bodies

Simeon Solomon and Algernon Charles Swinburne

Thaïs E. Morgan

> The other night I went to a bachelor's party to meet Rossetti and Swinburne at Simeon Solomon's ... As for Swinburne, he is without exception the most extraordinary man ... but the little beast will never I think be acknowledged for he has an utterly perverted moral sense. (George du Maurier, 1864, letter to his mother)

> The subtleties and harmonies of suggestion in such studies of complex or it may be perverse nature would have drawn forth praise and sympathy from Baudelaire. (Algernon Charles Swinburne, 1871, review of Simeon Solomon's work)

As the two above quotations suggest, the term 'perverse' and its cognates, such as 'perverted' and 'perversity', bore negative moral connotations (for du Maurier) as well as positive aesthetic connotations (for Swinburne) during the 1860s–70s in Victorian England. This simultaneity of contradictory cultural forces around the concept of the 'perverse' alerts us to an emergent way of thinking that differs strikingly from the traditional one. According to *The Oxford English Dictionary*, to be 'perverse' (from the Latin, *perversus*, 'turned the wrong way') primarily means to be 'wicked' or sinful within a Christian context: examples are given from the Bible, Chaucer and Donne (1971: 2144). This is the established ground from which du Maurier speaks when he condemns Swinburne's poems (those he was drafting for *Poems and Ballads, Series 1*, published two years later in 1866) as having 'an utterly perverted moral sense'. In contrast, when Swinburne praises Simeon Solomon's work as 'perverse' in the Baudelairean sense, he is speaking from the oppositional viewpoint of *l'art pour l'art*, within which all subjects, including same-sex eroticism and sado-masochism, can be made beautiful by an artist or a writer.[1]

Moreover, *The Oxford English Dictionary* suggests a basis for Swinburne's reorientation of the term 'perverse' from rejection to approval of an artist's work – the secondary meaning of 'perverse' carries over from the domain of moral judgement into that of aesthetics: 'Not in accordance with the accepted standard or practice; incorrect; wrong,' as instanced by the usage in R. Ellis's book on *Catullus* (1871): 'The experiments of the Elizabethan writers ... [are characterized] by that strange perversity which so often dominates literature ...' (1971: 2144). Ellis follows the conventional notion of novelty (in this case, that of the Elizabethans' metrical experiments) as a 'strange perversity', whereas Swinburne attempts to redirect the 'perverse' to an avant-gardist aesthetic declaration. The visual work of Simeon Solomon is 'beautiful and new'; the 'fair feminine youth' typical of his art as well as of his prose piece, *A Vision of Love Revealed in Sleep*, are 'suggestive of things hidden in secret places of spiritual reserve' (Swinburne 1926: 456, 447). The 'perverse' is aesthetically, perhaps even morally, good – but otherwise than in the usual sense.

Significantly, *The Oxford English Dictionary* does not list the medical meaning of 'perverse' or 'perverted' familiar today. Sigmund Freud's concept of homosexuality, sado-masochism, and fetishism as types of 'perversion' was not to become current until the early twentieth century.[2] Nonetheless, several influential studies of Victorian sexual behaviours and attitudes toward sexualities assume that male–male desire, presumably leading to genital contact, is a pathological 'perversion' and further assume that the Victorians themselves saw it as such. For example, Ronald Pearsall in *The Worm in the Bud* describes Simeon Solomon as 'unashamedly homosexual and perverse' for that reason (Pearsall 1969: 549). Noting that '[p]erversions occur when sexual impulses are diverted into other than heterosexual channels', he also judges Algernon Charles Swinburne to be incapable of 'any participation in normal sexual relations' because of his involvement in the practice of flagellation (Pearsall 1969: 427, 420). Pearsall is basing his survey of Victorian sexualities on Freud's definition of – and disparaging attitude toward – 'perversions'. Accordingly, he regards homosexuality and flagellation to be virtually synonymous as such.[3]

More complex are Peter Gay's observations on nineteenth-century European sexualities in his multi-volume history entitled *The Bourgeois Experience*. On the one hand, Gay analyses all historical data through psychoanalytic eyes. He presupposes Freud's notion of homosexuality as a perversion in classifying it as a 'problematic attachment' and characterizes late nineteenth-century laws against homosexuality as 'the return of the repressed in culture' (Gay 1986: 221). On the other hand, Gay emphasizes 'the unsuspected openness' of society to close and lifelong same-sex 'attachments' between men and between women 'before the 1880s' (Gay 1986: 212, 219). Paradoxically, he remarks, the 'delicacy that had governed the discussions about erotic aberrations [*sic*]' until the last quarter of the nineteenth century served to enable them (Gay 1986: 219).[4] Indeed, the idealization of same-sex friendship, which can be seen, for example, in the novels of Charles Dickens, 'permitted men to declare their love for other men – or women for other women – with impunity' (Gay 1986: 217). Still, although spiritualized and putatively free from the 'base desire' involved in the 'inferior' sexual relations between men and women, same-sex love had to keep within the bounds set for it by the predominantly heterosexual Victorian culture 'in which appearances thoughtfully preserved meant denials successfully sustained' (Gay 1986: 212).

The friendship between Simeon Solomon and Algernon Charles Swinburne, which lasted approximately ten years, produced some of the most aesthetically innovative and morally daring work of the 1860s and early 1870s. Both men 'were engaged in the production of revisionary masculine discourses' which pushed at the boundaries of the Victorian norm of heterosexual 'manliness' by exploring alternative forms of desire and love between men, and by celebrating these in art, poetry, prose and criticism (Dellamora 1990: 5).[5] The friendship between Solomon and Swinburne also raises the important question of whether or not we can locate a boundary between homosociality, as delineated by Eve Sedgwick (1985), and homosexuality, as defined by genital contact between men. Solomon's letters to Oscar Browning and to Swinburne, for example, indicate that he considered himself what today would be called a homosexual.[6] These letters as well as anecdotes about Solomon passed down to us through a variety of biographical materials and histories of the later Victorians show that he was quite open about his sexual orientation with his friends.[7]

The sexual practices and the self-identification of Swinburne are much more uncertain. Again and again, we hear that Swinburne made a 'victim' out of 'poor Solomon,' on whom Swinburne's 'interest' in anything 'perverse' – sado-masochism, lesbianism, homosexuality – 'had a deteriorating influence' (Gaunt 1945: 45–6). Solomon's demise, which began in 1873 when he was tried for 'buggery' and abandoned by most of his friends, including Swinburne, is said to have been caused by 'the influence of [the poet's] unstable character on the all too impressionable' younger artist (Reynolds 1984: 13). Yet, despite recurrent references to the pleasures of 'the birch' and the beauty of boys in letters between them, and despite the homoeroticism in some of his published as well as unpublished writings, Swinburne himself never disclosed his sexual orientation.

Thus, Wendell Stacy Johnson concludes that if Swinburne 'was largely or partly homosexual, or indeed was homosexual at all' must remain 'an unanswerable question' (Johnson 1979: 129). Cecil Lang, editor of *The Swinburne Letters*, concurs: 'Whether he was overtly homosexual, as a persistent oral tradition maintains, I do not know' (Lang 1959, 1: xlix). In contrast, Emmanuel Cooper suggests that '[t]o all intents and purposes [Swinburne and Solomon] may have been lovers' (Cooper 1986: 65–6). As some evidence for this, Cooper notes that Swinburne 'introduced' Solomon to Walt Whitman's *Leaves of Grass*. But whether or not their shared reading of Whitman signals a sexual relationship remains undecidable.[8] More recently, Richard Dellamora has suggested that 'whether Swinburne himself engaged in sex with other males or not ... in the 1860s he enjoyed imagining such possibilities' with friends such as Simeon Solomon and Walter Pater (Dellamora 1990: 69).

As Jeffrey Weeks reminds us, an 'identity is not a given in any particular historical situation but is the product of different social interactions' (Weeks 1989: 209). More important than ascertaining the declared or undeclared sexual orientation of Solomon and of Swinburne, then, is understanding the multiplicity of discourses on male–male desire and the beauty of the male body which circulated among the several social groups of writers and artists among which their friendship flourished.[9] Solomon's visual works (both those for public exhibition and those solely for his close friends) and his literary piece, *A Vision of Love Revealed in Sleep*, as well as Swinburne's published poetry and art criticism were nourished by and in the first instance addressed to these overlapping all-male circles of friends. What counts, I would suggest, in Solomon's and Swinburne's relationship is 'not [an] inherent propensity' to homosexuality, but 'the degree to which [each] man's activities and self-concepts were supported by the subculture' of Victorian aestheticism during the 1860s and early 1870s (Weeks 1989: 210).[10] An indication of the sometimes conflicting ideas about the representation of men – their bodies, their desires, their sexualities, their very 'manliness' – that had currency at this period in so-called bohemian circles is the seemingly irreconcilable gap between du Maurier's moral condemnation of Swinburne's 'perverted' poetry of the 1860s and Swinburne's enthusiastic approval of the 'perverse' as it informs Solomon's work up through 1871.

In histories of Victorian culture, Simeon Solomon is considered at best a minor footnote to the second wave of Pre-Raphaelitism which was led by Edward Burne-Jones and William Morris, beginning in the late 1850s, and at worst the creator of 'corrupt delicacies' who was 'ruined' by 'drink and perversity' (Welby 1929: 5, 58). Timothy Hilton, for example, opens his influential book *The Pre-Raphaelites* with a defense of the movement's importance in the cultural mainstream against 'the unwholesome and sexy gloom in the art of, say, Simeon Solomon' (Hilton 1970: 9).[11] While Dante Gabriel Rossetti, whom he met in 1857, and many of the techniques and subjects of Pre-Raphaelite art as it had been developing since the late 1840s provided an initial framework for Solomon's visual work, this is only one of the several contexts of male friendship and aesthetic effort in which his art and the prose *Vision* should be considered.[12] For, at the same time as he was becoming an intimate of the Pre-Raphaelites, Solomon was enrolled at the Royal Academy Schools where, for instance, he met George Boyce, Edward J. Poynter, and the future president of the Royal Academy, Frederic Leighton.

Boyce's diaries for 1857–72 record frequent evenings spent with men who were associated with the anti-establishment Pre-Raphaelite movement as well as with the dominant Royal Academy – gatherings at which Solomon was often present. In 1857, while visiting the painter Abraham Solomon, Boyce first noticed 'some remarkable designs' by Simeon (Surtees 1980: 17). During 1858 and 1859 Boyce socialized on several occasions with '[l]ittle Simeon Solomon' (Surtees 1980: 21). One day in April 1859, Boyce found Solomon and Poynter at their mutual friend's, William Burges, and Solomon gave him a drawing of William Morris and his wife. Seven years later, in 1866, Boyce was still running into Solomon: both were invited to Leighton's for breakfast with D.G. and William Michael Rossetti. While Boyce enjoyed these gatherings of artists of various persuasions, he also sought out the poet Swinburne's company. In March 1859, they both dined with some of Boyce's friends at Oxford; in July 1862 Boyce attended Swinburne's house-warming party in London; in November 1865 Boyce entertained Swinburne and the Rossetti brothers, among others, at his own lodgings. The point is that these men all knew one another, and they mingled freely and often, across lines of artistic affiliation and, apparently, across sexualities since Solomon made no secret of his exclusive desire for young men, while Swinburne always brought 'excitement' and 'intellectual cleverness' with his declamations of his risqué poems (Surtees 1980: 26–7).

Commenting on men's social relations from the 1870s until the early twentieth century, Jeff Hearn emphasizes the ways in which men both 'construct[ed] and were ... set within tensions' between individual 'experiences' and 'the elaboration of organizational monocultures' that were strictly all-male (Hearn 1992: 200). Their 'experiences' might include homoerotic attraction, if not the practice of homosexuality, but these were typically subordinated to 'the apparent ... asexuality' of such organizations. The 'public self' projected by most Victorian men would be determinedly heterosexual, as dominant 'patriarchal' institutions, built by the men themselves, required (Hearn 1992: 210). In fact, though, such all-male 'monocultures' were always 'also sexual cultures' with a 'sexualized discourse' that is simultaneously heterosexual and homosocial in import, with the latter interest placing the men in a given organization 'as the existent actors within [a] homosexual subtext' (Hearn 1992: 200–1). I would suggest that the frequent gatherings and close friendships among several of the men called the Pre-Raphaelites say, the Rossetti brothers and 'Ned' Burne-Jones – and several of the men aligned with the Royal Academy – say, Albert Moore, Poynter, and Leighton – formed a cross-organizational male monoculture.[13] Further, I would suggest that this sort of cross-organizational monoculture was particularly amenable to the 'perverse' aesthetic programmes which Solomon and Swinburne were, at first separately and then together, working out during the 1860s and early 1870s.

In particular, Solomon may have found that his homosexual preference was not discouraged but encouraged by the cliquishness among D.G. Rossetti's pals and by the comradeship provided by the Sketching Club he joined with fellow students from the Royal Academy, including Henry Holiday and Albert Moore, both in the later 1850s.[14] At the very least, these all-male 'monocultures' affirmed 'men's preferential desire for each other' and their 'mutual recognition as sexually similar' (Hearn 1992: 205). Indeed, Solomon fast became an intimate of D.G. Rossetti's circle, as evidenced by the 'spoof on Pre-Raphaelitism' which he drew in 1857, called *A Pre-Raphaelite Studio Fantasy* (Seymour 1986: 30–1). His sketchbook was passed around and 'admired by the Pre-Raphaelites' during the later 1850s (Kolsteren 1984: 62). In 1859 he wrote a parody for their mutual amusement, 'The PRB Catechism for the use of Disciples of that School' (unpublished; see Seymour 1986: 38–42). He also drew portraits of some of his friends and one of himself, this last in 1859 and showing what Simon Reynolds characterizes as an 'epicene sensitivity' (Reynolds 1984: 11).[15]

While enjoying the company and praise of D.G. Rossetti, 'Ned' Burne-Jones, and other Pre-Raphaelite associates, Solomon was becoming known to the Victorian art-viewing public as an artist specializing in dramatic scenes from the Old Testament and from the rituals of Judaism – the latter a relatively unknown subject. As Forrest Reid observes in his survey of Victorian illustrators of the 1860s, Solomon 'employed two absolutely different techniques': 'the Pre-Raphaelite method of his Biblical and Eastern designs' and the 'impressionism of his studies of contemporary Jewish life' (Reid 1928: 103).[16] In 1858 his first drawing was accepted for exhibition at the Royal Academy: *Sacrifice of Isaac*.[17] Yet some of his work was already suffused by homoeroticism, even though he kept it within the safe bounds of religious narrative. Thus, *David Playing before Saul* (1859) shows the younger man leaning sensuously against the king's back and shoulder as he plays his music; '... the protagonists are absorbed in some sort of vision' which could be spiritual or homoerotic or both (Collins 1991: 52). Similarly, *A Jewish Musician in the Temple* (1860) depicts a handsome young man, with a soft cloud of Pre-Raphaelite hair framing his face, wholly absorbed in playing a beautifully decorated hand–held harp, against the background of an Assyrian-style relief.[18] Such art conveys more than stock figures from biblical times: Solomon is moving towards the notion of appreciation of male beauty and the love of men for men as a form of spirituality which culminates in *A Vision of Love Revealed in Sleep* some ten years later.

Solomon's homoeroticism is not evinced in the designs he published in *Once a Week* and *Good Words* in 1862. However, these, and the ten 'Illustrations of Jewish Customs' he did for the *Leisure Hour* in 1866, are 'completely unlike anything else that was being done at this time' due to their 'strange, sad, exotic, alien' 'atmosphere' (Reid 1928: 103–4). To the almost exclusively Christian Victorian public who read periodicals and saw Solomon's illustrations in them, he was a contemporary artist specializing in the somewhat marginal subject of 'Jewish life and ritual' and offering them 'their primary source of knowledge about the unusual and the exotic' (Collins 1991: 85).[19] However, Solomon's awareness of his doubly marginal position as a Jew and a homosexual may be part of both the sadness and the so-called strangeness in his illustrations of Judaic topics. For even close friends like Burne-Jones referred to him as 'the Jewjube' – a jocose nickname not without its mark of difference against Solomon, who in return flaunted his Jewish looks and 'play[ed] up to and along with' the stereotype (Collins 1991: 86). Solomon's 'proclivity for fancy dress and costumes' might have been part of his way of coping with the anti-Semitism of Victorian England (Collins 1991: 86).[20]

Just what year (1862 or 1863?) and how (through Burne-Jones or Lord Houghton?) Solomon met Swinburne is a matter of some conjecture. Seymour says that Solomon met Swinburne through Burne-Jones in 1862 – a likely occurrence since all three men were familiars of D.G. Rossetti (Seymour 1986: 78). Equally likely, however, is their having met in 1863 at Fryston, the country home of Richard Monckton Milnes, Lord Houghton, 'a worldly politician and savant who delighted in the role of social catalyst' – or perhaps it was at his bachelor's quarters in London, which he held until he married at forty-two years old (Lambourne 1986: 25; Croft-Cooke 1967: 31). What is important is that their friendship began within the context of overlapping circles of men interested in the arts as well as in challenging the hegemony of Victorian respectability, either by their aesthetic work or their social behaviour or both. An anecdote about Solomon and Swinburne cavorting about, naked, at Rossetti's home in the early 1860s is often repeated, but its significance – other than testifying to their playful behaviour – remains in dispute. Thus, one biographer of Swinburne states that 'Solomon was an effeminate character with whom Swinburne formed a semi-homosexual [*sic*] relationship' (Henderson 1974: 57). Another biographer disagrees, reasoning that the 'fascination which sexual ambiguity held for Swinburne' – whether that of a dominatrix at the flagellation brothels he frequented or that of a homosexual youth who liked to wear 'exotic' costumes – 'seems beyond that of one who was consciously homosexual. He stands outside it, as he stands outside heterosexual commitment' (Thomas 1979: 76). In any case, Solomon and Swinburne were each perceived by their own friends to be 'perverse' or going against the grain in their art and poetry, respectively, and also in their sexual lives.

Boyce records in his diary for 16 August 1862 that he '[j]oined [D.G.] Rossetti at Swinburne's rooms, where they were looking over 'Justine', by the Marquis de Sade, recent acquisition of the latter' (Surtees 1980: 35). Much has been made of Lord Houghton's introduction of Swinburne to de Sade's works around this time.[21] Lionel Lambourne speculates that Swinburne's first encounter with the work of de Sade took place in 1863 at Lord Houghton's, in the company of a new friend, Simeon Solomon: 'the two young men experienced with mutual excitement' de Sade's erotic fantasies (Lambourne 1986: 25). The sheer range of outré activities in de Sade would have appealed to Swinburne, who was interested in all sorts of sexual behaviour, while Solomon would probably have responded most to the same-sex encounters detailed. Interestingly, Solomon exhibited a painting called 'Juliette' – perhaps alluding to one of de Sade's characters – at the Royal Academy in 1863. A critic for *The Times* thought Solomon's work 'clever' but 'perverse' in the aesthetic, if not also the moral sense, then current.[22]

Also, as Henderson notes, Swinburne 'had ... already written many of the poems that were to appear in *Poems and Ballads* (1866)' by the early 1860s (Henderson 1974: 54). It is significant, then, that in 1863 Solomon drew *In the Temple of Venus*, a departure from his early repertoire of biblical, Jewish ritual, and Pre-Raphaelite themes in the new direction of classical or classicizing scenes (Seymour 1986: figure 93).[23] Solomon's picture of two women standing by a wall, with flowers scattered on the ground might be compared to the lovers described in Swinburne's 'Laus Veneris': they inhabit the world of the goddess Venus, suffering here where 'Love shed fruitless flowers' (line 332). Although the couples in 'Laus Veneris' are heterosexual, the speaker of the dramatic monologue, Tannhäuser, often describes his love of the sadistic Venus in terms of flowers: 'Her eyelids on her eyes like flower on flower, / Mine eyelids on my eyes like fire on fire' (lines 107–8). Was Solomon commenting obliquely through his art on the suffering that could accompany same-sex love in the context of Swinburne's poem?[24]

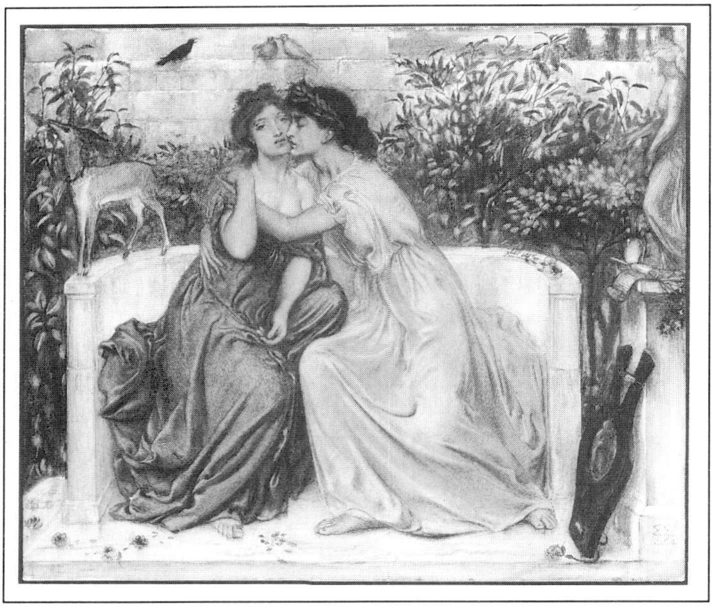

Figure 4.1 Simeon Solomon, *Sappho and Erinna in a Garden at Mytilene* (1864), watercolour on paper, $8^1/_2'' \times 6^1/_2''$
Tate Gallery, London, and Art Resource, New York.

Swinburne celebrates Sappho, the lesbian poetess of sixth-century B.C. Greece, in the dramatic monologue 'Anactoria', which details her (imaginatively) sado-masochistic relationship with the younger woman of the title.[25] This poem elicited much outraged criticism when it was published in 1866, but Solomon appreciated Swinburne's 'perverse' aesthetic. While Swinburne was writing the poem in the early 1860s, Solomon drew the head of Sappho (1862) in preparation for a painting he was planning (Reynolds 1984: plate 27). Solomon found in Swinburne's enthusiasm for the subject of lesbianism a novel opportunity for representing same-sex desire in a publicly acceptable form. Since classical subjects were recommended highly by the Victorian art establishment presided over by the Royal Academy, depicting sapphism was excusable under this pretext.[26] Solomon duly completed his painting, *Sappho and Erinna in a Garden at Mytilene* in 1864 (Figure 4.1). Seymour considers this to be 'one of the artist's most outspoken and open allusion[s] to homosexuality' (Seymour 1986: 95). She also observes that 'the marble floor is strewn with flowers' in this 1864 painting as it is in *The Temple of Venus* (1863), thus linking the two works visually (Seymour 1986: 96). I would further suggest that they resonate with the subject of passionate but sorrowful love between members of the same sex, safely set within a distant, partly mythologized past, and portrayed within the classicizing iconography familiar in Victorian art of the 1860s.

Sadism of the Sadeian kind may be represented by Sappho's aggressive embrace and partial disrobing of the apparently reluctant Erinna in Solomon's painting. Certainly the 'tender passion' of close friendships allowable among Victorian women has been succeeded by an undeniable eroticism in Sappho's gesture (cf. Gay 1986). Seymour sees Solomon's painting as a statement against the restrictions which the 'morality' of Pre-Raphaelite 'Aestheticism' imposed, and in favour of the more radical view that 'the beauty of a work of art was independent of its message, and might even be enhanced by its immorality' (Seymour 1986: 97). Swinburne had elaborated upon this avant-gardist programme in his review of 1862, 'Charles Baudelaire'. Besides its aesthetic ramifications, though, Solomon's *Sappho and Erinna in a Garden at Mytilene* pairs with Swinburne's 'Anactoria' in several other ways. For example, there are the Sadeian allusions throughout Swinburne's poem and in Sappho's sexually determined action in Solomon's painting. 'I would my love could kill thee', declares Swinburne's Sappho: 'I would find grievous ways to have thee slain, / Intense device and superflux of pain' (lines 23, 27–8). As if enacting these words, Solomon's Sappho almost grimaces with desire as she pulls Erinna toward her; Sappho's neck cords stand out tensely as she leans into Erinna who tries to delay the dominant woman's impulse by putting her right knee up between them.

Equally important is the foregrounding of same-sex relationships in Swinburne's poem and in Solomon's painting. Swinburne's claim that 'Anactoria' is a scholarly 'paraphrase' of Sappho's 'Ode to Aphrodite' in the wake of critical outcry when it was published in 1866 does not quite – nor was it wholly intended to – erase the fact that his poem glorifies the strong and ultimately transcendent passion of a woman for other women. As Swinburne himself says: 'I have striven to cast my spirit into the mould of hers ...' – a woman who loves women as the model for a man who loves men (Swinburne 1966: 20–1).[27] In a staunchly heterosexual (and heterosexist) society like Victorian England, the poem along with Swinburne's defence of it were quite bold statements on the possibility of alternative kinds of desire. Solomon's painting is no less daring. In his survey of nineteenth-century art entitled *Idols of Perversity*, Bram Dijkstra observes that *Sappho and Erinna in a Garden at Mytilene* is a 'relatively rare explicit early treatment of lesbianism' (Dijkstra 1986: 153). For Swinburne imaginatively and for Solomon vindicatorily, a female–female couple could stand in for a male–male couple. In particular, the lesbian poetess celebrated by Longinus as one of the most sublime writers was suited to head Swinburne's aesthetically as well as morally 'perverse' pantheon of great authors. At the same time, she had begun to 'assum[e] the role of patron saint of modern (homo)sexuality' for men from Solomon to J.A. Symonds (deJean 1989: 225).

The threads connecting 'Anactoria' with *Sappho and Erinna in a Garden at Mytilene*, Swinburne's interest in same-sex couples and Solomon's practice of homosexuality, were to produce further parallels between their work. In 1859 Solomon had done eight drawings for 'The Song of Solomon'; these had 'deeply impressed' Burne-Jones with their technique (Reynolds 1984: plate 13). His friend Swinburne's interpretation of 'The Song of Songs', however, was anything but orthodox. The poem 'Anactoria' features a brilliant if 'perverse' parody of this biblical text, a defiant gesture that brought charges of blasphemy down on Swinburne's head in 1866 when it was included in *Poems and Ballads, Series 1.* His Sappho describes what she would like to do to her lover, in this case, Anactoria:

> Ah that my mouth for Muses' milk were fed
> On the sweet blood thy sweet small wounds had bled!
> That with my tongue I felt them, and could taste
> The faint flakes from thy bosom to the waist!
> That I could drink thy veins as wine, and eat
> Thy breasts like honey! (lines 107–12)

If, as the biographer Henderson asserts, Swinburne was already writing many of the poems published in 1866 several years earlier, then Solomon would have known about the poet's lesbian version of 'The Song of Songs'. Sappho and sapphism, Solomon and male–male desire: a 'perverse' approach to 'The Song of Songs' or 'The Song of Solomon' which Simeon began to read otherwise, as a paean to same-sex love instead of heterosexual love.

During the early 1860s, when his friendship with Swinburne was increasing in aesthetic and personal intimacy, Solomon started to develop an aesthetic programme in which he makes 'The Song of Solomon' represent a central dilemma of Victorian culture: the Judaeo-Christian injunction to men and women to marry, and the actuality of intense male friendships in a patriarchal society whose very institutions encouraged homoeroticism.[28] Simeon worried this difficult topic again and again throughout his career, doing several variations on it. The most important instance is *The Bride, The Bridegroom and Sad Love* of 1865 (Figure 4.2), which questions the divine happiness supposedly to be found in marriage of man and woman, and indicates the presence of male–male desire beyond the bounds set by matrimony. The drawing shows the future husband embraced in a rather insistent head lock by his bride, with his left hand around her hip, both standing on the right side of the picture. Hanging back slightly, on the left side of the picture, is a winged male 'Love' who sorrowfully touches one finger of the bridegroom's right hand, in a gesture reminiscent of Michelangelo's Adam and God in the Sistine Chapel. The bridegroom is extending his right arm backwards in order to meet the male 'Love' 's hand: the groom accepts the male 'Love' but keeps him socially 'on the side'. In response to this ambiguous situation, the male 'Love' can only give the groom a 'sad', because resigned, reminder of the other commitment of his heart and soul. The male 'Love' is thus effectively marginalized in Solomon's drawing, which conveys a powerful message of protest against even as it acknowledges the hegemony of heterosexuality. Significantly, too, all three figures are nudes, with drapery covering the bride's and the bridegroom's genitalia, as Victorian convention would require, but with the genitalia of 'Love' only partially hidden by the meeting of the two men's hands: he is an interloper

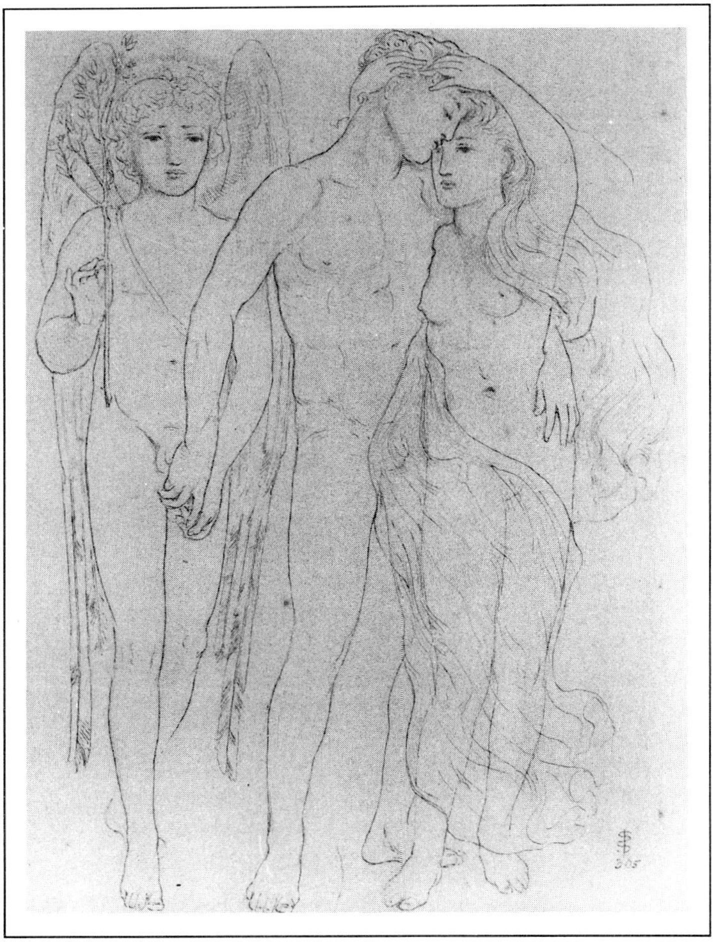

Figure 4.2 Simeon Solomon, *The Bride, the Bridegroom and Sad Love* (1865), 8″ × 10″
Art Resource, New York.

in the scene of future marital bliss both visually and morally. 'Love' when it occurs between men is 'perverse' and hence doomed to be 'sad'.

In 1868 Solomon continues thinking about the problem of sexualities, but his drawing entitled *The Song of Solomon* (Figure 4.3) shows his awareness of the moral conservatism of the Victorian art-viewing public because it tones down the implicit challenge to the marital norm by medievalizing and fully dressing its three characters. Yet the sorrowful kiss bestowed upon the bridegroom's hand by his friend, and the fact that the male friend holds a flowering branch erect while that carried by the bridegroom has shed its blooms on the ground and droops downward over the area of the bride's genitalia, betoken the artist's persistent critique of the exclusivity of heterosexual union in the Judaeo-Christian tradition upheld by Victorian culture. Solomon's ironic visual play on the authorization of love between man and woman in the biblical *The Song of Solomon* may be related to a joke which Swinburne makes in a letter to W.M. Rossetti (8 January 1870). Speaking of 'mystic bawdy poetry', Swinburne says that he still favours 'The song of Solomon – *ne pas lire* Simeon, as it is none of *his* canticle – though it might be called the *Nunc Emittis*' (Lang 1959, 2: 79; his emphasis). The currency of such puns evidences the strong current of homoeroticism running through the all-male monoculture of artists, writers and critics in which Swinburne and Solomon lived.

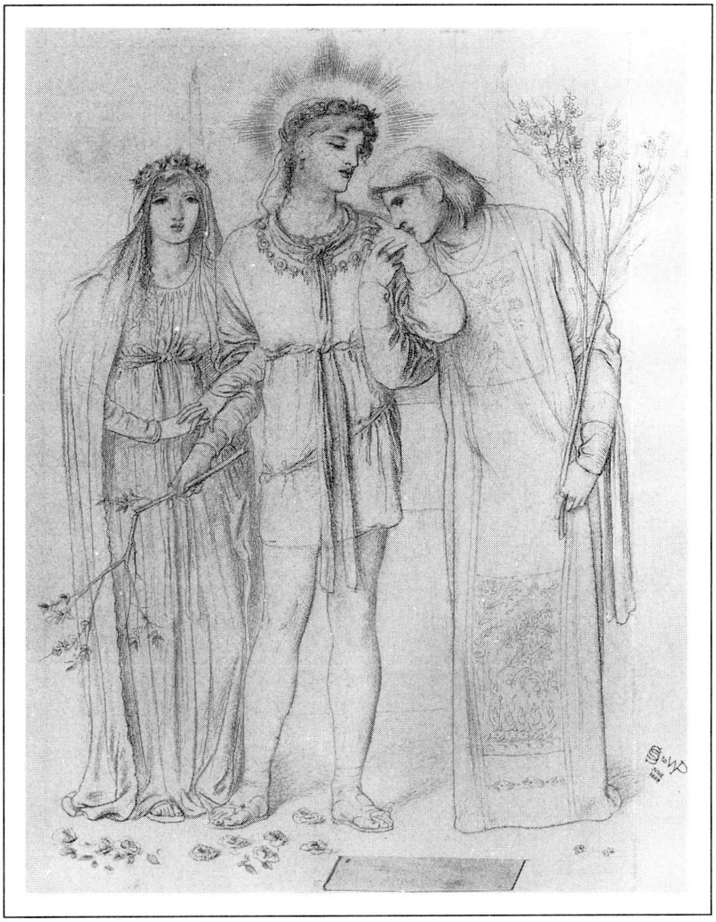

Figure 4.3 Simeon Solomon, *The Song of Solomon* (1868), 8″ × 10″
Hugh Lane Municipal Gallery of Modern Art, Dublin.

Solomon was deeply engaged with the problematic triangulation of figures in his visualization of the Song of Songs. He went on to do a watercolour as well as an oil entitled *The Bride, The Bridegroom and the Friend [of the Bridegroom]*, the latter of which he exhibited at the Dudley Gallery. He was attacked for this work in the *Saturday Review*.[29] Also in 1868, for his new acquaintance, Walter Pater, Solomon specially drew a version of *The Bride, The Bridegroom and the Friend of the Bridegroom*, which, following suit, 'alludes wittily to the situation of men with homosexual tendencies who get married' (Seymour 1986: 165). Several years later, in 1871, Solomon was still concerned with this subject: a painting with the same title was accompanied by two passages from the Bible which placed the work within the familiar context of biblical typology: one from the Old Testament, 'And behold, the bush burned with fire, and the bush was not consumed' (Exodus 3: 2); and one from the New, *'Qui habet sponsam, sponsus est; amicus autem sponsi, qui stat, et auditeum gaudio gaudet propter vocem sponsi!'* ('He that hath the bride is the bridegroom; but the friend of the bridegroom, which standeth and heareth him, rejoiceth greatly because of the bridegroom's voice!'). By some Victorian male art-viewers, however, these two quotations could be read otherwise, the first hinting at a passion not to be satisfied by heterosexual practice, and the second ironically underscoring the loss suffered by the friend who sorrows (like 'sad Love') when he hears the bridegroom's announcement of marriage.[30]

The keynote to Solomon's work in the 1860s, then, is the problem of the couple (heterosexual, socially sanctioned) and the triangular relationship (simultaneously heterosexual and homoerotic, if not actively homosexual) as experienced by a large number of Victorian men. The ideal, classicized and remote, sapphic couple gives way in Solomon's art to ever-changing combinations of three figures, most often two males and a female, as in *The Bride, The Bridegroom and the Friend.* Consider, as a variation on the dilemma of same-sex desire, *Shadrach, Meschach, and Abednego Preserved from the Burning Fiery Furnace* (1863; Wood 1981: 130). This watercolour is dominated by two strong triads: three comely youths, huddled together with expressions of resignation or fear (or orgiastic joy?); and a towering angel who embraces this knot of young manhood with his/her arms and great wings in order to protect them from the flames lapping at the sides of the picture frame. Intimate male bonding is here legitimized by biblical allusion as well as by visual composition. As in the more daring series on 'The Bride, the Bridegroom and the Friend', Solomon uses the Bible as a site for reevaluating male–male desire, attempting to spiritualize it without denying its physical beauty.

'Friendship with Swinburne provided Simeon with just the inspirational stimulus he needed' (Lambourne 1986: 25). But of what exactly did this stimulating friendship consist? Seymour asserts that 'Swinburne's sadomasochistic tendencies were shared by Solomon and ... must have created a bond between them' (Seymour 1986: 86). But can we be sure? Reynolds opines that Solomon 'is simply pandering to Swinburne's predilections' when, beginning in 1865, he does illustrations for his friend's novel, *Lesbia Brandon* (published posthumously), and the pornographic fantasy, *The Flogging Block* (Reynolds 1884: 14).[31] After all, Swinburne was an aristocrat and an increasingly well-known poet by the mid-1860s, an advantageous friend for a Jewish artist from a mercantile family. Croft-Cooke adds that Solomon 'was without educational background and was enormously impressed by his friend's knowledge of the classics ...' (Croft-Cooke 1967: 43). Perhaps, Croft-Cooke reasons, because 'Solomon was neither masochist nor sadist and Swinburne was not homosexual', the former was only 'play[ing] up' to the latter as an inferior to a superior when Solomon's art turned to sado-masochistic themes, whether Sappho or schoolboys.

Did Swinburne introduce Solomon to homosexuality, as is usually alleged, or the reverse? If genital contact was not part of their relationship, and if Solomon was not as keen as Swinburne on flagellation – 'my affections are divided between the boy and the birch', writes Simeon to Algernon in 1863 – they certainly shared an intense interest in young male bodies (Lang 1959, 2: 32).[32] In the same letter, Solomon describes for his friend's delectation an acquaintance of his 'who has excited so much sympathy and interest in your breast', a William Nesfield, the son of a watercolourist. He is 'a fat, jolly hearty fellow' who is 'very fond ... I deeply grieve to say of women' and who 'is not at all of the sensual temperament in your and my conception of the term ...' Now, what does Solomon mean here? What precisely is 'the sensual temperament' which he and Swinburne share? Assumedly, Swinburne would agree with Solomon that it is regrettable that the young man in question is determinedly heterosexual (although not adverse to homosocial ties, as his association with Solomon proves). Solomon himself passes quickly over this potentially hazardous moment of homoerotic union with his addressee. He immediately goes on to mention the relatively safe –

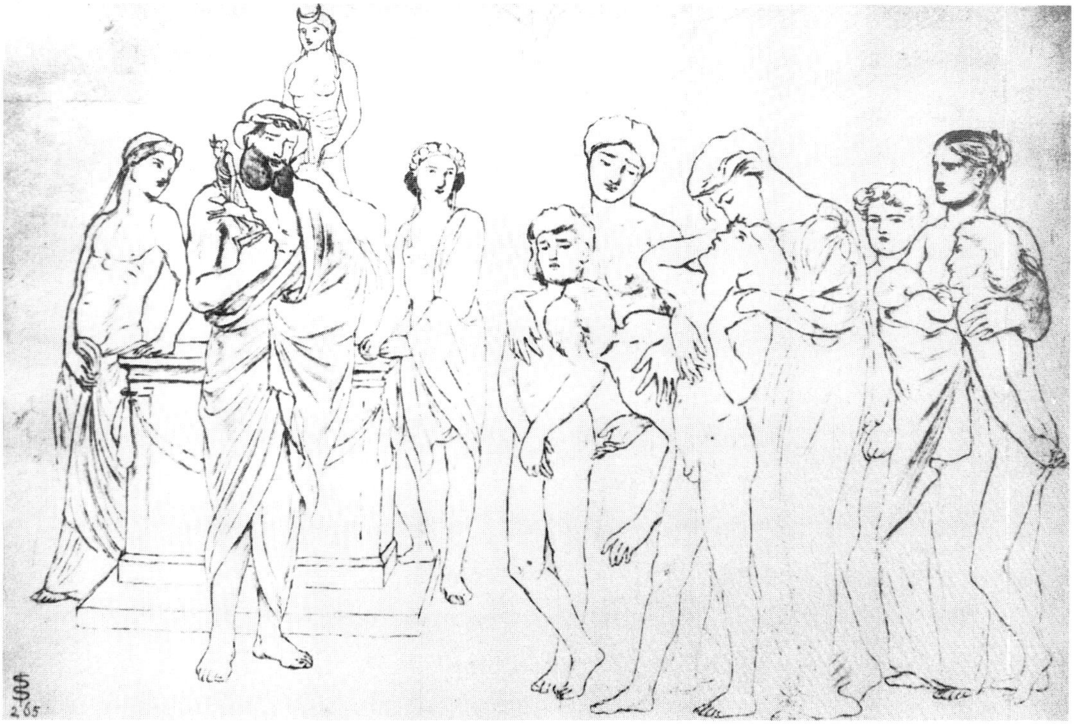

Figure 4.4 Simeon Solomon, *Spartan Boys about to be Scourged at the Altar of Diana*, drawing photographed by Frederick Hollyer (1865), 8″× 10″
Collection of the Miskan Le'Omanut, Museum of Art, Ein Harod, Israel.

because not solely homoerotic/homosexual – topic of flagellation. He has bought a copy of the pornographic penny paper, *Peter Spy*, for its front-page picture of 'a young girl in a highly resigned condition unlacing her stays' in preparation for a whipping by 'a shameless libertine' who holds 'a rod (I draw much better ones)' and by a woman who has another 'rod'. Titillating Swinburne still further, Solomon mentions that 'the paper has been suppressed. I have kept it to show you when you come to see me.'

In this as in other letters to Swinburne, Solomon skilfully segues from an object of homoerotic desire, usually a young man, to a multiply directed erotic fantasy of flagellation. Solomon thereby implies that Swinburne does not always prefer male–male sexual relations as he himself does. Later in the same letter, Solomon facetiously says that he has begun writing 'an autobiography of a man of irregular affections', by which he could mean sado-masochism or homosexuality or both: 'I do not sympathise entirely with the unaffected victims of passions which I blush and tremble to name ...' (Lang 1959, 2: 34). Swinburne, when reading Solomon's *tour de force* of ambiguity here, can take his pick of his friend's intriguingly 'perverse' statements on his own 'irregular affections'. The same applies to the drawing entitled *Spartan Boys to be Scourged at the Altar of Diana* (1865; Figure 4.4).[33] The high repute in which subjects from classical history were held by the Victorians furnished Solomon with a pretext for depicting naked boys and youths together. Indeed, one pair, a young man and a boy, is embracing as the former reassures the latter before the divinely ordained ritual of flagellation.[34] Of course, this drawing would also 'appeal to Swinburne's fascination with flagellation' (Reynolds 1984: plate 40). But the presence of mothers in the picture, who are bringing their sons for ritual flagellation, ambiguates the eroticism of the several male couples by re-admitting the norm of heterosexual reproduction and thus distracting attention away from the nearly all-male, naked or partially draped, handsome young bodies. Although pleasing his friend Swinburne was certainly a strong consideration in drawings such as this one which Solomon did during the mid-1860s, he was exploring the range of and possibility for representation of intimate male–male relations in art for the sake of his own interests as well.

Lang observes that the friendship between Swinburne and D.G. Rossetti was 'matched in English literary history only by the intimacy between Wordsworth and Coleridge' (Lang 1959, 1: xlv). I would argue that the friendship between Swinburne and Solomon deserves as much attention as either of these, both because it produced some of the two men's most aesthetically important works and because it offers us some insight into the 'continuum' of male relationships which existed in Victorian England of the 1860s–70s (see Sedgwick 1985). This continuum, as the variety of all-male social circles in which Solomon participated indicates, consisted of fluid contacts between men which cannot be distinguished 'on the basis of the "homosexuality" of one and the "heterosexuality" of the other' (Martin 1989: 182). The fact that Solomon's art and Swinburne's poetry converge increasingly upon the same kinds of topics during the decade or so of their friendship (1862–73), is testimony to this continuum, in that it is not determinable whether or not the two men enjoyed sex with each other, enjoyed fantasizing about same-sex relations, enjoyed sado-masochistic practices or representations of such among men and/or women, or all of these.

Wayne Koestenbaum has theorized that 'collaboration between men in the 19th and early 20th centuries was a consciously and anxiously homosocial act' in which the writers whom he studies seek to 'express homoeroticism' at the same time as 'they strive to conceal it' (Koestenbaum 1989: 3). One of the instances of 'the erotics of male literary collaboration' which he discusses is the complex bond between Wordsworth and Coleridge. Koestenbaum finds Wordsworth's obscuring of his very close tie to Coleridge in 'Tintern Abbey', for example, to be paradigmatic of the way in which the dominant one of a male–male couple 'snap[s] the bond between erotic entanglements and literary partnerships' (Koestenbaum 1989: 110). The relationship between Solomon and Swinburne – in their case, between an artist and a poet – may be understood in this light, although the fact of Solomon's avowed homosexuality complicates our understanding of their collaboration significantly.

For, after many years of working on parallel subjects, from 1862 to 1871, and after encouraging him in his art, if not his 'irregular' lifestyle, Swinburne was to repudiate Solomon on the basis of the latter's 'unmentionable' behaviour. Swinburne's volte-face in regard to Solomon has been a constant source of critical blame: the standard narrative of their friendship portrays Swinburne as a villain who led astray the (almost) innocent Solomon. True, Solomon's homoerotic art, depicting biblical and classical scenes as well as pornographic ones, fits Swinburne's programme of aestheticizing the 'perverse' in the 1860s, beginning with his review, 'Charles Baudelaire' (1862) and culminating in his review of Solomon's *A Vision of Love Revealed in Sleep* (1871). Why, then, did Swinburne break with Solomon in the early 1870s? The answers to this question are many. Certainly an important one lies in the 'highly ambiguous homosocial/homophobic' all-male monoculture – the friends who met at D.G Rossetti's home or at Solomon's studio or through the Royal Academy – to which both Swinburne and Solomon belonged (Hearn 1992: 175). Homophobia was (is) built into the continuum of close male–male relations itself as a safeguard against same-sex couples ever effectively challenging the hegemony of heterosexuality and the guarantee of 'bio-power' (Foucault 1978: 143–4).[35] Swinburne was susceptible to a strong homophobia: even though he cultivated Solomon's 'perverse' representations in art and 'perverse' chat in their correspondence, he remained 'caught within the terms of [a] negation' of conventional Victorian morality (Dellamora 1990: 83). The 'perverse' was a glorious avant-garde gesture to make, but the legal punishment and social ostracism awaiting the practising homosexual were inglorious in the extreme. This seems to have been Swinburne's position when, after Solomon was arrested for 'buggery' in 1873, he began moving away from his friend.

Yet during the 1860s, Solomon and Swinburne collaborated on several projects which were aesthetically 'perverse' and homoerotic in implication without raising suspicion on the part of the critics or the public, and without troubling Swinburne himself concerning his intimacy with Solomon. Granted, the connection between their work was not always obvious. Consider, for example, Solomon's watercolour, *And the Sons of God Saw the Daughters of Men that they were Fair*, and Swinburne's sonnet sequence, 'Hermaphroditus', both dated 1863. At first glance, Solomon's piece on a biblical theme and Swinburne's on a statue in the Louvre seem to have nothing in common. However, the 'hermaphroditic quality' of one couple and the 'ambiguous sexuality' of the angel in Solomon's visualization of the scriptural scene resonate with 'the fruitful feud of hers and his' in Swinburne's poem (line 18). Furthermore, heterosexual 'union' is treated ironically in both. Solomon's hermaphroditic figures undermine the very title of his piece, which alludes to the hallowing of sexual difference, while Swinburne parodies the Victorian idealization of marriage by highlighting the 'waste wedlock' of the two sexes in the sculpted hermaphrodite (line 19).

Another collaboration between Solomon and Swinburne went similarly unremarked by their contemporaries. If Swinburne had written most of *Poems and Ballads* before it was published in 1866, as Henderson maintains, then Solomon's painting *Habeat!* of 1865 should be interpreted in the light of their mutual interest in 'perverse' sexuality and in particular should be compared with Swinburne's poem, 'Faustine'. Bearing the epigraph *'Ave Faustina Imperatrix, Morituri te Salutant'*, Swinburne's long description reveals the sadistic pleasures which the beautiful Faustine takes in all sorts of 'perverse' activities. One of her favourites is watching 'games men played with death, / Where death must win' (lines 65–6) – in other words, the gladiatorial games. Swinburne's poem was much criticized for its supposedly unnatural, hence 'perverse', representation of Woman, who was idealized by most Victorians as gentle and loving. In contrast, Solomon's painting *Habeat!*, which depicts several women at a gladiatorial game, was well received as a dramatic contribution to the genre of classical subjects approved by the Royal Academy. A well-known contemporary, Francis Turner Palgrave, praised Solomon's 'striking' picture of 'the ladies of the Imperial household' as they give 'the order to despatch an unsuccessful gladiator' (Palgrave 1866: 111). The distinction between the 'languid air' of one woman and the 'fierce' look of another saves Solomon's painting from being judged 'perverse', whereas Swinburne's emphatic combination of feminine beauty and very unfeminine cruelty – in which Faustine even takes pleasure – drew critical censure. Nonetheless, Solomon and Swinburne are exploring the same ambiguous region of sadism and sexual identity.

A more explicit collaboration is Solomon's *Damon and Algae*, exhibited at the Royal Academy in 1866 with a passage from Swinburne's 'Erotion' (published in *Poems and Ballads*). Indeed, as he himself mentions in his review on Solomon (1871), Swinburne had written this poem specifically for Solomon's artwork. Swinburne's commentary on the meaning of this aesthetic pairing is open to differing interpretations: *Damon and Algae* and 'Erotion' represent the 'subtle passionate sense of mortality in love' which 'cannot quite ... eat away with the bitter poison of doubt' the pleasures it brings (Swinburne 1926: 453). Is this just a visual and lyrical reminder of the power of love between man and woman, or an ironic observation on the 'subtle' but 'bitter' feelings associated with intimate male–male bonds? Moreover, in the year Swinburne wrote his review on Solomon (1871) for the new monthly review, the *Dark Blue*, he and Simeon also appeared in print together in the same publication. Swinburne contributed a poem called 'The End of a Month' ('At a Month's End' in *Poems and Ballads, Series 2*, 1878) and Solomon a drawing of two (male/female or male/male?)

heads. The fact that this collaborative work as well as Swinburne's review of Solomon appeared in an Oxford periodical is significant because, as Linda Dowling (1994) has recently documented, Oxford was a mecca for Victorian men and youths interested in legitimizing male–male desire and male (as opposed to female) beauty through art, poetry, fiction, criticism, philosophy and history.

Their London circles of friends or Walter Pater at Oxford – both Solomon and Swinburne knew him – were ever hospitable to the 'perverse' in Solomon's art and Swinburne's poetry, but some in the Victorian establishment were beginning to notice the sexual ambiguities of Solomon's work. (Those of Swinburne were already legendary after 1866.) For one, Sidney Colvin, who knew Solomon as an artist through the Royal Academy, judged his recent work to be marred by a certain 'affectation' in the rendering of the human figure. Although generally laudatory, his article warns Solomon against 'insufficient manliness' and urges him to return to 'grave themes of the Biblical or Roman kind' (Colvin 1870: 163). Further, Colvin detects a 'sentiment bordering a little on the crapulous' in some of Solomon's images of 'the Dionysiac kind' which 'carried [such sentiments] about as far as they could go'. Not coincidentally, it is these same images – the head of *Bacchus* (exhibited at the Royal Academy in 1867) and the partly nude figure of *Bacchus* (exhibited at the Dudley Gallery in 1868) – which Pater was to single out in 'A Study of Dionysus' (1876) as especially fine for their depiction of ideal male beauty.[36]

Negative reaction to Solomon's art was starting to come from the literary quarter as well. Robert Browning, a friend of the Solomon family who had taken an interest in its younger son's work, went on invitation to Simeon's studio in London in 1870. Browning judged his pictures '[f]ull of talent' but 'too affected and effeminate'.[37] After D.G. Rossetti's *Poems* were published later in the same year, Browning fulminated against the 'effeminacy of his school, – the men that dress up like women' and particularly blamed Swinburne who 'started this'. As the critic Robert Buchanan was to do in his scandal-raising attack on D.G. Rossetti and his associates as the 'Fleshly School' in 1871, Browning includes Solomon in his condemnation of what he perceives as a 'perverse' trend in Victorian culture. Probably alluding to *The Bride, the Bridegroom and the Friend*, Browning expresses 'hate' for Solomon's representation of 'Love' 'as a lubberly naked young man putting his arms here & his wings there, about a pair of lovers, – a fellow they would kick away, in the reality'. The homophobia in Browning's remarks is unmistakeable. Colvin's admonitions stem from the same fear of homosexuality within the intensely homosocial society of later Victorian England.

'[T]he men that dress up like women': 1870, the year in which Robert Browning used this phrase, saw a sensational case involving two male transvestites, Ernest Boulton and Frederick William Park, along with some of their male friends/lovers.[38] Boulton, calling himself 'Stella', and Park, calling himself 'Fanny', were in full drag – dresses, wigs, jewellery, ladies' gloves – when they were arrested at the Strand Theatre in London. The charge was a 'felony' which 'meant sodomy and nothing else' (Croft-Cooke 1967: 54). However, when Boulton and Park were medically examined for evidence of sodomy, the doctor was so unsure what to look for that pedication was not conclusively determined: ' "there were some symptoms in these men as I should expect to find in men that had committed unnatural crimes" ' was all he could say (quoted in Pearsall 1969: 564–5). Furthermore, Boulton and Park never hid themselves when in drag but went out on the town in full view of everyone. When the case came to trial in 1871, the defence argued that '[t]he whole thing was a lark ... Boys will be girls and if they like dressing up and writing to one another as "darling" and generally behaving with exaggerated effeminacy, who is to say that any "felony" was behind it?' (Croft-Cooke 1967: 52–3). Therefore, since '[b]efore 1885 the only legislation which directly affected homosexual acts was that referring to sodomy or buggery', and since such could not be proven in the case of Boulton and Park, the jury found them not guilty (Weeks 1977: 11).

Solomon was keenly interested in the Boulton and Park trial, for the way the law handled them bore upon his own situation as a homosexual in the increasingly homophobic London of the early 1870s. Swinburne, too, was eager to hear from his friend Simeon about the trial, which the latter attended, but as a matter for distanced pleasure in the 'perverse' – men dressed as women being comparable to lesbians or 'masculine women', for instance.[39] As usual in his correspondence with the poet, Solomon relays some juicy tidbits from his experience. There was some 'disgusting and silly medical evidence' presented at the trial, but more noteworthy was Solomon's lunch with the main defendants: 'B[oulto]n is very remarkable, he is not quite beautiful but supremely pretty, a perfect figure, manner, and voice' (Lang 1959, 2: 144). This portrait of a drag queen in masculine clothing seeks the reader's erotic admiration but also an identificatory sympathy with him. In contrast, Solomon's letter about the Boulton and Park case to his lover in the late 1860s, Oscar Browning, is critical of men in drag and their admirers: 'the taste of such a thing is, to say the least, doubtful and I suppose they are a most disreputable set of young men.'[40]

Solomon's feelings about men in female drag were decidedly mixed. After all, when he himself wore Oriental costume at parties at Lord Houghton's, he remained a man in masculine attire. Yet Solomon seems to have made a short trip to Italy in 1870, the year of the Boulton and Park scandal. Edmund Gosse notes, in a letter written many years later to Robert Ross, that Solomon's own arrest for 'buggery', which ocurred in 1873, 'was not [his] *first* lapse: he had been suddenly obliged to leave England earlier ... I think in 1870' (Ross 1952: 315; his emphasis). Solomon had apparently feared prosecution for his homosexuality already in 1870, in the wake of the Boulton and Park scandal. The fact that he went away to Italy is, furthermore, significant both for our understanding of the allegorical cast of his work beginning in the late 1860s and for insight it affords into the all-male monoculture of later Victorian England, in which homoerotically interested and homosexually active men mingled freely. Travel abroad, away from the constricting requirements of Victorian respectability (including marriage), was one of the modalities of this monoculture that enabled male–male relationships (cf. Hearn 1992: 195–8). Specifically, Italy was a draw for those like Oscar Browning who invited Solomon on several trips there while they were lovers in the late 1860s. On one of these to Rome in 1869, Oscar and Simeon took along the younger Gerald Balfour – a potentially galvanizing triangle, except that Solomon fell in love with a youth in Rome and stayed there while the other two men went on to Sicily.

Two works issued from Solomon's infatuation with his Roman lover: *Portrait of an Italian Youth*, a watercolor done in 1869, incribed with a suggestive line from Swinburne's 'Hermaphroditus' – 'Love turned himself and would not enter in' (Reynolds 1984: plate 4); and the first draft of Solomon's prose allegory, *A Vision of Love Revealed in Sleep*, which would be his most important contribution to the celebration of male beauty and male–male bonds. The rich heritage of Renaissance art in Rome and Florence, both of which Solomon visited, had a definite influence on his visual art.[41] Thus, while in Italy in 1869, he began the series of allegorical pictures, featuring single male figures, pairs of male figures, or triads of male figures, placed within otherworldly contexts and given mysterious titles, which became the mainstay of his art from then on. For example, while abroad, Solomon did *Until the Day Break and the Shadows Flee Away* (1869), which alludes to the epiphany of male–male love in *A Vision* but which has been widely reproduced as typical of Solomon's reputedly pretty but negligible art (for example, Jullian 1971: 43). Begun in Rome but finished in London is *Dawn* (1870–1; at the City of Birmingham Museum), which one commentator describes as a 'winged hermaphroditic youth' reminiscent of the 'equally androgynous "Ignudi" of the Sistine Chapel' (Seymour 1986: 187–9). In 1870, when he was completing the final version of *A Vision*, Solomon exhibited *Love Bound and Wounded* at the Royal Academy, a semi-nude male figure which is a variant on another work, *Love in Autumn* (1866; Reynolds 1984: plate 1), both referring directly to his prose allegory. Ironically, then, just as the homophobic voice of Robert Browning and the stern warning of Sidney Colvin were being heard, or in 1870, Solomon reached his goal: the representation of male beauty and male–male love as aesthetically and spiritually superior to female beauty and heterosexual passion.

A Vision of Love Revealed in Sleep is as much testimony to the increasing presence of an all-male monoculture in which male friendship including homoeroticism was legitimized, around 1870, as it is a testament of the imaginative work, both written and visual, of Simeon Solomon himself. Analysing Solomon's illustrations for Victorian periodicals and books, Collins points to 'his immersion into a homosexual underground that ... allowed him to express feelings and thoughts that were condemned by society at large' as a major factor in comprehending his later work (Collins 1991: 87). More specifically, *A Vision* should be interpreted in the context of the efforts of writers and thinkers at Oxford engaged in the project of relating male beauty and male–male desire to the history, philosophy, and art of classical Greece. *A Vision* follows the male narrator and his male Soul through an elaborate series of allegorical scenarios from which Love – emphatically male – emerges triumphantly beautiful and beatific at the end. Solomon visited Pater at Oxford often after they met in 1868; Swinburne himself kept close ties with his *alma mater*, reading Benjamin Jowett's translations of Plato, for example – a central source for those interested in justifying male–male relationships as 'a mode of spiritual and emotional attachment that was ... innocent or asexual' (Dowling 1994: 115). Besides the encouragement of his project of elevating true love between men above 'the imperatives of heterosexual reproductivity or ... sodomy' from friends like Pater and Oscar Browning, Solomon was well versed in D.G. Rossetti's use of allegory to raise bodily desires to a spiritual plane, as in the sonnets constituting *The House of Life*, published in 1870 but composed during the 1860s when Solomon was a familiar of the Pre-Raphaelite circle.[42]

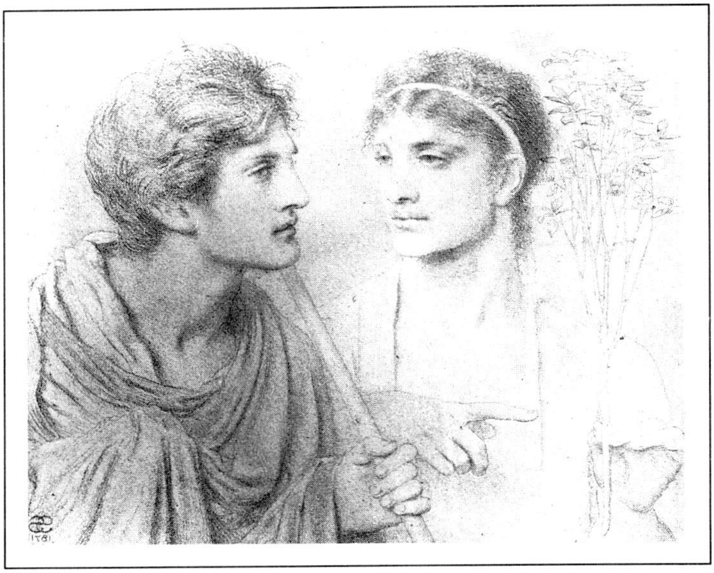

Figure 4.5 Simeon Solomon, *A Vision of Love Revealed in Sleep*, frontispiece (1871), 8″ × 10″
Courtesy of Special Collections, Arizona State University Libraries.

Solomon chose to accompany his prose allegory, *A Vision of Love Revealed in Sleep* (1871), with only one visual representation, the frontispiece, which bears a line from the text itself: 'Then I Knew My Soul Stood By Me, And He And I Went Forth Together'. Yet much of his art since 1869 depicts moments from *A Vision*, so that his work from this date onward can be largely interpreted as a pursuit in visual terms of the spiritualization of male beauty and male–male desire which comprises his prose allegory. The frontispiece to *A Vision* captures the essence of Solomon's central message (Figure 4.5). Two handsome, young men are portrayed standing close together. The dreamer–narrator leans slightly forward at the left side in the drawing, looking intently into the eyes of his Soul, as if for guidance. The dreamer–narrator's profile is strongly outlined, whereas his Soul, on the right in the picture, has lighter, etherealized features and turns his face towards his charge only partially, calmly, knowingly. The man grips the plain staff of a pilgrim; his male Soul delicately holds a flowering branch in his right hand while pointing with his left index finger to his right, directing the dreamer–narrator on his quest. (Compare the finger positions and flowering branch here to those in *The Bride, the Bridegroom and Sad Love.*)

Both figures are fully draped, implying the chastity of their spiritual union as male self and male Soul.

J.A. Symonds, another apologist for intimate male friendship associated with Oxford Hellenism, expresses his joy at discovering the validation of his 'own enthusiasm for male beauty' and 'the true *liber amoris*, the revelation I had been waiting for' in his reading of Plato's *Phaedrus* and *Symposium* (Grosskurth 1984: 99; see Dowling 1994: chapter 3). For Solomon, who had not had Swinburne's, Pater's, or Symonds' higher education, to produce *A Vision of Love Revealed in Sleep*, an allegory of love deriving from classical sources (second-hand) as well as from Pre-Raphaelite representations of the beauties of the body, made him an important member of these overlapping communities of male writers and artists. Moreover, Solomon's work, published in the spring of 1871, was set before the public in three reviews: the first by an anonymous critic in the *Athenaeum*, the second by J.A. Symonds himself in the *Academy*, and the third by his close friend Swinburne in the *Dark Blue*. The reviewer for the prestigious *Athenaeum* was frankly puzzled by Solomon's prose work, concluding that the artist 'intends the "Vision of Love" merely as a key to a series of pictures' (Anon. 1871: 368). He remarks upon the ' "white flame of youth, burning in ineffable perfection" ', at the end of the allegory, but he dislikes Solomon's 'somewhat affected style'.

Symonds's review in the *Academy* is considerably longer. Like the critic for the *Athenaeum*, he interprets *A Vision* as 'a key to the meaning of [Solomon's] drawings' but praises the 'perfect unity' between visual and verbal texts (Symonds 1871: 57). Symonds dignifies *A Vision* by treating it as a contemporary version of Dante's *Divine Comedy*, although he notes that the 'Love of Mr Solomon's *Vision* is quite distinct and unconventional' (Symonds 1871: 58). Indeed, Symonds continues, Solomon's allegory of a young man and his Soul 'is not the same' as Dante's canonical pilgrimage. Solomon's 'Love is not classical, not medieval, not Oriental; but it has a touch of all these qualities ...' (Symonds 1871: 60). Remaining within a safe corner of Victorian aestheticism – the spiritual yet fashionably new – Symonds suggests that Solomon's œuvre is marked by 'a vague yet intense yearning, a *Sehnsucht*, which...is essentially modern'. Less cautious, though, is one of Symonds's final comments: '[Solomon's] literary style, while it shares the delicacy and peculiar flavour of his pictures, has somewhat also of their profuse perfume and languor' (Symonds 1871: 63).

Robert Buchanan was to put it much more harshly in 1872, in *The Fleshly School of Poetry and Other Phenomena of the Day*, in which he declares that Solomon's œuvre partakes of the 'eccentricities of the Pre-Raphaelites', which include 'false and shallow mysticism', 'affectation' of all sorts, and, worst of all, 'effeminacy' (Buchanan 1872: 43, 49, 70). Buchanan's main targets in his pamphlet are D.G. Rossetti and Swinburne but his brief remarks on Solomon are characteristically venomous: 'English society of one kind purchases the *Day's Doings*. English society of another kind goes into ecstasy over Mr Solomon's pictures – pretty pieces of morality, such as "Love dying by the breath of Lust" ' (Buchanan 1872: 38). By the time Solomon had realized his artistic strategy of representing male beauty and male–male desire in allegorical terms, then, or in the early 1870s, conventional critics – determinedly heterosexist, homophobic ones like Robert Browning and Robert Buchanan – were becoming increasingly suspicious about that 'English society of another kind' which consisted largely of men who preferred the company, if not the sexuality, of other men.

It is in the interrelated, nearly simultaneous contexts of the Boulton and Park trial, rising public awareness of apologists for homosexuality at Oxford, pointedly homophobic criticism of Solomon's art, the publication of *A Vision*, further insinuations about the 'peculiar' cast of his work, and Solomon's openness about his own homosexuality among his many circles of friends that we must consider Swinburne's review article, 'Simeon Solomon: Notes on his "Vision of Love" and Other Studies' (1871). On 10 May 1871, Solomon writes to Swinburne: 'I want to know if you will write a little article about my book in connection with my pictures, *etc.*' (Lang 1959, 2: 143; his emphasis). The reviews in the *Athenaeum* (March) and the *Academy* (April) had already come out; Buchanan began to stir up the 'Fleshly School' controversy in a preliminary article in *Contemporary Review* only later that year (October). When Solomon humbly asked Swinburne for a review, therefore, the two that had appeared were passable but not brilliant; Solomon hoped that his more famous friend would compose an enthusiastic endorsement of his work, as he had already done for others. What Swinburne wrote, however, was a paean to the 'perverse' in Solomon's art and prose allegory. To 'English society of another kind' – Pater, Oscar Browning and Symonds, for example – presenting Solomon as the epitome of the 'perverse' in the Oxford periodical, *Dark Blue*, was an aesthetic compliment as well as a nod from one insider to another. To 'English society of one kind' or vociferously heterosexual and increasingly homophobic men who held hegemony in Victorian England, Swinburne's equating the name of Simeon Solomon with the 'perverse' was a social and economic disaster for the latter. As a worried Solomon wrote to Swinburne later in 1871, 'I saw that there were certain parts [in the review] which I could have desired to be omitted but I dared not ask you to eliminate or even to modify them' (Lang 1959, 2: 158).

The gap between Swinburne's iconoclastic ideas of the 'perverse' in aesthetics and sexuality, and mainstream Victorian society's notion of the 'perverse' as immoral and inartistic is nowhere more obvious than in his review article on Solomon. Swinburne either miscalculated the impact his words would have on most readers, or was oblivious to it, or, as most twentieth-century commentators on Solomon's 'tragic' career have decided, did not care. Swinburne begins with majestic generalizations about 'the manifold and multiform nature of beauty', focusing on the 'compound genius' who is able to fuse form with colour, 'spirit with flesh' (Swinburne 1926: 443–4). He elevates Solomon by placing him with John Keats as one of this group. But then the review turns to the ambiguities in Solomon's art and prose allegory. The beauty in Solomon's work has 'a new savour ... one strange and alien' (Swinburne 1926: 445). Even though comparable to 'the fair forms of godhead and manhood' in classical art, Solomon's figures 'know of something beyond form and outside of speech'. The faces he represents have 'a questioning wonder' which mingles 'a trouble' and 'a delight' (Swinburne 1926: 445). Swinburne's initial description of Solomon's work here may be read simply as lyrical prose which attempts to create an attractive air of mystery and novelty about the art and book of a friend. However, as an intratext in Swinburne's programme of aesthetic criticism, and in the immediate context of the all–male monoculture that was just at this time striving to present 'the fair forms of ... manhood' to the Victorian public as a worthy part of culture, these remarks are fraught with another meaning.[43] Thus, although Swinburne enshrines Solomon along with Charles Baudelaire as a master of the 'strange', and, later in the review, of the 'perverse' itself, he in fact does his friend no favour. Quite the contrary, by pointing out Solomon's 'alien' representation of mostly male figures, Swinburne directs the reader–viewer's attention to the artist's oblique but persistent 'suggesti[on] of things hidden in secret places of spiritual reserve' – in other words, the homoeroticism of the art and the homosexuality of the artist (Swinburne 1926: 447).

Swinburne is not particularly kind to Solomon when criticizing *A Vision*. A 'fragment of spiritual allegory', this prose piece 'seems to want even that much coherence which is requisite to keep symbolic or allegoric art from absolute dissolution and collapse' (Swinburne 1926: 445–6). Conceding that the allegories of his beloved William Blake – another artist/writer – are also sometimes impenetrable, Swinburne nevertheless finds Solomon's *A Vision* to have 'almost a superflux of images full of tender colour and subtle grace, which ... lead the writer into some danger of confusion and repetition' (Swinburne 1926: 446). Swinburne's critique of *A Vision* goes on for three pages: 'We miss the thread of union between the varying visions of love', he complains, adding that '[i]t might have been well to issue with the text some further reproductions of the designs' (Swinburne 1926: 448).

When he turns to Solomon's visual work, however, Swinburne is full of praise. Significantly, after mentioning 'a noble study of "Sleepers and One that Watches" ' (1871), he dwells on *Habeat!*

(1865), a 'masterpiece of large dramatic realism and live imagination' which the Victorian public liked (Swinburne 1926: 449). He hints at a collaboration between himself and Solomon by embellishing his description of the painting with the language of the 'perverse', adapted from his own poem, 'Faustine' (1866): the Roman women in Solomon's picture show 'the delicious thirst and subtle ravin of sensual hunger for blood' – but, he hastens to note, this is 'proper tragic beauty and truth and terror' (Swinburne 1926: 449). Next, Swinburne discusses Solomon's several 'Hebrew' series and his 'ceremonial bias' in pictures such as *Two Acolytes* (1863), almost all of which are filled with a homoeroticism which Swinburne names by mystifying paradoxes: 'the sadness that is latent in gladness; the pleasure that is palpable in pain' (Swinburne 1926: 450).

The pictures that exemplify for Swinburne 'some obscure suppressed tragedy of thought and passion and fate' in Solomon's visual œuvre are *Sappho and Erinna in a Garden at Mytilene* (1864) and *The Sacrifice of Antinous* (lost). The pairing of the 'masculine woman' Sappho and the 'feminine man' Antinous as 'types' of 'perplexities unsolved and desires unsatisfied' would have been transparent to that minority of reader–viewers, such as Pater and Oscar Browning, who recognized Solomon's work to be centred in their all-male monoculture and intended to represent same-sex desire and male beauty as suitable subjects for art. Swinburne's expatiation on the picture of the two lesbians also reminds us of his (in)famous poem on the same topic, 'Anactoria' (1866). Not coincidentally, the next picture he details emerged from yet another collaborative moment in his relationship with Solomon: *The Temple of Venus* (1863) which, as I argued (p. 73), parallels the poem 'Laus Veneris'. Equally pointed is his evocation of the 'perverse' around this apparently innocuous piece: 'As the Epithalamium of Catullus to his Atys, so is this bright and sweet drawing to the Sappho' (Swinburne 1926: 452). Adding more fuel to the fire, Swinburne celebrates the piece *(Damon and Algae)* Solomon exhibited in 1866, saying that his own 'verses called "Erotion" [were] written as a comment on this picture' (Swinburne 1926: 453). Although about 'the subtle passionate sense of mortality in love' with which anyone might identify, Solomon's artwork, Swinburne continues, mixes gender identities, so that 'the vows and kisses of these his present lips are not theirs but hers.'

Pater's ideal of the 'sexless beauty' of classical Greek sculpture, as discussed in his essay on 'Winckelmann' (1867), reappears in Swinburne's observations on the 'supersexual beauty, in which the lineaments of woman and of man seem blended' in Solomon's art (Swinburne 1926: 453). Like Pater, Swinburne especially admires *Bacchus* (1867) as 'a fleshly glory of godhead and bodily deity' (Swinburne 1926: 454). Yet a blending or transcendence of the two sexes is a rhetorical strategy, not an actual goal. In *Bacchus* (1867) and *Heliogabalus* (1866), we see not exactly a 'sexless' figure but a very attractive, young *male* who is associated with the divine. The goal, then, at least for Solomon, is to spiritualize male beauty and male–male desire. Swinburne's aim, in contrast, is to pursue his aesthetics of the 'perverse' through Solomon. The accumulation of sexually ambiguous examples from the artist's œuvre in Swinburne's review culminates in the revelation that '[e]ven in the glad soft grouping of boys and maidens by "summer twilight" ' we should be aware of the presence of the 'perverse' (Swinburne 1926: 455). Toward the end of his article, then, Swinburne effectively 'outs' Solomon. Referring to de Sade, Swinburne speaks of the 'mixture of utmost delicacy with a fine cruelty in some of these faces of fair feminine youth' in Solomon's pictures (Swinburne 1926: 456). Delivering what he considers to be the highest compliment, Swinburne states that '[t]he subtleties and harmonies of suggestion in such studies of complex or it may be perverse nature would have drawn forth praise and sympathy from Baudelaire' (Swinburne 1926: 456).

For Solomon, however, to be praised as 'perverse' by a writer who had become the *enfant terrible* of London after the scandal caused by *Poems and Ballads* in 1866 was the kiss of death. He writes to Swinburne in October 1871 that 'when the article appeared in print one or two very intimate friends said "eloquent and beautiful as it is, I think it will do you harm" ' (Lang 1959, 2: 159). Solomon, clearly hurt but always bearing in mind the greater stature of his aristocratic and well-known literary friend, goes on: 'You know, of course, my dear Algernon, that, by many, my designs and pictures executed during the last three or four years have been looked upon with suspicion ...' Why, he seems to be asking, has Swinburne exposed his artistic collaborator to further public censure by hailing Solomon as the paradigm of the 'perverse'? Yet Solomon holds his ground in the end: 'as I have been a false friend to myself, I have not sought to remove the impression, but I have gone on following my own sweet will; in pecuniary and some other ways I have had to suffer for it ...' Swinburne may think that he is intriguingly 'perverse', but Solomon has been and remains seriously committed to representing male beauty and male–male desire as morally and aesthetically acceptable.

Solomon was more right than he knew: he would indeed 'suffer' for his homosexuality and his homoerotic work. Buchanan included him in his widely publicized attack on the 'Fleshly School', published in the same month in which Solomon wrote this letter to Swinburne. At the end of October 1871, Solomon writes again to Swinburne, thanking him for understanding his misgivings about the import of the review, and admitting (again) that 'I have given grounds for the kind of remarks that have been made' (Lang 1959, 2: 162). He is frightened, though, and is deciding to return to what Colvin had called 'grave themes of the Biblical or Roman kind': 'I intend now to go in for a different kind of work and cultivate that element that was more prominent some years ago' (Lang 1959, 2: 162–3). Swinburne's side of their correspondence was destroyed, so we do not know what he replied.[44] However, Swinburne's ever-jocose letters to his homoerotically interested friend, George Powell, during 1872 show that the poet still considered Solomon an intimate: 'My love to Simeon', he closes in one, 'and say that I was sorry to be unable to see him again [recently]' (Lang 1959, 2: 191).

In February 1873, Solomon and another man were arrested for 'buggery' in a public place, under the Offences against the Person Act of 1861.[45] In the following month, Swinburne starts distancing himself from Solomon, wittily but definitely, in a letter to Powell. 'The aberrations' of 'our Wandering Jew' 'are a subject of real uneasiness and regret to me', he says, adding that Powell and he should 'give thanks ... that we are not as this Israelite' (Lang 1959, 2: 234). Solomon is suddenly now not a close friend and artistic collaborator, but the Other: homosexual and Jewish. In May, writing to his solicitor, Theodore Watts, about the 'prose' criticism he has so far published, Swinburne pointedly omits 'Simeon Solomon: Notes on his "Vision of Love" and Other Studies' (Lang 1959, 2: 242). Powell receives a nervous letter from Swinburne about Solomon in June. Swinburne has gone to Oxford 'where I saw and spoke with a great friend of poor Simeon's, Pater' (Lang 1959, 2: 253). Clearly, Swinburne is becoming increasingly concerned about his own reputation: promoting the 'perverse' in the 1860s was one thing, but trying to win a permanent place in English poetry, alongside Alfred Lord Tennyson and Matthew Arnold, in the 1870s was quite another.

Moreover, 1873 was the year in which not only Swinburne but most of Solomon's other friends disassociated themselves from him. Homosexual panic invaded the lives and correspondence of D.G. Rossetti and Edmund Gosse, among others (Reynolds 1984: 82–3). In June, Swinburne warns Powell to stay away from Solomon, as he himself will do:

> I suppose there is no doubt that the poor unhappy little fellow has really ... *done* things amenable to law such as ... would make it impossible for any one to keep up his acquaintance and not be cut by the rest of the world as an accomplice? (Lang 1959, 2: 253; his emphasis).

The underscoring of *done* seems to answer the question of whether or not Swinburne himself had ever engaged in homosexual 'things' with a resounding 'no'. He certainly takes the high ground in a December letter to Watts, warning him, too, 'not to be led away by any kindly and generous feeling towards' Solomon into 'a renewal of intimacy by correspondence or otherwise which might appear to involve [you] in equivocal or questionable relations with a man who has deliberately chosen to do what makes a man ... infamous in the eyes of the world' (Lang 1959, 2: 261). Swinburne somewhat hypocritically pleads his case, reminding Watts that he cannot 'be accused of lukewarmedness in friendship or pers[on]al timidity in the face of public op[ini]on.' But, when all is said and 'done', Swinburne repudiates Solomon as 'a – – – – let us say, a Platonist'.

The homoerotic friendship and artistic/literary collaboration between Solomon and Swinburne was ended by the latter, then, in 1873. Their relationship, though, was not, for afterwards, utterly destitute, Solomon sold some of Swinburne's risqué letters to him. Sedgwick theorizes that the contradictory structure of a patriarchy which encourages homosocial bonding but punishes homosexuality produces a 'residue of terrorist potential, of *blackmailability*' (Sedgwick 1985: 89; her emphasis). Swinburne's own homoerotic behaviour and the aesthetic of the 'perverse' in his writings laid him open to blackmail, should the letters which Solomon had sold be so used by the buyer. By the mid-1870s, Swinburne no longer wished to be associated with the 'perverse' as he had during the 1860s and early 1870s. Thus, in a letter to Gosse from his newly respectable home with the Watts-Duntons outside London, or The Pines, in 1879, Swinburne reacts explosively to the news of Solomon's having sold some of his letters. Appealing to 'the steady friendship and fidelity of honourable gentlemen' such as his addressee, Swinburne scorns 'such disgusting facts as that I hear of one person [Solomon] who was once my friend and is yet my debtor' (Lang 1959, 4: 107). The poet is keen to claim the aesthetic fruits of his collaboration with Solomon but even more anxious to disentangle himself forever from 'another, who is now a thing unmentionable alike by men and women'. Self-righteously condemning Solomon, Swinburne concludes his letter with a rhetorical flourish that sums up his homophobia: 'if I may respectfully venture on a parody of the Psalmist, it is all right with me ... as long as I can say, "Men are on my side: I will not care what beasts [e.g., homosexuals in general and Solomon in particular] may do unto me." '

'Perverse' male bodies: to Solomon, the possibility of a new aesthetic that would enable the representation of male beauty and male–male desire in many forms and contexts; to Swinburne, an avant-gardist programme that would win him notoriety and make him an important contributor to Pre-Raphaelism, Decadence, and, despite his later retrenchment, the minoritizing discourse of men interested in the looks, the literature, the art, the philosophy, and the sexual pleasuring of other men. Michel Foucault dates what he terms 'the perverse implantation' or the 'new persecution of the peripheral sexualities', including sado-masochism, homosexuality and lesbianism, from around 1870 (Foucault 1978: 42–3). Emphasizing that the growing currency of discourse about 'perversity' enabled 'a strong advance of social controls' on behaviour so labelled, Foucault wryly observes that 'it also made possible the formation of a "reverse" discourse: homosexuality began to speak in its own behalf' (Foucault 1978: 101). But, as George Chauncey, Jr has recently argued, 'we need to begin paying more attention to *other* social forms of homosexuality – other ways in which homosexual relations have been organized and understood ... named, and left deliberately unnamed' (Chauncey 1989: 315; his emphasis). Such may have been Solomon's and Swinburne's friendship and collaboration: an ever mobile eroticism, a 'perverse' play between fantasy and action, aesthetics and lifestyle.

Notes

The primary research for this essay was carried out through a fellowship (1992) from the Center for British Art at Yale University.

1 Swinburne elaborates his aesthetic position first in 'Charles Baudelaire' (1862), a tendentious review of *Les Fleurs du mal* which asserts the superiority of making art from 'strange' topics to the dominant tradition of limiting artists and writers to so-called respectable ones. See Morgan (1993: 317–19).

2 Freud first published *Three Essays on the Theory of Sexuality* in 1905. He considers 'perversions' in essay 1, 'The sexual aberrations', under the category of 'deviations in respect of the sexual aim', and defines them as 'sexual activities which

either (a) extend ... beyond the regions of the body that are designed for sexual union, or (b) linger over the intermediate relations to the sexual object...' (Freud 1962: 16). The heterosexist bias in Freud's definition (a) has informed discussions of Victorian sexualities until recently.

3 Pearsall discusses flagellation under 'Perversion' in chapter 7 and homosexuality as 'Against the norm' in chapter 10.

4 He adduces the case of Albert Dodd, a young American who, in the 1830s–40s, had several strong 'infatuations with male friends' (Gay 1986: 208). However, Gay declares with satisfaction, Dodd's 'masculinity triumphed over his homosexual appetites', for the 'biographical record' shows that he had ' "contemplated marriage" ' just before his untimely death (Gay 1986: 211).

5 Brian Reade concludes that there was 'a discernible wave of homosexual subculture, beginning around 1850 and closing shortly after the Wilde trials of 1895', as demonstrated in his literary anthology, *Sexual Heretics* (Reade 1970: 3).

6 For references to Solomon's relationship with Oscar Browning, including quotations from some of the former's letters to the latter, see Seymour 1986: 167–70, 172–3, 181–5, 189–90, 196. The two men's relationship is also discussed in Lambourne 1986: 26–7.

7 For a bibliography of writings about Solomon, see *Solomon* 1986: 86–7.

8 '... the closest that Swinburne ever came to acknowledging an investment in male–male desire occurs in a letter [dated 1866] in which the specified referent is Whitman' (Dellamora 1990: 89).

9 On the 'aesthetic minoritizing discourse' developed by Swinburne and Pater during the 1860s and early 1870s, see Morgan 1993.

10 The most thorough analysis of Victorian aestheticism, including 'the lives and writing, public and private, of men like Tennyson, Hopkins, and Swinburne', and culminating in Pater's essays which seek to validate male–male desire and male beauty on an aesthetic, even culture-wide basis, is Dellamora 1990.

11 In his final chapter, Hilton gives six lines to Solomon's work, stating that '[h]e painted many women [*sic*], generally with an unwholesome flavour to them' (Hilton 1970: 202).

12 Steven Kolsteren gives an overview of the 'the influence of Rossetti's iconography on Solomon', but fails to attach any significance to the fact that the younger artist's 'personal mythology' features not a Beatrice to guide Dante to heaven but a masculine Soul to reveal a male Love to the male dreamer (Kolsteren 1982: 35–6). See my discussion of Solomon's *Vision* below.

13 Hearn observes that 'the relationship of fragmentation [of individual experiences] and monoculture is especially complex in the creative arts' (Hearn 1992: 201).

14 Solomon joined the Sketching Club in 1856, the same year he entered the Royal Academy Schools. In 1858 he became part of another small group, the Junior Etching Club, and in 1859 he, Holiday, D.G. Rossetti, and William Morris formed the Artist Volunteer Corps. The chronologies in *Solomon* (1986: 83–4) and in Seymour 1986 (chapter 3: 'The Pre-Raphaelite circle') differ slightly. Holiday's relationship with Solomon may have been 'something more physical than the companionship which in later life he pompously recalled ... His own paintings ... suggest that ... he had rather more than the detached artist's interest in his own sex posed voluptuously' (Croft-Cooke 1967: 40).

15 See no. 41, 'Self-Portrait', in the catalogue in *Solomon* (1986). Croft-Cooke speaks of Solomon as '[p]recocious in the manner of a young homosexual free on the London streets' and a typical 'cockney queer' who 'developed the sophisticated wit' that would be recognized today as 'the natural campness of his kind' (1967: 39–40).

16 Seymour discusses some of Solomon's Biblical and 'Assyrian'-style pieces of the later 1850s (1986: 32–4, 36–8).

17 See no. 38 in the catalogue, *Solomon* (1986). This catalogue and the plates in Reynolds 1984 are complementary sources for reproductions of Solomon's work from the mid-1850s to the mid-1890s.

18 See Reynolds 1984: plate 21. This male figure is repeated, against a different background, in Solomon's *Hosannah*, later published in *Dalziel's Bible Gallery* (1880). Collins recognizes the 'theme' of 'homosocial behavior and its corollary of the androgyne' in this and several other biblical scenes by Solomon (Collins 1991: 88).

19 See Collins 1991: 79, 84–91 for an excellent discussion of Solomon's illustrations from the later 1850s to the early 1870s.

20 See, for example, the photograph of Solomon in Middle Eastern costume, *c.* 1870, reproduced in *The Pre-Raphaelite Camera*, with the following comment: 'Solomon was the only Jewish Pre-Raphaelite; in this he probably seemed exotic to [the photographer] David Wilkie Wynfield and the wayward strain in Solomon's personality would have made him seem more so' (Bartram 1985: 117). This photograph is also reproduced in Jeremy Maas, with a similarly disparaging remark: 'Although he was extremely talented he led a very disreputable life' (Maas 1984: 223). The photograph shows Solomon smirking; at a different moment, though, he looks into the camera sombrely (Reynolds 1984: plate 9).

21 Lang dates Lord Houghton's first loan of a book by de Sade to Swinburne to 1862 (1959, 1: xlvi–xlvii). Croft-Cooke ponders the long correspondence between Swinburne and Lord Houghton, concerning the works of the Marquis de Sade and the topic of flagellation, and concludes that the latter 'put up with much for the sake of Swinburne's confidence and never ... forgot his worth as a poet' (1967: 37).

22 Quoted in Seymour 1986: 83. She compares *Juliette* to Solomon's painting, *Beatrice*, finding 'an awareness of impending tragedy' in the former and 'an intimation of inner harmony and peace' in the latter. Seymour reads both in the context of D.G. Rossetti's work, in which the story of Dante and Beatrice is central. But can we be sure that Solomon's contrapuntal *Juliette* refers exclusively to Shakespeare's tragic heroine? Might not this painting covertly allude to de Sade as well?

23 See Collins for a discussion of Solomon's Pre-Raphaelite style (Collins 1991: 84–6, 89). Seymour mentions that *In the Temple of Venus* was owned by Lord Houghton (Seymour 1986: 85). Solomon did another version of it in 1865, this time featuring a single female figure (Seymour 1986: 102–3).

24 The image and word 'flower' was part of the emerging vocabulary recognized among homoerotically interested and homosexual men from the 1860s onward as connoting male beauty and its evocation of male–male desire. By the 1890s, Oscar Wilde is satirized for wearing a flower in his buttonhole, and John Addington Symonds is writing in his memoirs that the 'sexual relation between man and man' requires a special 'intimacy ... out of which the sexual indulgence springs like a peculiar plant ... which leads to no result of fruitage in the flesh of either, and which therefore exists only as the sign on both sides of particular affection' (Grosskurth 1984: 277–8).

25 For a discussion of 'Anactoria' as well as 'Laus Veneris' in the context of Victorian sexual politics, see Morgan 1984: 175–92.

26 On the predominance of classical Greek and Roman subjects in Victorian art, see Kestner 1989.

27 Swinburne makes this statement in his taunting *Notes on Poems and Reviews* (1866), reprinted in Hyder 1966. For an analysis of the intertextuality of Baudelaire's *Femmes damnées* and Swinburne's 'Anactoria' in relation to the problematic homoerotics in their representations of sapphism, see Morgan 1992.

28 For an insightful and thorough study of the institutionalization of homosocial and homoerotic relations in Victorian England, see Dowling 1994. Swinburne's devotion to Sappho, as a major classical author, would have been fostered by his education, first at Eton and then at Oxford.

29 Seymour dates *The Bride, the Bridegroom and the Friend* (sometimes also referred to as *The Bride, the Bridegroom and the Friend of the Bridegroom*) to 1868 but the negative review of it to November 1869 (Seymour 1986: 165, 177).

30 Seymour's disapproval of Solomon permeates her dissertation but is especially clear in her comment on this painting: she says that it refers to 'conjugal infidelity, and a homosexual one at that! [*sic*], (Seymour 1986: 167).

31 Pearsall discusses the dispersion of flagellation throughout Victorian culture as a 'perversion' in the Freudian sense (Pearsall 1969: 404–21). Swinburne is his prime example.

32 Lang dates this long letter from Solomon to 'My Dear Swinburne' to 1869. Seymour argues that it goes back to 1863, which I find plausible in light of the affinities between the two men's work and their close personal relationship at this time (Seymour 1986: 90).

33 Seymour puts this piece at the head of 'a series of drawings, many inspired by classical legends, which make clear references to [Solomon's] homosexuality and sadomasochism' (Seymour 1986: 104).

34 Dowling examines the centrality of the ancient Greek notion of 'the hearer/inspirer dyad of Dorian and Platonic love' to the justification of homoerotic friendship by writers and thinkers associated with Oxford in the later Victorian period (Dowling 1994: 150). Swinburne attended Oxford and retained friends there; Pater taught at Oxford and was a major voice in the attempt to legitimize homosexuality; Solomon was a friend of both.

35 '[N]o man must be able to ascertain that he is not (that his bonds are not) homosexual' (Sedgwick 1985: 88–9).

36 See the discussion of Pater's 'antihomophobic' use of Solomon's work in Dellamora 1990: 170–1, 177–8.

37 This letter and the following one by Robert Browning to Isabella Blagden are quoted in Seymour 1986: 185–6.

38 For detailed accounts of the Boulton and Park case, see Pearsall 1969: 561–8 and Croft-Cooke 1967: 47–55.

39 A biographer relates an anecdote from around the same period in which Swinburne is said to have been 'living on the sea-shore [on the Isle of Wight] in a field tent alone with a monkey dressed as a woman' (Henderson 1974: 148).

40 Quoted in Seymour 1986: 185. Note that Solomon's letter to Oscar Browning dates from the spring of 1870, just after Boulton and Park were arrested, whereas his letter to Swinburne coincides with the trial in the spring of 1871.

41 On the special importance of art at the Uffizi in Florence to the 'aesthetic minoritizing discourse' developed by Solomon's friends, Swinburne and Pater, see Morgan 1993.

42 Regarding Oscar Browning's influence on Solomon's *A Vision*, one critic asserts that he 'clearly had a hand in its composition' (Seymour 1986: 190). As for Pater, another critic finds that his 'influence on Solomon was as great as that of Swinburne or his artist friends Edward Burne-Jones and D.G. Rossetti' (Reynolds 1984: 2).

43 On Swinburne's aesthetic programme, see Morgan 1993.

44 'Swinburne enjoyed sharing homosexual jokes with Solomon – that is, before his disgrace in 1873 – and was anxious to have his own side of the correspondence destroyed' (Henderson 1974: 168).

45 For an account of Solomon's arrest, trial, and later life, see Seymour 1986: ch. 8.

References

Anon. (1871) Review of *A Vision of Love Revealed in Sleep* by S. Solomon, in the *Athenaeum* 2265: 368.

Bartram, M. (1985) *The Pre-Raphaelite Camera: Aspects of Victorian Photography*, London: Weidenfeld & Nicolson.

Buchanan, R. (1986) 'The Fleshly School of Poetry and Other Phenomena of the Day (1871–1872)', in Fredeman, W.E., Nadel, I.B. and Stasny, J.F. (eds) *The Victorian Muse: Selected Criticism and Parody of the Period*, New York: Garland Publishing, i–97.

Chauncey, Jr, G. (1989) 'Christian brotherhood or sexual perversion?: homosexual identities and the construction of sexual boundaries in the World War I era', in Duberman, B.M., Vicinus, M. and Chauncey, Jr, G. (eds) *Hidden from History: Reclaiming the Gay and Lesbian Past*, New York: New American Library, 294–317.

Collins, J.L. (1991) 'Prototype, posing, and preference in the illustrations of Frederick Sandys and Simeon Solomon', in S.P. Casteras (ed.) *Pocket Cathedrals: Pre-Raphaelite Book Illustration*, New Haven: Yale University Press, 79–91.

Cooper, E. (1986) *The Sexual Perspective: Homosexuality and Art in the Last Hundred Years in the West*, London: Routledge & Kegan Paul.

Croft-Cooke, R. (1967) *Feasting with Panthers: A New Consideration of Some Late Victorian Writers*, New York: Holt, Rhinehart &Winston.

deJean, J. (1989) *Fictions of Sappho, 1546–1937*, Chicago: Chicago University Press.

Dellamora, R. (1990) *Masculine Desire: The Sexual Politics of Victorian Aestheticism*, Chapel Hill: University of North Carolina Press.

Dijkstra, B. (1986) *Idols of Perversity: Fantasies of Feminine Evil in Fin-de-Siècle Culture*, New York: Oxford University Press.

Dowling, L. (1994) *Hellenism and Homosexuality in Victorian Oxford*, Ithaca: Cornell University Press.

Duberman, B.M., Vicinus, M. and Chauncey, Jr, G. (eds) (1989) *Hidden from History: Reclaiming the Gay and Lesbian Past*, New York: New American Library.

du Maurier, D. (ed.) (1951) *The Young George du Maurier: A Selection of his Letters, 1860–1867*, London: Peter Davies.

Foucault, M. (1978) *The History of Sexuality*, vol. 1, trans. R. Hurley, New York: Vintage Books.

Freud, S. (1962) *Three Essays on the Theory of Sexuality*, trans. J. Strachey, New York: Basic Books.

Gaunt, W. (1945) *The Aesthetic Adventure*, London: Jonathan Cape and The Book Society.

Gay, P. (1986) *The Bourgeois Experience: Victoria to Freud*, vol. 2: *The Tender Passion*, New York: Oxford University Press.

Grosskurth, P. (ed) (1984) *The Memoirs of J. A. Symonds: The Secret Homosexual Life of a Leading Nineteenth-Century Man of Letters*, New York: Random House.

Hearn, J. (1992) *Men in the Public Eye: The Construction and Deconstruction of Public Men and Public Patriarchies*, London: Routledge.

Henderson, P. (1974) *Swinburne: The Portrait of a Poet*, London: Routledge & Kegan Paul.

Hilton, T. (1970) *The Pre-Raphaelites*, New York: Oxford University Press.

Hyder, C.K. (ed) (1966) *Swinburne Replies*, Syracuse: Syracuse University Press.

Johnson, W. S. (1979) *Living in Sin: The Victorian Sexual Revolution*, Chicago: Nelson-Hall.

Jullian, P. (1971) *Dreamers of Decadence: Symbolist Painters of the 1890s*, New York: Praeger Publishers.

Kestner, J.A. (1989) *Mythology and Misogyny: The Social Discourse of Nineteenth-Century British Classical-Subject Painting*, Madison: University of Wisconsin Press.

Koestenbaum, W. (1989) *Double Talk: The Erotics of Male Literary Collaboration*, New York: Routledge.

Kolsteren, S. (1982) 'Simeon Solomon and Dante Gabriel Rossetti', *Journal of Pre-Raphaelite Studies* 2 (2): 35–48.

—— (1984) 'Simeon Solomon and the Romantic poets', *Journal of Pre-Raphaelite Studies* 6 (2): 62–8.

Lambourne, L. (1986) 'Simeon Solomon: artist and myth', in *Solomon: A family of painters*, London and Birmingham City Museums and Art Gallery, 24–7.

Lang, C.Y. (ed.) (1959) *The Swinburne Letters*, vol. 1, New Haven: Yale University Press.

—— (1959) *The Swinburne Letters*, vol. 2, New Haven: Yale University Press.

—— (1960) *The Swinburne Letters*, vol. 4, New Haven: Yale University Press.

Levey, M. (1978) *The Case of Walter Pater*, London: Thames & Hudson.

Maas, J. (1984) *The Victorian Art World in Photographs*, London: Barrie & Jenkins.

Mangan, J.A. and Walvin, J. (eds) (1987) *Manliness and Morality: Middle-class Masculinity in Britain and America, 1800–1940*, New York: St Martin's Press.

Martin, R.K. (1989) 'Knights-errant and gothic seducers: the representation of male friendship in mid-nineteenth-century America', in Duberman, B.M., Vicinus, M. and Chauncey, Jr, G. (eds) *Hidden from History*, New York: New American Library, 169–82.

Morgan, T.E. (1984) 'Swinburne's dramatic monologues: sex and ideology', *Victorian Poetry* 22 (2): 175–95.

—— (1992) 'Male lesbian bodies: the construction of alternative masculinities in Courbet, Baudelaire, and Swinburne', *Genders* 15: 37–57.

—— (1993) 'Reimagining masculinity in Victorian art criticism: Swinburne and Pater', *Victorian Studies* 36 (3): 315–32.

The Oxford English Dictionary (1971), vol. 2, Oxford: Oxford University Press.

Palgrave, F.T. (1866) *Essays on Art*, London: Macmillan.

Pearsall, R. (1969) *The Worm in the Bud: The World of Victorian Sexuality*, New York: Penguin Books.

Pre-Raphaelite Paintings, Manchester City Art Gallery, London: Lund Humphries.

Reade, B. (ed.) (1970) *Sexual Heretics: Male Homosexuality from 1850 to 1900*, New York: Coward-McCann.

Reid, F. (1928) *Illustrators of the 1860s*, London: Farber and Gwyer.

Reynolds, S. (1984) *The Vision of Simeon Solomon*, Stroud, Glos.: Catalpa Press.

Richards, J. (1987) ' "Passing the love of women": Manly love and Victorian society', in Mangan, J.A. and Walvin, J. (eds) *Manliness and Morality*, New York: St Martin's Press, 92–122.

Ross, M. (ed.) (1952) *Robert Ross: Friend of Friends*, London: Jonathan Cape.

Sedgwick, E.S. (1985) *Between Men: English Literature and Male Homosocial Desire*, New York: Columbia University Press.

Seymour, G. (1986) 'The life and work of Simeon Solomon (1840–1905)', unpublished Ph.D. thesis, University of California (Santa Barbara).

Solomon: A Family of Painters (1986), London and Birmingham City Museums and Art Gallery.

Surtees, V. (ed.) (1980) *The Diaries of George Price Boyce*, Norwich: Real World.

Swinburne, A.C. (1904) *Poems and Ballads, Series 1* (1866), in *The Poems of Algernon Charles Swinburne*, vol. 1, London: Chatto & Windus.

—— (1926) 'Simeon Solomon: notes on his "Vision of Love" and Other Studies' (1871), in E. Gosse and T.J. Wise (eds) *The Complete Works of Algernon Charles Swinburne*, vol. 15: Prose Works, vol. 5, London: William Heinemann, 443–58.

—— (1966) *Notes on Poems and Reviews* (1866), in Hyder, C.K. (ed.) *Swinburne Replies*, Syracuse: Syracuse University Press. 15–32.

Thomas, D. (1979) *Swinburne: The Poet in his World*, New York: Oxford University Press.

Weeks, J. (1977) *Coming Out: Homosexual Politics in Britain, from the Nineteenth Century to the Present*, London: Quartet Books.

—— (1989) 'Inverts, perverts, and Mary-Annes: male prostitution and the regulation of homosexuality in England in the nineteenth and early twentieth centuries', in Duberman, B.M., Vicinus, M. and Chauncey, Jr, G. (eds) *Hidden from History*, New York: New American Library, 195–211.

Welby, T.E. (1929) *The Victorian Romantics, 1850–1870: The Early Work of Dante Gabriel Rossetti, William Morris, Burne-Jones, Swinburne, Simeon Solomon and their Associates*, Hamden, Ct: Archon Books.

Wood, C. (1981) *The Pre-Raphaelites*, New York: Viking.

Chapter Five

Losing his religion

Saint Sebastian as contemporary gay martyr

Richard A. Kaye

> 'My dear, I've done some pieces which will delight you ... They're a new departure, newish anyway, and rather religious and full of feeling. One's a kind of *sacra coversazione* between Saint Sebastian and John the Baptist. The young man who modelled Sebastian was almost in tears when I showed it to him, it's so lovely.'
>
> 'How did you do the arrows?' I interrupted, remembering Mishima's arduous posing in a self-portrait as Sebastian.
>
> "Oh, no arrows, dear; it's before the martyrdom. He's quite unpierced. But he looks ready for it, somehow, the way I've done it.'
>
> (Alan Hollinghurst, *The Swimming-Pool Library* 1988)[1]

Set in a pre-AIDS idyll of casual *amours* and campy *badinage*, Alan Hollinghurst's *The Swimming-Pool Library* is the Pillow Book of urban homosexual life as played out in the clubs, cafés and homes of London in 1983. Saint Sebastian, the Roman martyr traditionally represented in Renaissance painting as a beautiful semi-nude youth pierced with arrows, is a recurring motif in Hollinghurst's novel as a kind of kitsch homosexual totem, a subcultural artifact guaranteed to bring an immediate smile to the knowing reader. And as this playful exchange between the novel's young hero William Beckwith and the elderly painter Ronald Staines suggests, even in the absence of the arrows that have so often defined Sebastian's position as the 'homosexual saint', the martyr retains his almost mystical associations of gay identity. Pierced or unpierced, Saint Sebastian has endured in the popular imagination as the patron saint of homosexual men, a figure who winkingly seems to mock religious ecstasy as an erotic put-on. Despite the ease with which writers such as Hollinghurst have exploited Sebastian's camp associations, however, it would be a mistake to see the martyr's incarnations as comprising little beyond an inside joke for self-consciously homosexual men.

In the following pages, I want to explore a constellation of instances in the representation of Sebastian in contemporary writing, painting, photography, film and performance art, noting, as well, Sebastian's nineteenth-century and *fin-de-siècle* associations, so decisive for subsequent perceptions of the Roman martyr. In addition to suggesting how the saint's history encompasses more than the role of aesthete's camp trope, I hope to explore some historically grounded bases for Sebastian's position as the most frequently renewed and successfully deployed emblem of homosexual consciousness. Whether he has served as the focus of a feature-length movie by the director Derek Jarman, of a music video for the rock group R.E.M.'s 'Losing My Religion', or, most recently, of a contentiously fought-over activist performance piece by Ron Athey, Saint Sebastian has emerged as the very distillation in art of an emotionally and politically fraught homosexual persona. Today, with the AIDS epidemic reviving the martyr's role in the Middle Ages as a 'plague saint', Sebastian's symbolic importance has intensified, as he has solidified his reputation as an emblem of modern gay identity *in extremis*.[2]

Just as each successive epoch has created an image for Jesus – rabbinical sage in the first century, 'universal man' in the early modern period, liberator of the people in the nineteenth century – many of the preoccupations of succeeding cultural eras may be linked to Sebastian's various incarnations. A Christian saint invoked against illness throughout medieval times, exquisite, beardless youth of Apollonian beauty in the Renaissance, 'decadent' androgyne throughout the nineteenth century, and self-consciously homosexual emblem in the twentieth, Saint Sebastian today has sustained his role as a distinctly 'perverse' martyr. Owing partly to the medicalization of homosexuality as a distinctly feminizing illness at the *fin de siècle*, Sebastian has come to represent the formation – and self-formation – of the modern male homosexual. Refusing to take his place with the obsolete icons of earlier epochs, he has enhanced his position as the single most successfully deployed image of modern male gay identity.

That status is powerfully complicated, however, by the enigma attached to Sebastian's solitariness of visual effect, in which, in a paradox essential to the martyr's enduring appeal, Sebastian's 'homosexuality' is assumed even as it is never explicitly articulated. Continually the focus of intense erotic fascination, Sebastian's sexual predilections historically have remained alluringly ambiguous, for, strictly speaking, however sexually potent his archetypal pose, there is nothing *necessarily* homosexual in an image of a youthful, handsome male shot through with arrows. This may be one reason a number of twentieth-century artists have felt the need to embellish their images of Sebastian with details that are additionally coded as gay. (In a 1934 painting, for example, the French artist Albert Courmes dressed his half-nude Sebastian in a French sailor's outfit, while the American painter Marsden Hartley's 1939 *Sustained Comedy – Portrait of An Object* presents an evident figure of the saint, equipped with tank top and tattoos of a butterfly, muscleman and a sailor, in a portrait that was considered so provocative that Hartley was advised not to exhibit the work publicly.[3])

Nearly all of the martyr's incarnations have emerged from a series of invented or embellished aspects of the myth of a saint who, in brave defence of his Christian faith and comrades, was said to have risked his life. Victorian religious thinkers sought to 'muscularize' Saint Sebastian along with a Jesus who they imagined had become, at the hands of Catholic fundamentalists, fecklessly effeminate. Later, mischief-minded 'decadents' discovered in the martyr Sebastian a semi-covert image of a homoerotic, boyish comeliness that often had been an unacknowledgeable component in Jesus's own iconographic appeal. Yet, as a subordinate theological player who had nonetheless become a pervasive Renaissance effigy of male beauty, Sebastian was more vulnerable to wilful, homoerotic 'misinterpretation'. Beginning in the twentieth century, Sebastian became, pre-eminently, the homosexual as beleaguered, existential hero.[4] Far more problematically, he has come to stand for the supposedly sado-masochistic nature of male same-sex eroticism. While generations of men of homosexual inclinations have understood Sebastian as a homoeroticized icon, for others he has denoted a homosexual eros that is menacingly narcissistic and suicidal in kind. In a paradox that goes to the heart of the saint's continuing resonance, contemporary gay men have seen in Sebastian at once a stunning advertisement for homosexual desire (indeed, a homoerotic ideal), and a prototypical portrait of tortured closet case.

This last conception confirms the common cultural dogma that sees the homosexual male as a death-tempting, Faustian experimenter in the fast lanes of contemporary erotic life. This evident paradox in the modern-day cult of Saint Sebastian (and one which a number of artists have continually sought to reconcile) indicates that the most salient emblem of homosexual identity is one with strong implications of compulsive sado-masochistic desire, erotic mayhem, and self-preening effeminacy. It is as if the most efficacious symbol of twentieth-century womanhood were Ophelia, or, that of Jewish identity, Shylock. Sebastian is (to borrow a term from the critic

Bram Dijkstra) an 'idol of perversity' continually chosen by homosexually identified men, who discovered in the Roman saint a figure of secret, deathly glamour.[5] In a nearly delirious 1983 tribute to Saint Sebastian, the French writer Michel del Castillo sees the 'pleasure of dying' as a key part of the appeal of the saint, a man 'abandoned in delicious and lascivious agony'. *Exulted Del Castillo:* 'Generations of smitten young men in the secret of their hearts, in their very being, have been caressed by the look and touch of his muscles.'[6]

Sebastian's complex cultural legacy suggests the ungovernable set of meanings generated by any given representation, a testament to the ways in which the offerings of high culture remain susceptible to popular appropriation as subcultural icons. Inadvertently having helped to spawn a figure of considerable homoerotic power, the mandarins of the Catholic church warily looked on as Sebastian escaped his legitimate theological role and became a trope for artists linked to the aestheticist movement such as Gustave Moreau, Odilon Redon, Wilde and Beardsley. In a failed attempt at recuperating Sebastian from those who would exploit him as a hero of perversity, the Catholic clergy condemned the 1911 Paris production of Claude Debussy's and Gabriele d'Annunzio's *Le Martyre de Saint Sébastien*, starring the famed Russian dancer Ida Rubinstein. Rubinstein's cries during her execution by arrows – 'Encore! Encore!' – marked a watershed year in Sebastian's devolution into decadent icon.[7] Images of Sebastian became a recurring source of irrepressible longing. 'The Church, in fact, excited more sexual wonderment than it repressed', the author Richard Rodriguez recalled of the religious icons dominating his Catholic Mexican–American boyhood. 'I would study pictures of martyrs – white robed virgins fallen in death and the young, almost smiling St Sebastian, transfigured in pain.' For Rodriguez, the saint 'touched alive some very private sexual excitement'.[8]

As either an emphatic or oblique symbol in the work of an astonishingly diverse range of modern artists – among them Pater, Wilde, Mann, Rilke, Kafka, Georg Trakl, Proust, Gabriele d'Annunzio, T.S. Eliot, Wallace Stevens, García Lorca, and Auden – Saint Sebastian has signalled sexuality beyond acceptable bounds. An attractive emblem for modernist poetics, Sebastian sometimes has been deliberately shorn of his homosexual affiliations in favour of a more generalized erotic 'perversity'. Indeed, while it is Sebastian's 'queer' dimension that has proven so crucial to his contemporary popularity, there have been attempts, not all of them homophobic in kind, to depict Sebastian as transcending associations of same-sex eroticism.[9] Nonetheless, Sebastian's fate in modern and contemporary representation is, above all else, the story of the mischievous appropriation of Christian symbolism and Renaissance imagery by homosexually identified men. More than any other figure of Christian iconography, Saint Sebastian has sustained a subculturally resonant homoerotic role. It is a reputation that was enhanced, long before deliberate appropriation became a benchmark of postmodernist representation, by continual borrowings from Italian Renaissance iconography.

Perhaps the most important question to ask in considering the figure of Saint Sebastian as a touchstone of distinctly homosexual implications is, why Sebastian? Precisely how, when and why did a relatively minor figure in Christian theology and the history of Christianity become such a significant marker of 'degenerate' eros and homosexual consciousness in the modern period? For Renaissance painters, for whom Sebastian was nearly as popular a subject as Jesus or Mary, the saint provided the occasion for a coherent accommodation of Christian and Hellenic strains in European culture, an enhancement of what the art historian Edgar Wind famously has termed the 'pagan mysteries' of the Italian Renaissance.[10] The multiplicity of contemporary meanings generated by the martyr's legend stem from this rich reservoir of Renaissance iconography but also from the murky, historically shifting nature of the details – nearly all of them apocryphal – concerning the circumstances of Sebastian's life. For a myth to prove as resilient as a cultural narrative as that of Sebastian, it must generate broad, multiple, and even contradictory meanings.[11] One obvious answer to the question of the martyr's continual appeal is suggested by the arrows that penetrate Sebastian in the classic renditions by painters such as Tintoretto, Titian, Guido Reni, Perugino, Botticelli and Bazzi ('Il Sodoma'), to name only the more celebrated versions by Renaissance artists.[12] The archetypal Renaissance image of the saint as ecstatically receptive to arrows suggests, of course, a desire for penetration and thus embraces associations of male homosexuality.[13] The penetrated (and therefore feminized) male in the Renaissance paintings of Saint Sebastian is, significantly, a figure of visibly triumphant bliss.

Saint Sebastian's homosexual status may by related, as well, to aspects of the saint's life as they have been relayed through various historical sources. The earliest reference to the saint can be found in the *Martyrology* of AD 354, which refers to him as a young nobleman from either Milan or Narbonne, whose official capacity was as a commander of a company of archers in the imperial bodyguard. Predictably, the Catholic Church has never given its assent to the 'homosexual myth' of Saint Sebastian, although, as the art historian James Saslow has noted, the Church's *Acta Sanctorum* does indicate an emotional bond between Sebastian and his commanding officers, noting that Sebastian 'intatum caras erat Imperatoribus Diocletiano et Maximano' – ('was dearly beloved of the Emperors Diocletian and Maximian').[14] Equally important is a description in the *Acta Sanctorum* noting that Sebastian came to the rescue of the Christian soldiers Marcellinus and Mark and thereby confessed his own Christianity. Diocletian demanded that Sebastian be shot by his comrade-archers. When these orders were carried out, Sebastian was left for dead. Miraculously, according to legend, he survived, owing to the aid of a woman named Irene. Diocletian was obliged to order a second execution, and this time Sebastian was beaten to death in the Hippodrome.[15] It is a testament to the extraordinary power of the figure of an arrow-pierced young man, to the concentrated force of what might be called an apocalyptic image, that this last detail of Sebastian's allegorical narrative, the miracle necessary for official sainthood, is rarely exploited or even noted by artists taking up Sebastian's legend. Yet it is exactly this spectacular survival that remains decisive to his homoerotic mythos as a masochistic figure whose actions, to quote the historian Edith Simon, demonstrated a 'miraculous invulnerability, showing that the saint could save himself if he would, followed by submission to mortality at the next attempt to execute him'.[16]

Another explanation for the correlations linking Sebastian with homosexual desire is related to developments in late-Victorian sexual theory. As a martyr with long-standing associations of disease (since classical times, arrows denoted divine wrath as expressed through plagues), Sebastian appears to have become a fitting embodiment of the transition whereby homosexual desire, once a theologically construed sin, was increasingly understood in the late-Victorian epoch as medical illness.[17] The image of an eroticized religious hero – simultaneously sacred and heretical in meaning – embodies precisely this historical transition. The elucidation of the homosexual in late-Victorian scientific discourse began as an understanding of Saint Sebastian as an object lesson in homosexuality as inevitably linked to sado-masochistic desire. The prototypal Renaissance image of Sebastian – his body willingly exposed to view, semi-clad, face averted in a frontally visible pose – was isomorphic with turn-of-the-century scientific, medical and anthropological representation of the individual. Like the late nineteenth-century representation of the hystericized female, who provided a dramatically visualized conception of medical illness for physicians such as Jean-Martin Charcot, the body of Saint Sebastian furnished a series of imagistically dynamic associations for the scientific conceptualization of the homosexual. As one who had endured near-death, Sebastian the survivor became a fitting visual embodiment of the psychological state of the psychiatry's hysterical male and, with the arrival of the First World War, the shell-shocked soldier. During the years of the Great War, the imagery of military accoutrements associated with Saint Sebastian inspired a spate of homoerotic poems revelling in the soldier Sebastian's aura of morbid sensuality.[18]

The pioneering German sexologist Magnus Hirschfeld, who had sought to locate a basis in biology for same-sex desire as a prerequisite for legislation favourable to homosexuals, placed 'pictures of St Sebastian', in the first rank of art works in which the 'invert' takes special delight.[19] Hirschfeld's observation forced a point that modern discourse surrounding the homosexual continually implied: it was not homosexual *acts* that constituted homosexual identity, but a desire or 'taste' in beautiful men, which might be understandable as a kind of homosexual aesthetic. In the absence of a 'community' of homosexual-identified men, Sebastian signified the possibility of a homosexual identity or, more abstractly, a homosexual sublime. Jean Cocteau, who as a young man had attended Rubinstein's performance and written a poem entitled 'Les Archers de Saint Sébastien', recalled that Proust left the self-imposed exile of his Paris apartment only once or twice a year – not to visit his fellow Parisians, whose anti-Dreyfussard sentiments repelled him, but in order to view a Saint Sebastian by Gustave Moreau in a friend's private collection or the version by Mantegna in the Louvre.[20]

From the huge Calvin Klein advertisements of physically flawless models that periodically loom over New York's Times Square, to their strapping male offspring in countless fashion magazines, from Victorian photographs of anthropological and medical subjects to the controversial 'posture photos' of American college students taken during the 1940s and 1950s, their torsos 'pinned' with rods and exposed for 'clinical' analysis, the imagery associated with Saint Sebastian has dominated the popular depiction of the human body. Affirming Sebastian's position as a solitary subject, contemporary psychoanalysis has frequently turned to the myth of the martyr as a way of conceiving of the precarious, concealed, or divided psychic self. Sebastian's titillatingly proffered promise of annunciatory revelation, a masculine fantasy of assuming a feminine role, has made the martyr an enduringly efficacious emblem of psychoanalytic self-revelation. Yet the saint signals his love of men only through his silent receptivity to arrows, as his 'confession' of homosexual eros is offered and withdrawn without the articulation of a sexual affiliation. In this sense, it is Sebastian's apparent assumption of a feminine role that dictates his 'perverse' status. Julia Kristeva has argued, in a highly suggestive formulation arising from an exploration of primary narcissism, that Sebastian is a paradigmatically modern 'soulosexual', one who will 'undergo martyrdom in order to maintain the fantasy that there exists a power, as well as its masochistic obverse–passivation, total "feminization" '.[21] The saint's role in the symbolic constitution of what might be characterized as the modern homosexual's 'subjective self' renders him an ideal focus for Lacanian analysis. In announcing a 1990 international conference on 'Traits de Perversions dans les structures cliniques', a poster for France's organization of Lacanian therapists, the Fondation du Champ Freudien, reproduced an image of Perugino's Saint Sebastian, now in the Louvre, around whose waist is casually draped a silky scarf and whose eyes contemplate the heavens as two arrows pierce his expansive torso. Sebastian the modern 'medical case' has reached his apotheosis as a poster boy for a leading school of psycho-analytic thought.

The martyr's self-absorbed detachment of visual effect is a fundamental aspect of his intricate mythology, for the archetypal image of an ecstatically self-preoccupied nude male would seem to grant erotic permission to nobody, and, yet, paradoxically, to every viewer. In rough psychoanalytic terms, then, the martyr provides the opportunity for an unobstructed, unmediated erotization, an opportunity notably diminished in, for example, an archetypal image of Ganymede, where a viewer (theoretically) would be required to 'triangulate' desire with the Greek god Zeus or (rather more awkwardly), the large eagle so characteristic in the Renaissance iconography of the myth of Ganymede. As with the solitary youth depicted in Michelangelo's *David* or Hippolyte Flandrin's *Jeune homme nu assis au bord de la mer* (both images that are frequently adopted as homosexual icons), Sebastian's basic narcissism provides for what might be termed a polymorphously perverse response on the part of the viewer.

The martyr's homoerotic associations also arise from his evident usefulness as a figure who replaced earlier, exhausted 'homosexual legends', particularly for those seeking appealing models of same-sex eros. As the English poet, author and religious eccentric Montague Summers declared in his 1907 volume *Antinous and Other Poems* (denounced on its publication as a 'cesspool of depravity'), Antinous and Aloysius are worshipped as Saint Sebastian in the modern era. Summers rejoiced: 'New gods arise, and antique alters fall'.[22] In Thomas Mann's *Death in Venice* (1912), Aschenbach, infatuated with an adolescent boy, embraces Sebastian as a 'new type of hero' of not 'merely passive beauty'.[23] The Japanese novelist Yukio Mishima's *Confessions of a Mask* (published in Japan in 1949 and in the United States in 1958) contains numerous allusions to homosexual figures in western culture (not only to Hadrian and Antinous but to Oscar Wilde), yet it is the figure of Sebastian that dominates Mishima's novel of adolescent homosexual self-awakening. If earlier classical and biblical 'homosexual myths' (most conspicuously, the stories of Hadrian and Antinous, Corydon and Alexis, Damon and Pythias, Theseus and Perithous, Zeus and Ganymede, and David and Jonathan) allowed for easy sentimentalization, the isolated, besieged figure of Sebastian suggests, instead, a deracinated mode of being.[24] Previous mythic tales of same-sex eroticism differ substantially from the Sebastian saga in that they are all largely reducible to narratives of love gloriously consummated (the myth of Ganymede) or else cruelly severed (Hadrian and Antinous, Damon and Pythias).

Sebastian's narrative, however, unlike these earlier fables, stands as a romantic counter-myth; the bare details of his tale resist a too-lachrymose rendition.[25] According to Michel Del Castillo, Sebastian's essence is reducible to the pressing dilemma: 'How to live without living, how to live without loving?'[26] Even the British director Derek Jarman's embellishment of Saint Sebastian's mythology in his film *Sebastiane* (1976) with a tale of Roman commander Severus's love of Sebastian turns into a narrative of Sebastian's obdurate *refusal* to reciprocate Severus's affections. The crux of the saint's mythic power for writers and artists of the last century comprises an evolving dynamic of the self in isolation, in which a young, accomplished soldier announces a 'true' self and is therefore punished for his self-incriminating candour. Sebastian thus could stand for homosexual self-revelation as opposed to homosexual affection, and as such he was a splendid vehicle for a new conception of same-sex desire, which, as numerous historians of sexuality have suggested, encompassed a shift from a stress on homosexual *acts* to an emphasis on homosexual *identity*. And in a polemical turn concomitant with the self-assertive stance of the contemporary gay rights movement, many homosexual men embraced Sebastian because of his potential unsuitability as an exemplary model, given that the martyr's obvious sado-masochistic connotations – his proudly perverse character – lend him charismatic power as a defiantly deviant figure.

Not least consequential among the elements in Sebastian's twentieth-century cultural history is the martyr's usefulness as a camp artist's vengeance on the citadels of high culture and the upholders of religious hypocrisy. The self-cognizant homosexual retaliating against a Church that continues to forbid same-sex activity has continually found in Sebastian a formidable ally, for Sebastian's presence in Christian iconography intimated at the Church's knowing accommodation of an illicit, possibly pederastic, sexuality. 'It was said that when Rome was most immoral', mused the American novelist Glenway Wescott in his *Calendar of Saints for Unbelievers* (1932), 'it became a convention for the popes and lesser ecclesiastical lords to have their boy-sweethearts painted as St Sebastian. Then, a good many immodest fantastic pictures must be regarded as portraits of personages of great consequence in church politics.'[27] However amusing it is to encounter such impish interpretations of sanctioned Church history (and they indirectly resonate as political gestures given the Catholic Church's historic intolerance of homosexuality), the 'camp tradition' in Sebastian worship heralded by Beardsley comprised only one module of the twentieth-century 'cult' of Saint Sebastian.

An altogether different note is struck, for example, in a series of remarkable *c.* 1906 depictions of the martyr that were executed by the turn-of-the-century Massachusetts photographer and self-fashioned aesthete Fred Holland Day, who was affiliated with the coterie of Whistler, Beardsley and other *fin-de-siècle* decadents (see Figures 5.1 and 5.2). To the extent that the photograph is linked to the aesthetic developments engendered by modernity, these images are the earliest 'modern' representations of Saint Sebastian. By the time he turned to Saint Sebastian as a theme, Day had become notorious in Britain and the United States for his 1898 Crucifixion series, in which an emaciated Day had photographed himself as Jesus on the cross.

What is notable about Day's images of Sebastian – some of a boy-saint, others of a Sebastian as an adolescent – is the extent to which they require the viewer to resist the familiar terms of camp aesthetics. Day's photographs generally have been viewed as aesthetically regressive in their kitschy reliance on Renaissance iconography's 'sacred subjects', yet, surprisingly, Day's depiction of Sebastian intensifies a highly popular tendency of the photographic medium at its inception, one which involved photographing the recently deceased as a way of preserving the memories of the living. Such origins intimated that the morbidly voluptuous Sebastian, who apocryphally had survived his initial execution, would be especially fitting for photographic representation. Early in his career as a photographic 'Pictorialist', Day worked in silver prints but he soon turned to platinum, which he combined with gum bichromate techniques to give himself more direct control over highlights and design effects. Bathed in soft hues, Day's images of Sebastian strive for a documentary-like verisimilitude, although the

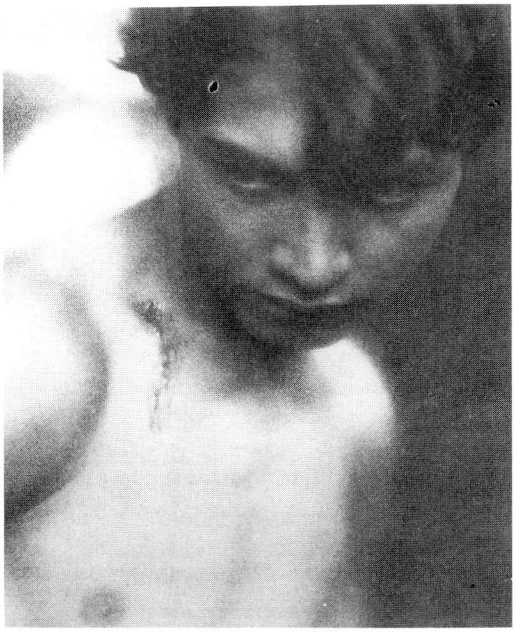

Figure 5.1 F. Holland Day, *Saint Sebastian* (*c.* 1906) Library of Congress.

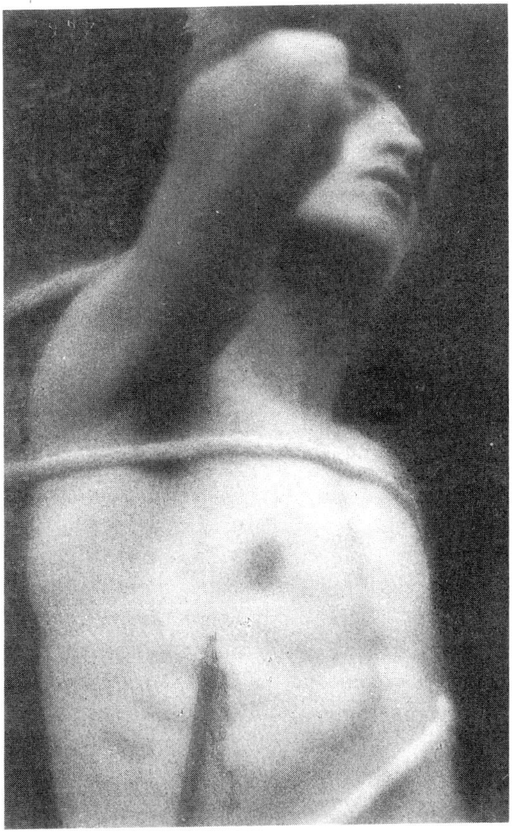

Figure 5.2 F. Holland Day, *Saint Sebastian* (*c.* 1906) Library of Congress.

photographer delicately altered his finished images by, for example, adding in pencil the wounds that can be seen on his young models. Just as Day had fasted himself in executing his Christ series to achieve greater 'accuracy' of effect, for his Sebastian study he selected working-class models, one of whom had an actual scar.

Viewed together, where they operate in a kind of sequence which seems to anticipate filmic movement, these photographs represent Sebastian as a maturing, physically mobile, dramatically charged figure in the throes of a final ecstasy – the capturing of fleeting instants in the martyr's protracted death-delirium. Day's pseudo-documentary approach record a series of private reveries, a closed-off world voyeuristically intruded on by the camera. His face momentarily obscured, Day's Hellenic ephebe is a spectral presence, but one whose homoeroticism must be projected onto an image by the viewer or else assumed as residing in an oblique code. In their seeming indulgence in isolated reveries, these Sebastians recall Narcissus, a time-honoured homosexual trope, but a Narcissus gone beyond simple self-love into masturbatory self-infatuation.[28] Day's Saint Sebastians are poised on a historical precipice in which homosexual desire was entering public consciousness but was inexpressible except in highly coded terms. By the time Day photographed his Sebastian series, the Wilde trials already had put an end to the homoerotic imagery pervasive in the British academic painting of Lawrence Alma-Tadema and Frederick Leighton.

Nonetheless, Day's iconography of homoerotic 'narcissism' allowed for the accommodation of a visually isolated, erotically charged male in lieu of a more emphatic depiction of eroticism between men. Moreover, Day's unique aesthetic of the camera, which held that the photographer must artfully invent rather than 'capture' a sensually available 'real' world, meant that each of his images had as much distinctiveness as a canvas by Perugino or Guido Reni. Yet, despite Day's reputation as a 'painterly' photographer, in his rendering of Saint Sebastian as a mobile figure he also freed the Roman martyr from the domain of Renaissance iconography. (George Bernard Shaw noted the new component offered by Day's work when, praising the 'fine sympathy' of the photographer's images as displayed in a 1901 London exhibition, he remarked on Day's avoidance of 'sham brush and pencil' effects in favour of an authentic 'photographic technique'.[29]) In addition to allowing Sebastian to enter the unruly age of mechanical reproduction, in which images of the physically resplendent Roman athlete became as everyday as baseball cards, Day's 'fictive' depictions of Saint Sebastian went to the heart of the martyr's deepening fascination at the beginning of the new century. Christian saints could be 'invented' as 'homosexual martyrs' just as the man of same-sex erotic preferences was being conjured up as a distinct category.

The caginess with which more than one artist characterized Sebastian's sexual temperament is also related to an impulse to render the martyr as a manly, solitary athlete. In Mishima's *Confessions of a Mask*, the hero pens an 'unfinished prose poem' on the life of Sebastian that includes the following speculations:

> When one considers well, it seems likely that many a time, even in the midst of a sweet kiss, a foretaste of the agony of death must have furrowed his brow with a fleeting shadow of pain.
>
> Also, he must have foreseen, if dimly, that it was nothing less than martyrdom which lay in wait for him along the way; that this brand which Fate had set upon him was precisely the token of his apartness from all the ordinary men of earth.
>
> Now, on that particular morning, Sebastian kicked off his covers and sprang from bed at break of day, pressed with martial duties.[30]

Mishima's carefully calculated ambiguity as to whom Sebastian has kissed, the intimation of a deathly trance in that kiss, the author's doting on the image of the waking military man, all of these details build to an eroticization of a figure who is notably prevented from assuming a transparently homosexual personality. It would seem to be, rather, the imaginary reader's desires that Mishima aims to shape in such passages, as the reader encounters the waking, brooding 'bachelor' Sebastian. Accentuating the bonds between the saint's pictorial and novelistic incarnations, Mishima's fantasy of Sebastian as a haunted 'soulosexual' replicates at the level of literary narrative the experience of viewing an image of a Saint Sebastian. Sexually aroused to masturbation by a Guido Reni Sebastian, Mishima's hero both worships and identifies with the martyr because 'In no way was his a pitiable fate. Rather was it proud and tragic, a fate that might even be called shining.' Mishima's narrator actually adopts Sebastian's gestures as he has gleaned them from Reni's painting:

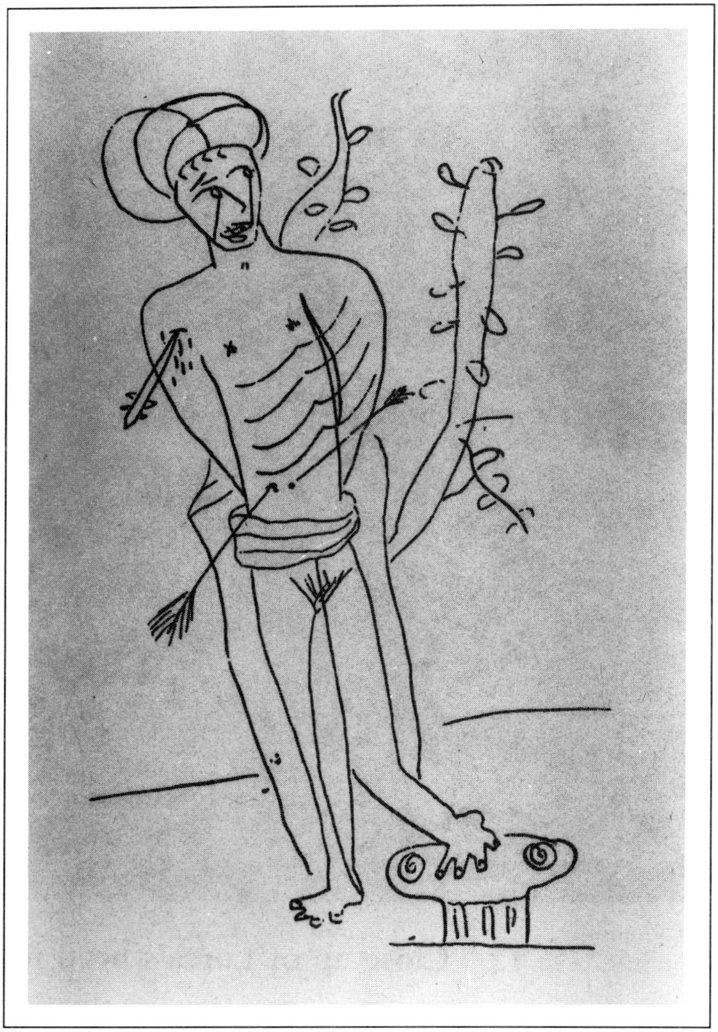

Figure 5.3 Federico García Lorca, *Saint Sebastien* (*c.* 1927). Drawing. By permission of Elizabeth Weisberg, ARS, New York, NY.

> Ever since becoming obsessed with the picture of St Sebastian, I had acquired the unconscious habit of crossing my hands over my head whenever I happened to be undressed. Mine was a frail body, without so much as a pale shadow of Sebastian's abundant beauty. But now once more I spontaneously fell into the pose. As I did so my eyes went to my armpits. And a mysterious sexual desire boiled up within me ... (Mishima's ellipses)[31]

There could scarcely be a finer example of a suddenly self-aware homosexual male deriving his self-conception – at the most basic self-constitutive level of unconsciously expressed behaviour – from the Renaissance iconography of Saint Sebastian. That the Japanese youth of Mishima's novel, yearning for a suitable outlet for his homosexual and masturbatory impulses, finds himself reaching for an icon from western painting suggests Sebastian's international symbolic resonance as a homosexual trope by the beginning of the twentieth century. Beyond its direct allusions to Saint Sebastian, *Confessions of a Mask* is studded with arrow and piercing imagery, usually surrounding its hero's increasingly violent sexual fantasies of stabbing a ravishing young man.

Mirroring the narrator's personal obsessions is the suicidally militaristic drive of Japan itself, propelling itself towards a global war that its citizens are depicted as neither supporting nor understanding. *Confessions of a Mask* is set during the war years, where Saint Sebastian emerges as a touchstone of a larger national crisis in the aftermath of the bombings of Hiroshima and Nagasaki.

Sebastian as representative of the generation confronting the Second World War recalls the doomed Sebastian Flyte of Evelyn Waugh's *Brideshead Revisited* (1944), while the reliance on the martyr as the corporeal exemplum had its campy beginnings in Ronald Firbank's *The Flower Beneath the Foot* (1923). Firbank's dandyish hero enjoys a bath in which he lies 'beneath the rhythmic sponge, perfumed with *Kiki*', where 'he was St Sebastian, and, as the water became cloudier, and the crystals evaporated amid the steam, he was Teresa ... and he would have been, most likely, the Blessed Virgin herself but the bath grew gradually cold'.[32] For a number of writers, imagining oneself as violently pierced suggests the traumatic crucible in which modern homosexual identity is forged. 'Like glittering, vicious footballs of ice, the huge diamonds struck his head', records the narrator Orvil of a 'terrifying and wonderful' dream in Denton Welch's *In Youth Is Pleasure* (1950), 'tearing the flesh till his eyes were filled with blood and he could feel the points of adamant ringing on white bone'.[33]

The camp dimension so integral to Sebastian's appeal stemmed from a comic view of the martyr's classic poses of exquisite satisfaction and pained detachment. In a 1927 essay on Saint Sebastian, the Spanish artist Salvador Dalí saw the martyr as representing the concept of 'Holy Objectivity', by which Dalí meant the modern artist's wry refusal to surrender to the cheaply sentimental. 'Irony ... is nakedness', noted Dalí, 'It is the gymnast who hides behind the pain of St Sebastian. And it is also this pain, because it can be recounted.'[34] Sebastian's nakedness, for Dalí, is also a mask. That Dalí was attracted to the iconography of Saint Sebastian is appropriate given the convulsive and arguably surrealist nature of Sebastian's image of death-in-life. Dalí's friendship with the poet Federico García Lorca was animated by droll references to Saint Sebastian. In addition to embellishing a photograph of Dalí depicting the painter as a Sebastian, Lorca drew his own version of the saint (Figure 5.3). The wry spirit of Lorca's sketch, in which a pained Sebastian – the Christian martyr as artist's doodle – uneasily totters on his pedestal, exploits the ridiculousness of Sebastian's celebrated role as upbeat survivor. This image is less a study in suffering than in nervous anxiety: Saint Sebastian having a particularly bad day.

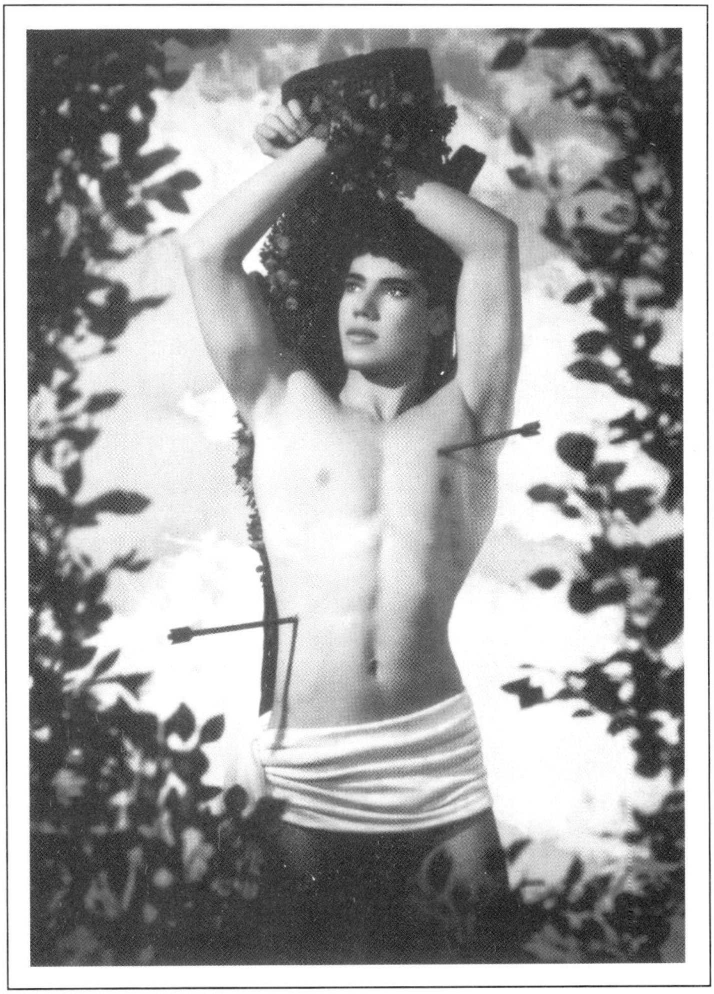

Figure 5.4 Pierre and Gilles, *Saint Sebastian* (1987), 40cm x 53cm, colour photograph
By permission of Samia Saouma Gallery, Paris.

Even when deployed by homosexual artists or as a homoerotic trademark, however, Saint Sebastian was often represented as palpable evidence of the dangers inherent in same-sex erotic relations. Tennessee Williams's 1958 play *Suddenly Last Summer* is best known in the celebrated film version directed by Joseph L. Mankiewicz starring Katherine Hepburn, Montgomery Clift and Elizabeth Taylor, with a screenplay by Williams and Gore Vidal. Mankiewicz's movie details the decline of Sebastian Venable, a young poet who courts death on the Playa San Sebastian in Cabeza de Lobo by preying on local boys, using his cousin Catherine (her name suggests Saint Sebastian's original saviour, Irene) as unknowing sexual bait. Here Sebastian signifies sexuality as unutterably beyond representation; Sebastian Venable is glimpsed only subliminally in a few frames. Viewed today, *Suddenly Last Summer* seems the apotheosis of Eisenhower-era camp sensibility.[35]

Such kitschy affiliations endure in our own time in the work of the French artists Pierre and Gilles, who produced a 1987 image of Sebastian as a tanned young man whose bee-stung lips and glassy eyes evoke the Hollywood motion pictures of Douglas Sirk, the popular religious art of Latin America, and, with roses dangling from his head to his mid-torso, a Saint Sebastian in Carmen Miranda drag (Figure 5.4). His cherubic innocence suggests a pop fantasy of 1950s serenity, in which Sebastian has become a technicolour dreamboat. The British artist Matthew Stradling sustains Sebastian's camp iconographic tradition in his 1991 *The Weeping Flesh*, which presents a red-haired, Firbankian Sebastian, accessorized with a pearl bracelet against a plush rose- and gold-décor backdrop, whose wounds drip drops of pearly tears (see Figure 11.1 page 141).

A number of poetic works, however, continued to emphasize a Saint Sebastian of palpably appealing sensuality. In one of his most memorable poems, written in 1960, the American poet Frank O'Hara offered a startling declaration to his beloved:

> Having a Coke with You
> is even more fun than going to San Sebastian, Irun, Hendaye,
> Biaritz, Bayonne …
> partly because in your orange shirt you look like a better,
> happier St Sebastian
> partly because of my love for you, partly because of your
> love for yoghurt …
> and the portrait show seems to have no faces in it at all,
> just paint
> you suddenly wonder why in the world anyone ever did them
> I look
> at you and would rather look at you than all the portraits
> in the world …[36]

Ecstatically asserting the primacy of experience over aesthetic apprehension, Saint Sebastian for O'Hara represents the dead weight of art history, an inert and inadequate means of expressing the swiftly-moving consummation of homosexual *amours*. Recently, the African-American poet Reginald Shepherd devoted a poem evoking the Roman martyr that begins as an invocation of Reni's Saint Sebastian but ends with a doting view of a boy shopping in a supermarket:

> In the painting by Guido Reni of Saint Sebastian
> in the Palazzo Rosso, which reproduction makes available
> to those who travel only on the page, the saint to be
> (he's not yet assumed by artifice, encumbered
> with perfections) endures continual martyrdom
> with a visual sigh, gazing almost directly upward
> as it to ask *What now my love*, or hum a chorus of
> *Is that all there is*, the body always some song …

> ... One grasps that sainthood is an attribute of youth,
> the wondrous fair, as in old ballads; they always end.
>
> The boy in the Eagle Discount Supermarket,
> for another, an apparition in a backwards baseball cap
> appraising cuts of meat in artificial light,
> deciding what he can afford
>
> to buy, how much each cut costs. *I love the ground*
> *where he stands.* His face? Unverifiable.[37]

Like Frank O'Hara, Shepherd is drawn to Saint Sebastian not so much as the aesthetic embodiment of an ideal male but as a martyr who inspires thoughts of other, actual exquisite men, in this case a fashion-conscious ephebe in a grocery store. The bedazzled poet–customer is a veritable curator of desire, discovering in his lust-object a visage as 'unverifiable' as that painted by a Renaissance master. 'Attribution', of course, here suggests questions of the young man's erotic predilections. For O'Hara and Shepherd, reproductions of Sebastian have become as banal as comic books, but real-life Saint Sebastians occupy hallowed ground.

How to render the intensely immovable figure of Sebastian in cinematic terms was a challenge facing the late British filmmaker Derek Jarman in *Sebastiane* (1976), which proved the director's most controversial film. Scripted entirely in Latin and shot on a rickety budget, filmed on location in Sardinia, *Sebastiane* was greeted with a furor reminiscent of that which met the 1911 *Le Martyre de Saint Sébastien.* (At the film's première at the Locarno Film Festival, shouting matches broke out among viewers.) Today, it is difficult to imagine how Jarman's slow-paced, almost hallucinogenic movie might have inspired such violent reactions. Interestingly, the film is by no means the exercise in anachronistic theatricality one might have expected from the director who allowed Elizabeth Welch to sing 'Stormy Weather' in his film *The Tempest* and Annie Lennox her version of 'Everytime We Say Goodbye' in *Edward II.* Although Jarman recorded his pleasure at finding in the actor Leonardo Treviglio a 'Saint Sebastian out of *GQ*', Treviglio's martyr – bearded, unmuscular, and ascetic in appearance – suggests a more austere, primitivist saint typical of the medieval iconography of Sebastian.[38] With the exception of several scenes in which Roman soldiers nostalgically recall their work in Cecil B. DeMille's motion-picture extravaganzas, Jarman favours a sombre, funereal steadfastness of technique. Owing to Brian Eno's eerily reedy score, a desolate desert locale and the general visual austerity, *Sebastiane* recalls the early films of Pasolini as well as Liliana Cavani's 1966 directorial debut, *St Francis of Assisi.*

The film narrates its subject's banishment to a remote outpost of the Roman empire and his persecution as a pacifist Christian who refuses to fight when called upon to do so by his brutal commanding officer Severus. (Diocletian makes a brief appearance in the film's prologue as a roué at a Bacchanalian orgy in which he orders the death of a young follower suspected of betrayal.) What sets off the call for Sebastian's execution, however, is his refusal to respond to the romantic attentions of Severus, who attempts to rape Sebastian while declaring his love for the young man he pursues obsessively. In a time-honoured move, Sebastian's own sexuality is left ambiguous. 'You will never have me', he tells Severus in Latin, leaving it unclear if others might. By turns kindly, high-minded, and ethereal, Jarman's saint is a child of nature who listens to seashells and only inadvertently inspires a destructive lust in Severus. It is Severus – blond, obsessed, psychotic – who is the true tormented sado-masochist of Jarman's movie. Rebuffed by his diffident charge, he arranges Sebastian's execution and forces the future martyr's fellow-archers to shoot their god-like leader. In its highlighting of Sebastian's loyalty to his comrades in the face of Severus's cruelty, Jarman's film extricated a latent, underexplored political element of the martyr's legend by emphasizing the bonds of class allegiance.

In the film's slow-motion last sequence, Sebastian's death-by-arrows is the symbolic acting out of an erotic penetration refused to Severus in life. The execution suggests a gang rape, in which a homosexual identity is forced on Sebastian metaphorically as Sebastian's tormentors become the necessary instruments of the martyr's homosexualization. In his memoirs *At Your Own Risk: A Saint's Testament*, Jarman characterized the martyr as an unwilling but ultimately receptive target: 'Sebastian, the doolally Christian who refused a good fuck, gets the arrows he deserves. Can one feel sorrow for this Catholic closet case? Stigmata who sports his wounds on a thousand altars like a debutante.'[39]

Despite the studied lugubriousness of Jarman's cinematic technique – a far cry from the subsequent, lushly realized style of *Carravagio* and *Edward II* – *Sebastiane* achieves moments of considerable mythic power. Jarman's decision to render Sebastian as the object of homosexual lust rather than as a 'homosexual martyr' not only echoed a rich tradition in the representation of Sebastian, it renders his film curiously orthodox in its approach to its subject. *Sebastiane* is, notwithstanding the controversy the film initially aroused, a religious 'life' of Saint Sebastian as a devout Catholic of homosexual leanings might have conceived it. Jarman should not have been too astonished when, as he noted in an earlier volume of his memoirs, a Catholic priest stopped him on the street after the film's première and told him how much he admired the film, its Latin dialogue in particular.[40] The director credited the turmoil surrounding his film with having inspired the rumblings of a gay movement in Switzerland. Uneasy distributors, meanwhile, kept the film out of circulation for a decade.[41]

Having crystallized as an explicitly gay symbol, Sebastian also increasingly signified the irreconcilability of disparate ideological tendencies vying for dominance in contemporary gay culture. However much homosexual aesthetes might embrace his image as an icon who struck masochistic chords while retaining the imprimatur of high art, for many the martyr continued to hold insupportable associations of a too-passive self-renunciation. The martyr's suitability as homosexual symbol in a period of post-Stonewall political self-assurance became shaky. 'Sebastian's lost his appropriateness as the official gay patron after the Stonewall riots', flatly noted one popular work of gay history. 'Modern Sebastians, after all, shoot back.'[42]

But with the burgeoning AIDS epidemic, Sebastian the historic soldier comes to represent the militant, newly politicized homosexual, beautifully exposed to his fate but non-passively, even militantly, *contra mundum*, a fantasy of the homosexual male as sexually appealing, manly activist. In the late 1980s and early 1990s, one witnesses a double transformation of Saint Sebastian: first, as a saint invoked to ward off the plague and thus of consoling value and, second, as a politically charged figure signifying not so much sado-masochism as government neglect and societal hostility. As such, Saint Sebastian symbolically encapsulates (and partly resolves) what the critic Douglas Crimp has identified as two vital, supposedly irreconcilable, components of gay culture in the age of AIDS: the labour of mourning and the work of political activism.[43]

As he collapsed his role as medieval plague saint and that of the gay man exposed to the threat of AIDS, Sebastian became an irresistible subject for artists. For the hypertalkative transvestite narrator Odette O'Doyle of James McCourt's 1993 'confessional' novel *Time Remaining*, the connection between the plague martyr of the late Middle Ages and modern homosexual identity hits with 'stunning force'. 'Does that not add a new and utterly eerie dimension to the configuration?' he asks.[44] That configuration was further enhanced given the disease's effect on intravenous drug users, whose needles and needle-marks symbolically resembled the arrows and arrow-marks of Sebastian. Nonetheless, 'martyrdom' seemed a rather troublesome term to characterize, even in metaphoric terms, the disease-besieged gay man or drug user in that the phrase seeks to designate as valiant those who may not be particularly heroic, but who are, no less sympathetically, simply sick. In Thom Gunn's 1992 elegy 'Lament', the poet invokes the state of martyrdom in tracing the evolution of disease in a friend yet finally eschews such terms in describing the ill:

Four nights, and on the fifth we drove you down
To the Emergency Room. That frown, that frown;
I've never seen such a rage in you before
As when they wheeled you through the swinging door.
For you knew, rightly, they conveyed you from
Those normal pleasures of the sun's kingdom
The hedonistic body basks within
And takes for granted – summer on the skin,
Sleep without break, the moderate taste of tea
In a dry mouth. You had gone on from me
As if your body sought out martyrdom
In the far Canada of a hospital room.[45]

Resisting the banality of conferring 'heroism' on everyone (a staple of such tributes to the dead as the 'AIDS Quilt'), 'Lament' instead addresses the desperation of sheer everyday survival, what Gunn calls 'This difficult, tedious, painful exercise' of illness. The sick crave health in 'Lament', not a martyr's canonization.

Borrowing much of the visual vocabulary of Jarman's *Carravagio* while appropriating the iconographic details of Russian Constructivism, the American rock group R.E.M. chose Saint Sebastian as the unifying figure in their 1991 award-winning video for the group's song 'Losing my Religion', in which the lead singer Michael Stipe sings and performs a solitary dance amid an array of Saint Sebastians modelled on pop images vaguely adopted from Renaissance painting. This lyrically emotive video, shot by the Indian director Tarsem, was at once a mournful meditation on the difficulties of revealing an illness, a lament on the results of announcing one's homosexuality, and a coyly knowing, autobiographical confession of gay self-identification at the heart of rock-music culture. With greater polemical intensity, the Los Angeles performance artist Ron Athey in his 1994 performance piece, 'HIV/AIDS Odyssey', part of his 'Martyrs and Saints' series, adopted the techniques of Artaud's 'theater of cruelty', to a self-enactment as a tattooed Sebastian (Figure 5.5). While passively receptive to invading arrows, Athey's body becomes a full-scale indictment of a neglectful public. In yet another reaction against

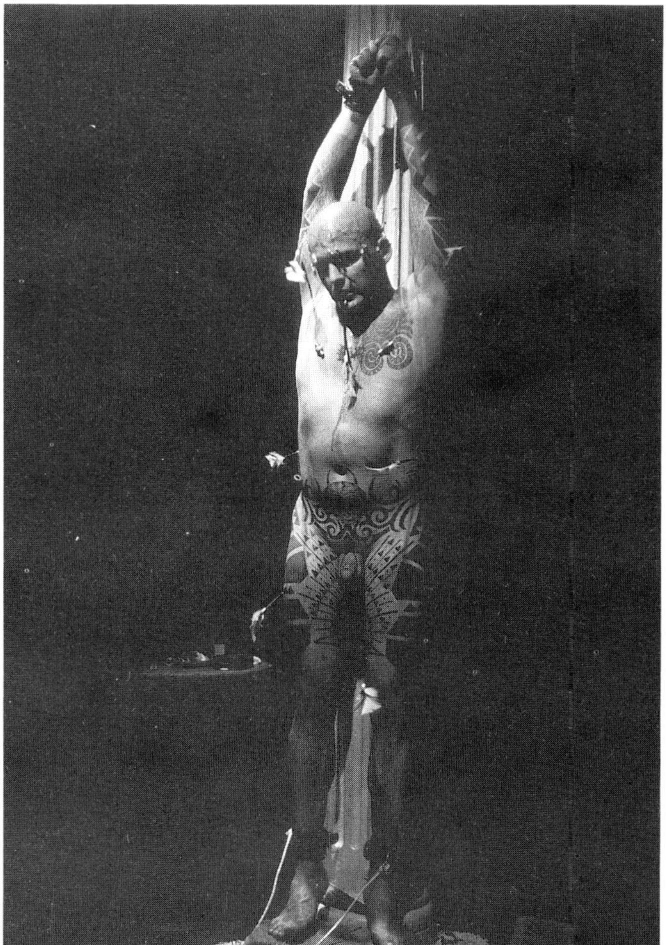

Figure 5.5 Performance artist Ron Athey, in *Martyrs and Saints* (1994) Photograph: Donna Ann McAdams.

government-funded gay art, Athey's performance became the target of critics of the 'new right'. One of the artist's 1994 works at a Minneapolis museum involved the drawing of blood from a young man sitting on stage, the blotting of the man's body with paper towels, and the hanging of those towels over the audience. Although the performance posed no dangers to members of the audience (the man was HIV negative), a Minneapolis newspaper implied as much, leading to an uproar in the US Congress given that a small portion of the performance was funded by the National Endowment for the Humanities. Athey became the focus of attacks by cultural conservatives, yet, in a notable departure from the practice of the Reagan–Bush years, the head of the National Endowment for the Arts lent her support to Athey and his work, declaring it an invaluable 'study of modern-day martyrdom as it relates to AIDS'.[46] Apart from its polemical force, the originality of Athey's conception lies in its aggressive renunciation of the martyr as impeccable Adonis. Several centuries of implied sado-masochism in the portrayal of Saint Sebastian are rendered overt in Athey's 'live' performance, next to which Mishima's self-portrait as an updated Sebastian by Guido Reni seems tamely stagy.

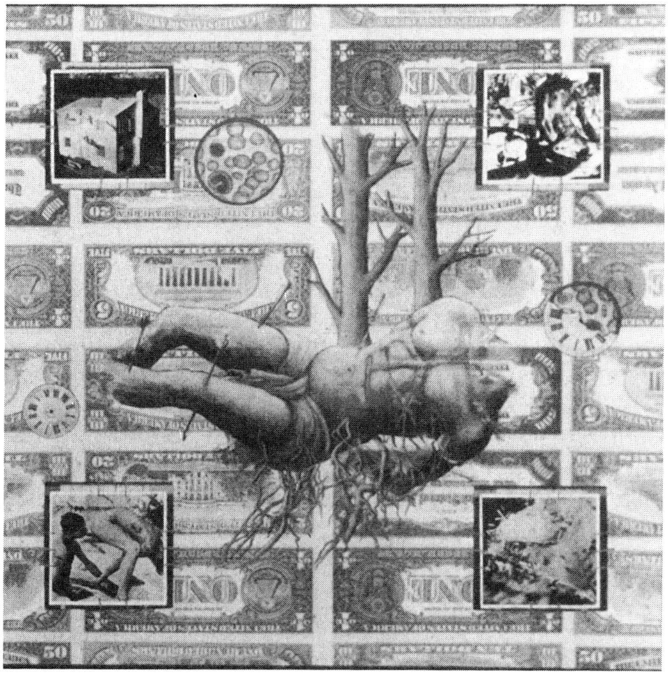

Figure 5.6 David Wojnarowicz, *Bad Moon Rising* (1989), acrylic
By permission of PPOW Gallery, New York City.

The vigorous politicization of Sebastian as contemporary plague saint assumed several forms throughout the 1980s and 1990s. A particularly compelling image utilizing Saint Sebastian is David Wojnarowicz's 1989 collage *Bad Moon Rising* (Figure 5.6), one of several works by the artist employing Saint Sebastian. (The spray-painted 1983 montage *Peter Hujar Dreaming: Yukio Mishima: St Sebastian*, is a homage to the Japanese writer.) As with the Pop artists he admired, Wojnarowicz typically 'uses borrowed imagery saturated with assumed meanings' in his work, as the critic Adam Kury has noted.[47] (The meanings of much Pop art may have been coded as homoerotic; Jaspar Johns's celebrated target paintings, as Kenneth Silver has noted, are an oblique allusion to the imagery of Saint Sebastian, particularly as in the 1955 collage *Target with Plaster Casts*, in which pieces of a plaster male body are positioned above the target.[48]) Wojnarowicz's work, however, retains an expressive gravity that Andy Warhol and such Warhol-indebted artists as Keith Haring coolly avoided. In a pointed diminishment of Sebastian as idealized virile athlete, *Bad Moon Rising* depicts the torso of a Sebastian image in which the head and feet have been eliminated as the saint's body is suspended horizontally against a tree and floats between four photographs pinned against a backdrop of US currency. Two of the photographs, pinned like snapshots at the bottom left and top left, depict what are evidently pornographic scenes. Another two images representing medical Petri dishes accentuate the saint's associations with illness. These free-moving juxtapositions serve to unite several thematic concerns:

Sebastian's subcultural homosexual meaning as an erotic icon, the undiminished threat of the AIDS crisis, and the urgency of finding a medical cure represented by a floating timepiece that is partly a Petri dish. It is the sheet of currency, however, that dominates the visual scheme of Wojnarowicz's montage, driving home the idea that a financial logic underlies and determines the fate of Sebastian and, by implication, that of the gay men he epitomizes. *Bad Moon Rising* registers the decomposition of an idolized queer icon before the effects of affliction and an inhumane money culture. It suggests, too, that a vigorously politicized art may borrow from a nuanced, recognizably homosexual iconography.

The multiplicity of examples of Saint Sebastian 'worship' I have discussed suggests not only the difficulty of assigning a single meaning to the Christian martyr but also the problem in viewing Sebastian as the symbolic property of any particular artist, individual or group. If the nineteenth century witnessed a battle over Saint Sebastian's appropriate religious character, as *fin-de-siècle* aesthetes battled with theological fundamentalists over the character of a Christian hero, more recent tensions concerning Sebastian reveal the competing interpretations of the martyr on the part of those who would see him as camp token, political comrade, or patron saint offering comfort against a new plague. And as his varying associations have accumulated over time, Saint Sebastian's homosexually inflected symbolism has come to suggest the intricate procedure through which is formed what we might call 'homosexual experience'. For it is not simply that gay men saw in Sebastian an idealized likeness of themselves. Rather, the Roman martyr helped form the very foundation for a sense of self that encompassed homosexual desire. This point is encapsulated in a 1987 poem invoking Saint Sebastian by Richard Howard, in which Howard hints at the perils of a too-close identification with the saint's aura of deathly ecstasy: 'Who else? What other throes could be/so eagerly submissive, so thrilling, so lewd?' Yet Howard went on to caution against a 'morbid appetite for arrows', noting that 'The moral is: *Don't pose as a Saint or you may become one ...*' .[49]

In an essay arguing against the historiographic tendency to see 'experience' as determining, in an unmediated fashion, the discrete identities of the subjects or groups neglected by traditional history, the historian Joan Wallach Scott has asserted that there is no foundational 'experience' that is without cultural mediation. There does not exist, Scott contends, a set of social or individual acts outside representation, which is to say, a discrete 'realm of reality outside of discourse'.[50] Scott's point could not be better illustrated than by an understanding of the complex ways in which gay-identified men have shaped themselves through representations of Saint Sebastian. In order to imagine themselves as 'homosexual subjects', men of same-sex erotic impulses turned to Sebastian, not just as Mann's 'new kind of hero' (that is, not just as a focus of hagiographic attention), but as a means of conceiving of the 'homosexual self'. For many of his ardent devotees, Saint Sebastian simultaneously served as an object of lustful devotion and a projection of an idealized 'homosexual self' – the idealized self as ideal lover. Yet, as Mishima's morbidly sensational identification with Sebastian indicates, such a relation to Sebastian did not always serve an enlightened conception of homosexual identity. Towards the end of his life, the Japanese novelist posed as Reni's Sebastian in a celebrated 1966 photograph, eerily anticipating – or even, one might say, hinting at – his own 1970 suicide by *seppuku*. Venturing to find a dramatic means of expressing his sense of himself as a reactionary outsider in the new Japanese social order, Mishima discovered in Sebastian the ideal western emblem for Japanese ceremonial suicide. In a grotesque culmination of his attraction for the homosexual artist, Saint Sebastian had emerged as a sado-masochistic exemplar to be emulated at any cost.

With the deaths of David Wojnarowicz, Derek Jarman and other gay artists, Sebastian has assumed what is arguably his weightiest role in his entire history as a homosexual emblem. Intensifying his value as an aesthete's token of perverse beauty and his usefulness as a politically freighted symbol, the martyred saint holds renewed emotional resonance for queer culture. In *Sebastiane*, Jarman had introduced a series of poems translated into Latin that summed up Sebastian's unique *mythos* as an exemplary martyr for those deemed social anathema.

He leaves the dark hours of the world.
See the arrows' wounds
His life blood drips in the sand
Marigolds spring up spreading their petals in the sun's
  rays, golden flowers of Apollo
Sebastian
Sebastian
Shower kisses on the young god with his golden eyes
Shower kisses on your beloved
And in the evening light
Remember this world of shadows.[51]

Given the evidence of his complex cultural legacy, the likelihood is great that the patron saint of homosexual men will not only remember, but that he will return yet again.

Notes

This essay is dedicated to the memory of Michael Sweas. Special thanks to Ron Athey, Richard Dellamora, Todd Shepard, Elaine Showalter, James Saslow, Jonathan Weinberg, and the staff at PPOW Gallery in New York. Thanks as well to Princeton University's Fund for Reunion, Princeton University's Committee on Italian Studies, and the New School for Social Research Faculty Development Fund, for financial support.

1 Alan Hollinghurst, *The Swimming-Pool Library*, New York: Vintage Books, 1988, 51.

2 Although there is compelling evidence that Sebastian held homoerotic associations as early as the Renaissance (Antonio's intense love for the youthful Sebastian in Shakespeare's 1600 *Twelfth Night* is a prime case), the possibility that Sebastian held homoerotic significance has been sharply disputed by scholars. See Wayne Dynes, 'Reply to James Saslow', *Gai Saber: Journal of the Gay Academic Union*, 1 (2), Summer 1977, 150–1.

3 See Jonathan Weinberg, *Speaking for Vice: Homosexuality in the Art of Charles Demuth, Marsden Hartley, and the First American Avant-Garde*, New Haven: Yale University Press, 1994, 185.

4 There were a number of attempts in the nineteenth century to retrieve Sebastian as a more robustly masculine religious image. In Cardinal Wiseman's 1854 life of Saint Sebastian, *Fabiola, or the Church of the Catacombs*, Sebastian is described as 'like a general on the battlefield'. Nicholas Wiseman, *Fabiola, or the Church of the Catacombs*, New York: P.J. Kennedy & Sons, 51.

5 Bram Dijkstra, *Idols of Perversity: Fantasies of Feminine Evil in Fin-de-Siècle Culture*, New York, Oxford University Press, 1986. For other explorations of 'decadent' mythological traditions of the nineteenth century, see Joseph Kestner, *Mythology and Misogyny: The Social Discourse of Nineteenth-Century British Classical Painting*, Madison: University of Wisconsin, 1988; Adrienne Auslander Munich, *Andromeda's Chains: Gender and Interpretation in Victorian Literature and Art*, New York: Columbia University Press, 1993.

6 Michel Del Castillo, 'Le Plaisir de Mourir', in *Saint Sébastien: Adonis et Martyr*, Paris: Editions Persona, 1983, 13. This volume, an illustrated tribute to the martyr comprised of impressionistic short articles as well as excerpts from art historical works dealing with the iconography of Saint Sebastian, is anonymously edited.

7 Robert Wilson launched a 1988 revival of the 1911 *Le Martyre de Saint Sébastien* at the Paris and Metropolitan Opera Houses.

8 Richard Rodriguez, *Hunger of Memory: The Education of Richard Rodriguez*, New York: Bantam Books, 1982, 84.

9 T.S. Eliot's poem, 'The Love Song of St Sebastian' (1914), eschews homosexual thematics for a depiction of a heterosexually inflected psychodrama in which the narrator Sebastian flagellates himself before a female beloved he eventually strangles. In a similar effort at 'heterosexualizing' the martyr, Wallace Stevens adopts Sebastian as a pagan image that eschews an aestheticism represented as effete in his 1944 poem 'Holiday in Reality'. See Richard A. Kaye, ' "Intangible Arrows": Stevens, St Sebastian, and the Search for the Real', *The Wallace Stevens Journal*, 19 (1), Spring 1995, 19–35.

The Polish novelist Gustaw Herling composed a remarkable 1960 novella on the theme of a modern-day Sebastian in his tale, *The Island*, a work that evinces no interest in the homosexual 'apocrypha' of the Roman martyr. Herling, *The Island: Three Tales*, New York: Penguin, 1993.

10 Edgar Wind, *Pagan Mysteries in the Renaissance*, New York: Norton, [1958] 1968.

11 In a classic statement on the art of film, the Russian director Sergei Eisenstein alluded to the transformation of Sebastian

from a purely aesthetic emblem to a figure of free associative meaning. Art, Eisenstein wrote, was essentially dialectical, a 'conflict between natural existence and creative tendency. ... Between organic inertia and purposeful initiative':

'Hypertrophy of the purposive initiative – the principles of rational logic – ossifies art into mathematical technicalism. (A painted landscape becomes a topographical map, a painted Saint Sebastian becomes an anatomical chart.) Hypertrophy of organic naturalness – of organic logic – dilutes art into formlessness (A Malevich becomes a Kaulbach, an Archipenko becomes a waxworks side-show.)'

In addition to identifying Sebastian's exceptional suggestiveness as an emblem – Sebastian as anatomical chart – the director positions Sebastian as the crux of his argument on art's dialectical conflicts. The martyr's admixture of 'organic inertia' and 'purposeful initiative' – his paralysis as an arrow-ridden body but his miraculous transcendence of death – becomes the very distillation of a film aesthetic. Sergei Eisenstein, 'A dialectic approach to film form', in *Film Form: Essays in Film Theory*, ed. and trans. Jay Leyda, New York: Harcourt Brace Jovanovich, 1985, 46.

12 While the most celebrated Renaissance iconography of Sebastian represents the saint as a semi-nude youth shot-through with arrows, a number of celebrated Renaissance painters did not depict Sebastian in this fashion. Raphael's version in Bergamo's Carrara Academy represents the martyr as a clothed young man proffering a single arrow in his hand. Antonello de Messina's rendition, also in the Carrara, depicts the saint without arrows. Giorgione's portrait represents a clothed Sebastian holding a single arrow, while Michelangelo's depiction of Sebastian in the Sistine Chapel depicts the martyr as an unpierced, muscular figure gripping a handful of arrows.

13 For an overview of representations of Saint Sebastian, particularly in Renaissance painting, see Victor Kraehling, *Saint Sébastien dans l'Art*, Paris: Editions Alsatia, 1938. See also the exhibition catalogue edited by Sylvie Forestier, *Saint Sébastien: rituels et figures*, Paris: Musée des Arts et Traditions Populaires, 1984.

14 James Saslow, 'The tenderest lover: Saint Sebastian in Renaissance painting. A proposed iconology for north Italian art 1450–1550', *Gai Saber: Journal of the Gay Academic Union*, New York, 1 (1), Spring 1977, 58–66.

15 *Acta Sanctorum* (Januarii), vol. 2, Brussels: J. Reiter, 1863, 629. See also *The Oxford Dictionary of the Christian Church*, ed. F.L. Cross, London: Oxford University Press, 1959, 1235.

16 Edith Simon, *The Saints*, New York: Delacorte Press, 1968, 69.

17 In the opening lines of Homer's *Iliad*, Apollo is said to have inflicted a deadly plague on the Achaeans through the arrows of the archer-god, Apollo.

18 See Paul Fussell, *The Great War and Modern Memory*, New York: Oxford University Press, 1975, 278–9 and 285–7.

19 Struggling with his homosexual feelings and himself obsessed with Sebastian imagery, the narrator of Mishima's *Confessions of a Mask* interprets Hirschfeld's observation as demonstrating that 'in the overwhelming majority of cases of inversion, especially of congenital inversion, the inverted and the sadistic impulses are inextricably entangled with each other.' Yukio Mishima, *Confessions of a Mask*, New York: New Directions, 1958, 41.

20 Jean Cocteau, *The Journals of Jean Cocteau*, trans. Wallace Fowlie, New York: Criterion Books, 1956, 77.

21 Julia Kristeva, *Tales of Love*, trans. Leon S. Roudie, New York: Columbia University Press, 1987, 78. Alas, Kristeva gives complete credence to a view of the Sebastian myth as paradigmatic of suicidal same-sex desire, commenting, for example, that homosexual men such as Pasolini 'mistaking himself for Sebastian', and 'allowing himself to be executed by a hoodlum on an Italian beach, carry to the limit the slavish moment of male eroticism appended to a deathful veneration of the Phallus'.

22 Montague Summers, *Antinous and other Poems*, London: Sisley, 1907, 9–20.

23 Thomas Mann, *Death in Venice and Seven Other Stories*, trans. H.T. Lowe Porter, New York: Vintage, 1955, 11. In P. David Ebersole's 1994 film *Death in Venice, California*, Mann's tale becomes a latter-day parable of suffocated desire in a sun-dappled West Coast setting. In Ebersole's film, Tadzio is an eighteen-year-old named Sebastian – a hunky pin-up version of Mann's saint – who brazenly pursues a repressed 'scholar of romantic literature'. Unloved, anxious to 'out' himself yet rejected by his would-be older lover, Sebastian seeks death in a perilous gay underground, where he dies in a murkily rendered final scene of self-sacrifice.

24 Oscar Wilde enacted this transition. As a youth at Oxford, Wilde adopted the role of Antinous, and might even be said to have played Zeus in his dealings with the Ganymede-like Bosy, ending the last years of his life in exile on the Continent as 'Sebastian Melmoth'. The name partly derives from Wilde's great uncle, the novelist Charles Maturin (author of the classic *Melmoth the Wanderer*) and partly from that of Wilde's favourite saint, particularly as painted by Guido Reni in a version in Genoa's Palazzo Rosso. For a brief mention of Wilde's fondness for Saint Sebastian, see Richard Ellmann, *Oscar Wilde*, New York: Alfred Knopf, 1987. On Wilde and Antinous, see Gary Schmidgall, *The Stranger Wilde: Interpreting Oscar*, New York: Dutton, 1994.

25 In his study of the sexual politics informing Victorian aestheticism, Richard Dellamora has established a crucial link between late-nineteenth-century aestheticism and the political aspirations of homosexually inclined men. According to Dellamora, many Victorian writers, poets and intellectuals found in the rhetoric of aestheticism a means of conjuring up an imaginary, idealized universe of same-sex relations. Pater's sentimentalizing of the Rome of Marcus Aurelius in *Marius the Epicurean*, Symonds's worship of a paganized Renaissance, and Swinburne's poem on Sappho, were all

coded endorsements of a homosexual eros otherwise unacceptable during the Victorian period. Richard Dellamora, *Masculine Desire: The Sexual Politics of Victorian Aestheticism*, Chapel Hill: University of North Carolina, 1991.

26 Del Castillo, 'Le Plaisir de Mourir', in *Saint Sébastien: Adonis et Martyr*, Paris: Editions Persona, 1983, 13.

27 Glenway Wescott, *A Calendar of Saints for Unbelievers*, Paris: Harrison Publishers, 1932, 22.

28 For an extended discussion of Day's work as it comprises a neglected counter-tradition in American photography, see Richard A. Kaye, 'Future shock: the photography of F. Holland Day', *Civilization Magazine*, July–August 1995. For details concerning Day, I am indebted to Estelle Jussim's study, *Slave to Beauty: The Eccentric Life and Controversial Career of F. Holland Day, Photographer, Publisher, Aesthete*, Boston: David R. Godine, 1981 and to Stephen Maxfield Parish, 'Currents of the nineties in Boston: Fred Holland Day, Louise Imogen Guiney, and their circle', doctoral dissertation, Harvard University, 1954.

Since Day photographed his Sebastian series, other photographers have cast Sebastian as a subject. In 1911, the French photographer and poet Jean Reutlinger, later to die in the First World War, photographed himself as Saint Sebastian. More recently, the photographer Everard attached small needles to a photographic transparency of the saint, as if striving for a wholly new dimension in effect in the representation of the martyr. Arthur Tress placed a dirt-smudged, modern-day Sebastian amid metal debris on a waterfront in a 1979 photograph, evoking a world of rough trade and river-front cruising: Saint Sebastian as urban gay cowboy.

29 George Bernard Shaw, 'On the London exhibitions', *Amateur Photographer*, October 1901. Reprinted in *Camera Work*, 1906, n. 14.

30 Mishima, *Confessions of a Mask*, New York: New Directions, 1958, 45–60.

31 Mishima, *Confessions of a Mask*, 88.

32 Ronald Firbank, *The Flower beneath the Foot*, New York: Penguin [1923] 1986, 60.

33 Denton Welch, *In Youth is Pleasure*, London: Vision Press, [1950] 1958, 9.

34 Salvador Dali, 'Saint Sebastian', reprinted in Ian Gibson, *Federico García Lorca: A Life*, New York: Pantheon, 1989, 183–6.

35 Describing Williams's play as a 'devastating statement about corruption in the world', advertising for the movie alluded to an unspeakable storyline, declaring that 'Cathie knew she was being used for evil'. As if to demonstrate that kitsch is not the final stage in the phylogenesis of a work of art, the 1992 television production, starring Maggie Smith and Natasha Richardson, powerfully recast Williams's play as a parable of a young woman's struggle to save her homosexual cousin.

36 Frank O'Hara, 'Having a coke with you', in *The Collected Poems of Frank O'Hara*, New York: Alfred Knopf, 1971, 360–1.

37 Reginald Shepherd, 'Black is the color of my true love's hair', in *Some Are Drowning*, Pittsburgh: University of Pittsburgh Press, 1994, 35.

38 Derek Jarman, *Dancing Ledge*, Woodstock, New York: Overlook Press, 1993.

Jarman's film foregrounded Sebastian's story as a tragic homosexual myth, but a number of other films have used Saint Sebastian as a unifying motif of a generalized erotic disorder, independent of same-sex desire. In Jacques Tourneur's 1949 horror classic *I Walked With A Zombie*, a loose adaptation of *Jane Eyre*, a young nurse arrives at the island of St Sebastian to care for her employer's zombie-mad wife. A voodoo ritual is the movie's climax, as the zombie-wife is stabbed with an arrow taken from a huge Sebastian figurehead. This puts an end to the wife's psychic torment and the intimations of incest dominating the family in a film overdetermined by references to Sebastian, a figure who here signifies the paralyzing psychic weight of the dead past.

In Brian De Palma's 1976 *Carrie*, the heroine, a withdrawn, doe-like Carrie White (Sissy Spacek) is berated by her fundamentalist mother and locked into a closet. Screaming to be let out, Carrie reverently lights a votive candle next to a small effigy of Saint Sebastian, whose gleaming white eyes suggest the torment of suppressed adolescent sexuality. In this high-school wallflower's vengeance picture, in which the telekinetic heroine uses her powers to destroy an entire gymnasium of students and teachers, Carrie takes revenge on her sadistic mother. When Mrs White tries to murder her daughter after the girl has defied her by attending the prom, Carrie telekinetically causes every knife in the kitchen to fly into her mother's body. The camera pulls back to reveal that Mrs White has become a Saint Sebastian herself. Here Sebastian represents the bottled-up sexuality of small-town American life transformed into a self-destructive fanaticism.

39 Derek Jarman, *At Your Own Risk: A Saint's Testament*, London: Vintage, 1993, 83.

40 Jarman, *Dancing Ledge*, Woodstock, New York: Outlook Press, 1983, 162.

41 Jarman, *At Your Own Risk*, London: Vintage, 1993, 86.

42 Martin Greif, *The Gay Book of Days*, New York: Lyle Stuart, 1982, 26–7.

43 Douglas Crimp, keynote paper, 'AIDS and the work of mourning', Gay and Lesbian Studies Conference, Yale University, 1991.

44 James McCourt, *Time Remaining*, New York: Alfred Knopf, 1993, 171.

45 Thom Gunn, 'Lament', in *Collected Poems*, New York: Farrar, Straus & Giroux, 1994, 465–6.
46 William Grimes, 'For endowment, one performer means trouble', *New York Times*, 7 July 1994; C. Carr, 'Washed in the blood: Congress has a new scapegoat', *Village Voice*, 5 July 1994; Hilton Kramer, 'N.E.A.'s good will tour turns into a bloody farce', *New York Observer*, 4 July–11 July 1994.
47 Adam Kury, 'The art of David Wojnarowicz', *Outlook*, 16, Spring 1992, 53–60.
48 Kenneth E. Silver, 'Modes of disclosure: the construction of gay identity and the rise of Pop Art', in *Hand-Painted Pop: American Art in Transition, 1955–62*, ed. Russell Ferguson, Los Angeles: Rizzoli 1992, 179–203.
49 Richard Howard, 'Concerning K', in *No Traveller*, New York: Alfred Knopf, 1989, 61.
50 Joan Wallach Scott, 'Experience', in *Feminists Theorize the Political*, eds. Judith Butler and Joan Wallach Scott, New York: Routledge, 1992, 32.
51 Quoted in Jarman, *Dancing Ledge*, Woodstock, New York: Overlook Press, 1993, 143.

PART II

Practitioners' statements

Chapter Six

Dyke! Fag! Centurion! Whore!

An appreciation of Tessa Boffin

Cherry Smyth

The frontispiece to *Stolen Glances: Lesbians Take Photographs* declares that, 'Tessa Boffin has been staging scenes, with the consent of others, for as long as she can remember' (Boffin and Fraser 1991). For me, this at once conjured the pleasure of play: the pubic pleasure evoked by the photographic 'scene' which Tessa constructed for the book, as well as the private pleasure of the sexual scenes that she conducted for herself and her partners. Tessa's work charted the line between her public and private personas with immense honesty and intense commitment.

'The Knight's Move', Tessa's series of black and white photographs reproduced in *Stolen Glances*, came out of her sense of frustration with the privileging of reality over fantasy. 'Staged scenes and photo-tableaux are all seen as second best since they are always self-consciously (and even unconsciously) constructed and played out' (Boffin and Fraser 1991). She used this work to investigate the paucity of lesbian role models and the need to appropriate historical fictions for our own ends. As Neil Bartlett recently wrote, 'If you asked me to write a list of the first ten homosexual people with whom I had conversations, the the first eight of them would be fictional characters ... . Our relationship to fictional, fantastical or historical material, is different to that of heterosexuals' (Bartlett 1994).

Tessa pillaged the past for images from which to reinvent an identity and articulate desire, and placed her characters 'into the great heterosexual narratives of courtly and romantic love: by making the Knight's Move – a lateral or sideways leap' (Boffin and Fraser 1991). Her invention of dramatis personae re-interpreted notions of history as well as the contemporary spaces lesbians can enter. The location of the piece, the cemetery, not only summons our dead heroines, from Janet Flanner to Gertrude Stein, but also vibrates with the frisson of public, outdoor sex. Gay male sex. Cruising cemeteries is more dangerous for girls. It's only in gangs that we can be seen there. The display beneath a tombstone of black and white photographs of women who have been claimed as lesbian heroes, emphasizes the necessity of visual representations for lesbians to claim and record our desire. The work then proceeds to create individual representations of historical fantasy figures: the indomitable knight, the earnest knave, the sorrowful angel, the haughty Casanova and the inscrutable lady-in-waiting. 'I could hardly find you in my history books, but now in this scene, you all come together' (Boffin and Fraser 1991).

Two of the figures hold placards naming other lesbian heroines, from Dorothy Arzner to Alice Austen, as if to ensure that these images will not be recuperated and lost to a heterosexual, historical narrative.

The knight is the most resonant image in the series (Figure 6.1). Despite our rigorous attempts to deconstruct the fictions of hetero-romance, many of us have heavily invested in the notion of love, of finding the right partner, of rescuing or being rescued. The larger-than-life knight with her shaved head and slicked back hair, her muscles exaggerated by a robust suit of armour, her face

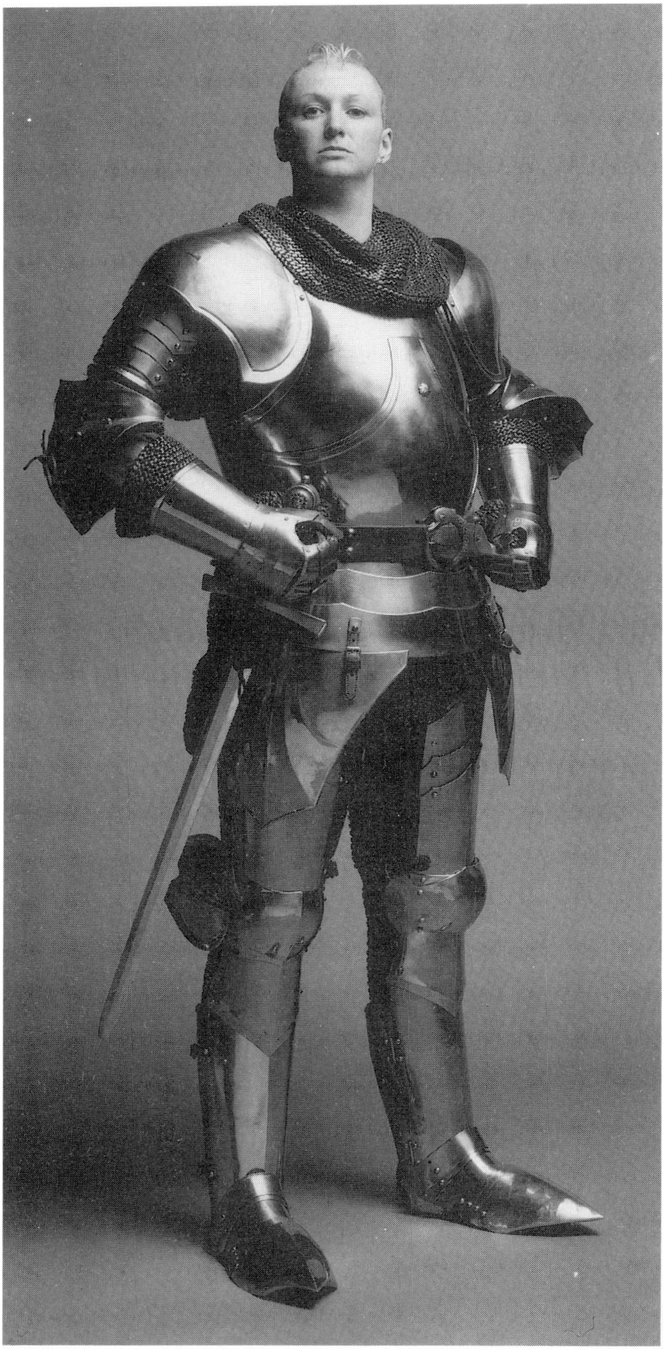

Figure 6.1 Tessa Boffin, *The Knight's Move* (1991)
Estate of Tessa Boffin.

defiantly expressionless, conjures the dilemma of dyke self-preservation: to be safe as women we often take on masculine guises, which then can result in homophobic attack, therefore compounding our vulnerability. The knight may have a forbidding presence, but as every lover of a butch knows, there is a pussy underneath.

Tessa's angelic rebel features not only in her series on safer sex in 1989, which was one of the first photographic pieces to confront the issue for lesbians (published in *Ecstatic Antibodies*, Rivers Oram Press, 1990), but also in *A Lover's Distance* (1986), where the female angel is unable to see in order to shoot cupid's arrow. Based on Roland Barthes' 'A Lover's Discourse', Tessa interrogated the themes of love and loss with a cool, precise detachment which belied the force of the passionate undercurrent in her work. In her attempt to pursue hopefulness beyond the pain of lost love, she created a style which became quietly distinctive. In her work notebook she talked of the need to create a layered ambiguity: 'I'm afraid of being too banal, too even, too ordinary ... not the realm of fantasy, of theatre, of spectacle which I am dealing with. It's strange how a style emerges, as if by accident and then you have to work within the confines you have set yourself' (Estate of Tessa Boffin).

Tessa developed the theme of the queer angel long before it went on to become the ubiquitous symbol of the late 1980s. This brave series contemplates the self-exposure required by love and the disillusion of rejection. In *Disposable*, a person of indeterminate gender is 'dumped' in a dustbin, surrounded by the broken bricks of the crumbled relationship. As in *The Knight's Move,* it comments on the projected image of resilience that we feel we must promote in the world as dykes, resisting the destiny of loneliness and sadness to which a hostile culture has designated us.

In the summer of 1991, I returned from New York, buzzing with the exhilaration of a new political movement which promised to embrace gender and race in a fight to challenge homophobia and heterosexual privilege. I wore my 'Queer Girl' badge with attitude, confounding and collapsing the label of 'lesbian woman' with glee. Later Tessa was to return from New York wearing a 'Queer Boy' badge, riding the edge of gender-fuck out further than I could. She described herself at that time as a queer dyke.

> I never identified with the word lesbian because it seemed quite medical, it was the word I used to come out to my mother and it seemed to have negative connotations. Queer was one of the ways of identifying with a mixed movement and challenging both separatism and misogyny at the same time. (Boffin in Smyth 1992)

When I danced into the early nights of Sadie Maisies, the first mixed queer SM club in London, wearing stockings, suspenders, a corset hugging my waist, Tessa was led in by a faggot, her neck in a dog collar, a huge plexiglass dildo swinging between her legs for anyone to suck. She delighted in the sweet contradictions of 'lesbian boyhood' and as Sunil Gupta wrote, 'her lifestyle became her art practice as she embraced "queer culture". The theory became the practice. She was the pervert faggot boy–girl drag queen'.[1]

In 1992 Tessa began working with her lover Nerina Ferguson. Together they conceived and performed the notorious 'Crucifixion Cabaret' at a nightclub called Purgatory, in which Tessa played a centurion in full costume, complete with red and gold cloak to Nerina's role as a gold-painted naked slave. It was one of the first mixed boy–girl, queer sex shows to be performed in London and shook several taboos by the throat: the taboo of lesbians being sexually explicit in front of and with gay men; of evoking Jesus as sexual and a skinhead dyke; of making master–slave roles visual and public; of cunt-fucking without latex gloves at a time when many pro-sex dykes still believed it was common practice to do safer sex; of fisting a woman who is menstruating.

Like all of Tessa's work, it was a beautifully orchestrated and carefully constructed piece, bathed in candlelight, the oiled bodies of the helpers, clad only in white loincloths, glistening in the honeyed light.

One of the drawbacks, however, was the extreme seriousness of the performance which inhibited response from a rather stunned audience. The chance to laugh would have facilitated a warmer reaction. Humour may have given the cabaret the touch of joy it seemed to lack and have prevented some of the hostility towards the performers which ensued. Sadly there was a lack of empathy towards the piece which seemed misplaced in a club and perhaps would have worked more successfully in a theatre setting or somewhere where the audience was anticipating a seriously provocative performance rather than a simply titillating one. But the performers deserve recognition for taking the risk to extend the confines of the space, for challenging the cosy complacency of the club scene which had its sex show formulas severely tested and disrupted on that occasion.

Tessa and Nerina then produced a wonderful homage to Jennifer Saunders, an eighteen-year-old dyke from Yorkshire who was sentenced to six years' imprisonment in 1991 for allegedly dressing as a boy and fucking two female lovers with a dildo without their consent.

In *A King's Trial*, Nerina, dressed in a T-shirt and jeans, packing a dildo, stands cross-armed, staring with a defiant gaze towards the camera. The black and white reportage style and the series of boxes with ticks alongside the image recall countless medical poster campaigns with a wry and subversive wit. The heading reads:

'This woman dressed as a man because:

a) she wanted to seduce other girls
b) her girlfriend was too frightened to tell her parents she is a lesbian

c) small towns have small minds
d) she is a gender-bending drag king'
Each option has a tick, deliciously compounding all the stereotypes and moving way beyond them into a celebration of something else. It's in that something else that Tessa thrived.

Tessa had just finished working on another safer sex, gender-fuck series, part of which is reproduced in *Lesbian Looks* (Scarlet Press, 1994) when she took her own life in October 1993. *The Wayward Sailor and the Showgirl* (1993) produced with Nerina and Denis Doran, testifies to the development of Tessa's work into a more collaborative stage, incorporating her desire to perform as many identities and sexualities as she could. This richly coloured piece consists of seven images arranged in a photo-story in which Tessa plays a sleazy tart posing in Piccadilly, out for trade. Only Tessa is no straight beauty in fishnets and wonderbra. She's decked out in two-inch long eyelashes, a mountainous black wig, a diamond-patterned, sequined, lurex dress and red feather boa. Just as Sandra Bernhard is proclaiming that women cannot be glamorous anymore, that glam has been stolen by drag queens, here comes Tessa, robbing back what was appropriated and putting icing on the top. As Marjorie Garber asserts, 'Transvestism is a space of possibility, structuring and confounding culture: the disruptive element that intervenes, not just a category crisis of male and female, but the crisis of category itself' (Garber 1993). Tessa was a walking, talking crisis of category and that was fascinating to witness.

Nerina appears as a fresh-eyed sailor called Sam, who's on shore leave and looking for 'girl pussy'. Little bubbles capture their thoughts as Shi-Shi, the call girl, tempts Sam into a doorway, but warns, 'I don't care how big your packet is honey, unless you've got a pack of three, you ain't coming in this port.' 'So', reads the caption, 'Sam slipped one on and they got acquainted.' The final shot shows Sam and Shi-Shi kissing under a neon billboard, Shi-Shi's leg hiked over Sam's hip, a queer fuck if ever there was one.

It's difficult to predict how Tessa's work may have developed, but I suspect she may have been a short step away from filmmaking, bringing her talents of accurate and precise framing, directing a cast of fantastical characters, working collaboratively and pushing boundaries of gender representation to another medium. I dream of what those movies may have looked like and the roles Tessa would have created for them. She was something else.

Note

1 Sunil Gupta, *Creative Camera*, 325, 1993.

References

Bartlett, N. (1994) 'Troublesome visibilities: reviewing queer strategies in contemporary theory and culture', unpublished paper delivered at St Martin's College, London, April 1994.
Boffin, T. and Fraser, J. (1991) *Stolen Glances: Lesbians Take Photographs*, London: Pandora.
Boffin, T. and Gupta, S. (eds) (1990) *Ecstatic Antibodies: Resisting the AIDS Mythology*, London: Rivers Oram Press.
Garber, M. (1992) *Vested Interests*, London: Penguin.
Smyth, C. (1992) *Queer Notions*, London: Scarlet Press.

Much of Tessa's work is profiled in *Tessa Boffin: Queer Photographer*, a video directed by Mark Harriott, 1994, available from video distributors Dangerous to Know, London (0171-735 8330).

Chapter Seven

The art of accompaniment

Robert Farber

> Art's job is to engage the viewer. Visual art makes that contact directly through the eyes, without the intermediary of speech. With such a connection the communication can be made on a profound level. If it is good art, it will invite the contemplation of things that cannot exactly be put into words: ambiguities that form the connective tissue in life, passing incidents that may hold great consequence, as well as sheer exhilaration and seering pain. When I recognize such things in a work of art, it helps me to feel less alone. Someone else has lived these things too. The solitude of individual existence is momentarily broken and the contact provides, as Nietzsche said, '... triumph over the frightening depths'. Art allows us to accompany each other. It is what I try for each time brush meets surface.

When I found out in the fall of 1989 that I was HIV positive, my life and everything in it changed for ever. I had just turned forty-one years.

After that, I felt that AIDS was the only thing I could or even wanted to paint about. I am sure that some of my motivation arose out of my involvement with the activist group, ACT-UP (from 1989 to 1992). Apart from going to meetings, participating in demonstrations, helping to organize benefit art auctions and so on, ACT-UP gave back to me an invaluable sense of the fighting spirit. I was *not* prepared simply to lie down and let the disease roll over me. It is this fighting spirit that has enabled me to continue to paint and make work about the AIDS epidemic even today, even in the face of my deteriorated immune system.

However, before I was able to make use of all that ACT-UP, family members and others gave to me by way of support, I went through a very dark period of several months shortly after I discovered my HIV status. Up until that point, I had been able to derive some sense of comfort from the idea that there was more to life than I could see. In other words, that there was a larger picture, so to speak; some grand design to the universe wherein even the most idiosyncratic phenomena fit into place somehow. All of that fell away from me when I realized that I had a fatal illness for which there was no effective treatment. Stripped of the garments of belief, I felt as if I had been left shivering in the harsh, cold landscape of existential despair. Nothing seemed to matter or mean anything. The phrase, 'what's the point?' kept coming back to me over and over. Nothing I might do was going to change my situation so why do anything? Certainly, why paint? Everything seemed pointless and without value.

I turned to philosophy to see if I could find my way out of the sense of futility that had begun to contaminate my life as surely as HIV was infecting cells in my body. I read Nietzsche, Camus and art criticism of all kinds with a voraciousness born of my hunger to find out how these nihilistic and existential philosophers managed – managed to continue living. I needed role models for moving on in a life of chronic emergency.

All of this had a profound impact on my thinking, my relationships and, of course, my art. It was the most important period of self-examination I had ever experienced. It forced me to look at the fundamental issues in my life and in my work as an artist. And it for ever changed both. I did not, however, emerge from this period with solid answers that once and for all silenced my sometimes frightened questionings. It is an ongoing process in an ongoing life.

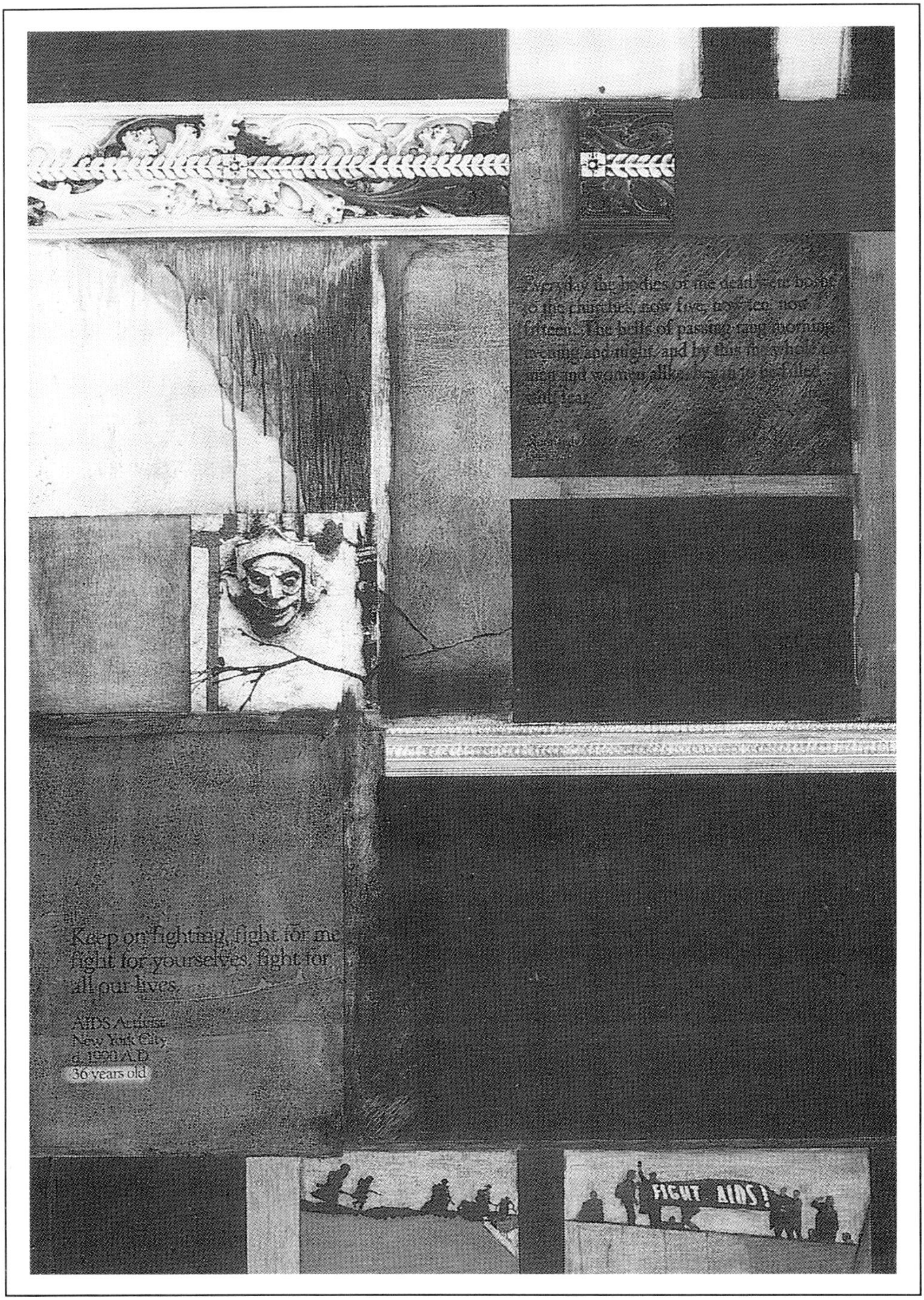

Figure 7.1 Robert Farber, *Western Blot No. 14* (1992), 62″ × 40″, mixed media on wood panel
Photograph: Jean Vong.

Nevertheless, I did come away with some insights that continue to help me both inside and outside of my studio. If I start off with the knowledge that one day soon I will die from AIDS, it means that at a certain point, I will not be here any more. Well, the first thing of value that arises from this idea is the fact that I *am* here today. That means that my time, while I am still here is of immeasurable value. I am keenly aware of how I use my time; what I choose to focus on. The clock is always ticking. I consider myself extremely fortunate that I have whatever talent I may as an artist, for it allows me a medium and forum through which I can try to communicate my thoughts about mortality and human frailty and, who knows, maybe that can help others as they go through their lives. In a strange way, my acute awareness of time allows me to be less anxious about the amount of time I spend puttering around in my studio. I've come to accept that that is part of my creative process; a necessary, if sometimes oblique, approach to a difficult subject. But none of it is wasted. While I may be attending to chores in my studio, I am simultaneously (though sometimes unconsciously) working on the painting before me. By the time I pick up my brush again, new ideas have already begun to coalesce.

Even more powerful than my newly developed sense of time, has been my attempt to formulate for myself what it means to say I *am* here today. For me, it involves bringing as much of myself as I can to whatever it is that's in front of me. Whether it's my work, a friend or a medical situation, I invite the entire sum of myself into play. I try to be genuine. This is not an easy task, so many things can get in the way of making a genuine connection. Few moments in life afford the kind of clarity and simplicity that allows for such a connection. But it is something I try for. It's almost as if I try to give each painting the gift of my sincerity which in turn brings another aspect to my work. My paintings have come to represent concrete evidence that I am here, in this place, at this time. To me, the brush-stroke, the photo, the formal arrangements of paint and panel are the footprints I leave behind. They show me the road I have travelled so far and the direction my particular journey has taken. If I have been able to achieve some degree of genuine-ness in creating these works, there is the chance that their authenticity might enable them to speak to others and even, perhaps, live on to tell future viewers something of what it was like to live through these dark times.

Before discussing the role AIDS has played in my recent work, I would like to bring to this discussion aspects from my personal history which I believe strongly influenced my development as an artist, my attraction to abstract art and my work process that continues to operate today.

I have never considered myself a 'gay' artist. I *am* gay and have been openly so for the last twenty years but I do not see or experience my work as arising from my sexual orientation. In fact, I do not believe that there is such a thing as gay or lesbian art. Having said that, I *do* know that for as long as I can remember, I always felt different from others and before I 'came out', the feeling of being different was a painful one. I never became used to the ridicule I experienced on a daily basis during my early adolescence in school. It always caught me by surprise and made me feel tremendous shame and loneliness. What was I doing that elicited the cruel jeering? I was accused of 'acting like a girl', but I was completely unaware of my behaviour in gesture or deed. I believe that my feelings of being different did, in fact, play a role in my development of an artistic sensibility. For the most part, artists have always felt outside of the mainstream. It is a vantage-point from which artists can observe and comment on what others take for granted as part of their daily commerce in society. But unlike artists who claim the role of outsider as part of their credentials for social critique, my own experience led me first to seek solace and relief in a world I could make.

This led quite naturally to my interest, as a young teenager, in abstract art, an interest that continues today. I think it has something to do with my wish to communicate things that cannot be described by linear narrative. Though, recently, I have included texts in my paintings, I still see myself as an abstract artist. It is through abstraction that I hope to 'speak' to the viewer.

I never know how a painting will look until it is finished. No matter how strongly I sense the image of a work, or how clearly I 'see' the painting ahead of time, I am always left solely with where the actual painting is taking me and what it is trying to become. There is no map. There is, for instance, no way to anticipate the accidents that may occur or their repairs which often enrich a work far beyond whatever I could imagine ahead of time. For me, the goal is to be in a state of readiness so that these unforeseen (and initially unwelcomed) painting events can be first recognized and then incorporated. At each of these junctures, the painting shifts direction even if just slightly. The conflict between what I want the painting to look like and what the painting is telling me it needs, is the basis of my daily work in the studio. It has taught me to approach my work more improvisationally and less wilfully. It has taught me to trust my intuition more than my conceptualizations. It has taught me humility. And, it has taught me to live with uncertainty and *that* is the most difficult lesson to learn because when all else fails (and it usually does) it requires faith that it will all work out somehow; even when 'somehow' means that a particular painting does not come together in the end. Well, there's always the next painting. It is living with a sense of uncertainty that goes against everything our society and civilization has fought to overcome. It is also what people with AIDS must live with every day.

The last five years of my work are a direct result of my endeavour to deal with my own health and the AIDS epidemic in general. I began creating this work after I had read about how the Black Death or Plague of 1348 devastated Europe, helping (along with other significant factors) to dismantle the social and political infrastructure of feudalism. There seemed to be so many similarities between the medieval experience of the Black Death and the experience of AIDS today, that I began to make paintings that compared these two epidemics. Even though they are entirely different diseases, epdimiologists point to the bubonic plague of the Middle Ages as a useful model when trying to calculate the scope and impact of the AIDS pandemic worldwide. I have taken as the title for this growing body of work the name of one of the tests used to detect HIV antibodies in the blood. The Western Blot, to use an over-simplified analogy, operates almost like an ink-blot. But as a title, it also suggests something of the foreboding I want to express.

In comparing the Black Death to AIDS, I have taken visual motifs from the late Middle Ages; fragments of Gothic architecture, gold-leaf, fresco-like surfaces, gargoyles, marble, etc., and juxtaposed them with elements of contemporary art such as photographic imagery of all kinds, modernist abstraction, medical paraphernalia and silkscreens.

In my research, I came across documents, journals and literature that chronicle the impact of the Plague on people who lived through it. I have placed quotations from these sources alongside quotes from today in order to exact an even greater comparison between these two catastrophic moments in western civilization. So some of the voices in my work speak from across six hundred years but their power and pathos are as immediate and urgent as those from here and now. They all communicate what it is like to face one's own death with an eloquence and power that could never be captured in an academic account or historical description. These are the voices of human experience and I consider it a privilege to find places for them in my work. I have tremendous respect for the courage of all those whose words I use and I feel a deep sense of obligation to create spaces in my paintings for these voices to continue to speak and resonate. It is one of the reasons I have taken so much care with these paintings, in particular, to use the most archival materials I can find. I take some comfort from the thought that some of these paintings might survive the current epidemic and provide the kind of documentation I uncovered from the late 1300s which helped illuminate for me the actual, individual experience of the Plague.

In placing the AIDS crisis in this historical context, it is my hope that people will begin to see the basic human tragedy underlying this or any fatal illness.

The various components that go into my work are evident in the two reproductions that accompany this essay. With *Western Blot No. 14* (Figure 7.1), I introduced military imagery for the first time (along the bottom of the painting). As I continued to read about AIDS research in the media and in scientific journals, I became increasingly aware of how we talk abut this disease, particularly in light of the failure of modern medicine to come up with anything approaching an efficacious treatment. We use the imagery and analogies of battle, war and combat. As just one example, *Time* magazine ran a cover story in May 1992 the title of which reads, 'AIDS: Losing the Battle'. We are constantly talking about the fight against AIDS. There is the fight to find a cure. There is the fight against homophobia, which has surely slowed our society's response to the epidemic and there is the most fundamental fight of all; the one that goes on inside my body twenty-four hours a day with or without my conscious attention. So I wanted to incorporate the element of battle into the work. In *Western Blot No. 14* I found I was able to place the First World War battle scene of soldiers silhouetted against an empty sky alongside a photograph I took while participating in an ACT-UP demonstration in Albany, New York in 1990. Here too, the figures, soldiers really, are silhouetted as they stretch a 15-foot banner reading, 'FIGHT AIDS!' across a highway overpass. Just above these images, to the left, I use a quotation from an AIDS activist who died, 'Keep fighting, fight for me, fight for yourselves, fight for all our lives.'

These two quotes (both visual and written) are counterbalanced by an excerpt in the upper right of the painting from a chronicler living in Normandy in 1349:

> Everyday the bodies of the dead were borne to the churches, now five, now ten, now fifteen ... The bells of passing rang morning, evening and night, and by this the whole city, men and women alike, began to be filled with fear.

With utter simplicity, his observations give chilling reality to what otherwise might fall into sterile, statistical formulations. Here, we have a bit of evidence that enables us to imagine what it was like actually to live through the Black Death. What a day was like. What people saw and heard. One of my goals as an artist is to provide that kind of information with respect to AIDS; something of the day-to-day experience of living with the disease. These are things that might never make the front page of a newspaper because, perhaps, they are not considered dramatic enough, but they are surely the things that PWAs (Persons with AIDS) wake up to every morning of every day: uncertainty, fear, physical discomfort, exhaustion and grief. Not to mention the arcane scheduling of dozens of medications that must be taken in such a way so as to minimize their potential for cross-reactivity.

I have tried to include this sense of the daily life with HIV in a variety of ways. Along these lines, with *Western Blot No. 19*, I have incorporated a graph (Figure 7.2). I printed the faint blue lines of the grid onto transparent film and then placed it over a panel which had an impression of my handprint. You can see this in the upper half of the painting towards the right. Numbers appear along the left side of the graph. Starting at the top, they descend from 400 to 350 to 300 and so on till they reach 0 at the bottom left corner. The graph line itself is plotted to coincide with these numbers as it plummets from 400 to 50 before it literally falls off the page. This is the chart of someone's diminishing T-cell count. For me it represents the kind of clinical data PWAs receive all the time. Without fanfare or theatrics, disturbing lab reports are given to me on a regular basis and there is nothing to do about them. I try to steel myself against hope and the disappointment that invariably follows. The new drug is not working. I move on.

To the left of the graph panel, which also has a veined marble square, I have used a quotation from a journal written in 1349. The author, John Clyn, lived in Kilkenny, Ireland:

> I, as among the dead, waiting till death do come, have put into writing truthfully what I have heard and verified. And that the writing may not perish with the scribe, I add parchment to continue it, if by chance anyone be left in the future, and any child of Adam escape this pestilence and continue the work thus commenced.

The chronicle *was*, in fact, continued, for just below this entry, in another handwriting, it goes on to say, 'Here it seems that the author died.'

I first used this quote in an earlier painting in 1991. At that time, I was profoundly struck with the courage and physical strength of the author who actually died while he was still writing. Because I have these texts made into silkscreens, I can re-use them. I returned to this particular quote in 1993 and my response to it was weighted differently. In the intervening years, my situation had changed, I had changed and John Clyn's words took on added meaning. Now I was moved by the sheer force of his desire to leave a record behind of his experience of the Plague which seemed to engulf his world. With the continuing erosion of my immune system, his valour and determination helped to reaffirm my own wish to leave a record behind. I drew inspiration from his words written

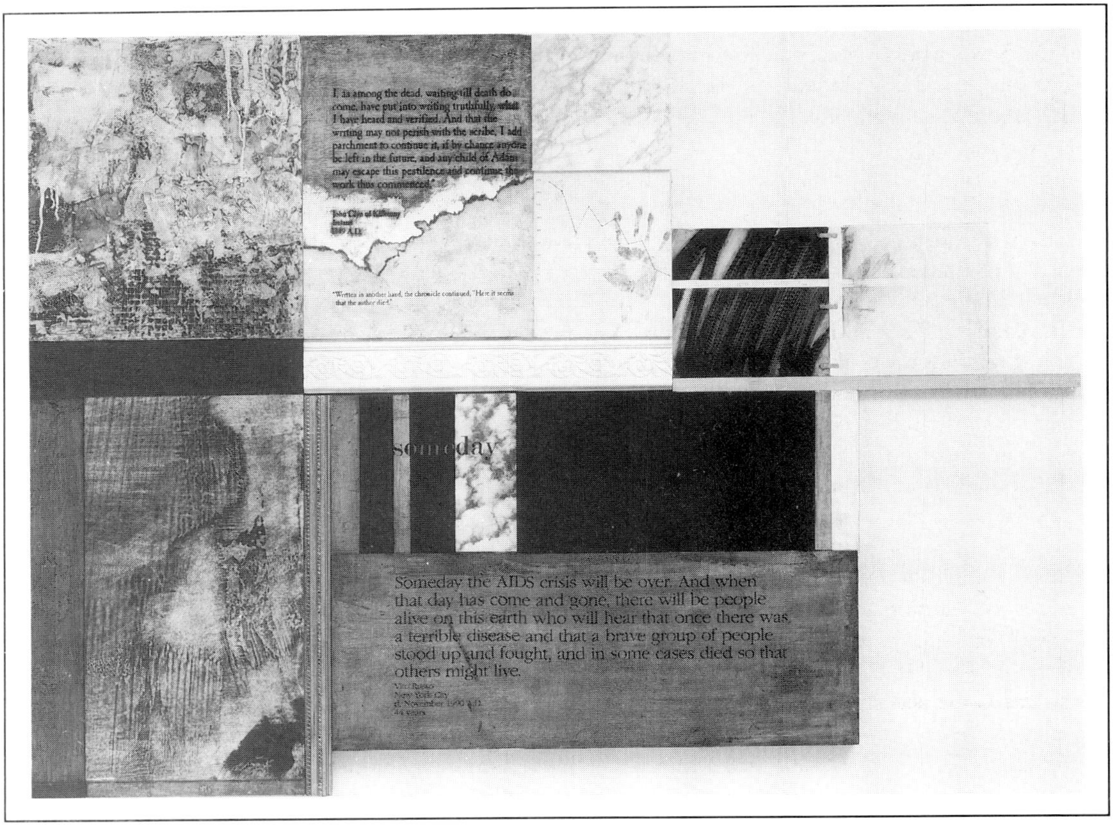

Figure 7.2 Robert Farber, *Western Blot No. 19* (1993), 60″ × 81″, mixed media on wood panel
Photograph: Jean Vong.

nearly 650 years ago. Out of this grew the section (to the right of the graph) which continues out beyond the main body of the painting. This section is made up of two separate wood panels. Reading them from left to right, the first panel shows where I used gestural brushstrokes to create a zig-zag pattern which veers off to the right (echoing the adjacent graph line). Through this passage I carved out a horizontal space that abruptly breaks the diagonal brushwork. Into this empty space I placed a portion of John Clyn's quote, only here using a modern typeface: 'I add parchment to continue it ...'. Immediately to the right I placed what amounts to an empty panel. It has been joined to the preceding one by some metal hardware. With this I am trying to put into concrete form my hope that the story of AIDS and its devastation will continue to be recorded long after I am dead. The extension of the wood beneath these two panels is there to suggest that more may follow. The story continues.

In the large panel below all of this, I placed one of my most treasured quotes. These are the words of Vito Russo who was a filmmaker, an archivist of gay video and film and an early AIDS activist. He died in 1990 at the age of forty-four. In accepting an award for his achievements he spoke,

> Someday the AIDS crisis will be over. And when that day has come and gone, there will be people alive on this earth who will hear that once there was a terrible disease and that a brave group of people stood up and fought, and in some cases died, so that others might live ...

For me, Vito's words embody all that I would wish for with my work; my hope that the paintings might survive and that the voices within them might shed some light on how we tried to cope with this disaster; the heroic effort to face one's own death, sometimes with insight, sometimes with great sadness.

I took the first word from Vito's quote, 'Someday' and placed it above the text so that part of the word appears over a colour photo of white clouds against a blue sky. I guess I wanted to leave this element open to interpretation. It could be a remnant of hope that some day things will be better, it could be the wish to fly away off into the clouds or it could simply be the ability to be able to conceive of a future day. I felt it was fitting that these two pieces of text were joined together in one painting. They both point to the future. But they also suggest something of the phrase, 'pass it on'. It reminds me of that incredible moment in a relay race when one runner passes the baton on to his or her team-mate, the next runner, who will then carry it until it must be passed on to the next and then the next and the next and on and on. Only here, the laps are not measured by metres and the baton is passed not when the laps are finished but when the runner, dying, exhausted and gasping for breath, manages to reach his or her team-mate and with an outstretched hand passes the baton on as if saying, 'Now it's your turn, run!' It is with that sense of responsibility that in some small way I feel the baton has been passed to me. I shall run with it for as long as I can.

Since writing the above essay over a year ago there have been significant changes in my life and art. I am still running, baton in hand, but my gait has slowed a bit and the track has shifted direction. Having been hospitalized with pneumocystis pneumonia (PCP), I am now for the first time dealing with full-blown AIDS. This has affected everything in my life; from my ability to get to my studio every day to the actual form my work has taken. When I finished *Western Blot No. 23* I felt it was time to move on. Now I needed to find shape and substance to express my daily experience of living with AIDS. I have found that with my return to abstraction. Using a variety of materials, oil, encaustic, concrete, etc., I feel more able to communicate in universal terms the themes of facing one's death, the diminishing of possibilities, fear and the search for relief.

Editor's postscript: since writing this last paragraph Robert Farber has died. It is a great sadness to us that the book was not in print in time for him to see it: his contribution was, from the beginning, very welcome and important. When the time it takes to produce an anthology is greater than a contributor's life expectancy, the urgency of making culture in the time of AIDS becomes ever-more evident. Our thoughts go out to Robert's family and friends.

Chapter Eight

Lesbian artist?

Sadie Lee

The issues surrounding the usage of the term 'lesbian artist' leave me feeling confused as I can see many arguments for and against. When, in 1992, my painting *Erect* was selected by the National Portrait Gallery for the poster advertising the BP Awards, no mention was made of my sexual orientation other than on the application form. There was a question which asked what my relationship was to the people depicted in the painting and I wrote 'self-portrait with partner'. The painting (Figure 8.1) was displayed on the posters as in the Gallery with no explanation as to its reasons for being and I like to hope that it was selected because it was a strong and interesting painting. If anyone were so interested in it that they wished to understand why I painted it then they wrote to me care of the Gallery, which they did by the dozen.

Although I am a lesbian and an artist I am also interested in attempting to challenge preconceived ideas of lesbianism. I believe that giving your imagined 'cross-section of society' audience too much initial information can determine how they feel about what they're looking at. There are advantages to being labelled a 'lesbian artist' as it provides a positive role model for other lesbians, helps create awareness and visibility and, in some cases of positive discrimination, artists are invited to exhibit their work primarily because they are lesbians. This is of course beneficial to the lesbian and gay community but may make it difficult to promote positive images of lesbians to those who are most prejudiced. I feared that some heterosexual people would shy away from my paintings as they might feel that they had nothing in common with lesbians and therefore would not be interested in art created by them.

While despising this form of discrimination I do admit to its existence and I had an idea that perhaps sometimes people may have to be lured into looking at something, allowed to decide for themselves whether or not they like it and *then* be told what it is they're looking at. Some of my images are deliberately ambiguous so that the messages are strong but can be read on different levels and mean different things to different people.

Because of my disappointment in the lack of information throughout history about artists who are women, I appreciate the importance of bringing an artist's gender to public attention. I believe that anybody who is gay or lesbian should be open and honest about their sexuality. I also can see the point that in labelling someone a 'lesbian artist' one is perhaps enforcing the belief that this is something which is not the norm and that, while it may show society that we exist, it may also suggest that we wish to separate ourselves from that society by remaining within our separate category. The artist, Maggi Hambling, refuses to even be referred to as a 'woman artist' for this very reason, believing that the term infers she should be singled out for special attention, good or bad, because of her gender. Often the 'lesbian artist' is seen merely as a producer of lesbian imagery rather than as an artist in her own right. I am interested in a lesbian artist's contribution to art as well as her contribution to lesbianism.

My paintings are very personal but are also documentary representations of the people around me who I am involved with and interested in . The majority of these people are lesbians. However, the images of these women and their sexual orientations are only part of my interest. I am producing large-scale detailed oil paintings, which have as much in common with other, sometimes heterosexual, painters as they do with lesbian activists.

One of the best things for me about the National Portrait Gallery poster was that it allowed my painting to stand for itself rather than as an advertisement for something with exclusively lesbian connotations. People were then able to respond to the image without information about who *I* am determining their reaction. This is an automatic privilege for most heterosexual artists, but because I am known to be a lesbian I am expected to constantly talk about and justify it, rather than letting the content of the paintings register or not, depending on the viewer.

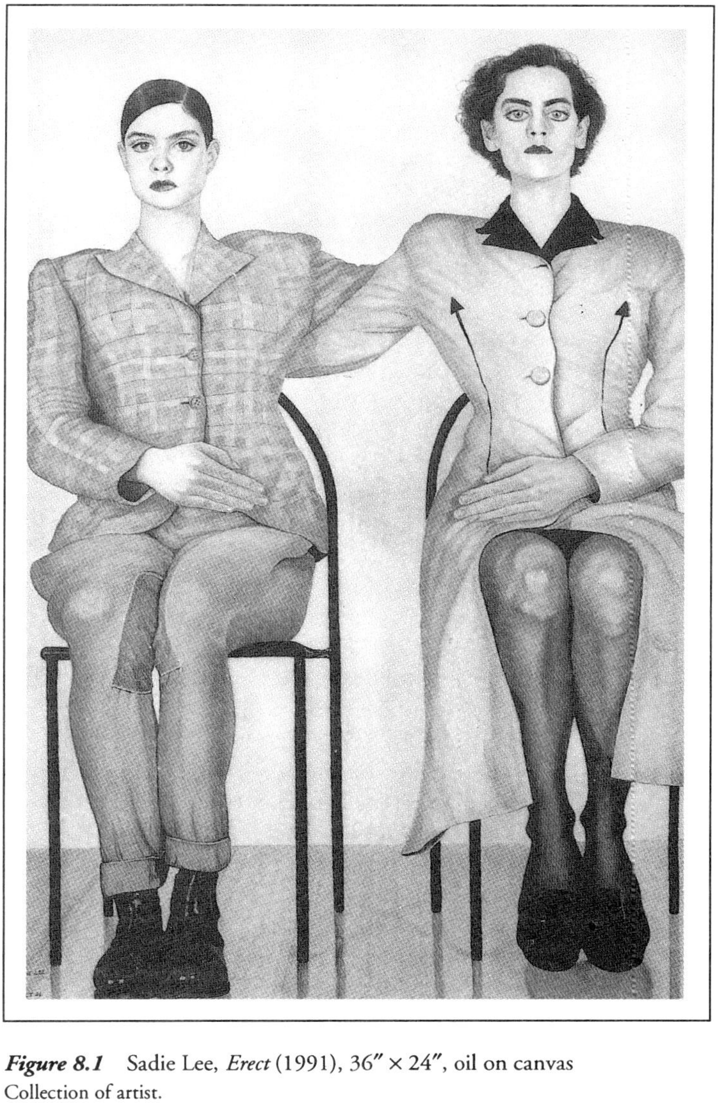

Figure 8.1 Sadie Lee, *Erect* (1991), 36″ × 24″, oil on canvas Collection of artist.

I was forced to consider these issues in more detail during my first one-woman show at Manchester City Art Galleries in September 1994. I was chosen by the Gallery as their contribution to the 'It's Queer Up North' annual arts festival. The exhibition was advertised in the gay publications and also through the Gallery's general catalogues. The Gallery has a superb collection and attracts hundreds of visitors a day, most of whom, willingly or unwillingly, found themselves in the middle of my exhibition, 'Venus Envy'. There were people who came from all over the country because they specifically wanted to see a lesbian exhibition but there were also many people who did not, and would not have looked at the work had they been given a choice. There were catalogues available which contained a small introduction to my work and statements from me about my desire to present these images (of lesbians) in good gallery spaces.

The comments book for my exhibition was very full and the Gallery estimated that approximately 80 per cent of the comments were positive. The ones that weren't generally complained that the gallery had given space to 'disgusting' art, or quoted homophobic passages from the Bible. The interesting thing is that within the Gallery's permanent collection are many paintings of semi-clad or nude women embracing, some in bath scenes, and there is even a large-scale portrait of Sappho. Of course, these paintings were by men and offered no explanations as to the meaning behind them or to the relationships between the women in the paintings. Needless to say, no complaints were made about these paintings. This made me start to question what lesbian art is considered to be – and I firmly believe that the problem is not with 'lesbian art' (that is images of women together), but with 'lesbian artists' (that is, when the viewer is told of the artist's gender, sexual preference and feelings towards the women she paints).

As the images in my exhibition were, in my opinion, fairly tame, I think that it was the information that accompanied it that created the majority of the disapproval. Of course I can only guess what a heterosexual viewer's reactions are to my paintings other than what they choose to tell me in the comments book, but I think that some were also disturbed by the contemporary dress, or, in the cases of the nudes, hair styles of the models, which somehow made the bond between the women, or the woman and viewer, more sexually threatening. Even at the time that they were painted most of the paintings in the Gallery's permanent collection showing women bathing together etc., portrayed them in old-fashioned, almost allegorical dress and settings, which helps to encourage the 'tastefulness' of the paintings and play down the sexual implications other than that in the imagination of the (male) viewer looking at it. Even so, the images in my paintings, although always considered challenging, had never attracted quite such a vehement response as that shown by the outraged general public in Manchester. It is unfortunate that I was not able to conduct an experiment and remove all explanatory information for a short period of time and compare the comments with previous ones when the public were told exactly what they were looking at.

It is not always essential to me that my work is properly understood by everyone. Sometimes the theories that people tell me they have about my paintings, although not my reason for making the painting, offer an added dimension that I hadn't even considered. Occasionally I finish a painting and the more I look at it the more I feel it says, even though my original ideas for it were very simple. I think that often the simplicity, spontaneity and immediate impact can get a bit lost in the discussions about the political implications behind it. However, often there are strong statements that I am trying to make and one of my interests is in examining the differences between men's painting of nude women and my paintings of nude women, as not only a woman, but a woman who is a lesbian.

It is generally believed that in a traditional painting of a female nude by a male artist the woman in the painting is 'arranged' in such a position as to appear available, unthreatening and entirely submissive to the male artist (and viewer). She either looks away, while her body language still invites the viewer's attention, thus making it easier for the male to voyeuristically observe her completely unchallenged, or she looks directly into the eyes of the observer encouraging the enjoyment of her body. The women are idealized to be safe and tasteful, which denies them any reality and sexuality of their own. The nipples are usually only suggested by a faint shadow and body hair merely hinted at, or else she is draped in such a way to conceal the genitals while giving an almost teasing reference to the forms that are hidden. This 'perfecting technique' turns the woman into a fantasy figure and instead of being a representation of a real person she becomes exaggerated and moulded into an ideal form for the spectator. By the suggestion that the woman is not real and has been redefined to improve on nature and conform to men's ideas of beauty in women, the female viewer is virtually excluded and may find it difficult to identify with the women presented.

The women (sometimes nude) in my paintings differ from nudes by male artists in that they are aware of their sexuality. In fact, their sexuality is so evident that their awareness of it gives them a challenging, threatening presence not shown in most traditional paintings of women. Where women have been seen to be in control of their sexuality in paintings by men, it is usually in relation to the man who is presumed to be looking at her, whereas although the women in my paintings engage the viewer by direct eye contact, their attitudes are depicted as confident, primarily within themselves. In addition to my interest in how the painted nude observes her observer (and vice versa) I also try to explore the relationship between women within the picture plane and am currently working on various couplings where one woman is clothed and the other naked.

I use the word naked rather than nude as often this transformation occurs when a figure's lack of clothes is contrasted with another's comparative clothed security.

I am very aware of the relationship between the painted woman and the viewer and try to set up a narrative in which both play a part. Sometimes I attempt to convey a mood or feeling about a woman using direct eye-contact, certain colour techniques, stance and size of the figure. In the painting *La Butch En Chemise* (Figure 8.2) my reasons for asking the woman to pose for me were very personal.

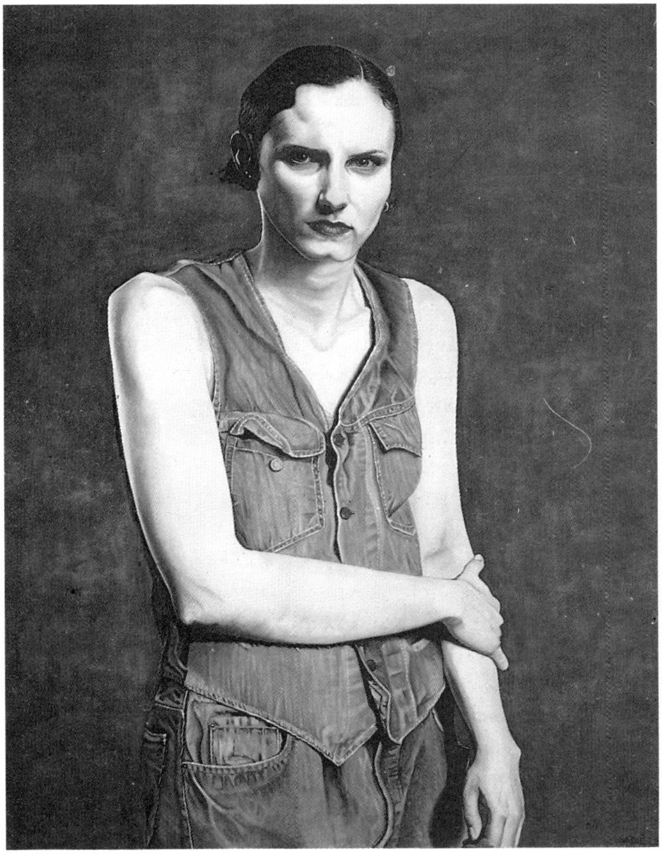

Figure 8.2 Sadie Lee, *La Butch en Chemise* (1992), 60″ × 48″, oil on canvas
Private collection.

I had seen a woman in clubs and secretly watched her over a period that lasted about four years. Because of the nature of London women's clubs it was quite possible for us to move in the same circles, have mutual friends, turn up at the same places at the same time and yet never speak to each other. Had I attempted to talk to her it would have meant that I fancied her. Although this was true, I didn't really want to shatter the illusion I had invented by actually getting to know her. Apart from this I have always been terrified of rejection and have very rarely approached anyone unless completely intoxicated.

Based on my observations I imagined her to be both hunter and hunted. Cruising about in the clubs she looked like a predator but she still retained an air of vulnerability. Nervously (and drunkenly) I managed to approach her and asked her to model for me. Of course she was nothing like my fantasy of her and although she is recognizable in the portrait I exaggerated her features and colouring to give more of a sense of how I perceived her. As in my painting *Raging Bull*, the portrait is large and fairly daunting. I am fascinated by the women that I paint but often find it hard to talk to them and when I do, we are usually uncomfortable in each other's presence.

I have always tended to make people nervous as I have difficulty relaxing with people I don't know very well and therefore make it unlikely that they should want to get to know me any better. I try to convey all this in my paintings of them and allow other people to feel as uncomfortable in front of the painted women as I do in front of the models themselves. The electric blue background draws attention to the nerve-jangling coldness of the woman, as I perceived her, in this particular painting.

The title came quite some time after the painting was finished and I saw a painting from Picasso's 'Blue Period' called *La Femme en Chemise.* The painting is of a woman shown from the waist up, in a sleeveless vest against a rough dark blue background. Although the two paintings are completely different these similarities made me want to draw a connection between them. 'La femme en chemise' means the woman in the chemise, but as 'femme' also means a 'feminine lesbian' in dyke-speak, as in 'butch and femme couple', I called this painting *La Butch en Chemise,* meaning 'the masculine lesbian in the chemise'.

To sum up, I am an artist who is a lesbian. My paintings explore my feelings towards the women around me, whether our relationship is sexual or not. It is my intention to produce paintings that show women in a positive, provocative, sometimes even sarcastic way, but I hope that they can be considered as technically accomplished pieces of art in their own right rather than simply visual examples of lesbian propaganda.

One of the fascinating things about the comments book at Manchester was that it gave me an opportunity to hear the opinions of people who I would not normally come into contact with. Apart from the expected misogyny, sour grapes and homophobia, it also revealed the expectations of lesbian viewers, many of whom had travelled to Manchester specifically to support a 'lesbian exhibition'. I found it interesting that some lesbians were angry about the women I had chosen to paint, and wrote that I had painted too many women who were attractive or who wore make-up. There were also demands that I should paint more women of colour, women with long hair or more women smiling. It is a strange feeling that in being known as a lesbian artist I have become the property of that community, who feel that they have a right to tell me who I ought to paint. I am painting likenesses of individuals who I find interesting and not all my paintings are intended to be taken as potential role models typical of a community. Most of these women who criticized my choice of subjects supported what I was doing, but were disappointed that they personally didn't feel represented in my work. I find it surprising that they would rather instruct one artist to do everything, than support another artist who they could identify with. I also grew up with virtually no positive images of lesbianism that I could relate to, and was forced to read mainstream images against the grain. I am now producing paintings that mean something to me, and am not attempting to represent every lesbian in the world.

Because prejudice is still rife in the art world there are relatively few well-known artists who are 'out' lesbians. This means that there exists a certain amount of tokenism where if someone were in need of a lesbian artist (for equal opportunity reasons or in an attempt to be 'alternative' or controversial) my chances of being selected are rather good. I am fully aware that had my paintings been criticized on technical merit alone and the lesbian content not been discussed, I would not have enjoyed even half of the exposure that I have had.

In a world of heavy competition sometimes it is necessary to work all the angles and highlight a unique quality that sets one apart from contemporaries. Simply because I am a lesbian artist I have been interviewed in national newspapers, including an unauthorized piece on page three of the *Sun,* appeared on television and radio, and had a one-woman show in connection with a lesbian and gay festival. The whole 'novelty value' and 'lesbian chic' craze has worked very well for me. Except I now have the added problem in that what was once deemed too controversial and specialized for general public consumption became suddenly hip and then unfashionable in the space of a year.

It is my hope that, by lesbian images becoming commonplace through soap operas, fashion magazines and art exhibitions, one day it may be useful, but no longer absolutely necessary, to use labels like 'lesbian artist'. If I were a heterosexual artist painting my partners I would not have these dilemmas. People would connect my work with others who had a similar style, not include me in a group of diverse artists who all happened to be heterosexual. I am very happy to be a lesbian but I wish that being a lesbian wasn't always positioned as different or 'Other' in contrast to heterosexual, which is unspokenly viewed as the norm.

Chapter Nine

Negotiating genres

Veronica Slater

... artists are often shy people ... They would feel priggish if they were to speak about 'expressing their emotions'.
(E.H Gombrich, 'Introduction' to *The Story of Art*, 1950, London: Phaidon)

When I first went to art college Gombrich's *Story of Art* was central to the understanding of what 'art' and 'artists' were. This perception constructed an artist's identity as elusive, ephemeral and almost sacred like the status of a saint. However, my actual experience of artists was far removed from Gombrich's 'shy' characterization; they were for the most part large male egos with plenty to say. It was from this point on that I gradually recognized the package that built the myth of a genetic gendered 'artist'. It became clear to me why I had such difficulty in calling myself an artist when it signified a history that seemed totally removed from my experience. Gombrich's story had excluded women and as a student I reacted with a sort of androgynous approach to the creative process in an attempt to be taken seriously.

On leaving Camberwell in 1980 my confidence was fragile and my direction confused. It was not until much later on that I began to understand how this experience had positioned my sense of self in relation to an artistic practice. My work began to focus on this relationship and feminism informed its development. The part-time MA course I took at Newcastle offered a theoretical framework which helped dismantle much of the myth-making process. The work became a dialogue that explored how the language of painting itself was coded. Painting was not a 'natural' process and 'expressiveness' was not the pure unmediated heroic act that Gombrich and Camberwell had led me to believe in. I was never going to be a hero of modernism; its 'universality' did not include the questions that became the content of my work. I became interested in the different strategies that artists used to challenge a dominant position that marginalized the 'Other'. These offered exciting possibilities in approaches to art practice and enabled me, at last, to occupy the space of an 'artist'.

This in turn led to recovering some of the more positive aspects of my art education, namely the practical experience of techniques and processes. In reconnecting with the physicality of painting I could be clear about how process relates to content and how this in turn defines intentionality. While theory provided useful tools in understanding the creative process I had to recognize that it too could become prescriptive and relegate the activity of painting to an illustrative role. The physical process of using paint externalizes not only the (intellectual/emotional) content but the human tactile expression of getting the work onto canvas. This activity of painting is about feeling connected to something, it is a trace of my being there and the spontaneity and unpredictability of the medium allows an exploration of the unfamiliar which makes the most unexpected and exciting links. This uses a sensibility that is not rational, it defines an internal chaos which is both separate from and connected to the outer chaos of what surrounds me. The identity of what I do (being an artist) is central to my work in that it connects to how I work (using paint) which articulates the content of my images. When I am the viewer I read an image with an awareness of this process and the many-layered meanings it constructs in language.

In assessing my educational experiences I can reflect on the institutions that provided the context in which I formulated my understanding of art practice. This relationship of the individual to their cultural framework has been so important to me and informs my role as an artist and as a tutor. It has also been critical in my understanding and confronting how that cultural framework perceives my sexuality as a lesbian. I see sexuality as a fragment of 'self' which is constantly re-encoded according to the situation in which it is experienced. To be actively involved in representing this experience of sexuality is to draw upon and evolve images that view the body as a site which is in a state of continual change. This is a process of questioning. It is an opportunity to challenge notions of 'fixed' identity and to discard the legacy of an ordered sexuality. For me, this is an important means of self-recognition. In negotiating representation, I am empowered.

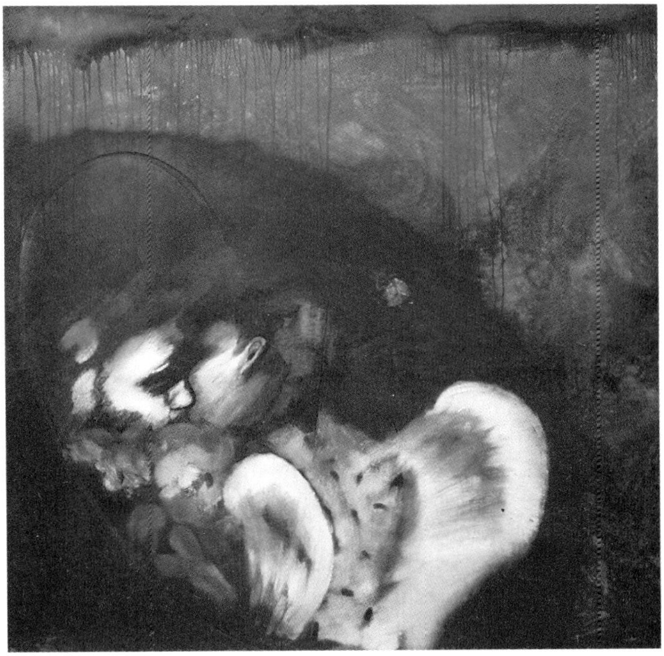

Figure 9.1 Veronica Slater, *Angel Lust, no. 2 (Wings of Desire)* (spring 1993), 48″ × 48″, oil on canvas
Private collection of Mr and Mrs Booth.

My previous work has been concerned with the family album and the way that the 'self' is documented by others. In my case this was dominated by conventions which sought to conform to the notion of an established, stable family but, in reality, it camouflaged the dysfunctional and chaotic relationships that existed within it. The anonymous narrative produced in such family album photographs creates a removed and fragmentary sense of the past and highlights the disparity between the experience of our histories and the representation of those histories. I began to explore these concerns in an exhibition called 'Intervening Spaces', commissioned by Darlington Arts Centre in spring 1993. The show involved five women artists working with installations that were interventions into public space; a disused Victorian pumping station provided the site for my piece *Sanctity and Sanitation*. The Gothic architecture for me symbolized the pseudo-divine role of the Industrial Father in purifying the town's drinking water. The installation comprised images of myself, my mother and my grandmother in holy communion dress. These were placed on light-sensitive perspex tubes and hung from the roof inside the darkened interior of the station. In our sanitized white glowing state we are daughters signifying purity. The pale images attempt to instil a powerful morality through the iconography of the sacred. In the same period I was also working on a diptych called *Angel Lust* which explored profane notions of desire and damage (see Figure 9.1). The paintings are of two androgynous figures that are locked into a threatening embrace: they are angels who lust, deviants who bear chaos. *Sanctity and Sanitation* and *Angel Lust* are contrasting images of the sacred and the profane as polarized states which together express the dichotomy that constructs fear and guilt.

My relationship to these polarized states permeated my sense of sexuality until I was able to unravel the layers that had constructed such poignant icons. *Genitals: External* (1989) was a triptych that evolved out of this process. It explored sexual identity using anatomical and religious imagery. The work is framed with gilt and the figures of Adam and Eve are on clear perspex laid over painted dissected sections of genitalia taken from a popular text *A Colour Atlas of Life before Birth*. In the centre piece of the triptych is a text describing the development of the genital tubercle which at nine weeks is neither male nor female but is referred to as the phallus. Even before gender is determined, social relationships are operating, and visibility of the phallus signifies its dominance. These myths and 'facts' inform our perception of the body: this piece of work foregrounds the difficulties we experience in unfolding cultural constructs like those that narrate our passage of birth, sexuality and death.

Body Paradoxes (1990) explores the relationship between art and anatomy further and examines their quest to reveal 'nature's secrets' with a mission to comprehend the living. This piece of work also uses the format of the triptych and with gold frames, gold overhead lamps and a gold plaque aims to create a 'preciousness' in order to deify the art object. The surfaces of the paintings are silky and the colours seductive, however the subject-matter disturbs this sense of sumptuousness through its portrayal of mortality with the anatomical mapping of a dissected head. The brain is scooped out from the skull, the casing for consciousness, and our identity is seen to be finally fixed by the anatomist's gaze. As I worked on *Body Paradoxes* I began to realize that I was exploring this 'mission to comprehend the living' in order to understand and come to terms with the post-mortem that my mother's body had gone through. This in turn heightened the sense of my own mortality and the eventual image of its identity. The ideas for this work initially centred on an exhibition called 'A Question of Identity' and was shown in Newcastle-upon-Tyne and later in a show called 'Pride' organized by 'Visible Images'[1] a lesbian and gay group in London.

In autumn 1994 I further explored the ideas around *Body Paradoxes* in a painting called *Portrait of the Collector*. The genre of artists portraying art collectors gave rise to a collaboration which used images of my collector's colon. These were looked at and jointly decided upon during the process of an endoscopic examination at a hospital. The painting was developed from these chosen 'stills', using the paint to 'probe' the physical space that the images mapped. Four orifices depict different stages of the journey as the camera retreats further down the colon. The process of painting has used these bodily structures to explore the absence and presence of abstract space in order to create a sense of this visceral journey.

'Visions of Paradise' was a solo exhibition commissioned by Oldham Art Gallery and shown in September 1992. It consisted of a series of fourteen paintings that set out to explore our relationship to nature. This series extended the concerns of earlier work by looking at the historical parallels that exist between the mapping of landscape and of the human body. The images were montaged from a range of collected resource materials and provided the framework in which to respond with a diverse set of approaches to processes in paint. The skills gained from this experience focused my understanding of the critical dialogue between the practical application of visual language and the eventual reading of its subject-matter. 'Paradise' is a means to examine 'man's' relationship to nature and it investigates how what is cultural is portrayed as natural. This series attempted to use the language of historical genres to question concepts of order and chaos as they are understood to exist in the spectacle of nature. I used this subject-matter to look at how icons are constructed out of familiar images so as to intervene, re-interpret and invent new meanings (see Figure 9.2).

This provided the key for me to understand my own positioning within a society that is dominated by heterosexual imagery. My experience as a lesbian is rarely reflected and often misrepresented.

I see my task as addressing that absence by manipulating and subverting the language that establishes heterosexual presence. The creative means of such re-invention are expressed continually within gay, lesbian and queer culture: the AIDS crisis has highlighted this through poignant and moving events. The reaction to the crisis of AIDS has in some ways been empowering as lesbians and gay men create their own responses to the passage of birth, sexuality and death. This made possible an understanding of how to come to terms with the death of my own mother. I needed the familiar symbols and rituals to deal with death but I did not want what, in my case, Catholicism represented. These were the destructive values that had set up the source of conflict between mother and daughter. Our relationship had been surrounded by such symbolism and in re-appropriating its meaning I could create my own rituals to grieve her death. Seven years on, I can understand what role my practice as an artist has had in externa-lising the confusion that emerges in making sense of the agencies that use the body as a site of control.

The cultural artifacts that document and inform our lives are a validation of the personal relationships in which we invest, and lesbian and gay archives contribute by visualizing a history so often denied in the 'family album'. *Soul Identified as Flesh* (1989) was the first painting in which I began to address aspects of identity and visibility. The painting was part of a touring exhibition called 'Along the Lines of Resistance' and is of my partner standing with repeated copies behind her of the painting *Self-portrait with a Cigarette* by Gluck (1925). This self-portrait appeared on the book cover for Radclyffe Hall's *The Well of Loneliness* and it was one of the first lesbian images I encountered. The aim was to create a lineage by placing Gluck's painting within a 1980s context, juxtaposing the two portraits within the one image. I also worked Gluck's self-portrait in a silk-screen mode so as to make a reference to Warhol's *Marilyn Monroe*, an icon of heterosexuality. At the time this was evidence of an uncomfortable relationship to the polarized representations of female sexuality. These contrasting feminine stereotypes (reproduced as Monroe and Gluck) appear anchored and fixed but the conventions that have placed them in opposition are re-appropiated in this work so as to reverse their meanings. By offering multiple readings of icons I try to dilute the impact of intended symbolism so as to present rich possibilities for creative intervention.

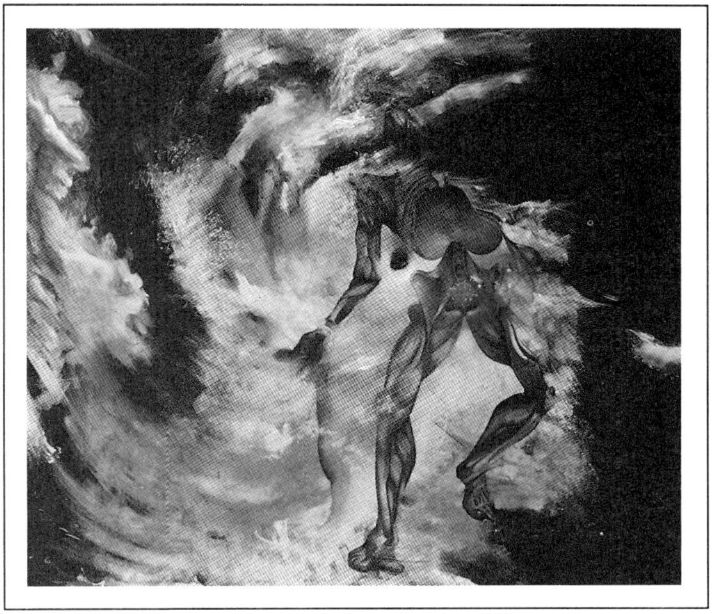

Figure 9.2 Veronica Slater, *Visions of Paradise, no. 5* (summer 1991), 72″ × 84″, oil on canvas
Collection of the artist.

The Mad Ballerinas (1993) is a series of three small paintings which continues to play around with this approach. The dancers have lost control and defy their 'feminine' sexuality through chaotic and disturbing choreography that is portrayed in bright colour and richly applied paint. At the same time I worked on *The Nude*, an eroticized figure which attempted to explore how images fetishize desire within the conventions of traditional subject-matter. *The Nude* (1993) is of a lover posed as a languishing muse but her passive gaze is disrupted by the fondling of an erect dildo between her legs. The figure looms out of a sumptuous dark crimson background, built up through layers of glazing. Ideas about passivity and activity are further explored in *Two Wrestlers after Muybridge and Bacon* (1994), a diptych that depicts two frames from Muybridge's wrestler series. The painting is worked with reference to Francis Bacon's re-working of this image which places the figures into a homoerotic context. I, in turn, have re-worked the gender of the wrestlers and used the paint to interact playfully with the movement and physical presence of the now female figures.

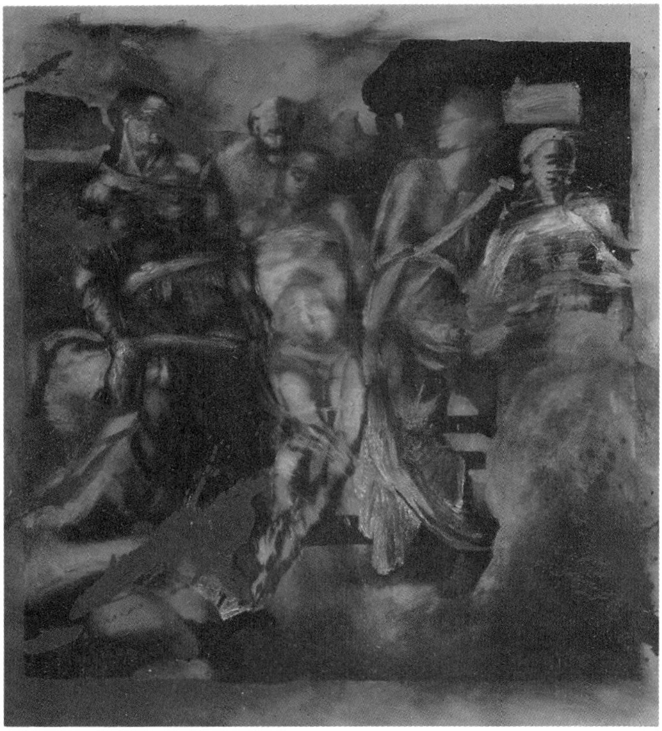

Figure 9.3 Veronica Slater, *Entombment, no. 1* (summer 1994), 72″ × 72″, oil on canvas
Photograph: Rachel Ara. Collection of the artist.

This approach was extended into a set of paintings which recently toured in an exhibition called 'The Borrowed Image', organized by the City Art Centre in Edinburgh. The series re-works Michelangelo's *Entombment of Christ* whose authorship is continually debated through interpretation and re-intepretation of the painting's content. The dynamics of the figures in this image and their relationship to each other trigger ambiguities that do not sit comfortably within the tradition of the subject-matter. The mourners have never been clearly identified and their androgynous nature sets up a charged relationship to the eroticized passive, almost 'camp' Christ. It signifies a diverse and complex representation of these icons at a poignant moment in this harrowing narrative. The painting interweaves a whole set of polarized positions and presents an opportunity to foreground further dialogue between constructed genres and re-invention.

This dialogue remains for me a vital area of debate as it opens up narratives which have imposed identities that are now negotiable. My practice uses the language of these narratives to make visible the position of 'self' in relation to the identities offered, the artist, the lesbian, the daughter. It is in the continual shifting between these that a recognition of 'self' emerges which the anatomist's gaze can never fix. This awareness is a means of dealing with the practical aspects of identifying within the polarized notions of sexuality in western culture. To be lesbian, gay, queer or bisexual is to be immediately marginalized by the values dominant in a heterosexual society. To challenge this dominant culture is still a political task which is hazardous from both a personal and global perspective. My experience is locked into these perspectives that continually negotiate the values of an art establishment and their perception of 'peripheral cultures'. It is through my practice as an artist that I want to address these issues and reflect back the apparatus which defines the origins of such perceptions.

Note

1 Visible Images was formed in 1989 and was an invaluable source of critical feedback as well as a supportive network for exhibitions. It provided a forum to discuss and develop ideas in art practice within the context of sexuality. Contributors were from a range of areas such as filmmaking, video, performance, painting, installation, sculpture, print-making and photography.

Chapter Ten

Rough trade

Notes towards sharing mascara

Lawrence Steger and Iris Moore

Iris Moore with her multi-layered texts, and Lawrence Steger with his eerie dramatic persona, have carved out reputations as consistently provocative performance artists. *Rough Trade* is genuinely transgressive, exploring gender roles and, more specifically, sexual preference and identification. Combining lip-synching, appropriation of popular culture, danger and constant subtle shifts in meaning, *Rough Trade* plays on stereotypes to create a haunting yet humorous and surreal world.

Two scripts, *Illusion of Conspiracy* by Iris Moore, and *Bliss* by Lawrence Steger, are each performed solo by their respective authors on the first night, while the second night is the 'trade' – Moore doing Steger's script and Steger doing Moore's. This simple trick reveals the preconception of gender-specific meaning, the full effect of each performance revealed by seeing both presentations. *Rough Trade* has been presented in the United States and toured the United Kingdom in 1994.

Achy Obejas, *The Chicago Reader*

The inspiration to work on *Rough Trade* came from the suggestion of a mutual friend who understood and witnessed the similarity between our approaches to performance: both on-stage and, through our genders, off-stage. In previous solo work, we shared an interest in dissecting and performing aspects of our individual personalities. We created personae through solo performances that focused on our individual desires and expectations. We spoke of our individual sexual desires through characters that simultaneously declaimed and declined their position of authority. Off-stage, we shared a cynically camp repartee. We were aware of each other's mistrust of an increasingly mainstream sexual politic (that is, the assimilation of gay and lesbian). Also, we developed performance tactics of bait-and-switch which reflected our individual dissatisfaction with gender roles and authority. Iris didn't feel that we were drag artists *per se*, but Lawrence felt we used our personalities as drag. The question arose: if our genders were fixed, did that mean they were our texts? And what authority did the text have, if any? Our friend who suggested the 'switch' recognized our similarities but didn't take into account the difficult territory of an assumed *We*. 'We' complicated our ambivalence toward the Self. We trusted each other's mistrust, but how would the mistrust of the other party fit if we each tried them on? If we had something to share, did that mean we would give something away and have it stolen at the same time and vice versa? We amused each other with passive/aggressive flips during improvisational banter – we were less interested in acting like each other than anticipating the next move, and the next one. On-stage, we could offend the audience and then engage them; we could indicate our gender and then re-name it. We were disinterested in a heterosexual exchange of body fluids – that would be nihilism given Lawrence's HIV-positive status and our sexual preferences. We mistrusted ourselves in order to trust the other.

We had each been working in a cabaret format for many years, primarily at Club Lower Links in Chicago. We enjoyed the luxury of working for an audience who was dedicated to a form and a club and who saw the work develop over a period of time. We didn't have the illusion that we were working for some illusive public or general audience. We're not *Angels In America*.

The form for *Rough Trade* came from cabaret and the amateur (low budget) style of drag shows. We approached the form as the true fiction of performance. We worked in dense and layered texts; some might say to the point of opacity. Iris's relationship to drag had been an exploration of femme as abject citizen. Where Iris constructed a world view from the position of abjection, Lawrence approached it as a means of constructing an image destined to fail.

Rough Trade developed as a series of vignettes that encompass the limitations of identity, authority, gender and sexuality from the perspective of the objectified performer. It contains sections that touch on the responsibility of the performer, the relationship of the performer to the audience, and the use of the language of the oppressor to convey experience that is invisible to 'Him'. From the beginning, we agreed to work under an assumption of our queerness(es) without positioning it in the foreground. It was never the subject-matter of the piece, but it formed the ground of the work. The piece would not have made sense without it. We were not addressing an abstract alienation; we were talking about our psychologies and how they were formed in relation to a culture that identifies us as deviant and unlawful. We embraced our criminality and started mapping out a territory for ourselves, sketching out an alternative to the 'free and healthy' world of the non-criminals.

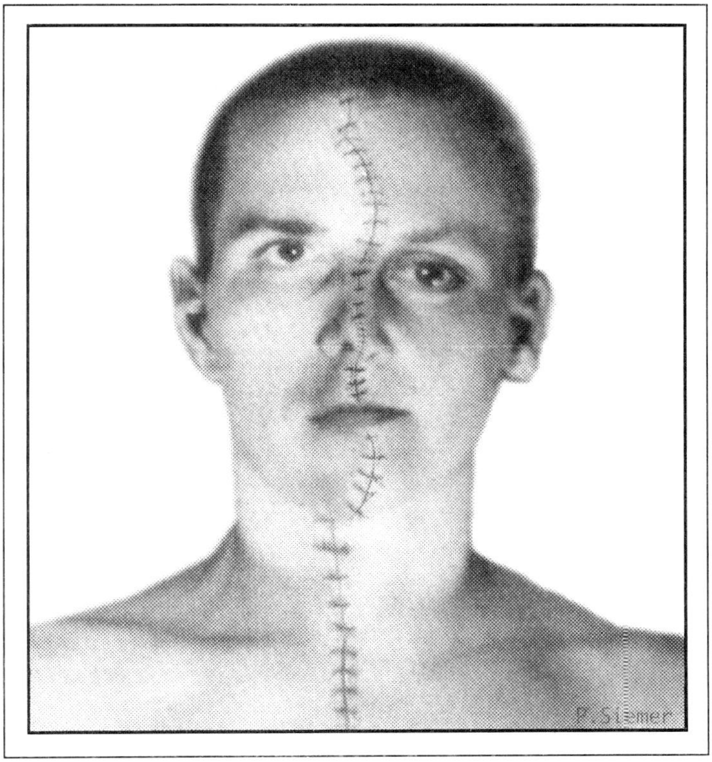

Figure 10.1 *Lawrence Steger and Iris Moore* (right). Photograph: Steve Lafreniere. Surgery: Patrick Siemer.

Of course, the attempt to create a new assumption in the audience has the built-in danger of slipping into the standards of a new status quo.

> The relentless apparant raises its ugly head and nothing is revealed but the Truth. Vexation, Anxiety and Instability fade into the border mist and we are left on known territory. (Iris Moore, *I Have Seen Things Which Make Me A Liar*, 1990)

Iris: I began examining a scene from the movie, *Basic Instinct*, as a representation of the male dream of the authority of femininity in which the lesbian/criminal Sharon Stone is interrogated by the detectives. In the midst of psychological warfare, she displays her cunt as a tactic in battle. Sitting centre-stage, wearing the now-famous *Basic Instinct* dress, we lip-synched the scene. The use, presence (and absence), of her sex is underscored by a chair that lights up from underneath when she uncrosses her legs. When Lawrence re-dresses the scene, it takes on the baggage of camp, revealing Sharon as the construction of femininity.

In the next section, the Sharon character talks about the nature of contracts and how the creation of the contract looms over its content. This describes the relationship between Lawrence and I (and between performer and audience) as somewhat antagonistic, critical, but unmistakably collaborative.

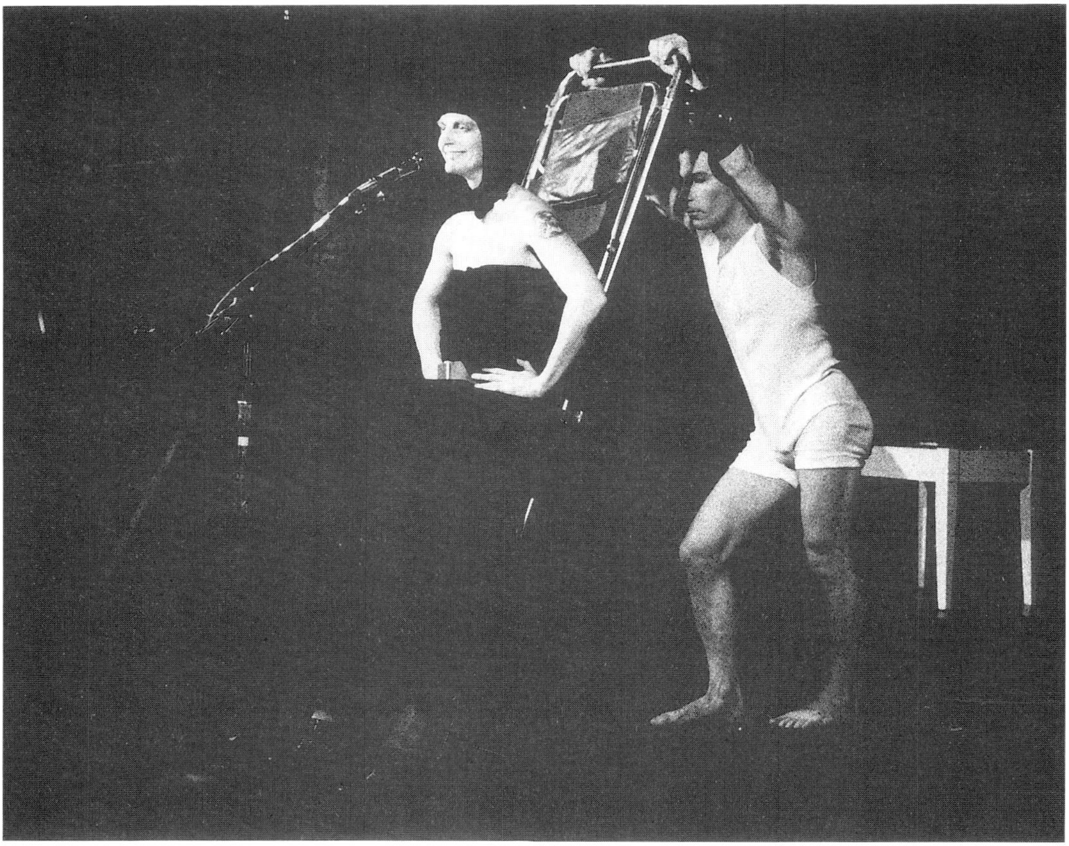

Figures 10.2 and 10.3 *Rough Trade i* and *ii*
Photographs: Debra E. Levie.

It also refers to that hated leap of faith that characterizes living in and using another's language.
Lawrence: Iris and I display these holy badges of queer, which in our self-professed status as deviant and outsider allowed us to align ourselves with other members who spoke from the margins of the social sphere – somewhat like the speakers of the underclass. In *Bliss*, my use of other authors' texts questioned the authority I took on in order to subsume other authors' ideas and make them *mine* and subsequently *ours*, which outlined our alleged memberships of the supposed subtribe. We described our rejection through the assumption of our not belonging to the dominant group. We became interested in outlining our position and abdicating responsibility for the authority it took to describe these roles. We agreed that we could bite the hand that fed us, but not exclusively.

> This is not the challenge of a son to his father. Not the desire to usurp power. Neither is it nihilism. I don't mean to mystify my project, but to name it would, again, put it at the service of my own interests.
>
> (Iris Moore, *Rough Trade: Illusion of Conspiracy*)

In spite of describing them, the sacrificial roles that we assumed were not meant to gain privilege through their public annunciation and articulation. I was particularly interested in writers who explored the nature of the social contract. More specifically, writers who described their own

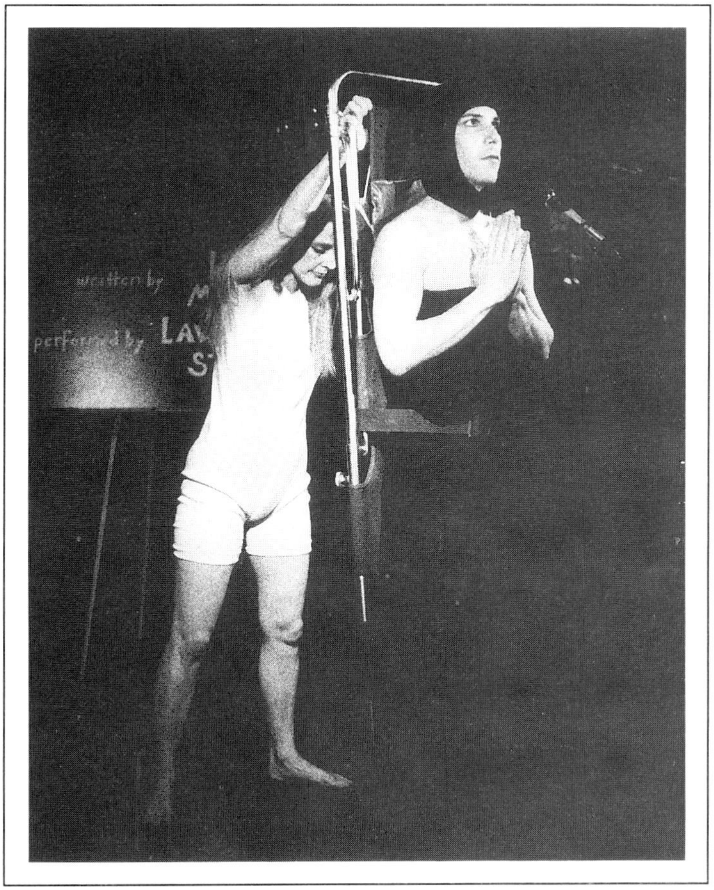

alienation from society, and in the process, create testaments of *disownership*. In thinking about texts that Iris and I were to share, I was seduced by the ambiguity of our ownership that represented the queer nationality they outlined and tossed away. We employed a certain level of denial to obtain duality and maintain an illusion of 'Self'. George Jackson's book, *Soledad Brother* seems to outline this dilemma:

> The prisoner must use the very language, the words, the syntax of his enemy, whereas he craves a separate language belonging only to his people ... It is perhaps a new source of anguish for me to realize that if I write something beautiful, pretty, it is in my enemy's language. ... It's his language that is enriched. ... I have only one recourse: to accept this but to corrupt it so skillfully that they are caught in my trap. To accept it in all its richness and to suffuse it with all my obsessions and all my hatred. That is my task.
>
> (George Jackson, *Soledad Brother*)

In my version of this text, it is delivered with the salutation 'Dearest'; and read as a letter that is procured from the inside pocket of the performer's dinner jacket – the jacket itself being shared with the other performer. The letter is sealed with a contractual (obligatory) gold seal. It is all things *Official,* leaving unanswered the authorship of the letter – was it left in the jacket from the previous performance? Is the reader the author? Is the author addressing the reader through written agreement? Is the reader actually the author and by reading it, reviewing it and reconsidering its terms? Is it a proclamation or a confession of a secret, something private? Why is it notarized? Made public? Is the accountability of content shared or unilaterally denied? The letter is punctuated at the end with the ironic phrase, 'Some task'. It remains unclear if the words 'Some task' are in the text of the letter or if they are a comment on it. 'Some task' seems to function as a subtext of *Rough Trade's* efficacy, articulation and/or purpose. We are describing our position to those who have denied us any position of authority. We are substantiating our own status as subclass. We are also divesting in our motivation and ability to describe our purpose. The *Soledad Brother* letter is then followed and signed-off with a host of possible endearments and goodbyes: 'yours', 'best', 'sincerely', 'yours truly', 'love'. This still doesn't indicate the name of the author and feels fraudulent. To eliminate the proof of its existence, the letter is immediately burned, resulting in a puff of smoke and the gold notary seal. No ash is produced and a simple, overused magic trick becomes a metaphor for the escape clause – words can be burned and the evidence of the contract destroyed. Through this act of disrespect for the written word, the performers enter a place of authority – their body is revealed as the source of truth (text), outlining that the contract or exchange occurs through the corporal body as it is linguistically conditioned and manipulated by the constraints of cultural constructs.

Iris: The appropriation of George Jackson's text is an illustration of the fear expressed in the original letter. The problems around using another's language, then using another's discontent with using another's language is presented as a queer issue. The letter is bracketed by an accusation and an apology with Lawrence flipping back and forth between rage and shame. His sense of self, always in flux.

> The white page is holy, but no one understands it. The black ink is holy, but no one understands it. The gold seal is holy but still no one understands it. And so we have our banner, but no one understands it. And we have an arena, in which our illnesses can face off. (Iris Moore, *Rough Trade: Illusion of Conspiracy*)

We had become dissatisfied with solo-monologue performance. We had exhausted our interest in a form that was being used by gay and lesbian performers in order to tell a coming-out story to a larger, looming mass. That *mass* is our nemesis. We were not interested in telling coming-out stories. We had each developed individual, distinct characters who were enhanced versions of *Selves*. We were not in the business of providing role models or proving how quantitatively normal (that is, healthy) we were. In addition to creating an environment that would allow for our differences, we also shared an interest in talking about our present condition and the dissatisfaction with the feigned and foreign language that it required. Our regular audience had become accustomed to us as sort of morbid, distressed, dissatisfied and pathologically queer. We wanted similarities between the scripts to appear but not seem forced or coerced. We wanted to write for an absent body and inhabit another. We wanted to create something that wasn't a proper play, something that couldn't be re-enacted by another actor. Our collaborative project would question the role of a singular author without levelling the material to a common ground. It was risky behaviour.

Lawrence: My own writing for performance had become increasingly reliant on appropriated texts of dead authors (largely those from the canon of gay, white male found in Naturalist/Romantic genres). This gave me the ability to rewrite, change syntax and subsume the authors' ideas into my body and make them come out of my mouth. This interest in histrionic ventriloquism carried over to *Rough Trade*. By writing in order to trade scripts, a contract of mutual ownership was built between us – one could never be performed without the other. Since the scripts were developed in the form of solo monologue, the performer would only allow the outsider or deviant to appear as a chimera or a ghost, or the kind of angel that is dark and hovering awaiting one's death. In essence, the author of the script would have to die a little when the outsider performed and would be periodically resuscitated and unplugged throughout the show. As performers, were were outlining the outsider's absence and subsequent resurrection. We were indicating our own failure in order to be open for possession. In the opening sequence of *Bliss*, a lip-synch to a Yoko Ono song becomes a ritual chant, a clearing of the space and a redefinition of the body in order for the rest to follow:

> Open Your Mind
> Open your mind.
> Open your legs.
> Open your heart.
> Open, Open, Open, Open, Open your thoughts.
> Open your cities.
> Open your trousers.

Open your mind.
Open your bodies.
Open your mind.

(Yoko Ono, *Hirake*)

Performed in underwear, this section first appears as an awakening but ends in exhaustion with the costume eventually being stripped off to reveal the new (old) body My interest was to provide a space for both bodies to exist. With this section serving as both a purge and an invitation, the performer could then be the proper medium for dual occupancy. The ambiguous author is partially introduced by revealing the sex of the performer.

Iris: We started out talking about the mutability of gender. In the three years of performing the pieces, the focus has given way to an awareness of the internal life of another person, a state of utter passivity in the face of a sentient experience that exists parallel to the critical one. The relationship evolved from the audience/performer to Lawrence/Iris. What does it mean when the audience is cut out of the loop? This transformation was invisible to the audience but has informed our subsequent work(s). I had been writing about femininity as illness for quite some time before I began this project with Lawrence. I was not comfortable with much of what I had written in relation to his HIV-positive status. It was too intimate and assumed a great deal about his feelings. If the writing was to remain personal, it had to be personal to both of us. The process of writing and then editing, so that the script resembled the voice in my head that created fiction about Lawrence's head. It was a trust game and a power exchange in an erotic sense. During the 'switch', the author is effectively muted and immobilized; frozen in a position of absence.

It's in my head but it comes out of your mouth.

One thing we do is act as stand-ins for each other. We emphasize the other's material and thoughts by highlighting or obscuring the absence/presence of their *sex*, their *self* and their *sexuality*. The overlay, of course, is the agenda of the second performer in the form of the other's *sex*, *self* and *sexuality*. It was my fear that in this forum, the job that I was trying to do would become impossible. In clearing that space for femininity to speak, and then occupying that space with a fag, I worried that femininity would again disappear. The tired, old argument, 'There are no women, only drag queens' would be pronounced. In the best interpretation, what happened was that femininity asserted itself as a separate entity, differentiating herself in the mass of material.

It's in my body and I want it out.

We relieve each other of the burden of authorship for a half hour. For a moment, all responsibility falls on the performer. S/he must own the text and exhibit the denial of the other's authorship. The contract required us to enable the other to do the work. An unexpected illustration of that idea occurred the last time we performed the piece. I was ill and had taken cold medicine. The effect of the medicine combined with my normal terror of performing dislocated the script from my head. The material was all there, but it was in no particular order. I opened my mouth and any part would come out. I would complete a scene and then Lawrence would help with props or costume change, all of which happened on-stage, but then he would tell me which scene to do next or tell me what I had skipped. It was a condition of letting Lawrence drive. In both pieces the body was displayed often; changing costumes on-stage, getting naked. A frequent comment was that we were reminding the audience of the fact that one is a boy and one is a girl. I thought of it as a way to hinge the spoken material onto the flesh, make it dependent on sexual attributes and eliminate any preconceived universality of experience or meaning.

In the years since we first wrote the pieces, living in different cities now, and having reunited to tour the piece in the United Kingdom, the material has taken on a deeper, less abstract meaning for both of us. We continue to act as stand-ins for each other; we inhabit each other's space, but now there is a critical perception of the difference between us. There is always the ghost of the other present and a sense of someone looking over your shoulder – ugly, pesky angels if you ask us. It is about a sense of responsibility and what we are entitled to assume about one another. Under what conditions are we allowed to invade the private territory of another person and what part of that can become public? What is the 'We' entity that we can safely agree on? What is the limit to our safety? The sentient body, the essence being on display in performance, is in itself only a semi-public event, not for mass consumption, best suited for basement cabarets and for those who seek it.

References

Jackson, G. (1971) *Soledad Brother*, Harmondsworth: Penguin.
Obejas, A. (1992) *The Chicago Reader* (June): 32.

Chapter Eleven

The aura of timelessness

Matthew Stradling

I define myself as an 'artist who is gay' as I feel the two aspects of the definition are inextricably linked; I am a gay man, proud of the culture I have inherited and I am an artist, whose sexuality informs and motivates my work. Despite this, my sexuality is not my only concern. Therefore I prefer to be called 'an artist who is gay' rather than a 'gay artist', since the latter implies '*Gay* artist', a categorization that suggests my work is only for the eyes of gay people and invites comparison with other gay artists, whose concerns are different from mine. I am very aware of the ghettoization of the gay and lesbian visual arts: labels only help to reduce the audience the work can reach. If, through my work, I am to be a representative of homosexuality, I want it to reach people of all sexual persuasions. This does not mean I wish to be a spokesperson for gay people;my work expresses my thoughts and feelings, however complicated and confused, as an individual gay man among many. Just as my work is a reaction to, and comment on, the work of many straight artists, I would hope it provokes a dialogue with others regardless of sexuality.

I feel that being gay is a privilege that has given me insight into ways of viewing the world that few straight people get the chance to explore. As 'outsiders', gay people can view society with an eye unclouded by conformity. We are not trapped in gender stereotypes. We have learned to play with'masks' and understand the value of artifice. Being confronted with heterosexuality on a daily basis leads us to question and define our sexuality. We understand the importance of sex in all areas of life and are creative in constructing relationships freer of convention. As a minority group, we have learned to deal with prejudice, humiliation, frustration, injustice and ultimately the challenge of being honest. I feel the 'gay experience' and gay culture has a lot to offer the straight world. My work is for whoever is open-minded enough to be interested in it; it is up to the viewer to cast aside prejudice. I feel it is my duty as a gay man to declare my sexuality in my art, thereby asserting gay people's worth as a group that has been ignored or denied its sexual freedom.

These days paintings are seen very much as products for commercial consumption. I still hold the, maybe idealistic, opinion, that painting is a medium, free of the pressures of social convention, in which an artist can be totally honest. I feel committed to being true to myself in my work and, as my sexuality is such an integral part of my individuality, I feel I must paint what interests and touches me as a gay man. Unfortunately it seems that galleries do not view paintings that deal with sexuality, or even worse, homosexuality, as a viable consumer product and so are reluctant to show my work. Coming out in my life and work has taught me that honesty is of prime importance to my self-respect. I am not about to get back in the closet for the sake of commercial gain.

Maybe if I had chosen a newer art form to express my ideas, such as photography or performance, my work might be better exposed. But what I like about painting is its aura of timelessness, which is lacking from most other art forms. I try to reflect this sense of timelessness in my work by avoiding placing figures in contemporary settings or in modern dress.I feel that the subjects my work addresses are ambiguous and do not need pinning down to a contemporary arena. With my work I am trying to make myself visible as a gay man within the painting tradition, and to reclaim the presence of past gay artists who have had an important role in furthering the development of our visual language.Therefore I hope the public perception of lesbians and gays is that not only are we around today, but that we have always been around and always will be.

As part of a minority group that has been underrepresented in the history of art, I find myself identifying with other groups who have suffered injustice. As a gay man I can identify to some extent with straight women and lesbians. Therefore I have found a lot of common ground with feminist critiques of the visual arts that are concerned with gender identity and its depiction in visual forms. Just as I am interested in inverting the traditional image of man as thinker and hero, so I am interested in subverting the depiction of woman as sexless virgin or servant to a male viewer. The women I paint are not painted for a heterosexual male viewer. (If they derive pleasure from them, then that is by-the-by.) They are embodiments of the female side of my identity; they connect me with womankind. They are also celebrations for women of their own beauty and power. The women I paint are individuals who are strong, sensual and in control of their own sexuality. Their gaze strips the viewer of their preconceptions rather than their clothes. I feel a gay man's view of womankind is as valid as anybody else's.

As I said earlier, I feel my work and my sexuality are inextricably linked. Gay people tend to be very visual; we are always looking, presenting and admiring. From clothes to bodies to interiors we are very aware of the language of appearance. From an early age art gave me an ideal world in which I could escape from the mundanity of real life. Galleries were the first places nudity was revealed to me without shame. Books of Michelangelo's 'ignudi' were my first porno mags. Art represented a world devoid of rules, where I could depict all the things I was not allowed to discuss. Similarly, painting for me now is a confessional experience: laying out my feelings, desires, thoughts and fears in visual form before the world is akin to coming out. Declaring my existence as a gay man through my work has empowered me. My sexuality has given me the motivation to paint and my painting has given me confidence in my sexual identity.

Throughout my art education I found myself surrounded by a visual language that meant very little to me. There was an emphasis on Abstract Expressionism and painterliness, regardless of content. The tutors were straight and mostly their concerns did not relate to my life. I began to challenge this claustrophobic heterosexual atmosphere by rejecting the dull intensity of their interests and delving into the world of kitsch and the banal. This involved much use of glue, dolls, plastic fruit and cartoon animals. I found that confronting the tutors and other students with work that was deliberately 'stupid' was a way of mocking their self-importance, while establishing a territory for myself that was concerned with wit, glamour, taste and beauty. I was beginning to define for myself a 'gay sensibility'. Having rejected notions of good and bad taste, I began to look at painters from the history of art whose work my education had rejected as worthless or just ignored. By claiming 'marginal art' as my inspiration I was declaring my marginality within the artschool setting. I discovered a tradition of camp that stretched from the Mannerists to Boucher to the Symbolists, which said more to me than de Kooning or Pollock ever could. I began to emulate the painting skills of the past and to cull imagery and symbols from classicism to create a personal mythology for today.

At this time I began to include male nudes within my work. With growing confidence they became the main focus of the compositions (as they were in my personal life). I came out in my work a long time before I did vocally. I felt liberated from the years of repressed desire and with a new-found freedom my work became a celebration of homoeroticism and sensuality. I lifted images of the male nudes from porn mags and 'elevated' them to 'high art'. They took on the role of gods by setting them within fantastical excessive tableaux, surrounded by the trappings of luxury: velvet, gold and jewels. Looking at pornography is often a liberating experience for gay men.To be allowed to look at desirable men,who will potentially love you, gives hope to men for whom looking can mean fear and humiliation. By depicting porn-models as icons within a luminous, timeless world, I wanted to elevate an art form that is regarded as base and dirty to that of high art with an almost religious significance, just as pearls are lumps of grit transformed into beautiful jewels. In so doing, I questioned the role of the nude in the history of art. I also wanted to present positive images of homosexual desire for a world that had made me feel bad about mine.

With the show 'Luxuria' at the Battersea Arts Centre, London, in 1991, I began to question the use of the stereotypical gay 'hunk' in my work. As I was maturing as a gay man I became aware that there was more to my sexuality than the purely physical. A lot of gay art depicts ideals, concentrating on looks, ignoring the person underneath, an attitude I was finding prevalent in the gay world in general. At this time I painted *The Mirror* (1991) as a comment on this attitude. The painting depicts a typical gay ideal based on the 'Venus with mirror' prototype of the Renaissance, gazing, frozen, at his own reflection in a bejewelled mirror. Although beautiful and sensual, with his imposing physique and good looks, the image is one of sterility; his genitals are dwarfed by his mass; his self-absorption closes him off from the world; he languishes on a mound of skulls, *memento mori* that remind us that looks will fade, or maybe they are the carcasses of those he has used up in his search for a love that can only be found in the mirror.

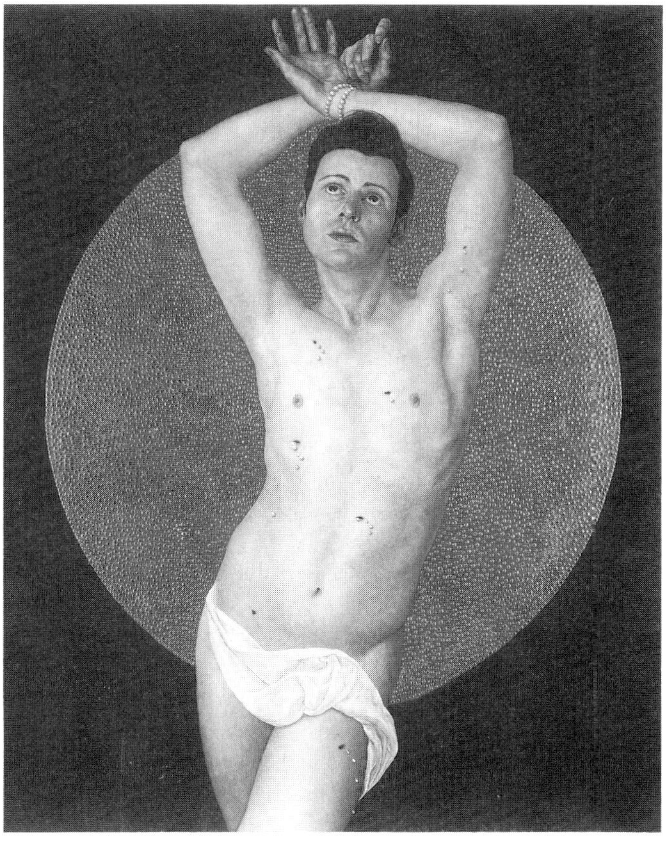

Figure 11.1 Matthew Stradling, *The Weeping Flesh* (1991), 48″ × 60″, oil on canvas
Collection of the artist.

Around this time I began using real people as models for my work. I took pleasure in playing with illusions of glamour and wealth by depicting ordinary modern people, friends and acquaintances, as divine figures, based on traditional painting prototypes, such as the Virgin Mary, Saint Sebastian, Narcissus, Danae, Christ, Atlas and Ophelia. The work for 'Luxuria' was a celebration of camp. I wanted the viewer to be wooed into a world of superabundance and luxury with the use of rich fabrics, sensual flesh and glittering jewels. But this excessive façade does not belie the serious intention of the subjects underneath; most of the traditional gender roles in the work are reversed, with the male figures assuming passive attitudes and the female dominant. The woman in *Lucina* (1991) is pregnant. She stares out at the viewer defiantly, while in her strong arms she holds aloft a giant pearl, reminiscent of the earth in depictions of Atlas. Seldom are pregnant women painted as being proud and glamorous.

Another painting depicts myself as the 'gay martyr' Saint Sebastian: *The Weeping Flesh* (1991) (Figure 11.1). I was interested in re-asserting the 'gayness' of this image; Saint Sebastian is a perfect icon for homosexuality. The writhing wounded man is sensual, vulnerable and passive. The penetration by spears is obviously sexual. The fact that he is in a religious ecstasy heightens the eroticism. The wounds can also be seen as symbols of the suffering endured by gay people in a homophobic society. In my representation, instead of blood pouring from the wound I have placed liquid pearls which solidify on the skin. They can be seen as tears or drops of spunk. Replacing the reality of blood with emblems of wealth and beauty is a way of transcending his suffering and gives him a magical significance. Despite the painting's sorrowful content it is intended to be a positive image: the saint's abjection is transformed into pride. He displays his suffering in defiance of the world. Of course it is an ironical image: by taking on the role of a saint I am dramatizing and mocking myself at the same time. The work has a sense of the ridiculous and theatrical which does not take itself too seriously. The presentation of serious subject in a non-serious way and vice versa encapsulates the spirit of camp, a way of seeing the world which, I feel, makes gay art relevant to a wider audience. Camp refuses to be didactic.

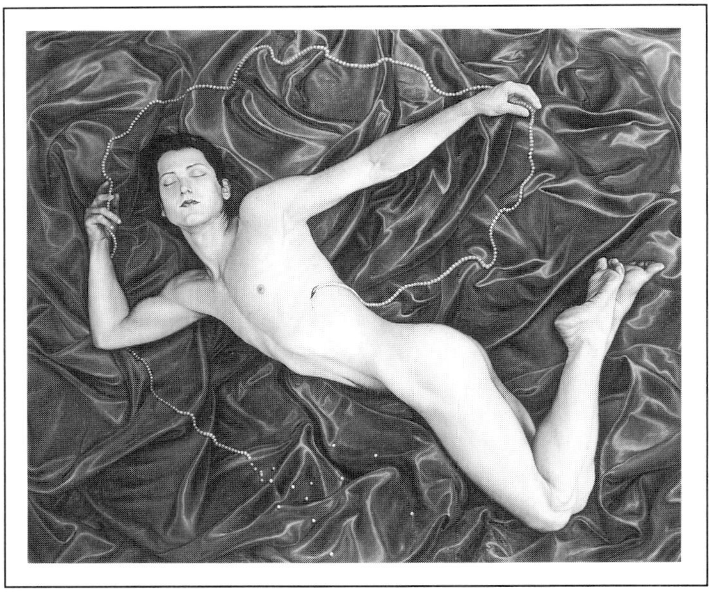

Figure 11.2 Matthew Stradling, *The Wound* (1993), 72″ × 60″, oil on canvas
Collection of the artist.

With the show 'Penetralia' at the Edge Gallery, London, in 1994 I continued to use the martyrdom theme in my work. Delving into the gay erotic experience, the work explored links between spiritual and physical ecstasy. It seems that the denial of sexual enjoyment in Christian morality has resulted in an imagery erupting with orgiastic fervour and extreme sensuality. I would compare this to the repression felt by gay people in a straight world, which results in the sexually charged, hedonistic nature of the gay scene. I found the irony of this comparison amusing and revealing, considering that homophobia is largely rooted in Christian morality. Therefore I placed an image of anal penetration, *Up and Out of the World* (1994), next to a quote from the writings of Saint Theresa in which she describes her religious ecstasy in highly sexual terms. Other paintings depicted details of sexual areas of the body set within icon-like frames: so that nipples, arseholes and vaginas became sacred objects akin to stigmata, symbols of fervent love. I felt it was important to show the arsehole as an erotic centre, to declare its sensuality without guilt, not only for gay men, but for lesbians and straights alike. By depicting such a taboo image, I wanted to be totally honest about what gay men do in bed. I find many gay artists are too coy and deflective about this area of our sexuality.

Other works dealt specifically with questions of gender identity. Several of the figures are hermaphrodite. The hermaphrodite transcends all gender stereotypes and can be seen as representing all of humankind, regardless of sexuality. In *Rebis (Double Thing)* (1993) I depicted a sexless, hairless, ageless figure emerging from a golden vagina. I wanted to depict an image of an innocent being, devoid of classification. Like a vision of the soul it is purely human and vulnerable, free of our struggles with the constraints of sexual identity. In contrast the hermaphrodite *Marissa* (1994) was painted to challenge these sexual constraints. The body of a beautiful young woman lies prone and inviting before our gaze, luxuriating in a setting of velvet, pearls and gauze. Like a love-slave she wears manacles of pearl, a collar and nipple-rings, enhancing her submissive pose. Only, from between her legs in a threatening manner rises an enormous erect penis. By depicting the alluring passive supine woman of 'titillating' boudoir art with the ultimate symbol of male aggression and dominance, the painting mocks the convention of female nude painting and questions the notion of male superiority. The painting can also be seen as depicting a gay man's state of arousal; he is passive and penetrable, yet he himself has the erection. Likewise, it could be seen as a lesbian fantasy in which she imagines what it is like to have an erect penis. Marissa stares out from the painting, questioning the viewer's desires and challenging them to believe in her reality.

The male nudes in the show also have an ambiguous sexuality; many have symbolic vaginas in the form of wounds in their flesh. As in the images of Christ, where the wound in his side seems to represent a feminine aspect of his personality, these wounds reveal a male vulnerability and passivity. In *The Wound* (1993) (Figure 11.2) a beautiful boy floats on a ground of blue satin, his body contorted in ecstasy or pain. From a gaping wound in his side pours a stream of pearls. His eyes do not engage the viewer, they are closed in euphoria or death. In this painting I was trying to unveil a fascination with death that seems to be at the heart of the erotic experience. Reaching the point of orgasm is like passing over into death; the self is annihilated. The wound in the boy's side could indicate that he is dead or it could represent a sexual orifice from which an ejaculation of pearls is shooting. The satin on which he writhes could be seen as bed-sheets or funeral shrouds.

In this time of the AIDS pandemic, the erotic brings us closer to death. For myself, and probably for many other gay men, sex makes me more aware of my own mortality and vulnerability. I am constantly touched by obituary columns and stories of loved ones who have died of AIDS. The gay world has been shadowed by the numbers of those that have died and those that will die. I feel this sense of mourning has filtered into my work. As I have become more aware of the AIDS crisis my paintings have become more sober, the imagery simpler and the content more expressive of sorrow. The nudes I paint have become portraits of individuals whose nudity expresses their vulnerability rather than celebrating their sexuality. The erotic for me is no longer only charged with excitement and liberation but also, now, tainted with a sense of anguish and loss. I feel my work is moving in a direction where the individuals I paint will be presented as 'real' people with 'real' imperfections; whose beauty comes from their dignity as human beings rather than from their physical perfection. I am more interested in creating a reaction in the viewer's emotions, as opposed to in their groins.

PART III

Production and consumption

Chapter Twelve

Promoting a sexuality

Law and lesbian and gay visual culture in America

Carl F. Stychin

This essay examines the relationship between lesbian and gay cultural representations and state funding of the production of culture in America. In particular, it looks at how, in the late 1980s, culture became a flashpoint of political and legal controversy centring upon the representation of sexual minorities. Arguments over the merits of particular cultural artifacts have occurred throughout the era of public funding. In recent years, though, the attacks on funding have become far more vigorous and sustained. As a consequence, cultural funding has been placed squarely on the political agenda. The debates surrounding funding have focused primarily on photography, performance art, comic strips and written description. What links these different media is that the content in question was read within dominant culture as 'homosexual' and, therefore, as obscene and indecent. The public funding context is particularly interesting because the discourses that surround the production of culture and constraints on its funding are not framed simply in terms of libertarian conceptions of free speech versus state censorship of expression. Rather, critics of public funding argue in favour of the public's right to oversee the expenditure of tax dollars and to make determinations of how revenue is spent. The central claim is that the public has a right to refuse to fund the creation of cultural representations which the vast majority view as offensive, obscene and indecent. At the same time, a second argument is made that emphasizes the rights of a religious minority of fundamentalist Christians to not be required to pay for cultural production which runs counter to the tenets of their faith. Furthermore, it is argued that government must make decisions all the time on what projects are worthy of its support, given that resources are necessarily limited. Is it not reasonable to discriminate on the basis of what the general public finds objectionable? Should taxpayers be forced to pay for culture that 'mocks' them, holds them in contempt, and discriminates against them based upon their religious beliefs? Of course, the makers of these arguments also claim to represent the voice of 'middle America' confronting the perceived elites – the urban art establishment, intellectuals and gay politicos.

Funding critics in fact deploy an array of arguments which stress the rights of variously constituted groups – religious minorities, middle America, and the nation as a whole, the moral fibre of which, it is claimed, must be defended. Such an approach is typical of arguments articulated by the radical right wing in American political discourse. When speaking on behalf of a singular national culture, they seek to define some cultural workers as subversive to the national interest. At other times, critics argue on behalf of specific constituencies within the United States against the competing claims of other groups. The slippage between arguments framed in terms of a monolithic national cultural sensibility, and a pluralistic and contested cultural space, thus is strategically manipulated by the right.

For arguments marshalled on the other side to respond effectively they must reach beyond mere cries against state censorship of cultural expression. The claims vary from the importance of maintaining an arm's length relationship between politicians and the funding agencies of government, to the inherent difficulty of defining what is obscenity and what is art. As a consequence, it is argued that particular funding decisions ought not to be interrogated by the legislature. This approach allows the proponents of funding to avoid a discussion of the merits of any particular cultural work. In addition, given that these cultural battles have been largely waged around lesbian and gay representations, the arguments emerging from that community have often been framed in the language of rights: the right to represent the lives of gay people; the right to be free from invidious discrimination in funding decisions; and, in the case of representations of safer sexual practices, the right to *life* through accurate and explicit information. Thus, a mixture of individual rights claims centring upon artistic freedom and claims of group rights grounded in communitarian language, form the basis of much of the pro-funding argument.

The funding context thus proves interesting because both sides ground their claims in the language of rights. Liberal assertions of group rights are met by a right-wing appropriation of that same discourse. Moreover, in this debate there is no scepticism expressed as to the importance of cultural representation in the construction of sexuality. Rather, everyone appears to agree on the crucial importance of visual culture and, in particular, lesbian, gay and queer cultural representation. In fact, the development of an openly articulated and confident lesbian and gay culture has served to galvanize the right-wing reaction.

I shall examine two controversies that dominated the political scene and which exemplify how legal discourse is employed to construct notions of individual and group rights, homosexuality and nationhood. The first is the debate surrounding funding decisions by the National Endowment for the Arts and attempts to restrict the range of projects which the Endowment was entitled to fund with public money. The second is the move in the late 1980s to preclude public funding of safe sex materials that 'promote homosexuality'. The two debates highlight how representations of the gay body are read as particularly problematic within dominant culture which demands no less than their erasure from the public sphere. The power of representation to promote and convert is apparent in the position adopted by funding critics and is combined with claims about the values that underpin 'America'. Lesbian and gay cultural production is perceived as holding the awesome power to undermine and destroy the core values that have shaped American society. The meaning of culture thus becomes singular and determinate and is read as perverse, pornographic and dangerous to the body politic.

THE FUNDING OF HOMOEROTIC ART

While the particular example focused upon here reached its zenith, in terms of publicity, at the end of the last decade, the National Endowment for the Arts continues to feature as an ongoing arena of controversy in relation to lesbian and gay sexuality. The contestation over arts funding heats up with a certain regularity and often with a fierce intensity, as in the campaign by Patrick Buchanan to unseat President Bush for the Republican presidential nomination in 1992. Claims that the President was 'soft' on arts funding for gay themed works were deployed as an example of weakness in the face of subversive forces at work within the nation. These arguments were not without some effect among the right wing in America. The NEA funding context thus is far from simply a matter of academic interest.

By way of background, the National Endowment for the Arts was created in 1965 as a means of public financial support for the arts through an agency with independent grant-making powers. The Endowment's mandate is to sponsor works of 'artistic or cultural significance' through grants to individuals of 'exceptional talent'. The Endowment was intended to be free from political influence in its grant-making decisions, which were to be based upon the recommendations of peer review panels of professional artists expert in particular fields. The final funding decisions have always rested with the chairperson of the Endowment: an appointment made by the President of the United States, with the advice and consent of the Senate.[1]

It is not surprising that funding decisions in the past have occasionally given rise to controversy. Since the creation of the Endowment, there has been criticism of individual funding decisions and general Endowment policy, often centring upon competing claims of cultural elitism and populism. In addition, dramatic budget-cutting in the name of national debt reduction produced an angry response in the arts communities in the early 1980s.[2] However, the vehemence of the reaction to two funding decisions that came to light in 1989 was unprecedented and underscored how a new cultural agenda was being set in place. The first was the posthumous NEA-sponsored travelling exhibition entitled 'Robert Mapplethorpe: The Perfect Moment'. This was scheduled to appear at the Corcoran Gallery in Washington DC, but was cancelled by the gallery in response to political pressure. The Mapplethorpe retrospective included his controversial *X Portfolio*, largely consisting of sado-masochistic gay male imagery. It also included the *Y Portfolio*, which comprised Mapplethorpe's frequently criticized photographs of African American men. The second work was by artist Andres Serrano who had received NEA funding for his *Piss Christ*, a cibachrome showing a plastic crucifix submerged in his urine.

In response to these funding decisions, Senator Jesse Helms intervened as a critic of the NEA. His attack alternated between the 'blasphemy' of Serrano's *Piss Christ* and the 'perversity' of Mapplethorpe's *X Portfolio*. In calling for an end to government subsidization of projects akin to these, Helms considered at some length the implications of Mapplethorpe's photographs. For the senator, this work 'ha[d] a political and social dimension':

> the art critics acknowledge that Mapplethorpe's obscene photographs were an effort to gain wider exposure of, and acceptance for, homosexuality – which happens to be the stated political goal of all homosexual pressure groups. For instance, the catalog for the Mapplethorpe exhibit at the Whitney Museum of Modern Art concedes that Mapplethorpe felt sadomasochism ... was an almost obligatory subject for him to treat and that 'he reported it not as a voyeur, but as an advocate.'[3]

Thus, it is the power of representations not only to expose a lifestyle to public view, but to further the acceptance and promotion of that lifestyle, which was particularly troubling for Helms. This is the political dimension of the work which provided the rationale for a political response to its subsidization by a governmental agency.

Senator Helms proposed a statutory restriction as a condition for the appropriation of funding for the Endowment, which he introduced on 26 July 1989. It provided that:

> None of the funds authorized to be appropriated pursuant to this Act may be used to promote, disseminate, or produce
> 1) obscene or indecent materials, including but not limited to depictions of sadomasochism, homo-eroticism, the exploitation of children, or individuals engaged in sex acts; or
> 2) material which denigrates the objects or beliefs of the adherents of a particular religion or non-religion; or
> 3) material which denigrates, debases, or reviles a person, group, or class of citizens on the basis of race, creed, sex, handicap, age, or national origin.[4]

Clearly, Helms sought to respond directly both to the Mapplethorpe exhibit and the Serrano piece. With respect to Serrano, clause 2) attempted to foreclose such a funding decision in the future. With respect to Mapplethorpe, the prohibition on the obscene and indecent, and the explicit references to sado-masochism, homoeroticism, and children cut a sufficiently wide swathe to include all of the photographs that Helms found offensive.

The original wording of the Helms amendment also was significant for the way in which it focused attention on group rights as a justification for restrictions on arts funding. Those groups that warranted protection from the 'harm' included religious minorities as well as racial, sexual and other groups. Clauses 2) and 3) explicitly deployed the language of group harm inflicted through expression. Previously, this argument had been used primarily by minority groups in the context of racial and sexual hate speech. Helms's appropriation of the idea of harm caused by representation also had a superficial resemblance to arguments developed by anti-pornography feminists.[5] In this context, though, the language of minority protection from hateful representations is re-worked in order to protect the sensibilities of mainstream America and the American Christian community. The supporters of the amendment sought to draw an analogy between the treatment of Christians at the hands of Serrano and intolerance directed against religious and racial minorities. As one congressman pondered, 'one wonders how many of those who are aggressively opposing the setting of these standards would be doing so, if it had been a photo of Martin Luther King or a symbol of the Jewish faith that had been submerged in a bottle of urine at taxpayers' expense.'[6] Furthermore, it was alleged that the constitutionally imposed separation of church and state was infringed by government funded 'anti-Christian' art. Opponents of the amendment also argued within a framework of religious faith, emphasizing not only their own deeply felt Christian beliefs, but also the dangers of religious fanaticism implicit in 'an amendment which would give an Ayatollah Khomeini or the like the right to veto the grants of the National Endowment for the Arts'.[7]

After congressional debate, the amendment was modified through the withdrawal of clauses 2) and 3) and the removal of the reference to indecency in clause 1). The focus thus shifted away from Serrano and religious offensiveness, and towards work that might be considered obscene. The justification for the amendment thus became more obvious and was clearly targeted at the Mapplethorpe exhibit. Simply put, it was argued that the taxpayer should not be expected to fund cultural work that is obscene, pornographic or, as Senator Helms argued, vulgar, sick and unspeakable. However, there also was included a new provision which stated that work which had serious artistic value was not precluded from receiving funding. But for those members of Congress supporting the bill (and indeed for most of those opposing it) there seemed no issue as to the artistic merit of *Portfolio X* itself, which one member claimed '99.9% of Americans would categorically define as obscene garbage'.[8] Some politicians went further, and attributed an overwhelming symbolic value to any representation of gay sexuality, finding that NEA funding decisions exemplified an ongoing battle against the 'eroding [of] the moral structure of our country' by something 'inherently evil'.[9] For one member of Congress, the battle lines were all too clear, and this controversy was:

> the symptom of a moral decay in a society that has lost the ability to say that there are standards in this world that govern mankind down through time and that are valid, traditional family values, where we have the courage as leaders of the country to stand up and say what is junk and what is good literature, what is pornographic, and what we are going to tolerate.[10]

In fact, the determination of what is unacceptable was explicit in the Helms amendment. The intent was to ensure that funds would not be made available to artists who would then produce a work that *might* be considered obscene and, given the definition, that meant anything that depicted the undefined 'homoerotic'. Moreover, because the amendment included in its list of prohibited representations, 'individuals engaged in sex acts', the further inclusion of the term 'homoeroticism' logically implied something other than the depiction of same-sex acts. It suggested rather that funding of any representation of lesbian or gay sexuality was foreclosed. Carole Vance has argued that the amendment had a particular 'linguistic elasticity' because it left unanswered the question of whether peer review panels should reject *all* proposals that might offend any group, and whether any representation that the proponents of the amendment would object to is then necessarily obscene.[11] Finally, the phrase 'may be considered obscene' suggested that the discretion left to the Endowment was sufficiently wide as to be beyond review in court.

There were other feats of linguistic gymnastics in the amendment. The exempting clause that permitted funding of works of serious value was difficult to square with the rest of the amendment. If a peer review panel determines that a project is worthy of funding, does it, by definition, possess serious artistic value which overrides the other statutory clauses? If that is the case, then the entire amendment becomes devoid of meaning since it merely reiterates what already was obvious, namely, that funding is to be awarded on the basis of artistic excellence. The amendment also implied that representations of sado-masochism, homoeroticism and the other examples necessarily are obscene by reason of content alone. However, in American constitutional law the definition of obscenity, which can be legally proscribed, is narrow and convictions under obscenity law are extremely difficult to obtain.[12] The narrowness of this legal test appears to be replaced by a much broader definition that turns on offensiveness to groups in general. Finally, as a symbolic matter, the grouping together of homoeroticism, sado-masochism, sexual acts, and the exploitation of children further reinforces the construction of lesbians and especially of gay men as perverse and degenerate.

Despite its apparent incoherence, the Helms amendment was far from ineffective both symbolically and practically. It easily passed into law and, in response, recipients of funding were required to certify that no federal funds would be used to promote material that could be deemed obscene, including, but not limited to, the various categories of representation prohibited by the amendment. Not long thereafter, Congress also enacted a number of structural changes to the National Endowment for the Arts. The composition of peer review panels was to explicitly reflect 'diverse artistic and cultural points of view' and include non-artists.[13] This was designed to allow for more representation of the views of middle America, in what was perceived to be the exclusive preserve of the East Coast artistic elites. Written records were to be kept of panel meetings and the chairperson of the Endowment was explicitly given final authority over funding decisions. Artists were required to file interim reports on their progress, and payments could be made by instalments, with a provision for reimbursement of funds that had been used to create a project determined by a court to be obscene. Clearly, these structural changes were aimed both at the funding decision stage (by ensuring review panels which would be less receptive to homoerotic work) and at the later stage of artistic production (by creating mechanisms to ensure closer monitoring of the content of the cultural production).

It also became increasingly clear that the focus of attention was specifically on the cultural production of the 'homoerotic'. This was apparent in May 1990 when then chairperson of the NEA, John Frohnmayer, overturned the recommendations of the NEA's theatre review panel and denied funding to four performance artists – Karen Finley, John Fleck, Holly Hughes and Tim Miller (the 'NEA Four'). Holly Hughes is openly lesbian and John Fleck and Tim Miller are out gay men, and the sexuality of all three forms an integral part of their performance art. Moreover, Karen Finley, although she does not identify herself as lesbian, creates work that tackles issues of sexuality, and it has been argued that her performances frequently are read within dominant culture as 'lesbian' because of her focus on 'policing displays of the body'.[14] As Finley explicitly employs her body (including orifices) in her performances, her art frequently is seen as 'unnatural' and, consequently, she is read as homosexual.

Although the NEA Four 'defunding' decision marked the height of the controversy and was followed by resignations by a number of expert panellists in different fields, subsequent events have suggested that these cultural contestations are far from over. In 1990 the Helms amendment was dropped by Congress, but in its place was inserted a provision which required the chairperson of the Endowment to ensure that 'general standards of decency and respect for the diverse beliefs and values of the American public' were a consideration in funding decisions; and that 'obscenity' (as judicially determined) was not funded.[15] In fact, the chair of the Endowment found himself increasingly unable to please critics on either side. In November 1991, Frohnmayer approved grants to Tim Miller and Holly Hughes. And, in early 1992, Endowment support for a New York literary journal, *The Portable Lower East Side*, publications of which included *Queer City* and *Live Sex Acts*, spurred conservative organisations to send excerpts to members of Congress. In the midst of Frohnmayer's conversion to support for the independence of funding decisions by the NEA panels, and in the climate of a presidential election campaign, he was forced to resign with effect from 1 May 1992.

The Republican administration elevated deputy chairperson Anne-Imelda Radice to the position of acting chair of the NEA. A few days after assuming office, Radice vetoed two grants recommended by the advisory panel for sexually explicit works: an art exhibit at the List Visual Arts Center at the Massachusetts Institute of Technology entitled *Corporal Politics*, which featured violence, castration and sexual fetishism; and a video and photography exhibit at the Anderson Gallery of the Virginia Commonwealth University called *Anonymity and Identity*, which included one work by photographer Annette Messager entitled 'My Wishes', which consisted of 'more than 100 tiny photographs of faces, lips, hair and, in one case, a penis'.[16] In protest, the Endowment sculpture panel announced the suspension of its grant meeting and the solo theatre arts panel resigned in protest. Two other panels criticized Radice's actions. But the Endowment was unmoved and in November 1992, during the final weeks of the Bush administration, it refused to award grants to three lesbian and gay film festivals on the basis of artistic merit.

Of course, the political climate changed dramatically with the election of the Clinton administration and especially with the appointment of actress Jane Alexander as chair of the Endowment. However, controversy still swirls around the cultural scene in America. Grant applications create heated debates in the NEA's advisory council meetings and, in a dramatic move, in August 1993 the county commission of Cobb County, Georgia, voted to end all of its arts funding because of the possibility of inadvertently supporting gay-related cultural works. The vote occurred after complaints about a production of the off-Broadway play *Lips Together, Teeth Apart*, which includes peripheral references to gay male sexuality. More recently, right-wing politicians have described as depraved and pornographic a performance by HIV-positive artist Ron Athey at the NEA-funded Walker Art Center in Minneapolis in April 1994. Athey carved symbols on the backs of audience members and made prints in blood of the patterns on paper towels. The performance has been cynically deployed as a rationale for threatened cuts to the NEA's budget.

Clearly, then, the political process has been a difficult arena in which to advance claims in response to the anti-funding critics. Arguments that taxpayers have the *right* not to have their money spent *promoting* lesbian and gay male sexuality through cultural funding generally get a receptive hearing at the legislative level. This is reinforced by arguments that lesbian and gay cultural representation *promotes* the destruction of the moral fibre and values of American society. Implicit in this position is the point that there is no right to governmental funding for any particular cultural endeavour, especially when the majority perceives it as obscene, indecent, pornographic and incompatible with the national interest. Finally, the funding of representations of lesbian and gay life, it is argued, would violate the rights of practising Christians not to have their tax dollars spent on promoting (simply through representation) a set of sexual practices they view as inherently evil. The rights both of mainstream America and a religious minority group thus are invoked simultaneously (despite contradictions) to marshall arguments in favour of restrictions on financial support for the arts.

This set of arguments, as formulated by the right wing, has forced proponents of lesbian and gay cultural representation to rethink their response. While claims can be made in terms of the rights of lesbians and gay men as a group to participate fully and equally in American cultural production, group rights arguments cut both ways. The rights of religious minorities and 'the American public' have partially neutralized arguments framed in terms of equal cultural participation. Moreover, this argument has frequently been met with the response that no artist has a right to funding and that the marketplace of ideas will ensure that work of value finds an outlet. The argument thus is made that artistic freedom is not limited by funding restrictions. Rather, only state subsidization is curtailed.

Interestingly, while the political process has been fairly hostile to claims of funding for lesbian and gay cultural representation, constitutional litigation has proven an effective means of eliminating funding restrictions. These 'victories' demonstrate the power of the doctrine of free speech in American constitutional discourse (the 'First Amendment') to trump other arguments also based in the language of rights. As Nan Hunter, a litigator in a series of cases dealing with restrictions on public funding of sexual expression has suggested, the argument has been made that cultural representations of lesbians and gay men are worthy of constitutional protection as speech of political and social value:

> Our claims set forth the first serious demand that speech about sexuality be treated as core political speech. This development marks a radical shift in First Amendment doctrine, provoking a category crisis of whether to treat sexual speech as part of a shared social dialogue or as second-tier quasi-obscenity. The change in legal doctrine has altered political thought as well. It signals the conceptualization of sexuality – and specifically homosexuality – as a political idea.[17]

Thus, while the legislative interventions have sought to define the 'homoerotic' as indecent, obscene and pornographic, the constitutional arena provides the opportunity to challenge that characterization and to assert a value in the expression of sexual minorities to which can be attached a constitutional *right*.

The issue of whether such restrictions on funding are a violation of the right of free speech raises one of the most vexed questions of constitutional law. On the one hand, it is well established that governments must make decisions all the time about what is deserving of funding (and what is not) and it is within the power of the legislature to determine that it will provide funding for some types of expression and not for others. To hold otherwise would mean that any attempt at public support of expression in America was unconstitutional. However, it also has been firmly established that the government 'may not deny a benefit to a person on a basis that infringes his constitutionally protected interests – especially his interest in freedom of speech'.[18] The difficult issue therefore is how to reconcile these propositions.

Two legal challenges in the context of NEA funding illustrate this difficulty and they both underscore the power of speech rights claims. First, in *Bella Lewitzky Dance Foundation v Frohnmayer*, a District Court judge held that requiring grant recipients to certify that funds would not be used to produce obscenity was unconstitutional.[19] Judge Davies found that the certification requirement was vague and created a 'chilling effect' on the speech rights of grant recipients.[20] He reasoned that there was no question of the government's right to place conditions on the award of federal funding, but that such provisions could not be unduly vague. As a consequence of this decision, the NEA dropped the certification requirement.

Second, in *Finley v NEA*, the 'NEA Four' challenged the decency clause as part of their constitutional appeal of the decision to deny them funding in May 1990.[21] Judge Tashima found in their favour, holding that the requirement that artistic merit and excellence be determined in light of 'general standards of decency' was vague and too broad in its sweep to satisfy constitutional scrutiny. He found the words 'decency' and 'respect' to be 'inherently subjective' and 'contentless'.[22] With respect to free speech doctrine, Judge Tashima reasoned that artistic expression 'is at the core of a democratic society's cultural and political vitality'[23] and that governmental funding criteria are limited to 'professional evaluations of ... merit'.[24] That determination of excellence did not encompass considerations of decency. Consequently, the decency clause was declared unconstitutional. In both cases, then, one can see rights claims based upon freedom of artistic expression overcome competing arguments.

The claims of indecency also highlight a deep ambivalence within dominant culture with respect to the representation of lesbian and gay male sexuality. The critics of arts funding for lesbian and gay visual culture assume without question that representations have a tremendous transformative potential which is sufficiently powerful to erode the dominance of heterosexuality in American society. Moreover, visual culture is seen as having the power to erode 'America' itself through the destruction of its traditional values. Proponents of these arguments implicitly accept the social construction of both sexuality and the nation state, in that each is capable of a radical reconstitution through cultural means. Nor is there any attempt made by the critics to question the relationship between the messages intended by the artist and the meaning received by the audience or to acknowledge the possibility of multiple, contradictory or ironic readings of any representation. There is, of course, an irony in the argument because, for Senator Helms and his supporters who have been an unanticipated audience for lesbian and gay visual culture, the works in question reinforce (rather than transform) their views about lesbian and gay sexuality. The solution offered by this audience is a truly conservative one, for they seek to stop any attempt at reforming public opinion through a denial of the material resources that are perceived as necessary for that project.

PROMOTING HOMOSEXUALITY: SAFE SEX EDUCATIONAL MATERIALS

Another area that has served as a flashpoint of controversy in roughly the same period is again public funding of gay visual culture, which comes to be characterized as obscene and pornographic. The function of the cultural work in question differs in that the content in this case is explicit 'safe-sex' information aimed at a gay male audience. Such material clearly remains a part of visual culture and is aimed at particular subcultural communities. Although I would argue that AIDS rhetoric implicitly infuses much of the discourse surrounding the NEA funding controversy, in the safe-sex debates that rhetoric becomes explicit and serves to ground claims that the public should not fund representations that 'promote homosexuality'. Thus, public funding for the promotion (realized simply through representation) of gay sexuality is argued to be intolerable for mainstream America and for religious groups. Within the terms of this debate, abstinence (or conversion to heterosexuality) is the only course that should be advocated and the only truly safe sex.

Furthermore, as in the later NEA controversies, a discourse of rights is invoked by both sides. For the anti-funding critics, the right of the taxpayer not to fund obscene materials that promote gay male sex and which corrupt the vulnerable was paramount in both instances. However, for advocates of public funding, rights claims were more immediately relevant in this context than they were to be in the NEA debates. In the case of safe-sex materials, the right in question is one of life, through accurate and accessible safe-sex educational material. Furthermore, the position is strengthened because, in this context, support is forthcoming from segments of the medical profession rather than from the arts establishment (although both sides invoke medical discourses to bolster their arguments). Finally, the funding argument is supported by the ethos of volunteerism in American society which is exemplified by the network of AIDS-related charitable organizations which produced the materials in question.

By way of background, in 1985 the American Centers for Disease Control commenced the funding of programmes aimed at changing sexual behaviour, including work undertaken by the Gay Men's Health Crisis in New York City. This organization provides educational and other services to the community. Some of these educational materials, aimed at sections of the gay community, included graphic descriptions of safe-sex practices. As a matter of course, GMHC used private funds to develop their most explicit materials. As early as 1986, the Centers for Disease Control, concerned about possible negative reaction to such strategies, developed restrictions on the content of programmes that received federal funding, requiring that any materials produced 'would be judged by a reasonable person to be inoffensive to most educated adults'.[25]

However, a single series of publications served to focus the debate in the United States. In 1986, GMHC produced a number of 'Safe-Sex Comix', which used cartoons combined with narrative to deliver safe-sex information aimed at a gay male audience. In keeping with the policy of GMHC, these publications were not produced directly with the assistance of federal funds. The comics were obtained by Senator Helms. In 1987, he introduced an amendment to an appropriations bill in Congress to prohibit the provision of federal funds through the Centers for Disease Control to either private groups or state and local governments which would be used 'to provide AIDS education, information, or prevention materials and activities that promote or encourage, directly or indirectly, homosexual sexual activities'.[26]

The debate on this amendment foreshadowed the NEA controversy. Attention was turned to the promotion of both gay male sexual acts and identities and the unreasonableness of the use of federal funds to support that lifestyle. The focus was not simply on the condemnation of sexual acts, but was more broadly based:

> I think it is appropriate for us to examine and find out a little bit more about how extensive the movement of homosexuality in America has become in terms of changing the cultural values of our society so that we will accept and equate homosexuality on a par with heterosexual life.[27]

Sexuality thus becomes culturally based, historically contingent, and therefore capable of promotion.

Moreover, gay male sexuality is not only dangerous because so easily promoted, but also because of its contagiousness. The metaphorical tropes used to describe homosexuality in conservative thought have long drawn upon the language of disease and infection. Consequently, gay male sexuality readily (and conveniently) is linked inextricably to the AIDS pandemic, such that the gay male body is *the* infectious vessel which contains and spreads HIV. According to Senator Helms, 'every AIDS case can be traced back to a homosexual act'[28], and more graphically:

> Many of the experts, self proclaimed, tell us that the source of the AIDS epidemic is the AIDS virus. That is like saying that the source of a fire set by an arsonist was the match that the arsonist used, rather than the arsonist who struck the match and set the fire.[29]

The promotion of homosexuality, then, leads to the spread of AIDS. In this explanation, safe sex cannot be gay sex, for the gay man is constructed as disease carrier. Funding of safe-sex materials contributes to the spread of AIDS because of the contagiousness of homosexuality as lifestyle. The only safe sex, for the incurably gay man, is no sex and that is what demands promotion. Finally, and inconsistently, safe sex materials were derided for their ineffectiveness since, according to Senator Helms, 'it still is not doing any good because the people who are spreading this disease do not pay any attention to it anyhow.'[30] Yet, at the same time, safe-sex representations were criticized for their power to promote the homosexual lifestyle and, moreover, were characterized as pornographic. In the context of these interventions, Helms's amendment easily passed the US Congress and was enacted into law.[31]

In response, the Centers for Disease Control adopted a strategy which foreshadowed the NEA's approach, and propagated guidelines which utilized a standard of offensiveness to a general, mainstream audience. Funding recipients were asked to draw up a peer review panel and to submit educational materials to it for prior approval. The panel would consist of a reasonable cross-section of the general public. Although the amendment was rejected the following year in the debate on the appropriations bill, and was replaced by a more 'neutral' clause that focused on whether AIDS educational materials were designed to encourage sexual activity in general, the CDC offensiveness restriction remained until 1992.

The legislative intervention in regulating safe-sex materials had a 'chilling effect' on the work of AIDS educators. The standard of offensiveness forced them to consider the directness and explicitness of information and, more generally, to ask whether 'realist portrayals of gay male sexuality are pornographic by definition to a main-stream culture that wants to hear nothing about it.'[32] The amendment provided a graphic example of how 'the specificities of gay men's health education needs are obliterated by the mandate of the heterosexual majority'.[33] It also has been argued that the restriction discriminated against the less educated, less literate and lower income populations for whom graphic representations may be more effective educational tools than more circumscribed explanations.

Interestingly, as in the case of the later NEA legislative restrictions, constitutional litigation proved an effective strategy for advocates of public funding in the safe sex controversy. The CDC guidelines were challenged on constitutional grounds in *Gay Men's Health Crisis v Sullivan.* The revised grant terms under consideration utilized a standard of 'offensiveness for a majority of persons outside the intended audience'. The United States District Court for the Southern District of New York found that standard to be outside the statutory authority of the CDC and the court also held the grant terms to be 'unconstitutionally vague' with 'no core meaning' (which also was the basis for the NEA decisions).[34] While the 'obscene' legitimately could be proscribed, Judge Kram held that obscenity and offensiveness were far from synonymous in the context of gay male safe-sex representations:

> Because the obscenity standard is inherently narrower than the offensiveness criterion, there is a vast amount of material that could be developed that would be deemed offensive, but not obscene. As such, the Court finds that reference to the obscenity standard offers no real guidance or clarification to either AIDS educators or PRP [peer review panel] members.[35]

The Court recognized the chilling effect on speech of such restrictions, citing evidence of self-censorship by AIDS educators. The guidelines thus were struck down as unconstitutional. Once again, claims of freedom of speech trumped competing claims about the right of government (and, by extension, the taxpayer) to choose what types of representation to fund. The use of rights language within the judicial arena proved a successful means of eliminating restrictions on the content of visual representations.

Within the context of restrictions on safe-sex materials, the link between the right to speech and the right to an identity is readily apparent. As Mark Barnes, a litigator who has specialized in HIV-related cases, has argued:

> explicit sexual images and the freedom to create and use them has been essential to the emergence of gay and lesbian cultures and identities over the past four decades. Explicit sexual images have allowed gay men and women to develop new eroticisms, to dismantle the view of homosexuality as pathological, to define a new culture apart from the dominant heterosexual ideal, and to establish new sets of norms and expectations. Censorship of sexual images – in the context of AIDS as much as in other contexts – therefore threatens the vitality and even the survival of gay culture.[36]

Prohibitions on funding for cultural representation are an attempt to re-establish a gay identity as pathological and, from a cultural perspective, to silence that identity by erasing it from the publicly funded domain. In that sense, prohibition constitutes a 'direct disenfranchisement' of members of the general public.[37] Within the context of American constitutional law, however, the right was framed as a right of freedom of speech; a strategy that ultimately has proven very successful.

CONCLUSION

The two examples analysed highlight a number of issues concerning the relationship of law, politics and lesbian and gay visual culture in America. The first is the *power* that is attributed to representations by the opponents of public funding. Any cultural representation of gay sexuality (and not simply gay sex) in itself is seen as having the capacity to promote that sexuality and to undermine the undefined values that underpin American society. The relationship of a representation to a social reality thus is extremely close. The critics of public funding also construct themselves as fighting a cultural battle for the soul of America. They hold the fort against the gay onslaught. The critique that they offer is far broader than the claim that lesbian and gay images offend public sensibilities. The argument rather is that such representations are completely contrary to the national interest and therefore to fund them from the public purse is absurd.

It is also worth noting how lesbian, gay and queer culture serve to galvanize the debates. While Serrano's *Piss Christ* also initially provoked controversy, the focus in the NEA debates quickly shifted away from arguments of blasphemy and towards an exclusive focus on sexuality. The anxiety over representations of the body and, in particular, the gay body thus came to shape the discourse. Furthermore, minority group rights are invoked by all sides. Claims of lesbian and gay rights of participation in public dialogue are met by arguments grounded in the right of religious minorities not to fund representations that contravene their deeply held beliefs.

Within the judicial process though, rights claims grounded in freedom of speech receive a receptive hearing. This speaks to the power of free speech as a claim in American constitutional law and highlights the complete absence of any parallel avenue for social change in the United Kingdom (as witnessed by the outcome of the Section 28 debates). Speech rights thus prevail over group rights grounded in religious intolerance and the claims of the mainstream American taxpayer to choose what his or her money is spent upon. Of course, the further response by politicians may simply be reduced spending on cultural production in general.

In addition, attempts to curtail lesbian and gay visual culture through a denial of public funding create unintended outcomes. The goal of cultural erasure can be achieved only by opening a space within public discourse for a debate over lesbian and gay culture. In this regard, the exposure given to performance art during the NEA controversies cannot compare to what it otherwise would have received. Queer culture was brought into the public arena – into the American Congress, courts and media – and, arguably, there was some success in 'queering' public discourse. The debate succeeded then in giving some visibility to gay lives, which is precisely what right-wing activists sought to suppress.

The attempts at restricting public funding to a significant extent also served to mobilize the lesbian and gay communities. This was particularly true in the case of restrictions on safe-sex representation. It became clear to many that their lives counted for less in the American political process than the moral values of the right wing, which thereby reinforced the claim that 'silence = death'. Social movements such as ACT-UP and Queer Nation thus may have been strengthened in their position within the gay community in this period as a reaction to Senator Helms and others. Cultural production within the lesbian and gay communities (and community support for its culture) also may have been enhanced.

In conclusion, then, the relationship of attempts to control cultural output through law and the outcomes of these processes are far from straightforward. Rather, they are complex and multifaceted phenomena. It is also clear that lesbian and gay visual culture will continue to serve as a point of contestation over the meaning not only of particular cultural artifacts, but also of the meaning of American culture itself.

Notes

1 The National Foundation on the Arts and the Humanities Act, Pub.L.No. 89–209, 79 Stat. 845 (1965).
2 On these earlier controversies at the NEA, see S.C.Dubin, *Arresting Images*, New York: Routledge, 1992, 278–83.
3 135 Congressional Record, 7 October 1989, S12969.
4 135 Congressional Record, 26 July 1989, S8806.
5 On Helms's and others' tactical appropriation of the language of group harm and minority rights, see generally J.H.Garvey, 'Black and white images', *Law and Contemporary Problems*, 1993, 56 (4), 189.
6 135 Congressional Record, 13 September 1989, H5633, per Rep. Rohrabacher.
7 ibid. at H5638, per Rep. Green.
8 ibid. at H5633, per Rep. Crane.
9 ibid. at H5637, per Rep. Dornan.
10 ibid. at H5635, per Rep. Dannemeyer.
11 C.S. Vance, 'Misunderstanding obscenity', *Art in America*, May 1990, 49.
12 The test devised by the Supreme Court of the United States in *Miller v. California*, 413 US 15 (1973) emphasizes three aspects: '(a) whether "the average person, applying contemporary community standards" would find that the work, taken as a whole, appeals to the prurient interest, (b) whether the work depicts or describes, in a patently offensive way, sexual conduct specifically defined by the applicable state law, and (c) whether the work, taken as a whole, lacks serious literary, artistic, political, or scientific value' (ibid. at 24).
13 20 USCA 959(c) (Supp. 1992).
14 L.Hart, 'Karen Finley's dirty work: censorship, homophobia, and the NEA', *Genders*, Fall 1992, 14, 1.
15 20 USC 954 (Supp. 1993).
16 W.H.Honan, 'Arts chief vetoes 2 approved grants', *New York Times*, 13 May 1992, C13.
17 N.Hunter, 'Identity, speech, and equality', *Virginia Law Review*, 1993, 79, 1695 at 1696.
18 *Perry v. Sindermann*, 408 US 593, 597 (1972).
19 754 F. Supp. 774 (CD Cal. 1991).
20 ibid. at 783.
21 795 F. Supp. 1457 (CD Cal. 1992).
22 ibid. at 1471.
23 ibid. at 1473.
24 ibid. at 1475.
25 Hunter, op.cit., 1710.
26 133 Congressional Record, 14 October 1987, S14216.
27 ibid.
28 ibid. at S14204.
29 ibid.
30 ibid. at S14208.
31 In addition, the amendment demanded that all safe sex materials 'emphasize abstinence from sexual activity outside a sexually monogamous marriage'. Failure to abide by the conditions could result in the refusal of further public funding for the offender. Labor-Health and Human Services Appropriation Bill for Fiscal Year 1988, Pub. L. No. 100–202.
32 C. Patton, 'Safe sex and the pornographic vernacular', in Bad Object-Choices (ed.), *How Do I Look?*, Seattle: Bay Press, 1991, p. 31 at 43.
33 E. King, *Safety in Numbers*, London: Cassell, 1993, 121.
34 792 F. Supp. 278 (SDNY 1992).
35 ibid. at 296.
36 M. Barnes, 'Toward ghastly death: the censorship of AIDS education', *Columbia Law Review*, 1989, 89, 698 at 720–1.
37 ibid. at 721.

Chapter Thirteen

These waves of dying friends

Gay men, AIDS and multiple loss

Simon Watney

Cities are our gardens, with their stench
and contagion and rage, our memory, our
sepals that will not endure
these waves of dying friends
without a cry. (Michael Lynch, 1989)

A witness accomplishes things that were not intended. (Czeslaw Milosz, 1991)

INTRODUCTION: THEORIZING LOSS

Those with sharp eyes attending the Eighth International AIDS Conference in Amsterdam in June 1992 might have noticed, among the material promoting the many thousands of talks and papers, a small but significant cluster of posters and other presentations dealing with the growing experience of multiple loss among gay men (Amsterdam 1992). For example, from San Francisco, Michael Gorman and others reported on suicide as the leading cause of non-AIDS mortality in a cohort study of local men, regarding suicide in the dry, defensive language of the social sciences as one aspect of 'the natural history of outcomes secondary to HIV itself' (Gorman *et al.* 1992). In other words, we are invited to distinguish between the *primary* medical symptoms of HIV infection, which are by now well established, and the *secondary* social symptoms caused by proximity to illness and death among one's friends and acquaintances on a constant, recurrent basis, over time.

A paper from Washington suggested from US data that young men who have attempted suicide 'engage in twice as many risk behaviours as those who have not attempted suicide' (Cunningham 1992). Another paper from Los Angeles identified a wide range of characteristics, understood to constitute what is now increasingly understood as 'Multiple Loss Syndrome' (Jacoby Klein 1992). These include: feelings of numbness, anger, isolation, guilt, abandonment, disbelief, depression, etc.; inability to emote; the expression of feelings of loss, by pessimism, cynicism, fatalism or insecurity; socially irresponsible behaviour with self-destructive overtones; withdrawal from support systems; preoccupation with one's own mortality; pathological grief symptoms; panic, self-doubt, loss of control; and resentment over never-ending memorial services. The 'coping mechanisms' also recorded in the paper seem almost pitifully inadequate for the scale of suffering in the situations with which they are supposed to help individuals to cope. They include involvement with support systems; lighting a candle to represent loss; volunteering to help the less fortunate; attention to self-care, grooming, exercise, nutrition and so on; and finally establishing a 'new place in life for the deceased'.

Writing from the perspective of a gay man living with AIDS, Leon McKusick identified three distinct processes involved in Multiple Loss Syndrome (a term discussed below) (McKusick 1992). First, grief and bereavement, 'feeling pain, disengaging from the dead and re-engaging with the living'; second, a process akin to Post-traumatic Stress Syndrome, involving either the intense re-experiencing of tragic events, or conversely, a protective dissociation, with symptoms of excessive coolness and numbing. Third, he describes burn-out, concluding on the subject of the need fully to feel and explore loss, in order to be able to re-adjust to the world of the living, and to redirect a sense of hope from the dead, as it were, to those who are still alive. This re-investment involves new ideas, new people, a whole new start to life. It is thus implicit that mourning on such a constant and protracted scale constitutes a completely transformative personal experience, after which one will never again be the person one was 'before'.

Writing this article, and others, is for me a part of an ongoing process of mourning, and in turn part of the far wider attempt on the part of so many of my generation to 'make sense' of what has happened to us (Watney 1994). This requires us to overcome reticence. Indeed, the strong feeling that one should not speak in public about questions of personal loss might be seen as one of the primary symptoms of multiple loss, whether or not one considers this a discrete, clinical syndrome. Here I want to explore some aspects of the ways in which multiple losses may be experienced, and to suggest that while distinct patterns of emotional and behavioural responses may indeed by established and classified, these do not necessarily lock together in any immediately apparent and uniform fashion. For example, the same scale of loss which may drive one gay man into workaholism and unsafe sex, may render another incapable of work or sex of any kind. Furthermore, such symptoms may change unpredictably over time. While there may at first sight seem to be some advantage in drawing an immediate parallel between the primary medical symptoms of Acquired Immune Deficiency Syndrome (AIDS), and the secondary socio-psychological symptoms of a closely associated Multiple Loss Syndrome, the analogy strikes me as initially misleading, and part of a wider contemporary tendency to conceptualize supposedly distinct syndromes (Air Hi-jack Victim Syndrome, Falklands War Syndrome), rather than considering and confronting death and disease as necessary aspects of the human condition. Neatly classifying our various responses to the AIDS crisis as a syndrome, we run the risk of finding yet another way *not* to talk about pain (Scarry 1985; Sedgwick 1993; Hacking 1995).

SEROPREVALENCE AND MULTIPLE LOSS

In Britain we are still in many respects in the 'early stages' of the full-scale experience of high AIDS mortality rates. It is thus of some practical significance to consider multiple loss as an experience which will predictably sadly affect increasing numbers of gay men, and others, in the coming decade, in order to be able to plan and resource adequate service provision and other forms of community-based support for those in need. At the same time it is equally important not to exaggerate the scale of multiple loss in the United Kingdom, compared to countries such as the United States, Canada or France, where HIV is far more widely prevalent among the various well-known risk groups, and where levels of immediate loss are already being experienced among gay men on a scale which we are, fortunately, most unlikely to experience in the United Kingdom.

Within the United Kingdom, the effects of AIDS-associated mortality have been overwhelmingly concentrated among gay men (King 1993). Thus, as of the end of 1993, 76 per cent of all reported AIDS deaths had been of gay and bisexual men, a total of 4,291 fatalities. The next single largest number of deaths in any other social constituency was the 381 heterosexual women and men infected by 'high risk' partners. These made up 7 per cent of the total. In other words, in the United Kingdom HIV/AIDS have had an impact among gay and bisexual men which is incommensurate with the effects in other risk groups, let alone among heterosexuals (PHLS 1994). Of the 9,218 cases of AIDS diagnosed in the United Kingdom since the beginning of the epidemic, 7,334 resulted from unprotected sex between men, or 80 per cent of the total figure (PHLS 1994). No less than 74 per cent of these cases have been among gay and bisexual men aged between 25 and 44, and it is therefore in this group that we may also reasonably expect the experience of multiple loss to be most concentrated, bearing in mind that another 21 per cent of HIV and AIDS cases have been among men over 45.

With some 75 per cent of all British AIDS cases being in London, it is also clear that multiple loss is fundamentally an urban phenomenon, closely related to the networks of friendships established over many decades in the lives of gay men in London. Taking the North West Thames region of London alone, we may note that 840 men aged between 15 and 64 died of AIDS in the years 1991–2, compared to 54 women (Ward and Hickman 1994). The great majority of these men were gay or bisexual, and it is within their immediate social environment that multiple loss is most frequently experienced, often by men living themselves with HIV or AIDS. It should, moreover, be understood that AIDS thus threatens to corrode the most fundamental level of social 'belonging' in most gay men's lives, namely those bonds of friendship and shared personal histories that constitute our sense of gay identity. All too often it is imagined that gay identity functions in this crisis like some kind of magical prophylaxis, whereas in reality self-confidence and self-esteem may be radically undermined rather than strengthened by the prolonged experience of illness, suffering and death all around one. For AIDS devours not only one's past, in the sense of ex-lovers and friends from one's earlier life, but also one's future, especially perhaps in the loss of so many of those younger friends who in happier times one might casually imagine as the friends of one's own middle and old age. That is, if you are not yourself infected. In this context I well remember the words of an old friend of mine, now in his late forties, while nursing his first lover (with whom he had lived for many years two decades ago) through his final illness in the early 1990s. Describing to colleagues at work within an academic institution that a 'friend' was dying, he was met with little understanding or sympathy. 'Friendship' among gay men is not frankly widely understood outside our own communities, just as the scale of our losses is rarely acknowledged by most heterosexuals, who seem often to prefer to imagine that HIV is some kind of 'equal opportunities' virus, affecting everybody equally, as so much official AIDS education continues misleadingly to insist.

Thus, for example, we may note a widespread cultural concern about so-called 'killer viruses' and their theoretical implications, in films such as *Outbreak*, and the writings of Richard Preston concerning the Ebola virus, while the actual, extensive impact of HIV among gay men is never publicly acknowledged, let alone regarded as tragic, or even regrettable (Preston 1995). Indeed, AIDS is frequently presented to heterosexuals as a 'warning' of other potential threats in such a way that the direct impact of HIV itself is displaced or ignored. Hence it is still possible for a leading British medical journalist to write casually of HIV as a virus which is:

> not particularly infectious, but its delayed action combined with its transmission during the most compulsive human activity can cause the complacency and denial that make it such a great threat. (Connor 1995)

For most heterosexuals in the United Kingdom, HIV is indeed a most remote statistical possibility, and this is precisely why they are generally so ill-equipped to understand or comment upon the situation confronting gay men, as the third decade of the epidemic in our midst looms into sight. Thus throughout the extensive social scientific and popular medical literature of AIDS we may find frequent references to the supposed dangers of 'denial', referring to the imagined refusal or inability of gay men to recognize the 'realities' of the epidemic, and to avoid *all* possible risk of infection. By this logic, gay men are thus deemed personally responsible for contracting HIV, while at the same time there is no consideration whatsoever of the possibly contradictory impact the epidemic has had in our lives. Nor is there any consideration of the many years of irresponsible journalism which has repeatedly insisted that there is no association whatsoever between HIV and AIDS, and even in effect that there is no such thing as an 'AIDS epidemic' at all (King 1993).

Rarely is there any understanding of the great difficulties facing gay men entering intimate personal relationships against the background of epidemic illness, which for many remains largely anecdotal and distant. Nor is there much interest in how we sustain our relationships over time, or the specific difficulties of ending relationships. So-called 'denial' is sternly admonished, but there is rarely any question of how gay men manage to 'get through' the epidemic, or any note of sorrow or loss concerning those who don't. 'Complacency' is a marvellously convenient term for those who have not felt or exhibited the slightest concern for gay men's lives throughout the entire history of the epidemic. Writing of the 270,000 military fatalities among British armed service personnel in the Second World War, and the 60,000 civilians killed in air-raids and so on, historian David Cannadine has observed that death in postwar, peacetime Britain tends to be thought of as 'either general and in the future, or individual in the present' (Cannadine 1981). AIDS has been posed as a largely abstract, imaginary horror for most heterosexuals, and there has been little attempt to consider it 'from the inside' as it were, as it affects those for whom HIV has long been a complex everyday reality, continually changing in its significance and meaning. Besides, 'denial' is a singularly inappropriate and insensitive term with which to try to make sense of the wide range of ways in which fallible human beings may respond over time to the escalating prevalence of HIV and AIDS within a relatively small social constituency such as gay male society. Who is to say what the 'reality' of HIV should be to a teenager 'coming out' in 1996, or to an older gay man who may have already lost over forty personal friends and long-term acquaintances, who are likely to include many ex-lovers and ex-sexual partners who subsequently became 'friends', with all the ordinary complexity the word implies. How is one supposed to live an ordinary, 'healthy' gay life with the knowledge that up to 20 per cent of one's community may already be infected, and that the worst years, in terms of deaths from AIDS, still lie ahead? It seems to me that these things are not currently being sufficiently discussed within the field of gay culture, from theatre and film to the gay press.

Such problems are exacerbated at a time when some gay intellectuals can still claim that AIDS is merely 'one issue among many' facing gay men, as if questions of reducing HIV transmission, and dealing with illness and death on an unparalleled scale in modern times were somehow strictly comparable with such issues as anti-gay discrimination in public housing or in the workplace (Annetts and Thompson 1992). Such issues are of course of great importance, but they are not commensurate with AIDS. These same attitudes are also reflected in the fashionable Wanna-Be-Julie-Burchill school of so-called 'Post-gay' and 'Anti-gay' journalism, which significantly flourishes in publications such as *Time Out* and the *Independent* newspaper, which are only too predictably happy to publish 'Post-gay' or 'Queer' journalists attacking the very idea of gay collectivity, or community values of any kind. In an epidemic, such attitudes also amount to cultural symptoms of the crisis in our midst, complex displacements of anxiety, uncertainty, and so on. Such attitudes also usually stem from those who have happily been largely spared the full impact of disease and death in their immediate social environment, and for whom spurious comparisons between incommensurate issues may often form their own type of personal defence against an otherwise unbearable reality.

The challenge here is not so much that of dealing with 'denial', imagined as a voluntary personal fault, as of meeting the dangers posed by the very psychological mechanisms that may serve to make life tolerable in the context of unevenly experienced illness, when the direct experience of asymptomatic HIV infection is far more common among gay men than that of death. Indeed, the crude social amnesia and exaggerated emotional detachment on the part of those gay men who complain that 'too much' is said about AIDS are themselves probably best understood also as

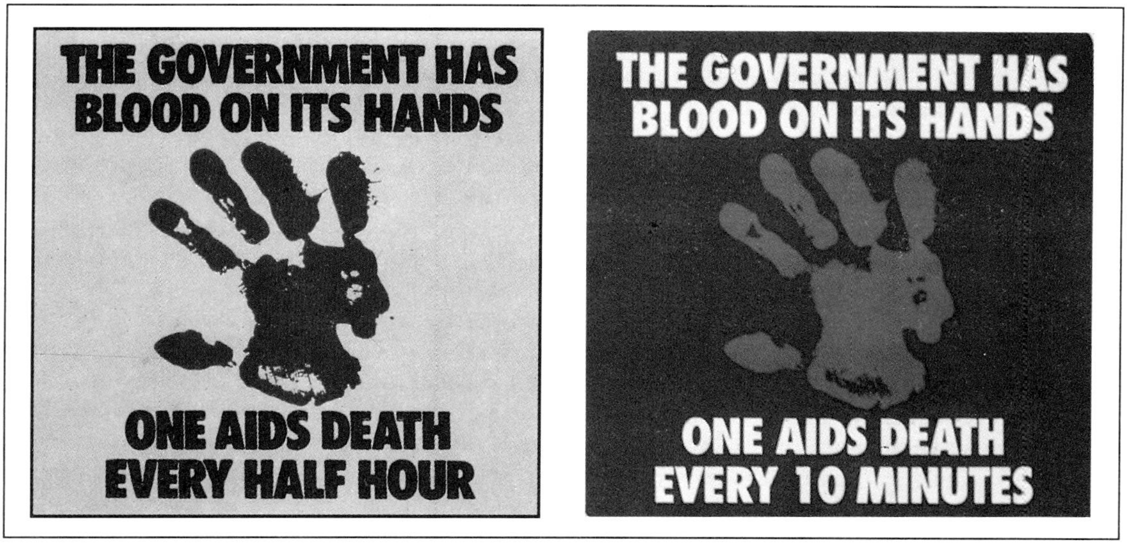

Figure 13.1 *Gran Fury*, stickers (*left* 1988, *right* 1990). Such activist stickers were widely distributed around New York from the mid-1980s onwards, and their starkly changing statistics spelt out the worsening crisis.
Photograph: Simon Watney.

displaced cultural symptoms of the epidemic, as it unfolds in our midst. This unevenness of experience of *all* aspects of HIV/AIDS is one of the major characteristics of the situation in the United Kingdom, unlike that in countries with much higher levels of seroprevalence. Thus the probability of multiple loss may be roughly calculated from local seroprevalence rates as they translate unpredictably into the daily lived experience of individuals and groups. With approximately 12,000 cases of AIDS in Britain up to mid-1995, and around 6,000 deaths, it is impossible accurately to assess how many gay men are currently experiencing multiple loss, though it is certainly several thousand. To this figure should be added the many thousands who have many friends living at various stages of HIV infection and related pre-AIDS illness. As the epidemic develops in time we may thus detect a common narrative, involving the gradual multiple experience of HIV illness, and AIDS, prior to the experience of death on a large scale. It is thus of the greatest importance that we recognize the essentially *slow-motion* impact of the epidemic among gay and bisexual men, bearing in mind that the average rate of progression from HIV infection to symptomatic illness is ten years, with a further uncertain future involving many potential different sequences and combinations of illnesses in the lives of people with AIDS.

We should therefore expect widespread cumulative emotional distress from the largely unpredictable course of illness and death surrounding us. At the same time, we should recognize the wide disparity of the experience of illness, death and mourning among gay men in Britain. Furthermore, it is statistically unlikely that younger gay men will have shared the same experience of illness and death as older gay men. This may serve to make death harder to talk about, and to share. In the coming decade however, death will increasingly affect those moving through their twenties and into their thirties, as infected contemporaries sicken and die. It should be noted that for several years approximately 1,000 gay men annually are discovering that they are infected. Indeed, one reason for criticizing those who wilfully exaggerate the actual numbers of gay or homosexually active men in Britain is that exaggerations such as 'one in ten' obscure our understanding of the likely future impact of the epidemic. While many of those who find themselves infected each year will not necessarily be cases of recent infection, it is none the less only too tragically clear that in the absence of more effective anti-retroviral treatment drugs, a steady rate of symptomatic illness and death will remain dispersed among gay men for at least another twenty years. The cumulative effects of such terrible losses can hardly be imagined, which is precisely why we need good research as this stage of the epidemic, in order to be able to respond to future needs.

The steady death-rate from AIDS among gay men is also likely to have important consequences for HIV education and prevention work, not least in relation to the growing potential for personal fatalism which the long-term experience of the epidemic may induce. And since illness and death are not evenly distributed among gay men, especially outside London, it is also likely that HIV and AIDS will remain largely theoretical for many gay men, whether or not they are actively involved in the social gay scene. Thus individuals experience the risk of HIV in very different ways, according to complex changing personal experience. For some this may result in feelings of magical invulnerability. For others it may conversely lead to the feeling that with so many of one's friends infected, or ill or dead, one has no right to be alive and uninfected oneself. Future health promotion campaigns will need carefully to monitor and evaluate the changing perceptions and experience of the epidemic in the gay community, since it is clear that no single strategy can be adequate. If gay men think that such work is already taking place on an adequate scale, they are sadly deluding themselves. Education which was effective at one stage of an epidemic may be irrelevant or even counterproductive at later stages. In this context, the likelihood that multiple loss may increase some gay men's potential vulnerability to HIV must be considered very seriously.

At the same time we may be confident that nothing will be clarified or adequately explained by those who claim there is a type of 'death-wish' intrinsically connected to homosexual desire, and always of course conveniently unconscious (Guibert 1991; Gehler 1994). How gay men managed to survive before the advent of HIV is never of course considered by such fatalistic theories, which present illness and death as the direct by-products of individual or collective gay pathology, 'problems' only for those who are innately 'predisposed' to premature death. From such a perspective the entire personal impact of the epidemic among gay men can be largely, if not entirely, ignored, together with any serious consideration of ongoing HIV education or treatment research, since presumably nothing can be done to help the innately 'predisposed' to protect themselves or one another. Such attitudes are frequently combined with the assertion that safer sex is really very simple and easy, and that vast amounts of well-researched, effective education work has been developed for and by gay men. Nothing could be further from the truth.

REPRESENTING LOSS: NEGOTIATING LIFE

No two deaths are ever the same. To live through the slow, and frequently painful, deaths of close friends, one after the other, and sometimes at the same time, over many years, is an experience for which nobody can be adequately prepared. For many of us, the epidemic has unfurled in more or less distinct stages, including stages in our experience of death. First, the early deaths, isolated, inexplicable, shocking, surrounded by mystery. These were the deaths that motivated many into HIV/AIDS-related work in the voluntary sector in the early and mid-1980s. Then deaths began to accumulate, though still scattered: sudden deaths, entirely unexpected deaths, as well as deaths which were fought long and hard, to the very last breath. Many now have quietly prayed for many friends to die. Many have marvelled at the strength of young hearts in prematurely aged and emaciated bodies. Deaths overlap. Sometimes the death of a comparative stranger is felt more deeply than that of an old flame. Names disappear, and surely few have time to honour all the anniversaries of deaths? Many weeks and even months would be packed with little else. Sometimes entire groups of friends are swallowed up as if they had never existed. Looking through old photos one becomes aware of a growing army of the dead. You learn to avoid certain streets, certain towns, certain cities. Often bars and clubs feel intolerably thick with ghosts, though they usually encourage one to have a good time. To avoid ghosts it is necessary to find new social haunts, but nowhere remains ghost-free for long. Then you learn to stop trying to avoid them, for their messages are important. I keep a kind of personal iconostasis where I work, with photographs of the living and the recently dead, and some now long-dead. We develop our own private rituals. There are some deaths, or dyings, one just cannot deal with. As a gay man in my mid-forties I find I am currently most deeply upset by the continued new infections and illness among younger friends and colleagues, from the generations which followed mine, which had been the generation of gay liberation in the early 1970s. They feel in a way like our children, and it sometimes seems that our most brilliant children were also the most vulnerable. Thus one also comes to mourn for futures that can never be, as much as for the 'pre-AIDS' past, which now seems all but unimaginable – locked far away behind gates guarded by angels holding blazing torches. For many, drugs serve their efficient narcotic function, blocking off the intolerable – for a while.

And sometimes, when death has become more or less completely normal, and is almost taken for granted and continuous with everyday life, death may, as it were, 'reach out' in ways that we have hardly begun to consider. Certainly morbidity and frankly self-destructive behaviour are likely to be frequent symptoms of cumulative loss. Some may indeed become wholly stupefied by the scale of death around them, while others painfully learn to adapt, make new friends, retain their sexual appetites, their self-confidence, and so on. As we move through the last years of the second decade of the epidemic, it is more apparent that the long-term emotional impact of HIV and AIDS is likely to be increasingly deeply felt among more gay men, as the direct impact of illness and death becomes inexorably wider, and the gaps in experience begin to narrow, like the isolated rings of ripples from individual raindrops on the surface of a pond, gradually overlapping as the rain sets in.

It is precisely in order to avoid fatalism and morbidity that we need to be thinking and talking more about death and dying in our communities at this stage of the epidemic. We have not chosen this terrible catastrophe. We do our best to control it. But it is there, and it is not going to vanish overnight. Somehow we have to come to be able to live with AIDS deaths without letting death overwhelm us. Alongside the struggles for effective health promotion, and better treatment drugs and services, we should also recognize the serious danger of widespread HIV/AIDS-associated clinical depression and other forms of mental illness throughout our communities. Bland talk about 'burn-out' does not begin to do justice to the complexity of the issues involved, not the least of which concerns the ways in which cumulative loss may undermine gay identity, returning individuals to private hells of shame and loneliness from which we thought we had long since escaped. Yet our contemporary gay and 'queer' culture seems to find it infinitely easier to deal with body-building than with soul-searching. Nor does the world of lesbian and gay politics seem to have anything much to say on these growing problems associated with cumulative loss in our communities, and has more or less surrendered the whole issue of 'feelings' to a motley crew of New Age gurus, who doubtless provide some people with some help.

For example, I have been struck by the reading of a late Victorian prayer by Henry Scott Holland at three funerals or commemoration ceremonies I have attended in the past year:

> Death is nothing at all. I have only slipped away into the next room. I am I, and you are you. Whatever we were to each other, that we still are [...] Put no difference in your tone, wear no forced air of solemnity or sorrow [...] Why should I be out of mind because I am out of sight? I am waiting for you, for an interval, somewhere very near, just round the corner. All is well.
>
> (Scott Holland 1992)

I think this is an appalling prayer. I think it makes mourning impossible, because it so trivializes and sentimentalizes death. At each of the three occasions on which I heard it read, in relation to the lives of socially active, politically committed, gay men I wanted to shout out loud: '*No!* Death is *not* "nothing at all". It's the pits, the worst. You are not who you were, as I am not who I was. You are dead, and I am devastated. All is not well at all. They are not just there having a quick smoke in "the next room" before opening the door to come back in. And I will be as embarrassingly "emotional" as I fucking well choose!' Providing only false consolation, the Scott Holland prayer (and the New Age culture that it typifies) strikes me as a positive barrier to mourning, and the slow, painful acceptance of loss that mourning involves, if it is not to turn into melancholia, unable to 'cut off', unable to incorporate the dead person into one's new, changed, diminished life.

Thus the cultural challenge of adequately memorializing the dead is always intimately connected to the widely shared yet generally private, individual experience of grief and cumulative multiple loss. Yet what kind of memorials might we need? Certainly it would be a disaster if we were to drift into a kind of victim mentality, along the lines of vague and generally misleading metaphors of the Holocaust. Surely lesbian and gay culture already suffers from more than its share of 'victim politics', with regular ritual shamings of the 'impure', and so on, and its upside-down hierarchies of victimhood status? Yet with so much grief in our private lives, we need opportunities for its shared expression, as well as the need to celebrate and affirm the significance of the lives of those who have died. We may perhaps eventually be able to rescue something meaningful from the annual platitudes of World AIDS Day, but at present our only two major national memorializing projects are both imported traditions from the United States – the Candle-lit Vigil, and the UK Quilts Project, and

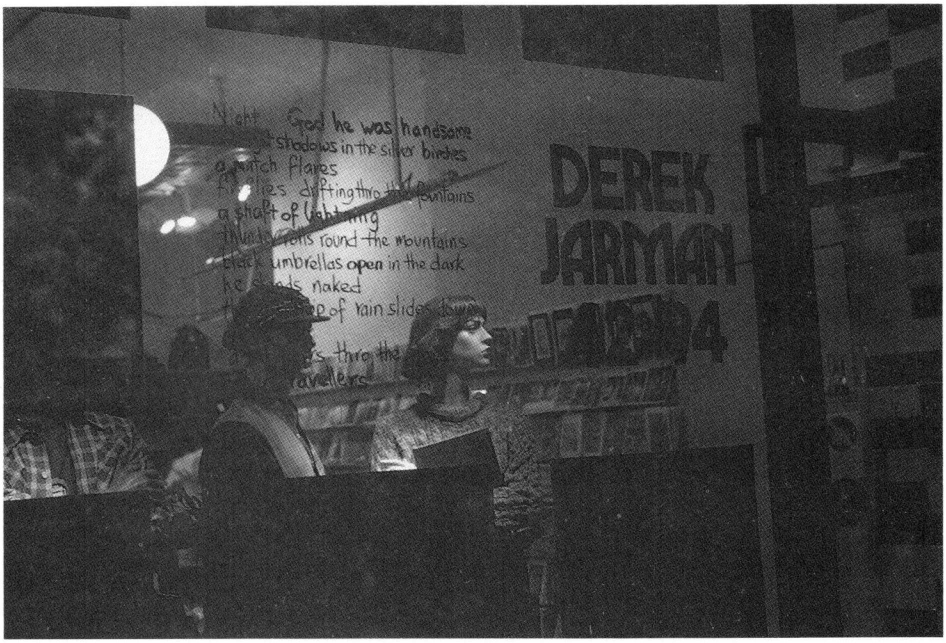

Figure 13.2 Shop window, Old Compton Street, London, February 1994
Photograph: Simon Watney.

while both have doubtless provided many with a means of public mourning, neither has seized the national imagination at the level of national cultural symbols. Indeed, it may well be that they were, as it were, 'premature', arriving in Britain from a country which has experienced a vastly higher death-rate from AIDS than the United Kingdom.

Perhaps some of our most effective memorials will be essentially local, like the light shop in New York's West Village, whose windows contain an ever-changing display of photographs and obituaries and personal tributes to local people who have recently died from AIDS, or like the images and texts by Derek Jarman which appeared in shop-windows up and down Old Compton Street in the heart of London's West End gay 'village' the day after he died (Figures 13.2, 13.3 and 13.4). A street that he had travelled almost daily for many decades now mourned his passing, and even today, more than two years later, there is still a shrine with fairy-lights behind the counter at his favourite Soho café, the Maison Bertaux which he, like me, had known since the 1960s, when it had been under the formidable rule of old Madame Bertaux herself, and next door there was a very proper hardware store, with neat, diligent apprentices. Derek would fight his way to the upstairs tea-room even after he could hardly walk (Watney 1994).

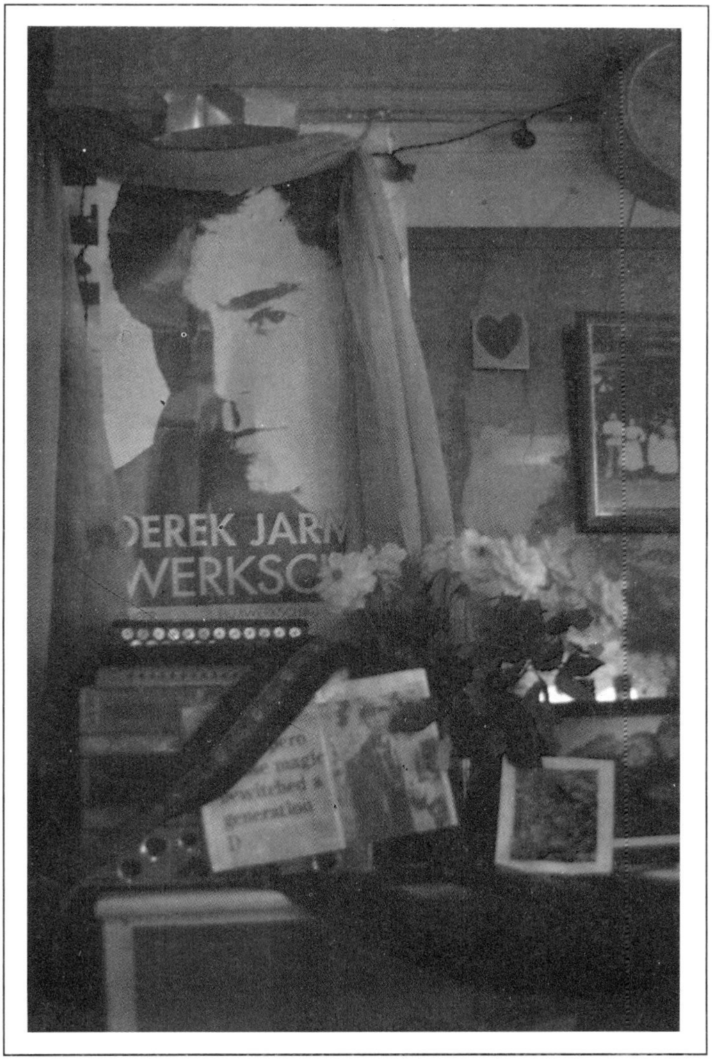

Figure 13.3 Interior, Maison Bertaux, Soho, London, February 1994
Photograph: Simon Watney.

Many will by now be familiar with the types of secular funeral and commemorative ceremonies which are such a feature of the immediate social gay response to the epidemic. For example, I suddenly recall walking through west London two years ago behind a magnificent horse-drawn glass catafalque carrying an ex-lover to the crematorium, and the wonderful release in the chapel as Barbra Streisand belted out 'Comin' in and out of your life', using our culture to affirm our lives and our feelings. Or, more recently, walking into another packed chapel, to the wonderfully appropriate and infinitely moving strains of Lou Reed's 'Take a walk on the wild side'. In this context it is worth perhaps also considering the way in which so much recent techno music has, in effect, revivified and reconstructed so many of the gay disco 'standards' and anthems of the

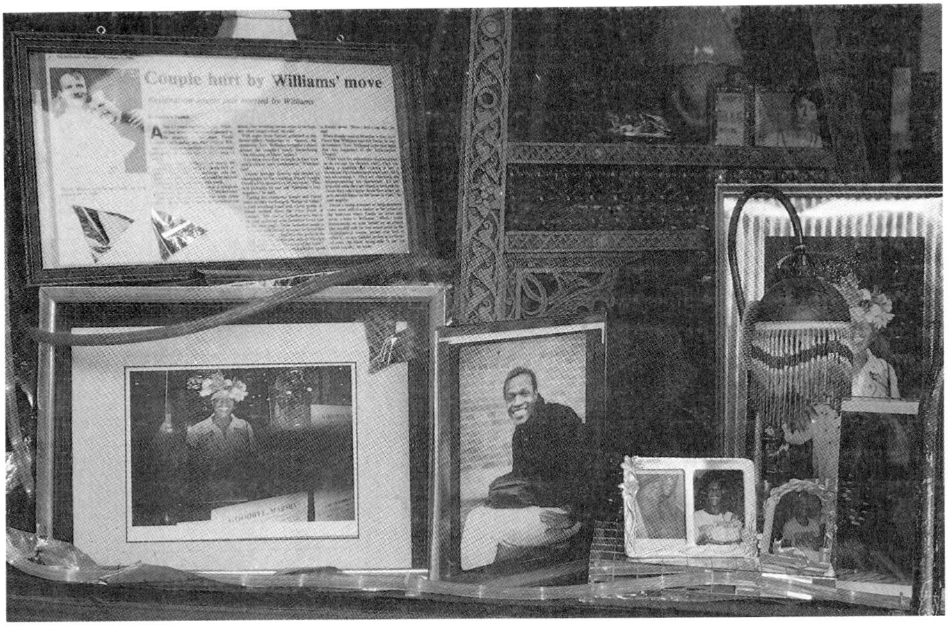

Figure 13.4 Shop windows with obituaries, Hudson Street, New York, 1990
Photograph: Simon Watney.

pre-AIDS era as new re-mixes, insisting as it were on the unbroken continuities of pop music and dance culture. Such continuities affirm the underlying tenacity of gay culture, and its deeper will for life and happiness, in spite of the growing presence of death all around us.

In such circumstances we should probably at least try to observe the anniversaries of our friends, or else life itself can begin to seem unreal and devoid of value or purpose, because we have been unable to integrate our dead into our new, changed lives. Questions of spirituality are much in the air, and it seems important not to 'give' this ground over wholly to purveyors of psycho-babble, or to spurious New Age religiosity. One of the measures of the strength of our culture will be reflected in the ways we learn to take care of ourselves and of one another, emotionally, and in every other way. Gay culture and self-confidence is very young, and we have little to draw upon by way of models. Nor can it be sufficiently pointed out that nothing quite like this has ever happened before – the steady haemorrhaging of a significant percentage of a marginalized social constituency which is itself widely blamed for the disaster in its midst.

At at time when mental health care and service provision is under fire throughout the statutory sector and the National Health Service, existing institutions should recognize the strong likelihood of steadily increased demand for both emergency service provision and for long-term counselling, group-work, and so on. For just as we were initially most at risk from HIV at the beginning of the AIDS crisis at a time when nobody knew HIV was out there, so today we are also most vulnerable to the long-term emotional and psychological consequences of living cheek by jowel with death in an epidemic of such duration, from all the varieties of clinical depression, to frankly suicidal behaviour. I can only conclude that it is our capacity to seize onto life and joy and happiness that will be most needed to carry us through the grim years ahead. We go clubbing on Friday night not out of 'denial', but in order, among many other things, to mourn. This is the complex nature of urban gay life in the 1990s, and it is already inseparable from the epidemic in its midst. How we are to share all this, and come through, only time will tell.

References

Amsterdam, Eighth International AIDS Conference Abstracts (1992) *Track D: Poster Social Impact and Responses*, D465.

Annetts, J. and Thompson, B. (1992) 'Dangerous Activism?', in Plummer, K. (ed.) *Modern Homosexualities: Fragments of Lesbian and Gay Experience*, Routledge: London, 227–36.

Cannadine, D.(1981) 'War and death, grief and mourning in modern Britain' in Whaley, Joachim (ed.) *Mirrors of Mortality: Studies On The Social History of Death*, Europa: London, 238.

Connor, S.(1995) 'The terror is infectious', *Independent*, section two, London, Thursday 20 April 1995, 31.

Cunningham, R., *et al.* (1992) 'AIDS risk behaviour: a new way of committing suicide?' Eighth International AIDS Conference, Amsterdam.

Gehler, M. (1994) *Adam et Yves: enquête chez les garçons*, Grasset: Paris.

Gorman, M., *et al.* (1992) 'Suicide as the leading cause of non AIDS mortality in a cohort of men in San Francisco', Eighth International AIDS Conference, Amsterdam.

Guibert, H. (1991) *To The Friend Who Did Not Save My Life*, Quartet: London.

Hacking, I. (1995) *Rewriting the Soul: Multiple Personality and the Sciences of Memory*, Princeton NJ.

Jacoby Klein, S. (1992) 'AIDS related gay grief: an update including multiple loss syndrome', AIDS Project Los Angeles, Eighth International AIDS Conference, Amsterdam.

King, E. (1993) *Safety in Numbers: Safer Sex and Gay Men*, Cassell: London; Routledge: New York, 1994.

Lynch, M. (1989) 'Cry', *These Waves of Dying Friends*, Contact Publications: New York, 82.

McKusick, L. (1992) 'The epidemiology and psychology of multiple loss in our communities', session 61, Eighth International AIDS Conference, Amsterdam.

Milosz, C. (1991) *The Late Show*, BBC-2, Monday 25 November.

Preston, R. (1995) 'Back in the hot zone', *New Yorker*, 22 May 43–5.

Public Health Laboratory Service AIDS Centre (1994) *AIDS/HIV Quarterly Surveillance Tables*, 25, Data To End September.

Scarry, E. (1985) *The Body in Pain: The Making and Unmaking of the World*, Oxford University Press: Oxford.

Scott Holland, H. (1992) 'Death is nothing at all' in Stewart, Liz (ed.) *Daring to Speak Love's Name*, Hamish Hamilton: London, 141–2.

Sedgwick, E.K. (1993) 'Epidemic of the will', *Tendencies*, Duke University Press: Durham, NC, 130–43.

Ward, H.and Hickman, M. (1994) *The Epidemiology of AIDS and HIV in North West Thames*, London: Academic Department of Public Health, St Mary's Hospital Medical School.

Watney, S. (1994) 'Acts of memory', *Out Magazine*, 15, New York, 92.

Chapter Fourteen

Culture wars

Race and queer art

Sunil Gupta

Some news on the Internet from Vancouver:

> The next day I went to the movie, *Pulp Fiction.* The movie, although a kick – it is largely a rapturous ode to the joys of injecting coke – is vilely homophobic. There is a scene where two of the movie's main characters, a small-time hood and the crime boss he's crossed are interrupted in their chase to kill each other, bound and gagged. They are hostages to a couple of gay S & M freaks. The crime boss is trussed over a gymnast's horse and fucked in the bum. We see this, more or less, after the hood, played by Bruce Willis, left in the antechamber to the torture room, frees himself. Hearing the screams of his adversary, instead of leaving his deadly enemy to his situation, he decides to rescue him. It's when the door flings open that we see the 'torture' whose victim's anguished screams we've only heard until now. This awful torture is, as I've already revealed, a little anal penetration. A scene more or less like a Tom of Finland drawing – except for the withdrawal of the passive actor's consent. Pause for a second to ask what, in the fiction of *Pulp Fiction,* could have motivated the Bruce Willis character to risk his own life to save someone he otherwise wanted dead? It must be that the screams from the torture room struck deep instinctual and cultural chords in him. The horror of anal penetration threatened worse for him than the loss of his life, the loss of masculine identity. As they dispatch the homosexual sadists together – by shooting them in the balls – heterosexual bonding is restored at a deep level and a peace is struck, revealing another level of the character's 'humanity'. Murdering queers and the satisfaction that brings is the ground on which the characters establish their truce.
>
> In an inverted sort of way, to carry this further, the S & M sadists are quite incidental. They are surrogates to act out the suppressed passion the men have for each other (which has led them to want to kill each other) and their murder of the queers is a kind of rite by which they take the passage back from the dark chamber where they've made love to [the] world of light and men.[1]

The last decade in the west has seen a growing interest in identity within cultural politics. The avant garde on the one hand and class issues on the other have been called into question in relation to race and sexual politics. Simultaneously there has been a 'coming out of the closet' for lesbian and gay artists dealing with issues of their own identity. London's Institute of Contemporary Arts has hosted at least two conferences around the notion of a 'gay sensibility in the arts' and Robert Mapplethorpe's work has been widely seen in America. In Britain we live with homophobic laws and a mindless censorship of so-called 'pornography'. The Thatcher era coincided with the birth of the Black Arts Movement during which the hegemony of white art, its history and institutions have been challenged. Having been the subject of mainstream practice; defined, codified and catalogued, queer artists and artists of colour have said finally enough is enough, and have spear-headed demands for autonomous control of their own cultural product.

In Britain we have witnessed an unresolved debate about whether there is a queer sensibility in the visual arts and whether there is more life in queer cultural activism rather than in the gay art world. Postwar Britain saw the creation of the welfare state and the 'swinging sixties' which led to the liberalization of the law concerning sodomy between two men over the age of twenty-one. Since then there has been a marked reduction in gay civil rights accompanying an increased exposure in the popular press, which some like to believe is a liberalization of attitudes towards gay men and lesbians. AIDS in the 1980s began to coalesce gay men of different political persuasions into some kind of direct action. However, efforts to deflect blame for the origins of the 'gay plague' to Africa proved divisive as Black gay men felt deserted by their white gay spokesmen. With its origins in the meetings of the Black[2] Gay Group in London a Black cultural activism was born.

Activism around gay politics leaning as it does on feminist politics and the history of the Black civil rights movements in the United States and Britain, came full circle as Black gay cultural activists began finding their voices not within a gay milieu but within an umbrella of funding for Black Arts. Black Arts were by definition confrontational and slogans like 'No art but Black art'[3] were to lead to almost insurmountable gulfs between gay cultural activists of different colours. The 1990s have ushered in an important new initiative in public-sector arts funding by the consultative process and development stage of the INIVA[4] (now known as inINVA: the Institute of International Visual Arts) project, which seeks to create a dialogue between what is perceived as the white mainstream and the world of Black arts practitioners.

The history of Black Arts in the United Kingdom is a brief but chequered one. As a documented movement it is invisible until the early 1980s when it appeared at the tail-end of the metropolitan initiatives by Labour-controlled local city governments who sought to create a rainbow coalition between artists and pensioners, races and genders. The radical politics of 1968 in Europe gave way to a left cultural agenda in the 1970s which brought together visual art and media studies. Photography, art and politics came together, spawning influential degree courses, galleries, workshops and publications. In all the frenetic activity of community groups, writings and exhibitions two features were missing: race and homosexuality. There was work done about Britain's racial minorities and the discrimination they faced in housing, employment and education; but all the work was being produced by white practitioners.[5]

The new radical elite, having fought for a slice of the funding cake, having evolved a rhetoric around critical theory borrowed from literature and film and with its own stars, was still unapproachable by Black practitioners. Even its language was so couched in jargon as to be incomprehensible to the Black punter in search of sustenance away from the doggedly white-only, male and heterosexual mainstream. Looking back, there is an embarrassing feeling that 'oops! they forgot about race'.

The early 1980s, into the Thatcher period of national politics, the increasing inner-city tensions of race and the emergence of local government bodies such as the Greater London Council as strident champions of women's rights, lesbian and gay rights and a host of other marginal groups' rights, which began to fund cultural activities as a strategy to empower these groups and win their political support, eventually saw us at the crossroads of Black Arts.

A number of issues got simultaneously raised. Why such exhibitions so late in the day? How had the gallery system managed to ignore this work for so long? And, where were the work and the artists going on to (since, by then, the demise of the GLC at the hands of Thatcher was a foregone conclusion)?

A direct consequence of the movement was to bring together a number of Black artists who began raising these and other questions. The transition of local funding to the Arts Council and the consolidation of a Black Arts movement including other art forms to replace the politically impotent notion of 'ethnic minority arts'[6] precipitated an overdue policy change – 4 per cent of Arts funding was to be spent on Black Arts.

The 'Black Experience' exhibition[7] went into limbo when the curator declined to tour it without adequate support. Meanwhile a simultaneous series of meetings in London took place, co-ordinated for a while by David A. Bailey, where Black photographers tried to map out a strategy. As time, arguments and the lack of money took its toll only a few remained after a couple of years when the time came to submit a grant application to the Arts Council to form an Association of Black Photographers.[8] This has gone on to become Autograph, a London-based group attempting to serve the needs of the national community.

In the interim, a group of Black women managed to get out a one-off magazine called *Polareyes*, and a group calling itself D-Max organized another touring exhibition of the same name. *Polareyes* was partly symptomatic of the emerging gender-based differences among Black photographers and D-Max, as an entirely Afro-Caribbean photographers' exhibition, revealed the problem between cultures under the Black Arts umbrella. D-Max, however, made significant links with the United States in terms of contact with organizers, curators and photographers, particularly in New York.

Meanwhile the first National Photography Conference in the United Kingdom, held at the University of Salford in 1987, nearly disintegrated over race when the keynote address (by Jo Spence) attempted to side-step the issue. By the second conference in 1989, Autograph: the Association of Black Photographers had established itself sufficiently to host the presence of Deborah Willis of the Schomburg Center for Research into Black Culture in New York as well as programme a series of workshops addressing in detail issues within the Black photography community. These issues have *particularly* represented the interests of Black women and Black lesbians and gay men as being the cutting edge of radical cultural politics. No longer were these to be relegated to the fringe.

The lesbian and gay issue has come to the fore because of the general direction of pluralism in the political climate of the Left, combined with the threat on the representation of lesbian and gay lives through Clause 28.[9] At the same time AIDS began to be reported by the British press with an extremely obvious homophobic and racist subtext. Finally a younger generation of artists, photographers and filmmakers was coming into its own and a number of them have had sexuality central to their work. Isaac Julien of Sankofa Film & Video made *The Passion of Remembrance* and went on to make *Looking for Langston* and *Young Soul Rebels*. Pratibha Parmar made *Reframing Aids* for Converse Pictures, a lesbian and gay video group, going on to make *Flesh & Paper* and *Khush* for Channel 4's *Out on Tuesday* programme. The radical lesbian and gay magazine *Square Peg* began publishing work by Black photographers such as Rotimi Fani-Kayode.

At the same time, throughout the 1980s, the Gay Black Group had met at Marchmont Street in London, providing a different kind of grassroots support and another kind of meeting-place for Black cultural practitioners. In fact, towards the end of the GLC, its Ethnic Minority Unit had been persuaded by its lesbian and gay workers to sponsor a day conference on Black lesbians and gays which was held in Brixton around the time of the first Black-funded photography exhibition,[10] 'Reflections of the Black Experience'. It was not coincidental then that the 'Black Experiences' issue[11] of *Ten.8* magazine carried a number of pieces about sexuality by lesbians and gay men.

The separatist politics of the 1970s had given way to both a demand for a Black cultural space and a closer and more equal link between the genders and the races. Having won our spaces the unspoken tensions between the races under the Black umbrella then began to simmer. Funding was inadequate, groups like Autograph exist by the skin of their teeth, across the art forms Black groups found a lack of skilled administrators and had to take on that onerous task. The rhetoric of employment and training for Blacks in supporting roles nearly sank some groups and a furious debate now rages whether white skills ought to be enrolled into the promotion of Black arts. The inspiration found in Black American cultural politics lacked the cultural specificity of the South Asian experience and suspicions were aroused with two US/UK photography shows in quick succession that involved only African/Caribbean artists from the United Kingdom. In the context of America's hegemony in mainstream culture and visual art practices, Blacks in the United Kingdom

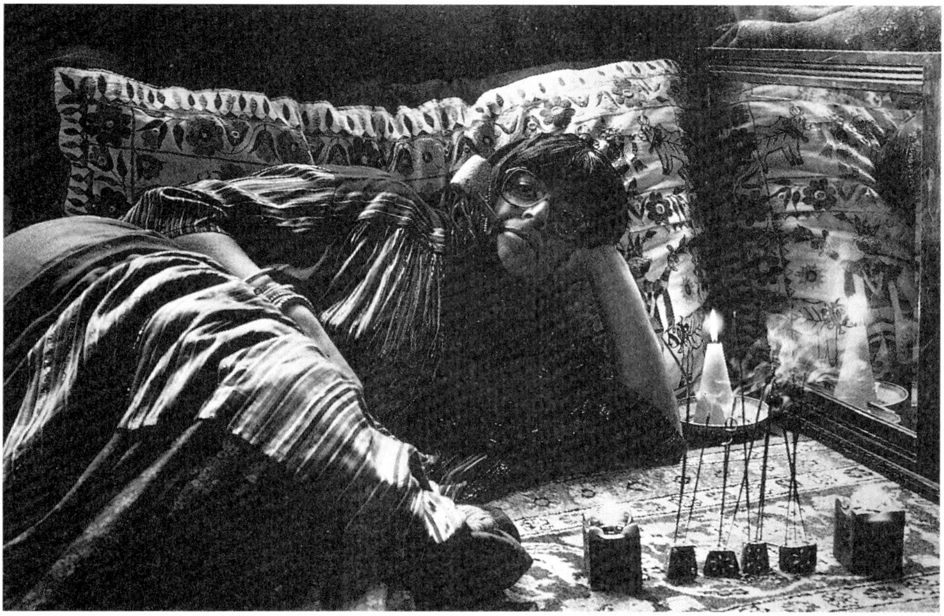

Figure 14.1 Mumtaz Karimjee, from the series 'In Search of Self' (1989), 8″ × 10″

are looking more closely towards their new role as Black Europeans as the economic borders of the European Community come down. Whether 'fortress Europe' will be good for us remains to be seen, but it is certainly the area from where future funding will come and from where comes the hope of reviving local social democracy .

Lesbian and gay artists have been with us since the invention of representation, but it is only since the emergence of the politics of representation that they have been allowed to participate in the cultural agenda. Black artists, always on the defensive since they inevitably have to speak for the race and fend off attacks from those Black spokespeople who have a vested interest in preserving the Black family as the site of Black experience, have been loath to 'come out' in their work. Increasingly, however, in this decade they have been doing so.

Some of the practitioners have included Mumtaz Karimjee, Ingrid Pollard and Rotimi Fani-Kayode. The most recent solo exhibition has been that of the Black gay photographer, Ajamu.[12]

Mumtaz Karimjee was born in Bombay and has lived in Britain for some time (see Figure 14.1). While doing a course on China at the Polytechnic of Central London she made extended field trips to that country and used a camera to record what she observed. She was one of the photographers selected for the 'Black Experiences' commission by the GLC. In that exhibition she made her work about the South Asian, particularly Bangladeshi, presence in London's Whitechapel area. She has been closely connected to the Black feminist movement in London and makes careful works not always for consumption by a general audience. She has shown her work in women-only venues such as the Sisterwrite bookshop.

Mumtaz Karimjee has taken on administrative roles and in 1988 was one of the organizers of 'Spectrum', the women's photography festival. She curated the first exhibition of Indian women photographers in this country, which was held at the Horizon Gallery (1988). Her piece, *My Mothers, My Sisters*, was included in the 'Fabled Territories'[13] exhibition, a survey of photographic works by South Asians in Britain.

She made a piece called *The Eastern Disease?/The Western Disease?* in which she assembled images of herself as a lesbian in search of an identity. The piece is very culture-specific; three landscape format black-and-white self-portraits in Muslim dress arranged vertically opposite three self-portraits in a reading of a Western lesbian stance around a central image of herself cowering under a tree. Text accompanies each photograph beginning with 'The Eastern Disease?' as the first and 'Western Disease?' as the last. The other images have quotes from western travellers describing eastern lesbian women within the classic framework of 'orientalism' and powerful quotes from lesbian feminist writers.

The piece is a direct challenge to cultures that have historically sought to blame the Other for the 'habit' of homosexuality. It has particular resonance in Britain today, living as we do in the throes of the Salman Rushdie affair. The media and the state have been sending out messages urging us that the new Satan is Islamic fundamentalism. Conservative community leaders have taken up the challenge in terms of reviving ancient tradition to keep their youngsters in tow and the whole affair has left the Left in shambles. The only voices making a rational appeal are those of a small group of 'Women Against Fundamentalism'.

In this heightened atmosphere Karimjee's work is a brave attempt to reclaim a space for herself, caught as we are in a climate of blame and the instant threat of excommunication from the culture/race. As the first published piece of 'out' lesbian work by a Muslim woman in this country it is historic.

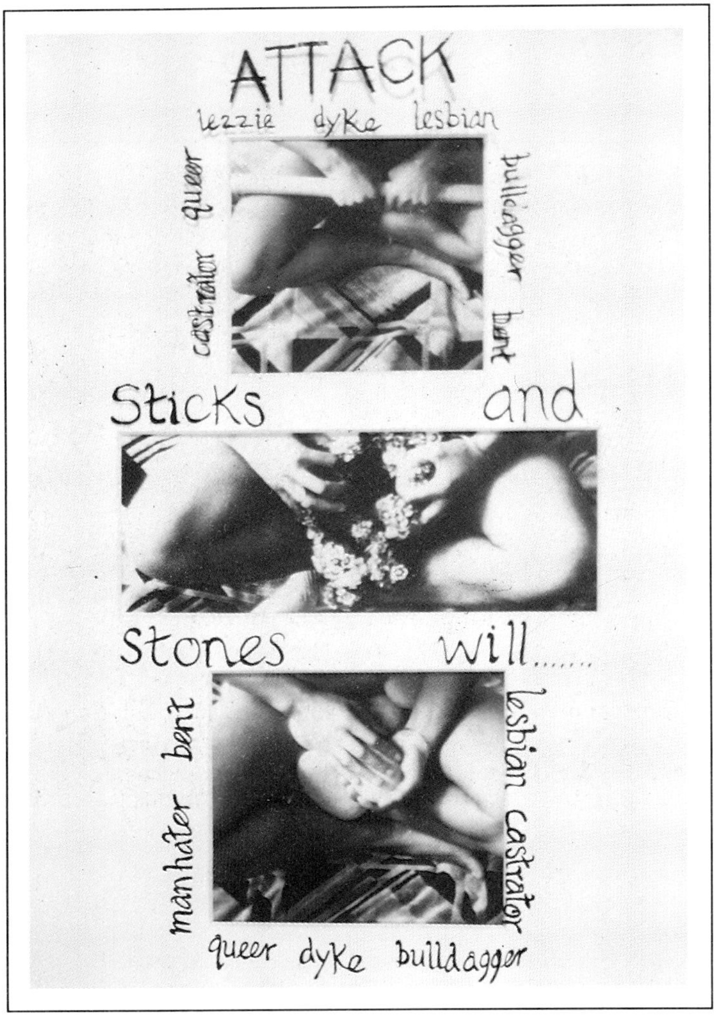

Figure 14.2 Ingrid Pollard

Ingrid Pollard has been continuing to make work about herself as a Black woman in Britain but now as a lesbian as well (Figure 14.2). Another photographer commissioned by the 'Black Experiences' show, she has gone from there to participate in a wide range of shows including D-Max, US/UK, and, 'Transatlantic Dialogues' (curated by Kellie Jones of the Jamaica Arts Center, New York). She was included in the big postwar survey of British photography at the Barbican Arts Centre in 1991, 'Through the Looking Glass', and was one of the women commissioned by the Photographers' Gallery to make work for their Black women's show 'Intimate Distance' (1989). For Autograph she curated an exhibition for CEPA Gallery in Buffalo, New York (1992).

These images contained in her work are fragments and studies towards pieces that appeared in a book edited by Tessa Boffin and Jean Fraser called *Stolen Glances*[14] and exhibition that collected work by lesbian photographers from the United States and the United Kingdom about lesbian representation, theory and practice. Her fragments of self-image are based on the body, framed within words which come, sometimes from popular black names for lesbian and sometimes from discussions Ingrid has had with her mother.

As with other Black practitioners, lesbian and gay work about self-image appears to become possible once artists and photographers have proved themselves in the more general arena of race and demonstrated beyond doubt their loyalty and commitment to it.

Rotimi Fani-Kayode and Alex Hirst had lived together for many years and had begun to make work together publicly in the two years preceding the sudden death of Fani-Kayode. In a sense their story touches upon a number of issues (see Figure 14.3).

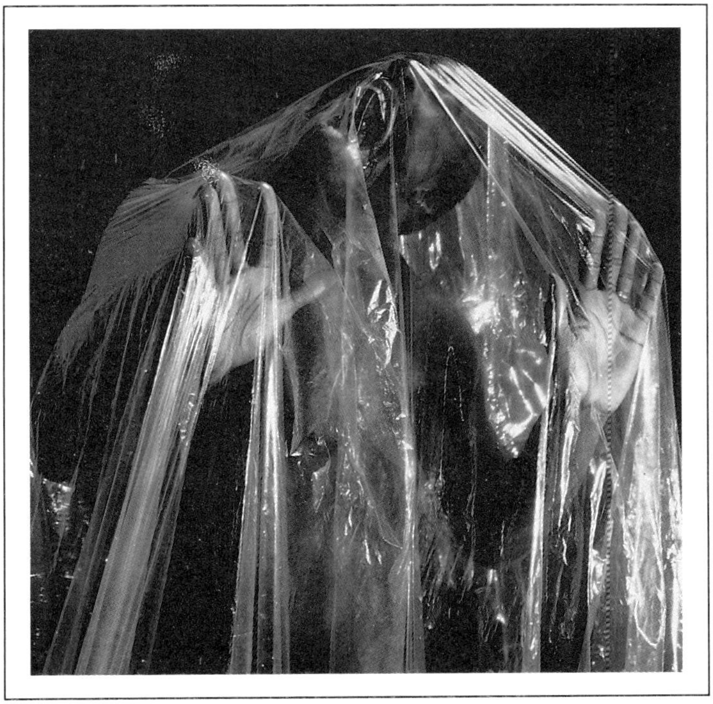

Figure 14.3 Rotimi Fani-Kayode, untitled (1988), 12″ × 12″.

Fani-Kayode was born in Nigeria and trained at the Pratt Institute before coming to live in Britain, where he met Hirst, a white Englishman who was to be his partner. Although one had trained as a painter and a photographer and the other as a writer, they came to be mutually supportive and the last pieces were seen to be a truly collaborative effort. Fani-Kayode brought his Nigerian, Yoruba references to the work and Hirst his background as a writer on the gay left and with the Square Peg collective in London.

They situated themselves on the Black gay front-line of Railton Road in Brixton, London and from there made photographic works that challenged the restrictions on representation of homoerotic imagery in Britain as well as of the work of Mapplethorpe. Their last published piece of work was commissioned by the project 'Ecstatic Antibodies' which opened at Impressions Gallery, York in 1990. A book[15] of the same title was published simultaneously. The exhibition was censored in the United Kingdom on the grounds of Clause 28.

Fani-Kayode was an active member of Autograph and its chair until he died. His commitment to the creation of a Black gay image, to anti-racism and to extending his work to photographing women friends was leading the way in which British lesbian and gay Black photographers were now expressing their confidence in their work. Their confidence was not going to be shaken by arguments of betrayal to the race; this confidence would allow for collaboration with white

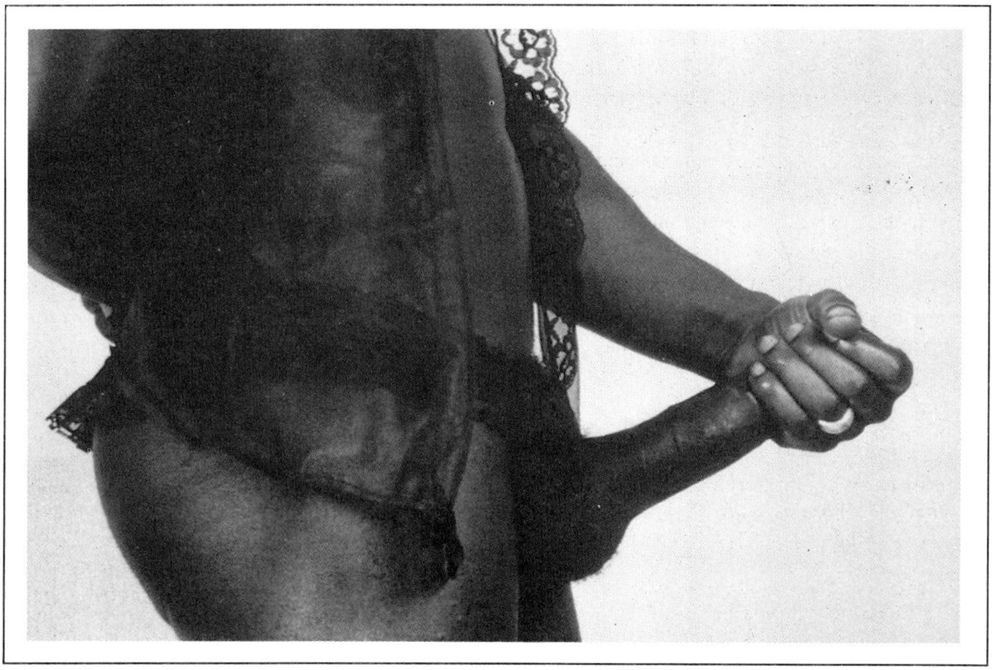

Figure 14.4 Ajamu, untitled (1992), 2″ × 3″.

practitioners and the forging of new multi-cultural alliances, based on mutual respect and equality, in the face of a brutal swing to the right by the state and shifting strategies by funding bodies.

So where do we go from here? Should Blacks be shouted down for homophobia and gays for racism, as happened as recently as the 1991 ICA gays and art conference? Should Third World gays walk away from the years of ignorance and disenfranchisement experienced at the hands of white gay cultural gurus? Should gay artists give up trying to be traditional gallery-based artists and take up a more direct-action approach, producing fanzines, postcards, and so on, as do the Manchester-based Homocult?

One possible response is a non-confrontational approach being taken by the London-based Institute of International Visual Arts. Here it was hoped would lie a live debate around the interaction of Black arts, gay art and the white mainstream. Here it was envisaged that not only Black audiences and work would be developed but lesbian and gay audiences and work as well. 'Mirage' an inIVA collaboration at the ICA during May–June 1995, included works by both Glen Ligon and Lyle Ashton Harris. Harris had been shown in London already in the first Autograph show, 'Autoportraits',[16] at Camerawork in 1990.

But what of censorship and the underlying fear of gay men's sexuality as outlined by Scott Watson's reading of *Pulp Fiction*? Kobena Mercer has written in his 'Notes on Ajamu's photographs' (Figure 14.4):

> For every action there is an opposite and equal reaction. Now that black gay men's sexuality has been demonised as the ultimate 'Other' to liberal humanist ego identity … . Ajamu draws deeply from multiple sources of resistance that enable us to survive such attacks, whether they come from the political establishment or from those who would cheerfully beat us up on the street. No we are not expendable, or marginal, or exotic, or quaint: we are black and queer and have always been here.[17]

There is a growing disquiet now that the heady days of activism and town hall funding have given way to Arts Council and Channel 4 funding. Assimilation and mainstreaming have exacted a toll on the activism side. The continuing rise of the 'new right' in America (long a source of queer cultural activist inspiration) and its threat over all arts funding is creating a contradictory time for us now. There is quite a lot more cultural production but the fundamental disquiet about queers and their arts remains unchanged. Black arts no longer exist in quite the same cohesive way as a movement. The larger body politic has insured the promotion of individual careerism over community involvement. The movement has not reconstituted itself and its individuals are working in an increasingly international setting. Perhaps it is because the local gay audience remains, as always, only marginally interested in issues of race and queer culture. A trip to your local gay pub will confirm this. Perhaps the 1990s will usher in a significant international movement that can capture the imagination of a local gay audience.

Notes

1 Scott Watson, Director/Curator, University of British Columbia Fine Art Gallery, Vancouver, Canada, in an e-mail distributed March 1995. Watson testified in the trial of 'Little Sisters', a local lesbian and gay bookstore.

2 Black for the purposes of this piece is to be understood in the British sense as representing people of African, Caribbean and South Asian descent. Originally the 'Colours of Black' at the Greater London Council included the Irish; its final political weight came to rest with the two main immigrant communities of colour.

3 Eddie Chambers (1993) *Black People and the British Flag*, Bristol: a collaboration with Cornerhouse, Manchester and City Gallery, Leicester. For many years a slogan imprinted by Chambers in the catalogues for the shows he curated; e.g. his first INIVA exhibition above.

4 Wason, S. and Jantjes, G. (1991), *The Institute of New International Visual Arts* (Final Report), Arts Council of England.

5 For example the radical exhibition at the Hayward Gallery curated by Hill, P., Kelly, A. and Tagg, J. (1979), *Three Perspectives on Photography*, London: Arts Council of Great Britain.

6 The notion of 'ethnic minority arts' was highlighted by a report produced by Naseem Khan for the Arts Council entitled *The Arts that Britain Ignores*, which led to the formation of MAAS, the Minority Arts Advisory Service, till early 1995 publisher of *Artrage* magazine.

7 Curated by Baker, M. (1986), *Reflections of the Black Experience*, London: Greater London Council, Brixton Art Gallery.

8 Unpublished discussion paper *African, Caribbean and South Asian Photography*, presented to the Arts Council by Similola Coker and Devdan Sen, 1986. This research study formed the basis of creating a structural foundation for Autograph.

9 Clause 28, part of an Act of Parliament limiting the powers of local government, specifically prohibits the 'promotion' of homosexuality as a 'pretended family relationship'. It has raised a whole area of censorship with respect to depicting lesbian and gay lives. Most visual art venues in the United Kingdom are subsidized by their town halls.

10 Curated by Baker, M. (1986), *Reflections of the Black Experience*, London: Greater London Council, Brixton Art Gallery.

11 It is interesting to note the shift from issue 16 (1984), *Black Image/Staying On*, Birmingham: *Ten.8* Magazine/ Photographers' Gallery, to issue 22 (1986), *Black Experiences*, Birmingham: *Ten.8* Magazine, where from a complete absence of discussion around homosexuality it becomes a central issue in just two years.

12 Catalogue, Ajamu (1994), *Black Bodyscapes: Photographs by Ajamu*, London: David A. Bailey.

13 *Fabled Territories: New Asian Photography in Britain*, exhibition and catalogue researched by Sunil Gupta for Leeds City Art Gallery, 1989.

14 Tessa Boffin and Jean Fraser (eds) (1991), *Stolen Glances*, 1st edn, London: Pandora Press.

15 Tessa Boffin and Sunil Gupta (eds) (1990), *Ecstatic Antibodies: Resisting the Aids Mythology*, Rivers Oram Press: London and Boston.

16 *Autoportraits*, the first Autograph touring exhibition, was curated by Monika Baker and Sunil Gupta for Camerawork, London, 1990.

17 Kobena Mercer (1994), 'The camera as kinky machine: notes on Ajamu's photographs', *Black Bodyscapes: Photographs by Ajamu*, London: David A. Bailey, 4–8.

Chapter Fifteen

Ad(dressing) the dyke

Lesbian looks and lesbians looking

Reina Lewis and Katrina Rolley

INTRODUCTION

This article stemmed from our realization that a lifetime's commitment to reading fashion magazines was neither a solitary nor an un-lesbian activity. Not only were lots of other lesbians doing it, but we all seemed to like the same spreads. A straw poll of who had cut out what to stick on or in which wall/desk/wallet revealed a commonality of visual pleasures. This led us to explore what it was about these particular images which attracted lesbian viewers. We should be clear from the start that this 'survey' is highly selective, based on our own readings and on opinions gathered from friends and responses to conference papers. The magazines we sampled were all mainstream high fashion magazines from the 1990s – *Vogue, Vogue Italia* ,*Elle* and *Marie Claire* – since we were interested to analyse the possible lesbian visual pleasures offered by fashion imagery in a field of cultural production that is understood to be aimed at an exclusively female (and overtly heterosexual) audience. We have not, therefore, entered into the realm of the more avant-garde 'lifestyle' magazines, such as *The Face* and *iD*, since these address a mixed audience and are often deliberately provocative in content and imagery.

This article approaches the lesbian gaze from a variety of angles: the first section explores how the fashion magazine functions as a mainstream space in which a plurality of possibly deviant sexual positionings can be expressed/explored; the second addresses theories of narcissism and female visual pleasure; and the third examines the specifically lesbian pleasures offered by a series of mainstream fashion images. While the third section of this article was jointly authored, the first two parts were written by one or other of us, in the context of shared discussion.

THE QUEER SPACE OF THE FASHION MAGAZINE (Katrina Rolley)

Before we analyse the apparently subversive readings available to the lesbian viewer of fashion magazines, I want to explore the forms of pleasure offered by fashion images to both heterosexual and lesbian women. During the course of this exploration I will suggest that fashion magazines function as a form of (homo)erotica for all women, making the lesbian's ostensibly seditious pleasures supplementary, rather than necessarily oppositional, to the predicated readings. This contradiction stems from the fact that due to its impeccable (heterosexual) credentials, the high fashion magazine offers a space within which rules can be broken: it is a fascination with this normative and subversive duality that animates our analysis of this material.

Responses to the recent proliferation of erotic images aimed specifically at women (be it men's bodies in mainstream advertising or lesbian erotic magazines) tend to ignore the fact that a form of sexualized female visual pleasure already existed in the form of the fashion image. Indeed, prior to the recent emergence of the patently desirable male nude within mainstream cultural production, sexual desire and desirability were predominantly signalled in terms of the female nude: imagery that was understood to function for both men and women. Thus women have long been tutored in consuming other women's bodies, in assessing and responding to the desirability of other women. This process has often been understood as one of passively identifying with the woman who is the subject of the active male gaze/sexuality (as will be discussed in greater detail later). However, I would suggest that this process potentially involves far more complex forms of identification and desire and that it is difficult, if not impossible, fully to separate admiration from desiring to be and from desiring to have.

According to popular wisdom, women are generally understood to be more critical and perceptive with regard to dress and appearance – especially that of other women – than the majority of men: hence the plethora of jokes about men not noticing new hairstyles, new dresses, and so on. Indeed this 'fact' was brought home to me recently when attending an exhibition entitled 'Chambre Close', featuring Bettina Rheims' photographs of naked and semi-naked women. My male companion – despite being sophisticated, visually aware and very appearance-conscious – perceived all the pictured women as professional models, whereas I was immediately intrigued by the fact that this clearly was not the case since the women's faces and bodies, while attractive, just were not 'perfect' enough to fulfil current codes of model good looks.

The specificity of my visual response was hardly surprising given that from an early age women are encouraged to develop a potentially obsessive concern with their own and other women's appearance. One of the primary socially sanctioned – and indeed quintessentially feminine – mediums through which women develop this skill is the fashion magazine. These magazines are comparatively freely available regardless of income: they are passed around at school, are a staple of every waiting room and may be flicked through at any large station, supermarket or stationery shop. Girls and women consume fashion images in a way similar to the male consumption of 'hobby' magazines (bikes, sport, computers); this activity, together with group shopping trips and experimenting with hair, dress and make-up, plays a primary part in adolescent female bonding. Similarly, as a group activity, the eroticized pleasures of reading fashion magazines correlate to the teen male consumption of porn.

The magazines thus consumed are *a priori* a 'world without men', and 'world' is often the word used to describe the milieu they invoke ('your *Cosmo* world', etc.). Both the producers and the consumers of these magazines are presumed female. If a contributor is male it is often integral to the purpose of the article; in general, it is only exceptional men, such as the subject of a 'star' profile, who feature within their pages. Thus, within this matriarchal subculture the mainstream is turned upside-down, leaving men, as opposed to women, in the role of the mysterious 'Other' whose alien characteristics are obsessively catalogued, dissected, criticized and ridiculed.

Therefore fashion magazines are fundamental to a socially prescribed and formative feminine experience. Either individually or as a group, the regular 'flicking through' of magazines in which women are the exclusive subject of almost every image effectively tutors women in actively consuming the female body and appearance. What is also undeniable is that sexuality is fundamental to the production, consumption and content of these magazines. Sex in one form or another pervades women's magazines and thus surrounds the fashion images, especially those in *Elle* and *Marie Claire*. In addition, while heterosexuality is still the norm within mainstream magazines, articles on homosexuality and/or lesbianism are now commonplace: the majority of magazines will reference lesbian and gay sex/sexual issues and lesbian and gay couples, in their general articles on sexuality and relationships. Similarly, while the sexuality of the magazine's models, staff and readers is still predominantly predicated as heterosexual, the line between hetero-and homosexuality is often a fine one: a good example being Kate Puckrick's 'Confessions of a Female Skirt-Chaser' in *Elle*

(Puckrick 1994: 17). Here, the author admits that '[w]hen I see a woman who's thrown down the gauntlet to conventional cuteness in order to celebrate her own unique sexiness, I can't contain myself. And there's no one kind of woman who'll make me want to scratch 'n' sniff': although Puckrick (re)assures the reader that 'seeing a fine foxy lady exploiting her potential just fills me with button-popping pride that I'm a woman, too.'

In addition to being a pervasive issue for the reader of a fashion magazine, sexuality is also integral to the production of the fashion image. Despite some notable exceptions, the majority of fashion photographers are still male, and an element of sexual attraction between model and photographer is generally understood to be an important part of many photo shoots (remember the fashion shoot in the film *Blow Up*?): thus Jeanloup Sieff said, of the photographer PeterLindbergh (*Independent On Sunday*,13 March 1994, 11), '[i]t is obvious in Peter Lindbergh's photographs that he loves women who love him back.' This 'love affair' between photographer and model means that the success of many fashion images supposedly resides in the photographer's communication of the model's sexual response to 'his' gaze. However, what does it mean when this gaze is then replaced by that of the female viewer of the fashion magazine? Does her perception of the model's sexual response (to the now absent male photographer) trigger her own desires? In this context it is also interesting to note: the number of eminent (male) fashion photographers who also produce erotica/pornography (David Bailey, Norman Parkinson, Helmut Newton, Stephen Meisel and others); the number of 'supermodels' who are now constructed as overtly sexual objects of desire and who pose (semi)-naked for male magazines, posters and calendars; and the way in which the 'quality' press use fashion spreads (especially those featuring lingerie and swimwear) to titillate the (male or female?) reader.

In *Women and Fashion: A New Look*, Caroline Evans and Minna Thornton argue that:

> Fashion imagery like fashion in general, tends to be trivialized ... Fashion takes its revenge against its trivialization: it gets away with murder. Extraordinary liberties are taken precisely because it is 'only' fashion. The 'evidence' lies in the photographs themselves ... . Here the outrageous, or the transgressive, particularly in relation to female sexuality, find covert expression. (Evans and Thornton 1989: 82)

Individual fashion spreads might occasionally become the focus of concerned debate, but such attention is rarely seen as a serious problem by the magazine in question and the more avant-garde magazines often appear to court controversy. As 'LA' pointed out in the *Observer* (30 May 1993), it was only because Corinne Day's photographs of Kate Moss in her underwear appeared in *Vogue*, the respectable bible of couture fashion, that they became the subject of such widespread discussion. In other words, the main problem was aesthetic. Day's representation of 'generation X' kids in their natural 'unglamorized' environment – already commonplace within magazines such as *The Face* and *iD* – shocked *Vogue*'s very different readership.

However Day's photographs do raise a number of interesting questions around the acceptable and unacceptable face of sexuality in fashion images. While media debate focused on the apparent youth of Moss, and the images' potential appeal to (male) paedophiles, no one questioned the role of these supposedly overtly provocative images in a magazine aimed at women. What was the assumed response of the female readership to these images? Were they presumed immune to such seduction? And, of course, what these photographs also represent are potentially erotic images of a woman taken by another woman – in this case a friend of the model – for consumption by women. In other words, while the feminist and lesbian movements have made a self-conscious, and much vaunted, effort during the past decade to produce a woman-centred erotica, fashion photography has been offering this pleasure to women for the last fifty years, via the work of female photographers such as Louise Dahl Woolf (who began working in the 1930s and who also produced sensuous nude photographs of her fashion models whenever possible), Sarah Moon, Deborah

Turbeville and Ellen von Unwerth (among others), all of whom have produced overtly sensual/erotic images of women for women.

Thus it appears that the fashion magazines' established place within the heterosexual mainstream – together with the fact that fashion itself is understood to be both inherently heterosexual and inherently trivial – allows both creators and consumers of the fashion spread to explore potentially subversive and challenging representations of female sexuality. The lesbian consumer might feel herself to be reading against the heterosexual grain in her response to certain fashion photographs, but I would suggest that not only do many fashion spreads overtly and covertly play with provocative lesbian themes, but that to some extent the magazines themselves almost invite – indeed educate – the reader into something very close to a lesbian response to much of their imagery of women in general. Heterosexual women, or women constructed as heterosexual, do themselves desire the women in the magazines. They have been trained into it. So what is set up is what we might call a paradigmatically lesbian viewing position in which women are induced to exercise a gaze that desires the represented woman, not just one that identifies with them.

THE LESBIAN GAZE (Reina Lewis)

This raises the question of whether/how far one can distinguish an overtly lesbian gaze, that self-consciously desires the represented woman, from a narcissistic one that identifies with the represented woman as an object of a presumed-to-be-male desire? It is possible that for the heterosexual woman viewer the temporarily lesbian mode of viewing can be contained if she remembers that the logic of the magazine positions the desired woman as ultimately the object of male desire. On the other hand, the self-consciously lesbian viewer can take what the codes of the magazine offer and add to that an extra-textual knowledge that presumes the existence of other lesbian readers. This shifts her to a position of either desiring for herself the represented woman or/and desiring to be the woman who is desired by other lesbian readers. Thus the social context of reading that we have previously argued is fundamental to the establishment of the magazines' logic, can also include a recognition of interpretive communities with reading habits that go against the grain of the magazines' heterosexist rationale.

Several writers (Brooks 1982, Myers 1982a, b, Evans and Thornton 1989) have commented that the peculiar situation of the female viewer looking at fashion images of women problematizes the sexuality of the female gaze. Two main themes recur in these discussions; distancing, understood as objectification, and narcissism. The first is concerned with the distancing effects of the (male) gaze that objectify (read dehumanize) women, and the second with an (over)identification between viewer and image, that is, with the opposite of distancing. In both cases the possibility of a female visual pleasure based on a sometimes voyeuristic gaze at images of the female body raises the question of pornographic or eroticized pleasures that are difficult to accommodate within accounts which assume a solely heterosexual positioning.

What interests me is how lesbian responses to selected fashion images may be both objectifying and narcissistic (identificatory). Here, I am thinking of object and objectification in psychoanalytic terms, that is, in relation to the processes of objectification that bring, or are imagined by the subject to bring, pleasure. A heterosexist analysis – in keeping with the generally trivializing attitude to the aspirational qualities of the fashion magazine – would assume that the female pleasure in fashion magazines was purely narcissistic in that the female spectator wanted only to *be* the object. However, I am concerned with the double movement of a lesbian visual pleasure wherein the viewer wants both to be and to *have* the object.

In Freud's account, narcissism is not merely the desire for a reflection of oneself, but of what the self 'would like to be'. This explains the obvious pleasures of identification with the model and entire world of high fashion imagery. Further, a narcissistic desire is not simply a desire for identification with the object of one's own desiring gaze, but also a desire to experience oneself being loved by others (Freud 1914). So although narcissism is sometimes understood to mean simply self-love, Freud makes it clear that narcissism is not an inability to objectify, to engage with an object outside of the self. It refers instead to a tendency to objectify that which reminds one of oneself or of the self as one would like to be/have been (for example, as the self was when the mother loved you). It is not that pleasure is not gained via object-love; object-love exists, but it requires an object that has some fantasized relation/similarity to the self.

Thus the devices that would satisfy a narcissistic desire are those that enable the fantasy of identifying with an ideal self and/or those which enable the fantasy of being desired/being loved. In consuming the magazine, then, the female viewer can potentially enjoy a variety of narcissistic pleasures: the object of the woman's (desirous) gaze is both the female body and the glamour of the high fashion world that transforms a female gendered body into an ideal. In this way, the fashion context, like the glamorous woman on film, is perfect for facilitating the spectator action necessary for the fantasy of experiencing oneself as the object of the desiring gaze. In effect the female viewer in imagining herself as the model places herself as the beloved object (since, as Freud points out, investing in one's beauty is the main avenue to satisfaction open to women in an unequal world; Freud 1914: 88–9). But, unlike film, this desire to be the beautiful object of the fashion magazine is lesbian, since the viewer who gazes at the beautiful model is undeniably female, unlike film where the audience is assumed to be mixed.

This is in contrast to Laura Mulvey's analysis of the female gaze in relation to classic Hollywood films. For her, the female gaze, in order to be active, must become transvestite, since male characters are seen to control the action while female characters are constituted and presented to the camera as the passive recipients of a male gaze (Mulvey 1975, 1981). Therefore, for a woman viewer who wants a pleasure not based on a passive masochistic identification with the female character (which is how narcissism would be inflected here) the only alternative is to assume a transvestite positioning as male - there is no room in Mulvey's formulation for a woman to make an active identification as female let alone to actively desire a woman from a female position. It is interesting that Mulvey's notion of transvestism, in terms of the lesbian gaze, would adequately describe the classic Freudian description of the lesbian who desires other women from a masculine position: an identification with the father and a rejection of the mother's position. (As Elizabeth Wright points out, there is no space in Freud's scenario for a lesbian to desire other women as a woman, only as a man; 'there is no trace of female–female desire: rather female homosexuality is likened more precisely to male homosexuality' [Wright 1992: 216].)

Evans and Thornton argue that, in the case of the fashion magazine, the female gaze at the fashion image can be identificatory *and* voyeuristic from a female position rather – or indeed, as well as – transvestite and masculine (*qua* Mulvey): a 'desire to look' that vacillates between 'narcissistic identification' and 'voyeuristic pleasure' (Evans and Thornton 1989: 10). I would add to this that the identification is not just with the women in the picture ('I want to look like that') but with their state of being looked at ('I want to be the object of the desiring gaze') by a *female* viewer. This radically re-situates John Berger's formulation, 'the surveyor of women in herself is male: the surveyed female', into a female surveyor of images of women whose pleasure lies in being the object and owner of a gaze that can only be female, and that is implicitly lesbian (Berger 1972: 47).

I think that we can use the example of fashion imagery to problematize negative pairings of narcissism and lesbianism by emphasizing the plurality of narcissistic placings and lesbian identifications (see also Merck 1984). If we allow that the lesbian gaze is narcissistic – based on reflexivity, recognition, identification and being looked at – then we have a lesbian gaze in which the pleasure of looking is experienced simultaneously with the pleasure of being looked at by a woman. Indeed the narcissistic desire for identification is a desire to be the desired object of a female gaze at the same time as experiencing the pleasures of deploying the gaze. Thus we can postulate a female and lesbian gaze – at the female object – that can be active from a female position without recourse to transvestism. Evans and Thornton argue that the fashion image is double-coded, allowing for the simultaneous signification of two autonomous languages, so that both transvestite/masculine and narcissistic/feminine positionings can be achieved. I would argue, instead, that in the case of the lesbian viewer the fashion image is multi-coded in that it allows a reciprocity of pleasure that is about both desiring the image and desiring to be the image, that is, an object choice that is both anaclitic (relating to someone or something outside the self: that recalls the early source of self-preservation, for example the breast) and narcissistic. I make this move towards both anaclitic and narcissistic object choice since to talk only of a narcissistic formation implies that there is only one kind of lesbian viewer. Psychoanalytic accounts see lesbianism as a process of desire for the same (implicit in the label of narcissistic) that does not allow for the differences between lesbians. Indeed, if we follow Judith Butler's lead (Butler 1990) in thinking about sex and gender as ambiguous and performative, then, we can move beyond a polarized position that sees female transvestism as the temporary assumption of a male positionality. The transvestite denotes a gender that is ambiguous, being irreducible to either male or female. This means not only that the female viewer may look *as* a lesbian whether or not she actually is/considers herself to be lesbian, but that the self-identified lesbian viewer may look from a variety of borrowed and invented positionalities too.

When we begin to map a self-consciously lesbian viewer onto the discourses of fashion and psychoanalysis we introduce another set of identifications that problematize the heterosexual binarism of psychoanalysis. The varieties of lesbian positionings and forms of 'sexual consciousness', to borrow a phrase from Lisa Walker (Walker 1993: 16), raise other questions: how, for example, would a self-consciously butch lesbian react to the prospect of being the glamorous model; do different images allow different narcissistic positions for different lesbians? Consuming fashion imagery may not involve identification with the image as one that is desired, so much as an investment in the activity of looking – and desiring – in itself. It is here that we need to think about what bell hooks, in her analysis of the black female film spectator, calls the 'pleasure of interrogation'; an oppositional reading that recognizes that while the racism and sexism of mainstream films refuse a pleasurable identification for black women viewers, the experience of watching such films while 'on guard' can afford an alternative pleasure and power in making a reading against the grain(hooks 1992). In our instance, we have a form of representation that is implicitly structured around a female narcissistic and identificatory gaze, but which can be read from a viewing position that refuses this invitation solely to identify and retains the possibility of desiring, or of experiencing both forms of connection (simultaneously or in flux). And we know by now that the desire – though perhaps coded as such – is about more than just wanting a certain garment. Indeed, in hook's analysis the collectivity of other black viewers engaged in similarly subversive modes of spectatorship is implicit in the pleasures of the interrogative gaze. For the self-consciously lesbian magazine reader, the knowledge/assumption of other subversive readers reinforces and claims as lesbian the homoerotic codes of the images.

This implicit recognition that the lesbian gaze does not operate alone nor outside of the social context, allows us to think about a variety of lesbian viewing positions (all of which may be occupied within the viewing experience of any one woman). In other words, the discussion of the lesbian gaze denotes a shifting spectatorship that can include both what we have characterized as a paradigmatically lesbian position (open, but not exclusive to, women coded as heterosexual) and, although I hesitate to use the word 'actual', a self-consciously, self-identified, lesbian viewing position (occupied by women conscious of themselves and others as lesbian). This latter positionality, which is in itself never singular or fixed, relies on both the codes of the images and the acknowledgment of a community of lesbian readers.[1] This, then, can also accommodate the significance of visibility in the lived experience of lesbians without ruling out the complexities of a feminist anti-fashion inheritance. The importance of dress as a signifier of sexual identity, and of looking, as a social, identifying and *sexualized* activity in the lives of lesbians, coalesce to provide a supplementary pleasure to the activity of consuming fashion magazines. As Walker points out, 'looking like what you are' in terms of self-presentation is crucial for a recognizable lesbian identity and structurally central to the theorization of marginal identities. In this instance, looking like a lesbian means viewing *as* a lesbian, but the demand for the imaged women to look like they *are*, or could be, lesbians remains important: not any image will do. Indeed, I wonder whether it is a prerequisite of exercising the desiring gaze that one also identifies with the idealized object, that is, is it just the codes of the fashion magazine which allow this actively desiring lesbian gaze, or does the lesbian assume an identification with the idealized object even if the acknowledgement of it is suppressed?

Our straw poll and personal predilection centred on images which seemed to offer particularly lesbian pleasures. This is not to deny that the polysemy of all images would in theory allow for diverse visual pleasures, but that some images caught lesbian eyes more than others. This is where

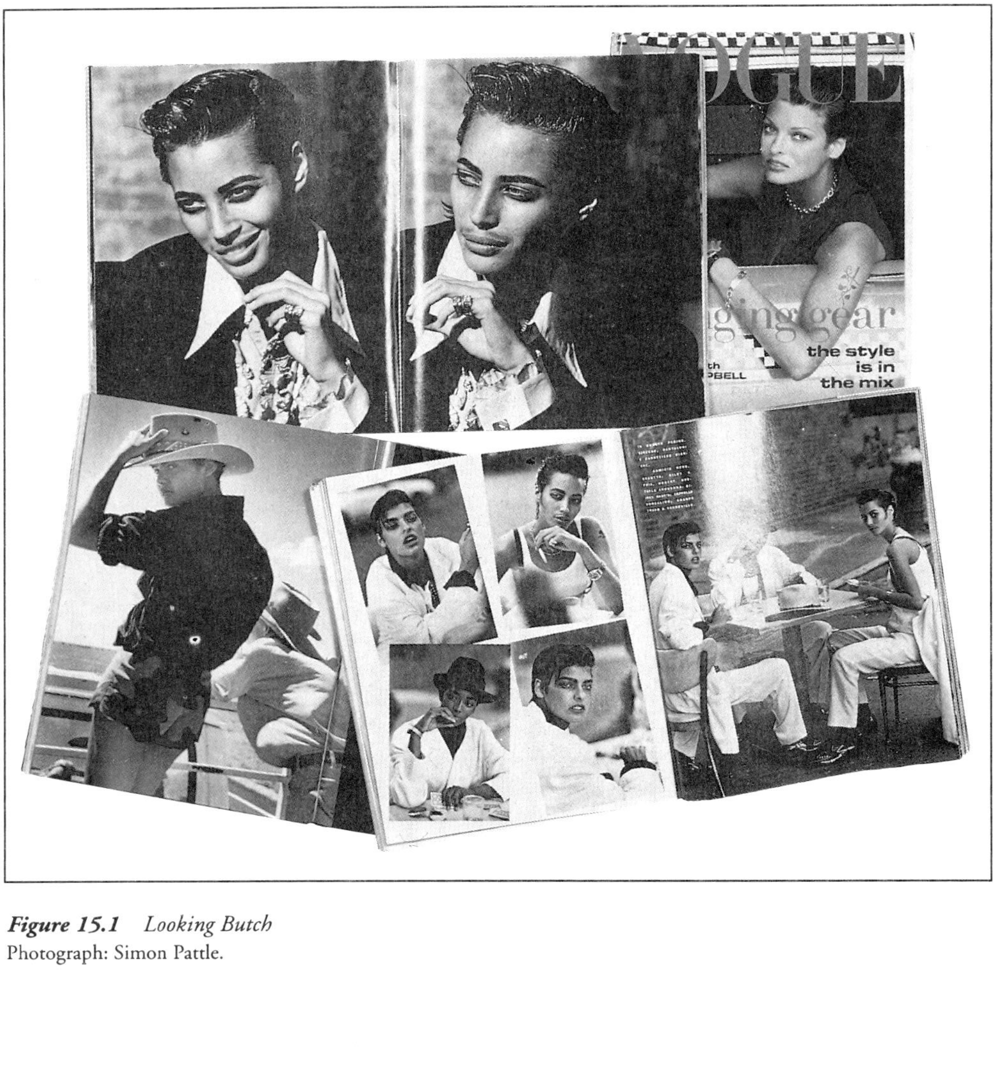

Figure 15.1 *Looking Butch*
Photograph: Simon Pattle.

the experiential exigencies of looking, as part of lesbian lives and subcultures, come to the fore. While the current interest in lesbians and high fashion is contingent – we certainly would never have written about this ten years ago – the habits of looking continue. One might expand the survey to include an assessment of how many lesbians who would never dream of reading *Vogue* have posters of kd lang on their walls or bought a copy of Sadie Lee's National Portrait Gallery poster *Erect.*[2]

THE IMAGES

Looking butch (Figure 15.1)

The spread from *Vogue Italia* (top left and bottom right) sets up a narrative of multiple transgressions and/or subversions that opens it to the sort of self-conscious lesbian appropriation we have been discussing. Most obviously it centres on cross-dressing combined with a narrative of criminality and a racialized Italianate mafiosi setting. Unlike conventions of male impersonation, these figures make no attempt to pass as male – they do not hide their breasts – but read clearly as cross-dressed women. This reading is enhanced by the fact that the reader recognizes these women (Naomi Campbell, Linda Evangelista, Christy Turlington) as supermodels: women with an iconic status as ideals of (hetero)sexual desirability. However, cross-dressing keys directly into lesbian traditions of butch in which, according to Joan Nestle, it is the wearing of male garments on a female body that functions to communicate an active lesbian desire:

> None of the butch women I was with ... ever presented themselves to me as men; they did announce themselves as tabooed women who were willing to identify their passion for other women by wearing clothes that symbolized the taking of responsibility. Part of this responsibility was sexual expertise. (Nestle 1987: 100.)

The cross-dressing in this spread is set within a clearly articulated narrative that relies for effect on its two other themes: criminality and racialized difference. The form of masculinity portrayed and parodied is clearly coded as Italianate gangster, drawing on styles and gestures associated with popular cultural representations of gangsters in general and the mafia in particular (pencil moustaches, sideburns, greased hair, heavy gold jewellery, vests). This brings with it not only a frisson of illicit activity and street-smarts (perceived now as one of the signifiers of butch bar-dyke culture of the 1950s) but also a culturally specific stereotype of masculine sexuality as aggressive, objectifying and public. Thus the presumed-to-be-female viewer of these images finds herself subject to a desirous/hostile appraisal by figures whose raiment and pose signals masculinity but who, in the last instance, cannot but be recognized as female. Moreover, the mode of masculinity they mimic is one that is regularly, albeit covertly, homoeroticized in popular culture, thus activating another set of transgressive associations.

Gendered couples (Figure 15.2)

Where Vogue Italia used gangster-style cross-dressing in an all-male ensemble, a few months later British Vogue featured a gangster spread (top left) by the same photographer (Peter Lindbergh) that involved a clearly gendered couple: Bonnie and Clyde. However, while the theme of criminality remains, the loss of the sexualized Italianate cultural codings and gritty, sweaty realism leaves these images clearly framed (literally) and containable as innocent charades. That the same photographer produced two so very different gangster spreads may be in part explained by the different editorial policy of the two magazines: *Vogue Italia* is widely recognized as being at the cutting edge of contemporary fashion photography, while British *Vogue* has undergone a transformation to (safer) American standards (Coleridge 1988). Thus, when the gendered couple appears in *Vogue Italia*

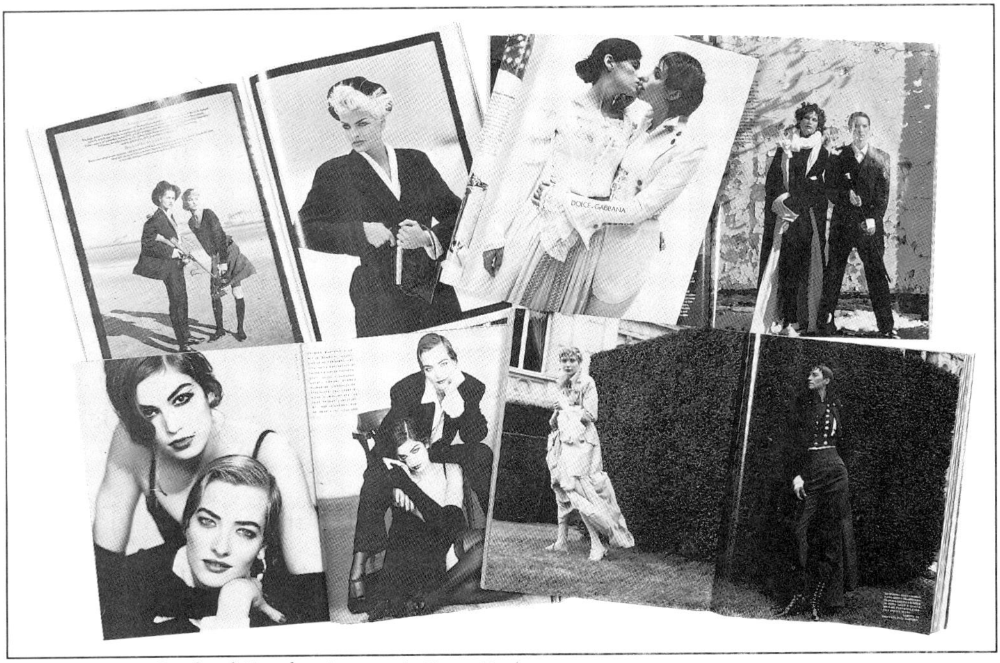

Figure 15.2 *Gendered Couples* Photograph: Simon Pattle.

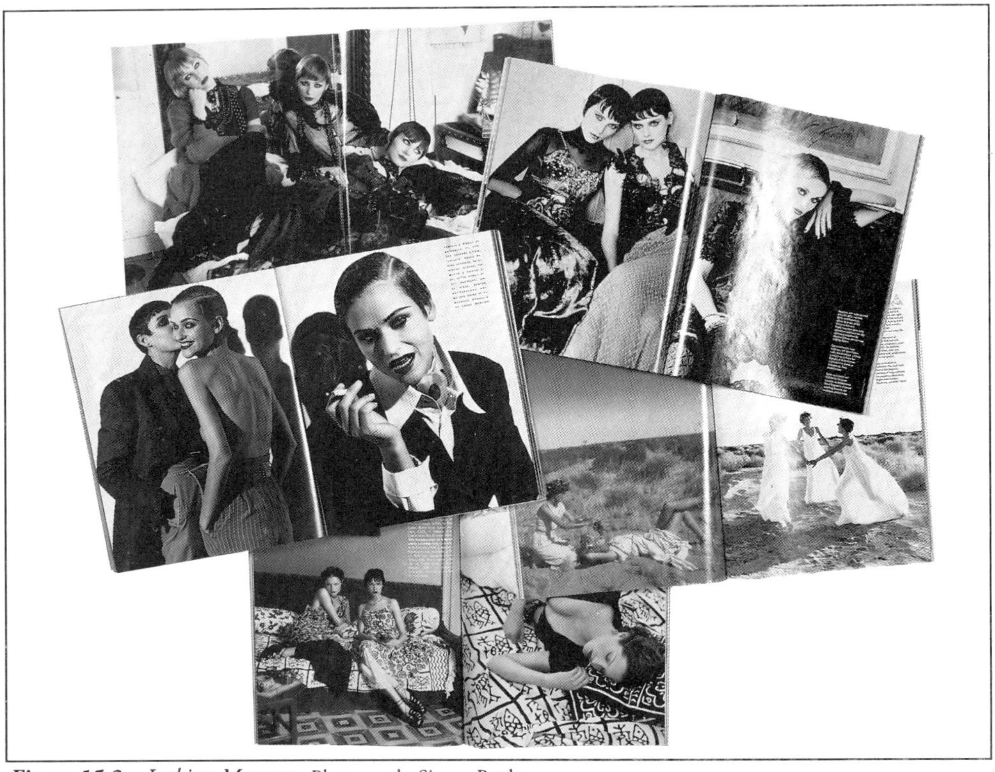

Figure 15.3 *Lesbian Moments* Photograph: Simon Pattle.

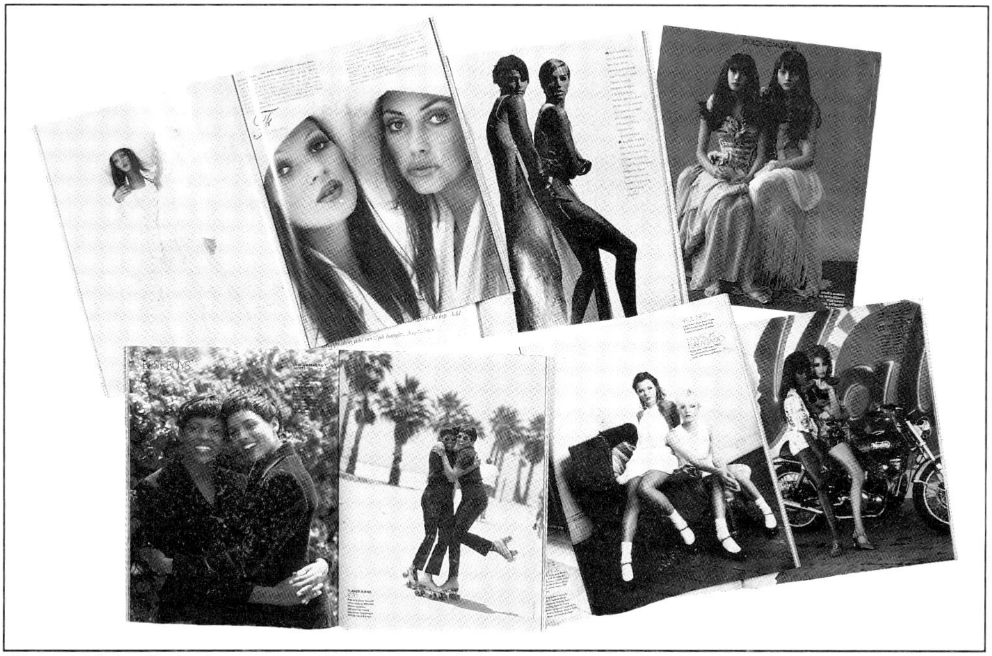

Figure 15.4 *Twinning* Photograph: Simon Pattle.

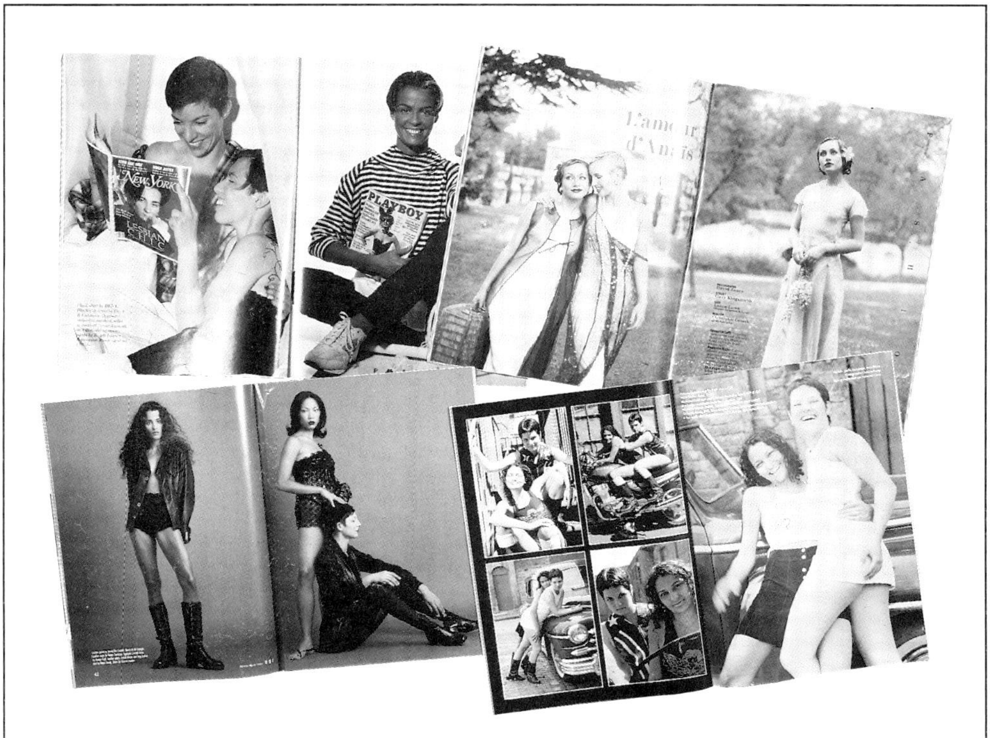

Figure 15.5 *Overt Pleasures?* Photograph: Simon Pattle.

(bottom right) – as Napoleon and Josephine – the narrative is, to us, far more effectively sexualized. This success may also be due to aspects of the feature's styling – short greased hair, red lips, strong features – which can be recognized by the urban/style conscious lesbian reader as elements of self-presentation popular within contemporary lesbian communities. It should also be noted that both these spreads key into long-established and potentially racialized codes within visual culture, in which the active sexuality of the (male) partner is signified by swarthiness, dark hair and rugged looks in contrast to the pale blonde passivity of the heroine.

Lesbian moments (Figure 15.3)

In these instances the lesbian referents are neither butch women nor gendered couples but historical eras, locations and figures which have a particular significance within accounts of lesbian history (Bloomsbury, inter-war aristocratic leisure, Vita Sackville-West) and/or associations with sexual deviancy within mainstream history (Weimar Germany, Brassai's Paris, brothels, Sappho's Lesbos). In these spreads, while the women tend to look unproblematically feminine, the perception of a lesbian subtext is prompted by the combination of a lesbian evocative *mise en scène* and the relationships between bodies and gazes: enclosed spaces, physical proximity, bodily contact and caresses, and a sexually provocative yet challenging gaze directed at the reader. The gaze, which is a determining feature in most of the spreads we have selected, is transformed in this context by the emphatically feminized appearance of the models. Unlike the butch gazes of *Vogue Italia* which sexually assess the (female) viewer but keep her firmly excluded from their camaraderie, these women both challenge the viewer's voyeurism and invite her into the picture as a (lesbian?) participant.

In many of these images the look directed at the viewer is strongly reminiscent of that employed by models in mainstream soft porn. Given the frequency of the brothel setting, where does this leave the presumed heterosexual female viewer who, within this narrative, can surely only be positioned as either client or colleague? But, for the lesbian viewer, the enclosed spaces and enforced leisure pictured here raise the possibility of lesbian activity in a world without men. Scenarios which offer this reading tend to draw on two main cultural stereotypes, artistocratic leisured dalliance and commercial sexual deviance (figured here as prostitution and/or cabaret). For the lesbian viewer, versed in the subcultural reclamation of the brothel as a site for lesbian relationships, these images offer a supplementary pleasure in which the gaze from within the fashion image can be received as coming from a friend or lover, thus bypassing the negative associations of viewing potentially pornographic imagery.

In addition, these periods in history and their key characters have been publicized and popularized by mainstream and alternative cultural productions (such as the films *Orlando*, *Vita and Violet*, *Cabaret*).[3] Contemporary versions of the fashion images associated with each of them have acquired an iconic status within lesbian material culture. Thus, in viewing these spreads, lesbians are able to recognize a (recently constructed) narrative of the lesbian past along with popular looks from the lesbian present.

Twinning (Figure 15.4)

> Our heart is the same in our woman's breast,
> My dearest! Our body is made the same ...
> With the power of my love, I understand you:
> I know exactly what pleases you. (Renée Vivien, 1877–1909, Vivien 1982: 73).

This paeon to Sapphic sameness reminds us of other modes of lesbian coding. While the issues of butch/femme and difference have recently been the focus of great debate and controversy within academic lesbian studies, the lesbian community and lesbian popular culture as a whole, it should not be forgotten that the current focus on difference that so tangibly informs our (lesbian) responses to visual culture is historically specific. Rather than evacuate sexuality from these 'twin' images, which now might be read as sisterly rather than sexual, we can draw on the long lesbian tradition of eroticized sameness to recognize their possible lesbian visual pleasures.

Despite the possibility of lesbian sexuality, these images are marked by an ambivalence that is more profound than in the other spreads. This is often determined by the look from the models to the camera and to each other: for example, in *Elle* 1993 'Best Buys' (bottom left) the emphasis is on girls having fun and with boys in some shots (not illustrated), this inflects the look as sisterly and friendly rather than sexual; however, the sultry, provocative and potentially challenging looks and clothing of 'Baby Belle' (*Elle* 1994, centre bottom), sexualize the images and play up the potential lesbian connotations. The use of similar dress and physical proximity in these images clearly constructs an emotional unity, but any tendency to read this as asexual is destabilized by the direct gaze of the models. Like Manet's *Olympia*, the impassive gaze that challenges the viewer bespeaks a knowing sexuality which, in these images ,works to exclude the viewer from the private relationship between the two women. Thus, where 'Baby Belle' is provocative but open to the fantasy of viewer participation, the Dolce & Gabbana advert (top right) and two spreads from British *Vogue* (top left, bottom right), present an image whose pleasure lies in empathy.

Conclusion

Having analysed the woman-centred visual pleasures offered to both heterosexual and lesbian women by mainstream fashion magazines, do the fashion spreads published within the recently emergent lesbian and gay lifestyle magazines (Figure 15.5) provide any additional pleasures? As self-confessed magazine addicts, we were both somewhat disappointed: while the financial constraints on the low-budget queer magazine cannot fail to impact, it seems that fashion is once again trivialized. Fashion operates as a sideshow rather than the main event: the detail, luxury, styling and thought that produces such fecund visual pleasures in mainstream magazines is generally missing. However, what would a satisfying gay fashion spread look like? Are we simply hooked on the transgressive thrill of eliciting a lesbian pleasure from mainstream fashion images? Perhaps the discomfort and guilt about the exploitative base of the fashion industry that can be avoided by the activity of subverting the nominally straight aesthetic of the mainstream magazine are brought to the fore when the gay magazine invites an overt rather than covert participation in fashion consumption? Both the newly recognized configuration, and buying power, of the pink pound and the 'critical mass' of images of lesbians in the mainstream (Briscoe 1994) should be situated as socially contingent (Hennessy 1993: 969). Lesbian chic and postmodern theory have only highlighted what was already going on: that buying, reading and sharing fashion magazines is for many an indispensable part of being a girl.

Notes

1 Of course, our characterization of the self-conscious lesbian reader who is aware of other such readers, does not rule out the readership of a woman reader conscious of her own same-sex desire, but who reads in social isolation, without a sense of the reality of other such readers. The 'I thought I was the only one who felt like this' syndrome common to many lesbians' experience, would not preclude a heightened sense of same-sex eroticism in the consumption of the magazine image, but might militate against the additional pleasure of understanding reading as an experience shared with other (unmet and anonymous) readers. Equally, though, the fantasy of a body of similar readers ('I hope I'm not the only one who feels like this ...') might produce a similiar effect.

2 This painting of two lesbians sitting was plastered all over London when it was used as the promotional image for the BP Portrait Award exhibition at the National Portrait Gallery in 1992. Copies of the poster soon sold out. See also Sadie Lee, this volume.

3 Apart from the long-standing deviant referents of the film *Cabaret*, the early 1990s saw the release of Sally Potter's film *Orlando* based on Virginia Woolf's book, and British television screened the story of Vita Sackville-West's lesbian affairs in an adaptation of Nigel Nicolson's *Portrait of a Marriage*.

References

Berger, J. (1972) *Ways of Seeing*, Harmondsworth. Penguin.

Briscoe, J. (1994) 'Lesbian hard sell', *Elle*, May, 57–60.

Brooks, R. (1982) 'Sighs and Whispers in Bloomingdales', *ZG*, 3.

Butler, J. (1990) *Gender Trouble*, New York: Routledge.

Coleridge, N. (1988) *The Fashion Conspiracy*, London: Heinemann.

Evans, C. and Thornton, M. (1989) *Women and Fashion: A New Look*, London: Quartet.

Freud, S. (1914) 'On Narcissism: an introduction' in the *Standard Edition of the Complete Psychological Works of Sigmund Freud*, trans. and ed. J. Strachey, London: Hogarth Press, vol. 14.

Hennessy, R. (1993) 'Queer theory: a review of the *Differences* Special Issue and Wittig's *The Straight Mind*', *Signs: Journal of Women in Culture and Society*, 18 (4), Summer.

hooks, b. (1992) *Black Looks: Race and Representation*, London: Turnaround.

Merck, M. (1984) 'Difference and its discontents', *Screen*, 28, 1.

Mulvey, L. (1975) 'Visual pleasure and narrative cinema', *Screen*, 16, 3.

—— (1981) 'Afterthoughts on visual pleasure and narrative cinema, inspired by *Duel in the Sun* (King Vidor 1946)', *Framework*, 15/16/17, Summer.

Myers, K. (1982a) 'Fashion 'n' passion', *Screen*, 23, 3–4.

—— (1982b) 'Towards a feminist erotica', *Camerawork*, 24.

Nestle, J. (1987) *A Restricted Country: Essays and Short Stories*, London: Sheba.

Puckrick, K. (1994) 'Confessions of a female skirt-chaser', *Elle*, March.

Vivien, R. (1982) 'Union', *The Muse of the Violets: Poems by Renée Vivien*, Tallahassee: Niaid.

Walker, L.M. (1993) 'How to recognize a lesbian: the cultural politics of looking like what you are', *Signs: Journal of Women in Culture and Society*, 18, 4.

Wright E. (1992) *Feminism and Psychoanalysis: A Critical Dictionary*, Oxford: Blackwell.

Index

Page numbers in *italics* refer to illustrations

Essentials of Legal Services